Genie

Clothing Alteration

Secrets

Revealed

1st Edition

**A step-by-step practical, up-to-date,
illustrated book for the beginner
or the experienced seamstress
covering the most common types
of clothing alterations.**

by Judith Turner aka genie

Genie Products Pty Ltd
ACN 116 997 141
Australia

A Genie Products Book

Copyright © 2007

Published by
Genie Products Pty. Ltd.

Genie Clothing Alteration Secrets Revealed

National Library of Australia Cataloguing-in-Publication data:
Genie Clothing Alteration Secrets Revealed

646.4

ISBN 978-0-9803525-0-4

Conceived, designed and produced by

Judith Turner

website - www.geniecentre.com

Author - Judith Turner, Genie Products Pty. Ltd.,
Queensland, Australia
email - judith@geniecentre.com
mobile 0011 61 417 369 339

Graphic Artist - David Peake, Graphix Plus,
Western Australia, Australia
email - graphix@arach.net.au
0011 61 8 9434 1599

Printed by Midas Printing (Asia) Limited, China

Acknowledgements

This book has taken nine years to write. It has been rewritten more than fifty times. We all have a passion, and my passion has been clothing alterations. I have enjoyed writing this book, and there are a number of people I would like to thank.

First would have to be my customers. Over the years I have had the privilege of serving some wonderful people. The problems they had with their garments, and helping them to find a way to look great given their body shape and the garments they chose. I have, at times, given people advise that they might not have liked to hear, but they took it on the chin, followed the advise, and thanked me for it.

Some of my customers endured photos being taken of them, which were later converted to illustrations for this book. Thank you for your patience and understanding.

To my dear friend Carol Sciacca. Because of you I began my new career in clothing alterations, and for that I am eternally grateful.

I would also like to thank David Peake of Graphix Plus in Perth. I lived in Perth for a little while, and whilst I was there found David, and he began converting my photos to illustrations. We certainly had some challenging times, but he always managed to remain patient and professional. David's wife is a seamstress, and his twin daughters also sew, so I think they had a hand in some of the illustrations as well.

I would like to thank a very dear friend, Bishop, who has always been there for me. We spent fifteen years together, and whilst we are no longer a couple, we are good friends and will remain so for as long as I live. Bishop helped me create some of my shops, and worked on the design of the Jean Genie. He is an extremely intelligent human being and I am priviledged to have him as my friend.

To my brother Doug, his wife Gloria and their two daughters Kristie and Shannon. My brother helped me build my first shop in Sydney when times were tough, and without that shop this book would never have been started. Shannon joined me when she was 15 years old, and became an integral part of the team. She would have to be one of the most experienced clothing alteration seamstresses around. A lot of people thought she looked too young to know what she was talking about, but she was always patient and just went ahead and did her job, and always to the best of her ability.

To my first employee, Robyn Walden. I remember the day your mum came in and asked if I would take on her daughter for work experience. I was doubtful of the idea, but went ahead anyway, and Robyn joined me. She worked as a casual, coming in after school. Robyn began full time when she eventually left school. It was a pleasure to work with you Robyn, and I wish you every success in your life.

My mother is 83 years of age at the time of printing this book, and she is an inspiration to me. She has certainly been through some tough times, but she has kept herself active, and she still loves sewing. I remember watching her make clothes for the family, and she even made my first bra. I think my sewing skills were ingrained in me when I was very young.

To my beautiful daughter-in-law Amalia. I am so lucky that my son chose you for his wife, because you have become the daughter I never thought I would have. I love you dearly Amalia, and thank you for all your advise and comments, which I took on board to help this book become more user friendly.

I have dedicated this book to my son Daniel Turner. I was single and living life to the full when my son came into my life. You were the best thing that ever happened to me, and you are an inspiration to everyone around you. Your attitude to life is commendable, and your determination to achieve your goals is admirable. When times got tough, you were always there telling me to get up, brush off and keep going. This book was created because my son said to me "Sell your knowledge". Thank you my darling son.

To everyone who purchases this book, I hope you find it useful and valuable in your quest to alter your clothes. I certainly have enjoyed writing it for you.

Judith Turner

About the Author

My passion for clothing alterations began in the 1990's when my dear friend Carol gave me a job in her fabric shop.

This was a time when my world was in a mess. At the time I thought "What am I doing sewing? This is not what I want to do." But you know what? Forces were in play here that I knew nothing about.

I found that I had a natural gift at altering clothes, and eventually in 1997 I moved to Sydney with my 15 year old son, where I opened a few shops.

I began writing my manuals on clothing alterations for the staff back in the early days of 1999. I wanted everyone to be altering the clothes in the same way, and I also wanted to give my customers a 100% guarantee that the garment would be altered to their satisfaction. This meant I had to have a system.

Customers were plentiful, and the shops blossomed, however I made some bad mistakes financially, which cost me dearly.

In the last few years, I have been quietly finishing my book, whilst running a clothing alteration shop in the Gold Coast, Queensland.

The shop was successful, and this time I didn't expand, but rather stayed with the one shop and worked hard.

I sold the shop in January 2007, and went full time on the book.

I now realise that this is what I love doing. In the beginning back in the 90's, I did not see the big picture.

My passion is alive and well, and whilst sometimes I feel a little strange saying I have written a book on clothing alterations, I believe in my heart that the time is perfect for this book.

I have tried to cover as many general aspects of clothing alterations, including Tips and Helpful Hints.

There are 400 illustrations in the book. I began with photos, but realised a few years ago, that the photos could not explain what I wanted you to do well enough, so I employed a graphic artist by the name of David Peake - Graphix Plus to convert the photos to illustrations.

This in itself was challenging for David and myself, but he has a wife and daughters who sew, and I think they have helped along the way.

This is the beginning of a Series of Books on Clothing Alterations. The Jean Genie is the first in a Series of Genies to come onto the market. My products will be informative, and innovative. I wanted to launch the Jean Genie, and I thought that this book was an innovative way to achieve that.

My goal is to create a standard in the clothing alteration industry. No more disaster stories. I would also like to pass on the secrets of clothing alterations to the next generation.

Clothes are so inexpensive to buy. It is cheaper to shorten or alter pants, jeans or evening gowns, than it is to buy a pattern, buy the fabric and accessories and make the garment.

I do hope you find this book worthy and that it helps you to alter your clothes in a safe and professional manner.

I have taught many people how to complete clothing alterations, and I truly believe that this book is the most comprehensive guide to clothing alterations on the planet.

I am constantly looking at ways to speed up the way clothing alterations are executed, and it will continue to publish books and create innovative products to help people perform their clothing alterations in a professional manner.

I hope that you find this book of help when you begin altering your clothes.

Happy sewing

Judith

Judith *aka genie*

Contents

Introduction

Forty years ago I was 13 years of age, and my mother made all my clothes. It was cheaper for her to buy the fabric and make my clothes (and my three brothers clothes) than it was to buy them. Here we are forty years later, and the world is a very different place.

It's cheaper to go out and buy a pair of pants than it is to buy the fabric, the pattern and make it.

You can buy a reasonable pair of pants for A$39.95 (or cheaper) because most clothes are "Made in China", where labour costs are minimal, compared with the western world.

In some cases it is more expensive to alter a garment than it is to buy it. Shortening a pair of pants is the most common alteration, however there are other alterations such as taking in a garment because it is too big, or letting out a garment because it is too tight.

The fashion industry changed when China become such a large player in clothing manufacture.

Whether the garment is cheap or expensive, the majority of clothes need to be altered, because we are all different sizes and body shapes.

Which brings me to the next point. How many people know how to take up the hem on their pants? I don't mean folding up the hem and stitching it into place. I mean learning the correct length to wear pants, how to mark up the pants, cut the pants and finally sew the new hem into place. There are a lot a variables to take into account. This book covers those variables.

There are many books on the basics of sewing, dressmaking, pattern making, and designing clothes. You can even go to classes and learn how to sew.

HOWEVER, to my knowledge no one has put together a comprehensive book covering most aspects of clothing alterations.

Many dressmakers and tailors will say they prefer to make from scratch rather than buy a garment and alter it.

I believe the only reason people shy away from clothing alterations is because there is no specific technique developed which explains how to alter.

Please note that I am not a dressmaker, nor do I enjoy dressmaking. I believe I have an advantage because I have no preconceived ideas or habits.

When I opened my first clothing alteration shop, I wanted my staff to be pinning, preparing and sewing the same way. That meant I had to create a system which everyone followed to achieve a finished alteration that was 100% accurate.

My first partner in life was a carpenter, and my second a telecommunication expert who was a jack of all trades - type of person. I learnt the importance of accurate measurements, so I adopted the same technique in fabric that is used in carpentry.

This book is about taking down measurements and transferring those measurements onto the fabric.

One of my goals in life is to create a standard in the clothing alteration industry.

I would like to help people learn some basic practical skills which will help them alter their own clothes.

I have tried to cover the most common type of clothing alterations, however it would be impossible to cover every variation.

If you don't want to personally alter your clothes, this book will save you a lot of time by teaching you how to pin the clothes yourself. You can then drop them into a clothing alteration shop, and because of the techniques you will learn from this book you will be able to tell the seamstress/tailor exactly what you want and demand 100% accuracy.

If you are at home and would like to earn a little extra money, learning how to do clothing alterations professionally could mean extra income for you and/or your family.

If you would like to comment on the book, contact me at judith@geniecentre.com

Happy sewing

Judith

What you will need

You will need the following equipment.

Blade

The blade is a fast way of slicing through the original thick jean hem. Details on how to use a blade is at the end of the book under Helpful Hints.

Bowl for pins

Use a bowl that is wide at the top so you can reach in and get the pins out with ease.

Chalk

I use four chalk colours : -

White chalk on light coloured fabric
Yellow chalk for white or light coloured fabric
Blue or red for darker coloured fabric

Cotton

Try to match the cotton colour to the fabric colour. Use the standard cotton for normal sewing. Don't try using the thick cotton, as most domestic sewing machines can't handle the thickness.

Use two cottons rather than one thick cotton for jeans and casuals.

Domestic sewing machine

It doesn't matter if the machine is 30 years old or brand new. All you need is a machine that does straight stitching and zig zag.

Needles - Hand Stitching

There are a number of needles you should buy.

I prefer a long needle with a reasonable size eye for the thread. There are small needles, but I find them difficult to hold (maybe I have bigger fingers than most).

Needles - Self threading

The self threading needle is wonderful for those of you who are challenged with the eye sight. All you do is push the thread onto the needle at the top, and the needle is threaded.

Needles - Sewing machine

One of the biggest mistakes people make is using the wrong needle for the fabric they are sewing.

I usually sew with a 75/12 Stretch needle. You can use a 70/12 or 80/12 for medium weight fabric, but personally I find the stretch gives a beautiful stitch for most fabrics, including cotton, linen, stretch, lining fabrics, and woollen fabrics.

I always switch to a 90/14 Jeans needle when I am sewing denim. If you want to sew Leather, then buy yourself some Leather Needles. They are like a scalpel blade and are 100/14 in size. The needle slices through the leather, and you will be able to sew with ease.

Nippers

Snipping threads after sewing. Easy to handle and use.

Over locker

Although you can do clothing alterations without one, if you want a professional finish then you will need an over locker. Buy a second hand machine if money is tight. Garage sales are great for picking up second hand machines.

One little trick for over locking normal fabrics. Only attach three threads, even if it is a four thread. Take the needle out of the right hand-side position, and leave the needle in the left hand side.

This gives a wider over lock, and it looks more professional. Don't worry about having no cotton in one of the reels. The machine will sew well. This technique can be used on most fabrics except lycra.

Pencil and paper

The pencil and paper are for writing down your measurements.

Pins - Hat

When altering jeans or garments with thick fabric, you will find the hat pins are stronger.

If I was taking in the back on a pair of jeans, or a pair of pants with a thick band, I would use the hat pin at the top and the quilting pins further down.

Pins - Quilting

I find it easier to use the 1.5 cm quilting pins rather than the smaller type of pin. You save time because you do not have to put so many pins into the garment.

Quick Unpick

For when you need to unpick seams or over locking. I prefer the Clover quick unpick because the blade is very sharp.

Scissors

Always make sure your scissors are sharp. If you buy yourself a good pair of scissors, they will last you for a lifetime. Never use these scissor to cut paper, only use for fabric.

Sewing Machine

There are many varieties of sewing machines to choose from. All you need is a machine that sews straight stitch and zig zag. You do not need anything fancy. If money is tight buy a second hand machine at a garage sale or look in your local newspaper under For Sale.

Tailors pencil

When preparing the garment for sewing, you will use the tailors pencils to mark where you will sew.

Tape Measure

This gives accuracy to your clothing alteration. I prefer the imperial measurements to be in 1/8th of an inch increments. I explain why under Helpful Hints.

Tweezers

To help threading needles on sewing machine. I have acrylic nails, and I find it easier to use a pair of tweezers to thread my sewing machine needle, than it is to try and push the thread through with my fingers.

Even if you don't have nails, but are challenged with your eye sight, you might find this an easier way to thread your machine.

Wrist pin cushion

Makes pinning easier. I made a elastic band to fit my wrist with velcro sewn on the top at one end. I used the male part of the velcro (harder) on the wrist band and sewed the female velcro (softer) onto some little pillows which I stuffed with wadding. (Sew the velcro on before you sew the pillow up)

I glue a small strip of male velcro to my sewing machine/s. Usually on the right hand side below the dials. It must be in a position that will not get in your way.

As I sew I take my pins out of the garment and stick them into a spare pillow. This way I always have my pillows ready for another pinning session with a customer.

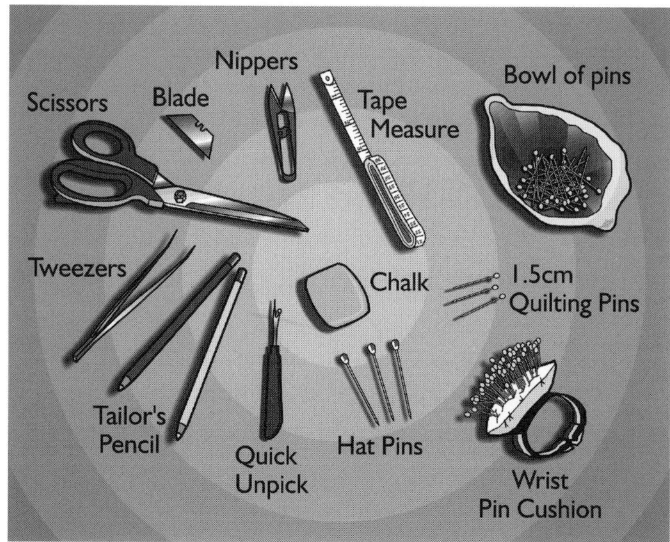

How to use this book

The majority of Clothing Alterations is covered in two areas:-

1. Taking Up

This could relate to shortening the hem on a a pair of pants, jeans, dress, evening gown, jacket, shirt, skirt, tee shirt or top.

2. Taking In

This would relate to taking in almost all types of garments that are too big for you. It may be you have lost weight and your clothes are too big, or you may have bought a garment that does not fit you correctly.

---oOo---

The layout of this book begins with Taking Up a pair of pants.

You may think it is a simple procedure to shorten a pair of pants, but there are many variables to it. The type of shoe you are going to wear, and the style of pant all have a bearing on the length you will finish up with.

I have used Dress Pants to explain my Taking Up Technique. This covers the Pinning, Preparing and Sewing of a garment.

I refer back to the Taking Up Technique from time to time in the book when a garment is being altered in the same way.

Casual Pants are also included in this section.

We then move into the Take In section. First, I explain my Taking In Technique. This technique will be used on all garments when they are being taken in.

If you follow this way of Taking In a garment, your alterations will always be perfect.

The first garment I use as the example is taking in the back on a pair of Dress Pants.

I then move on to all the different ways a pair of pants can be Taken In. In these sections I mainly cover the pinning aspect of Taking In because as you will see with my system, if your pinning is accurate, your alteration will be accurate.

The last section on Pants covers how to replace a zip in a pair of Dress Pants. This cover each and every step of replacing a zip.

The next section covers Jeans. Jean hems are totally different from Dress Pants. This is where the Jean Genie is explained and covers instruction for use.

As a bonus I have also included how to Take Up a pair of jeans and put the Original Finish or European Finish back on. Taking In the back of a pair of jeans is different to Dress pants, and Replacing the zipper in jeans is a little different from replacing the zipper in Dress Pants.

I have then moved into garment types. The first is Dresses, Gowns and Skirts, followed by Jackets. The last garment section is on Shirts and Tops.

In every alteration you do you will be unpicking seams. There are quick ways and difficult ways to unpick seams. This next section covers Seams and how to unpick them.

You could not alter a garment successfully unless you knew the right way to read and use a tape measure. Some of you may not need this section, but I felt it was important to explain Imperial and Metric to the novice.

I have included a small section on the most common fabrics you will come across. There are some great books out on fabrics, so if you want to know more, check out your local book shop.

The last section covers Helpful Hints and Tips. I have covered an A - Z on this, so I hope that this section is helpful.

Pants

Taking Up

"Where I pin

is

Where I sew"

Introduction

Shortening the length on a pair of pants is one of the most common type of clothing alterations required by our society.

Because we are all different heights, it is not possible for manufacturers to provide each pants style in the many lengths required for every person on the planet.

The first step in Taking Up a pair of pants is to know how to get the right length, based on the pants style, the shoes you are going to wear, and the person's personal preference for length.

If you are altering for yourself, you will need the help of a friend.

You can try to pin it yourself, however you will find that when you bend down, the hem will rise, and when you stand up straight again the hem will move down again, so you will be going up and down, and whilst it will work eventually, it is a lot easier to have someone help you.

Moreover, let me say that there is a right way and a wrong way to pin. If you get the pinning wrong, you **will** get the clothing alteration wrong.

I always tell my customers -

"Where I pin is where I sew"

I mean this literally. By the time you have read this book, you will understand the extent of those seven words.

The first section I cover is Shoes and Styles of Pants. This explains how the style of pants and the shoes you wear determines the length you will choose.

The next section on Mistakes People Make is exactly that. It covers some of the mistakes people make when shortening their pants.

I have created my own Pinning Technique which I call "The Knuckle Technique" and I explain this to you in a Step by Step Section, along with illustrations to explain your steps.

The section following this is all about the Taking Up Technique.

This covers Writing down measurements, Preparing and then Sewing the pants.

Whilst the Taking Up Technique is based on Dress pants, I have also included a section on Casual Pants, because the hem is slightly different.

I also felt it was important to dedicate a chapter to Dress Pants for both ladies and men.

Further on in the book you will find more on Taking Up Jeans and Dresses etc., but for now we cover standard pants.

I wish you every success in shortening your pants.

Judith

Judith aka genie

Conclusion

When you make a pair of pants, the hem is included in the pattern. Shortening pants after they have been made is different from working from a pattern.

In most cases the hem will not fit back into the pants without opening out seams, or if the pants are flared without closing seams.

You have to work backwards to unpick, then forwards to make your changes, and depending on how the garment is made, you will have to unpick in a certain way to achieve a professional finish.

Don't take short cuts. I have a saying -

"Good enough - isn't"

Reference points on pants

Before we get into Shoes and Pant Styles, I would like to cover the important area of reference points.

Let's take a look why you need to have a reference point and the advantages of writing down the measurements.

Scenario

A friend, family member or customer asks you to take up (shorten) their pants by 4".

You have not been involved in the pinning process, and the person giving you the pants says it's alright to just take them up that amount.

You do what is asked of you, and the person comes back and says that the hem is too short!!

An argument begins. You can probably supply them with the cutoff to prove you took them up 4", but that will prove nothing.

Solution

When the person comes to you with a pair of pants and asks you to take them up 4", take a pin and measure up 4" from the original hem and place a pin on the outside or inside leg.

Measure from the top of the band to the pin
=
Outside leg measurement = OL

Measure from the crotch/fork to the pin
=
Inside leg measurement = IL

Write this measurement down on a piece of paper, and if you are really concerned with the persons belief, ask them to sign the paper. That's going to an extreme, but I have found that if a customer expressed a concern that a mistake not be made, it was better to put their mind at rest by explaining how I operate and what reference points are about.

My customers walked out the door knowing that

if I made a mistake, and the finished length was different from the length on the docket, then I would replace the pants.

That is a 100% guarantee to my customers.

No more disaster stories!!!!!!!!!!!!!!

The following illustrations covers all reference points for a pair of pants. At this point you are only concentrating on the inside and outside leg length.

The other reference points will be discussed further in the book.

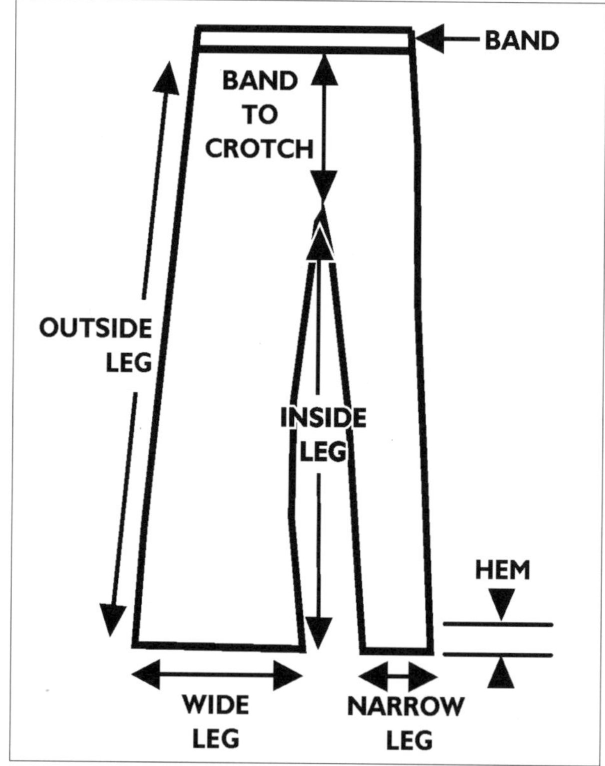

Conclusion

There is absolutely no way you can guarantee the finished length on a pair of pants without a reference point.

That is why I developed a technique which worked on facts. The facts are if you have a reference point that everyone is working on, there can be no mistakes.

Pants

Taking Up

Shoes & Styles of Pants

"Pin hem length with low heeled shoes first."

"Pin as long as possible without touching the floor."

"Try on high heeled shoes to see length is ok."

Different heel heights

Shoes are extremely important when it comes to the finished length on a pair of pants.

The height of the heel will determine whether the foot is on a steep angle or is sitting flat in the shoe.

This illustration shows how the height of the heel affects the angle of the foot.

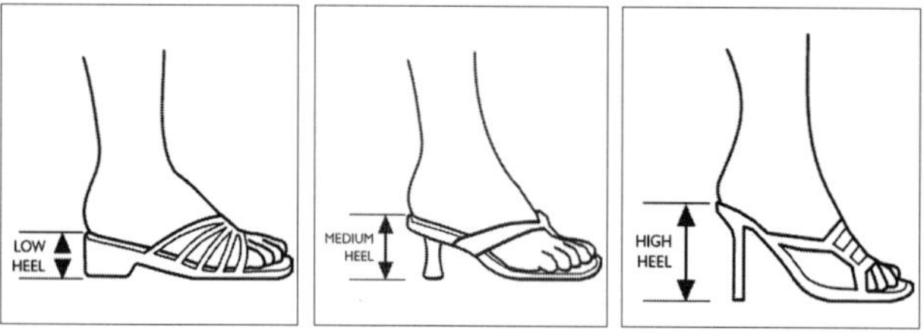

As I stated before, I always have the person try on the pants with low heeled shoes first, then try on the higher shoes.

The following illustrations are from photos taken of a person wearing the same pair of pants with low-heeled shoes on first, and then she changed to the medium-heeled shoe, and last to the high-heeled shoe.

Notice how the pants get higher from the ground as the heel gets higher.

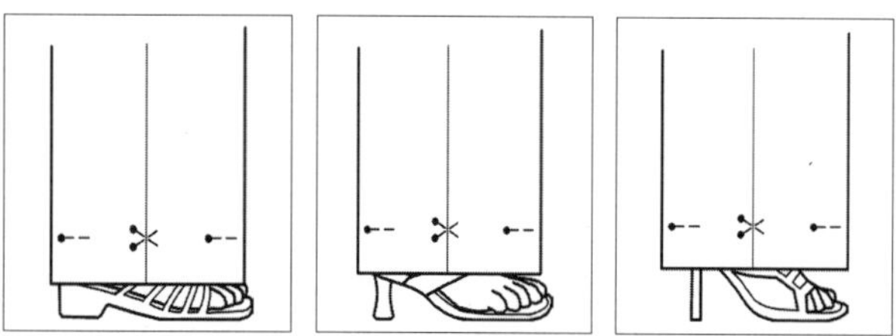

Conclusion

The width at the base of the pants will determine how long or short the pants should be, and finally the type of shoes the person is wearing will determine the length.

How many times have you had a pair of pants taken up, only to find that the pants are too short with a particular pair of shoes?

Hem length options

Wearing low or high heeled shoes with the same pants

If you want to wear pants with low heeled shoes and high heeled shoes, always have both shoes available at the fitting. Put on the low heeled shoes first.

Pin the hem as low as possible without the pants touching the floor. Make sure your pins are holding the excess fabric up inside the pants.

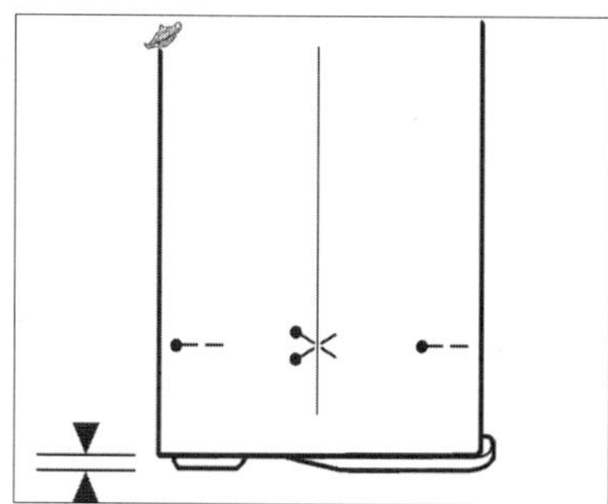

Now try the high-heeled shoes on and see if you are happy with the length of the pants with these shoes.

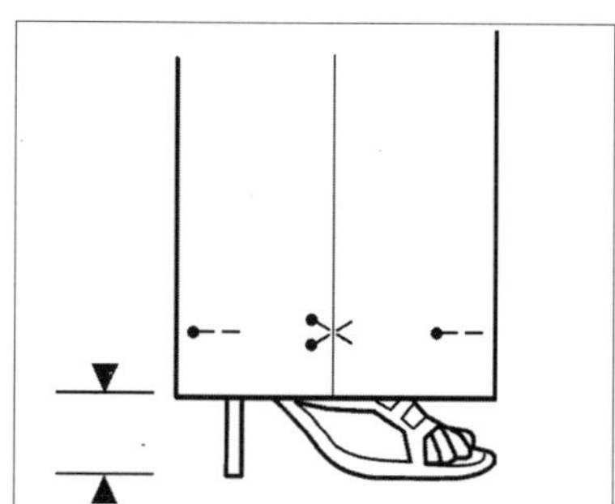

If you find that the pants are too short with the high heeled shoes, you will have to think about whether you will only wear high heeled shoes with these pants and for-go using the low heeled shoes.

I find that usually the pants look ok, however I have had situations with customers who have very high shoes, and the pants don't look right being that short.

Short length

Our senior citizens tend to prefer the shorter length. I think the main reason is that they don't want to trip over their hems, and cause themselves an injury.

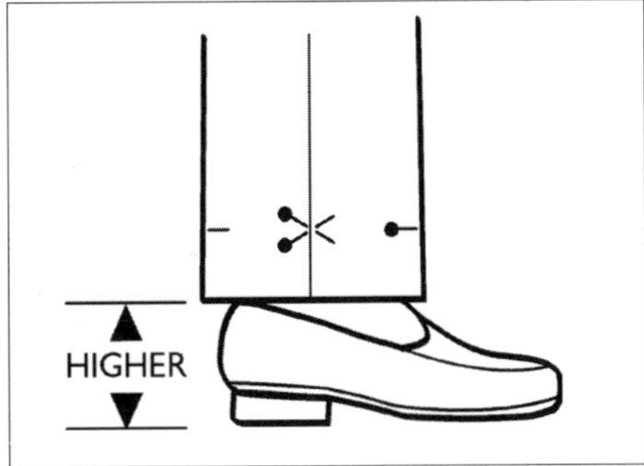

I have also found that it is harder to find out the length an older person would like their pant hems, because they may be too shy to let you know what they really want.

I usually take the time to talk to the person before I get down and do any pinning. You can see how shoes make a big difference, so think about that before you go pinning the length.

If you want your pants short, make sure you have a belt on for the fitting, because a belt will tend to make the pants sit higher than without a belt. A belt will only be worn if the pants have belt loops.

Another thing is to keep in mind that some fabrics can shrink after the first wash. Example - 100% cotton usually shrinks. Particularly if the garment is put into a dryer.

Some of the track suit pants on the market shrink a lot, so if in doubt wash the pants BEFORE pinning up the new hem length.

I bought a pair of track pants once and altered them before I washed them, and they shrunk by over 2".

Read the care label on the pants if you are not sure.

Medium length

When you have your pants hemmed to this length, it generally means that the pants are flared or box leg.

It would be difficult to have this length for a slim fitted pant. It would bunch in the front.

This length means that you can cater to wearing a low-heeled shoe or a high-heeled shoe or boots.

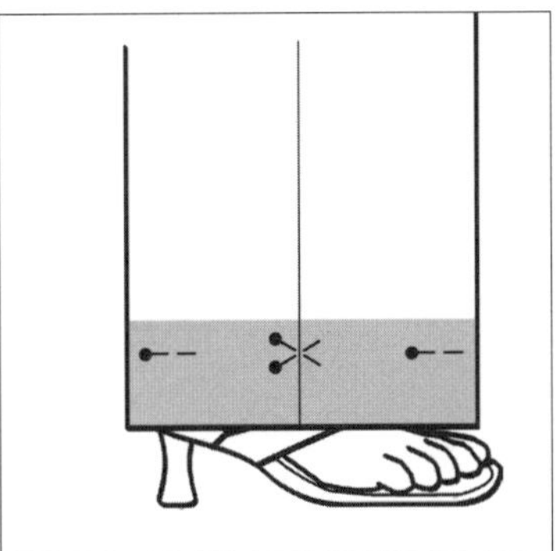

Long length

A lot of people prefer their pants long. The long length generally means 1/2" or 1 cm from the floor.

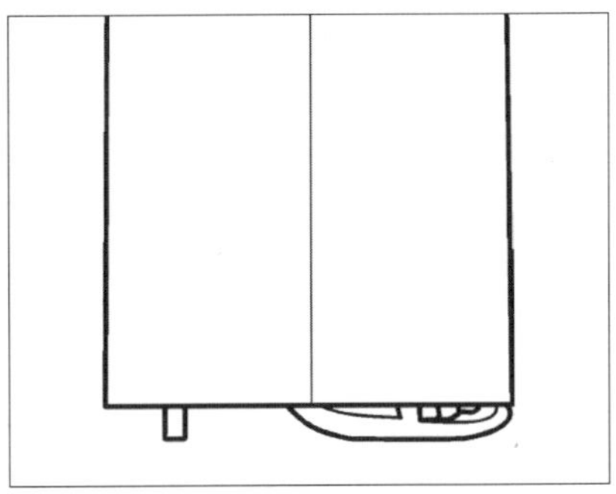

People who are short can look taller if they have their pants as long as possible. It gives the illusion that they have longer legs.

Young people also prefer their pants long.

If you want your pants long, buy pants that are wide at the base of the hem.

Dress Pants

There are three length options for dress pants.

Option 1 - Mid length

Front of pants to sit on the top of the shoe, which means the front crease is straight from the waist to the top of the shoe.

This can only happen if the pants are reasonably wide at the base of the pants.

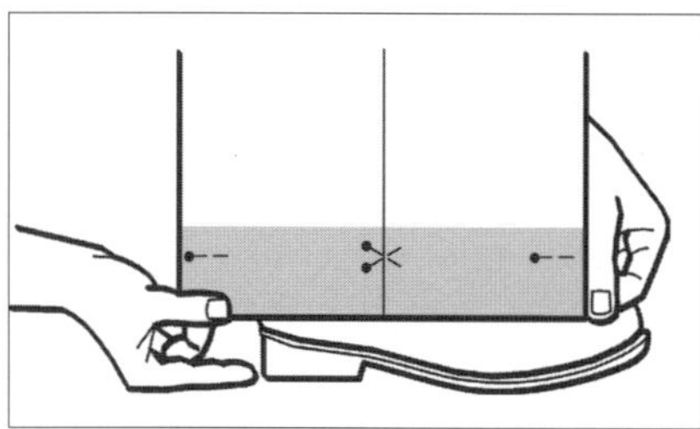

Option 2 - Long length

The pants are a little longer than the first option, therefore the front of the pants are longer at the top of shoe. This causes the pants to create a crease or break at the front of the pants.

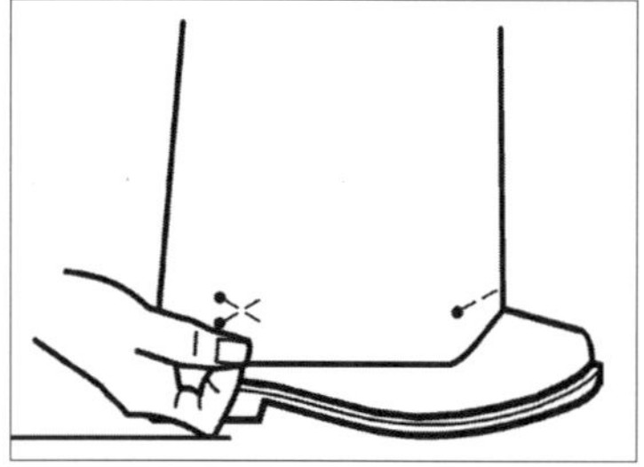

Option 3- Very long

For pants to be very long, the width at the base must be wide. Pants should be at least 1/2" or 1 cm from the floor, or as long as possible without touching the floor.

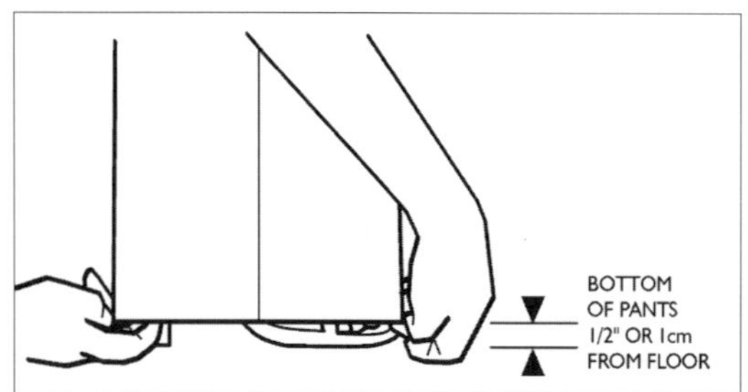

Cuffed Pants

Cuffed pants are usually hemmed with the front of the pant sitting on the front of the shoe.

Have the pants resting on the front of the shoe, the same as dress pants.

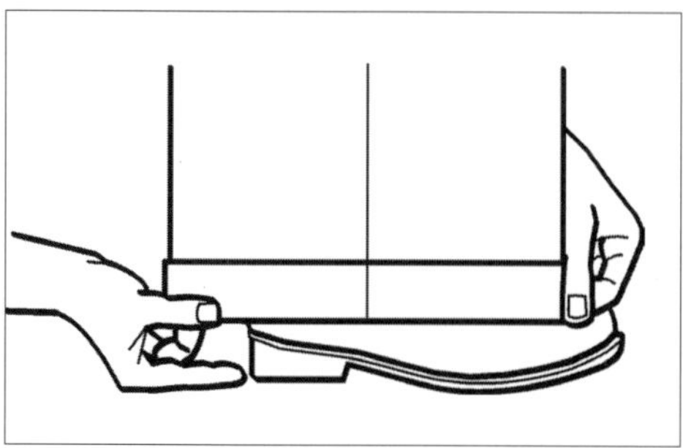

If you want the pants to be longer, then there will be a break at the front of the pants.

When you are altering pants with a cuff, the manufacturer may have had the cuffs permanently pressed, which means if you take them up by half a cuff, you will have a crease line through the new cuff.

Try to take the pants up by a full cuff length at a time. This may not be practical, because it may make the pants too short. If you need to take up by half a cuff, try ironing out the cuff crease on the pants before you work out the new length. The crease should come out of most woollen fabrics and some cotton mix Check the label and care instructions.

As a general rule, men's pants have a 1 1/2" or 4 cm cuff size.

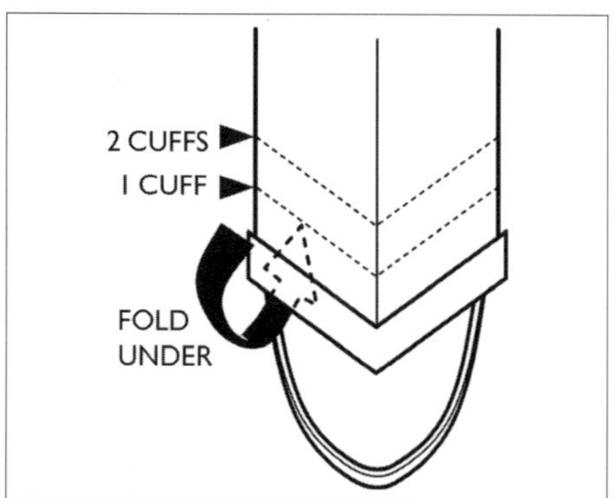

The full measurement to allow for cuffs of this size is 4" or 10 cm.

If the pants are being shortened a lot, then the existing cuff may not be an issue, but if you are only going up one or two cuffs, then it could be an issue for you.

I sometimes get asked to put cuffs on men's pants that did not originally have a cuff. I am only too happy to oblige, however I always measure the amount I am taking up the pants, plus the old hem allowance, to make sure I have enough fabric to put professional cuffs back on.

Stove pipe

Stove pipe pants hug the leg around the ankle. If they are very tight around the lower leg, then the pants can be pinned either above the ankle or just below the ankle.

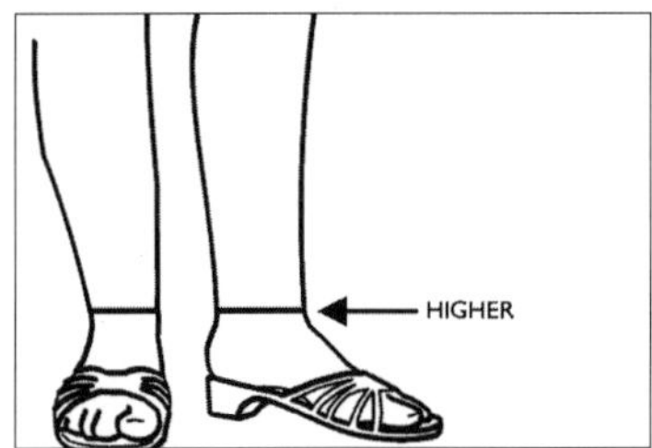

The above illustration shows the narrow pants leg is higher at the ankle than the pants below, therefore I would pin the pants on or above the ankle.

The pants below are not as tight fitting and therefore can be pinned a little lower.

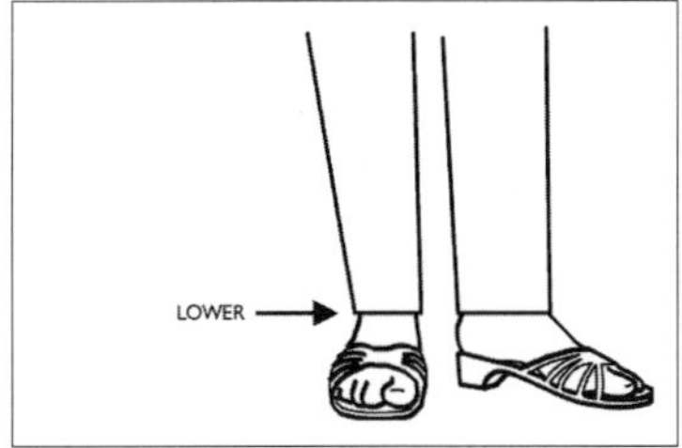

Narrow width leg

There are two situations that can occur with narrow legged pants.

The first is that it is very difficult to wear narrow legged pants long.

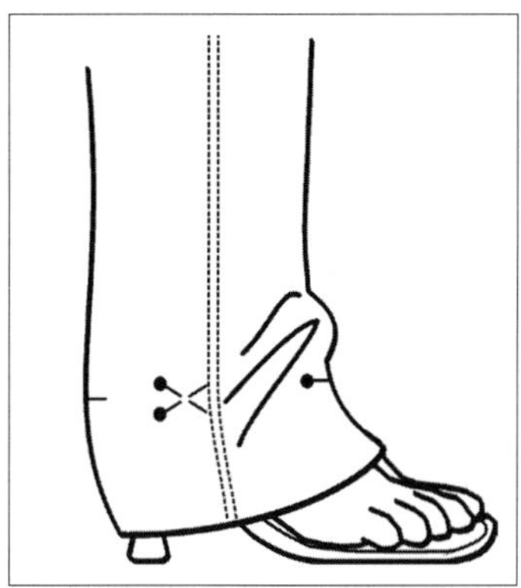

You can see from the above illustration that the pants do not sit over the shoe.

If you pin the pants too long, the fabric will just bunch around the ankle and they will not feel comfortable to wear.

In fact they will eventually ride up and will just sit bunched around the ankle.

This particular type of pants leg needs to be shorter than a wide legged pant.

You can see from the following illustration that the pants sit better by being just at the edge of the back of the foot or just below.

Shoes will make a difference, because it will place the foot on an angle which will mean if you wear high heeled shoes, you can have the hem longer.

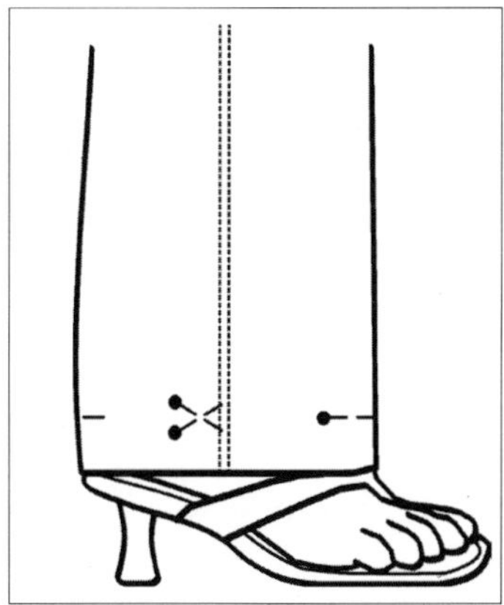

The second problem with narrow legged pants which are made of a thicker quality fabric, like heavy denim or thick cotton, the bunching will not just stay around the ankle, but rather the pants will be baggy all the way up to the thigh area.

This gives the impression the pants are too big.

When a customer came to me complaining that their pants were too big around the thigh area, I always asked them to try the pants on before I commented.

Some of the time I would just fold up the excess fabric at the hem area, and pin the new length, and the pants would drop down, and this bagginess would go away.

Another reason pants may seem baggy at the thigh area, is because they have been folded with creases at the side seams, and this forces the fabric out at the sides.

Iron your pants with a crease down the front or if you prefer no crease, iron the pants so there is no crease at the front or the sides.

If the person wears shoes that are slingback (no back) they may prefer the pants to finish at the bottom of the heel so that the pants do not work their way under the foot as the person walks.

I find that the narrow pant looks good being worn at this length (with high heeled shoes), but a wider legged pant tends to look too short and flaps around the ankle as you walk.

Flared leg

Jeans, casual pants and track suit pants can be flared. The flare at the base of the hem is wider than the knee or thigh area. Flared pants can be worn as long as the person wants.

Depending on the height of the shoe, try for a finished hem length in the middle of the shoe just below the top of the heel.

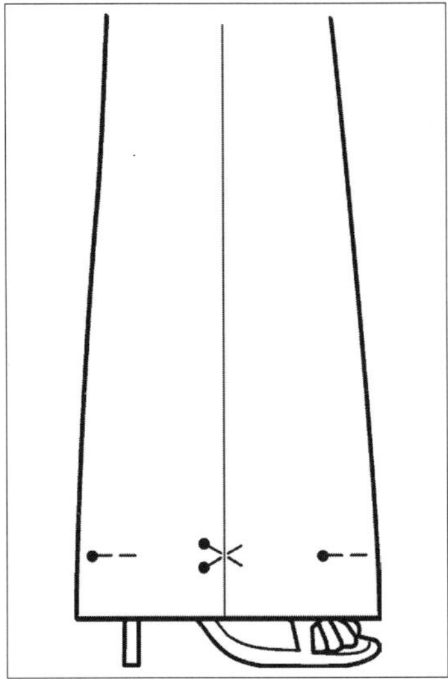

If flared pant hems are left too long, the hem will touch the ground, and the hem will fray. To fix the frayed edge could mean making the pants shorter than you would have originally wanted. It could take just one time of wearing the pants too long for the hem to fray.

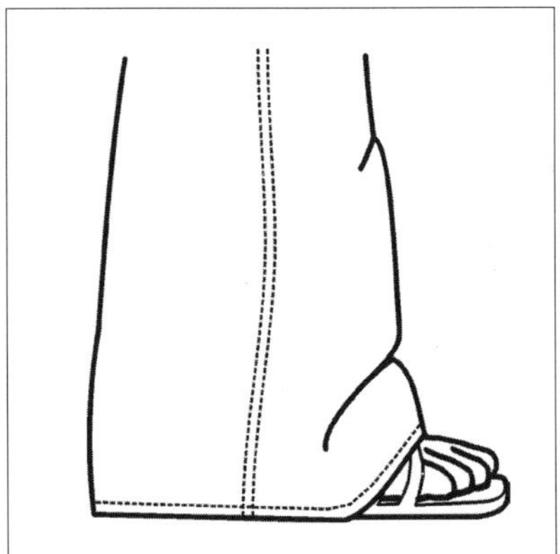

Most people want jeans to be as long as possible without the hem touching the floor. To eliminate fraying, always have the hem taken up BEFORE wearing the jeans.

Fun lengths for Pants

Fashions are constantly changing, however, whilst there are some fads that are seasonal, we really can wear whatever we like.

There is a way to work out what the final length should be for hem lengths between the ankle and just below the knee.

I call these the Fun Lengths for Pants, because we usually look relaxed and casual with pants hems at these lengths.

So have you ever wondered how to work out where to have your capri pants?

It's really an easy process once you follow my technique.

Have a play with this with long pants that have been sitting in your wardrobe for a while. If you don't wear them long, why not shorten them to a Fun Length and you may find you will wear them all the time.

You can also do this with pants that have been taken up too much. You probably won't wear them anyway, so shorten them to a Fun Length, and get some wear out of them.

So let me help you to work out those Fun lengths without stressing about what is right and what is wrong.

Try any of the following lengths. If you fold the excess fabric under, and pin, then look in the mirror, you will see which length is best for you.

What is important is to understand your leg shape, and work with what you have to show off your best leg features.

All you need is your tape measure and pins.

Have fun.

¾ length

This is a very flattering length because it shows off the curve of the leg from the slim ankle to just below the knee.

This length suits people with a slim ankle and shapely calves.

It also can suit a short or tall person.

Step 1 - Place the beginning of your tape measure over the centre of the ankle.

Step 2 - Measure up 9" (20.3 cm) from the centre of the ankle working up the leg towards the knee. Place a pin at this measurement.

Step 3 - Fold the excess fabric up into the pants on the outside seam.

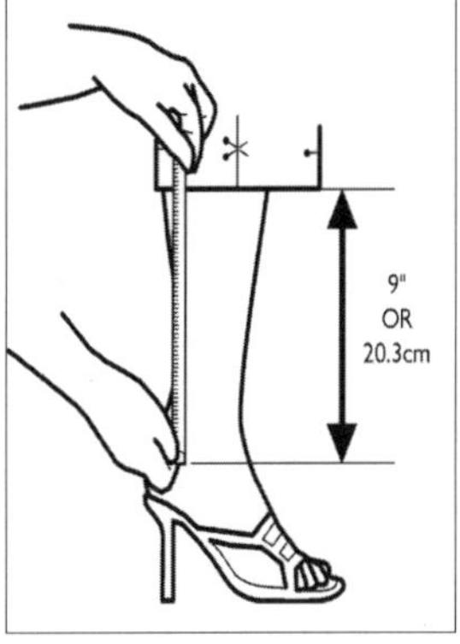

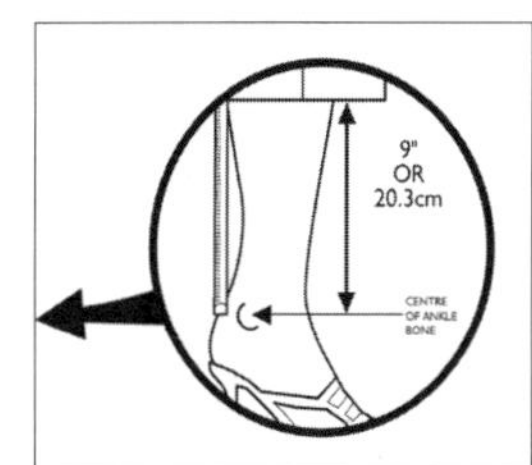

Step 4 - Place two pins in a cross at the outside seam. If there is a lot of fabric folded under, then place another pin above the crossed pins to keep the fabric up there.

Step 5 - Move around to the inside leg seam and place a pin to hold the fabric up.

Step 6 - Place a pin at the front of the pants.

Step 7 - Place a pin at the back of the pants.

Step 8 - Proceed to Taking Up Technique page 32 - 39.

7/8th length

The 7/8th length can be another flattering length for the female leg. This style shows the slimness of the ankle moving up to the curve of the calf.

This length suits shorter people, and if you are carrying a bit of weight on the tummy, but have great ankles and calves, then use this length to help you look slimmer.

Step 1 - Place the beginning of your tape measure over the centre of the ankle.

Step 2 - Measure up 6" 1(5 cm) from the centre of the ankle working up the leg towards the knee.   Place a pin at this measurement.

Step 3 - Fold the excess fabric up into the pants on the outside seam.

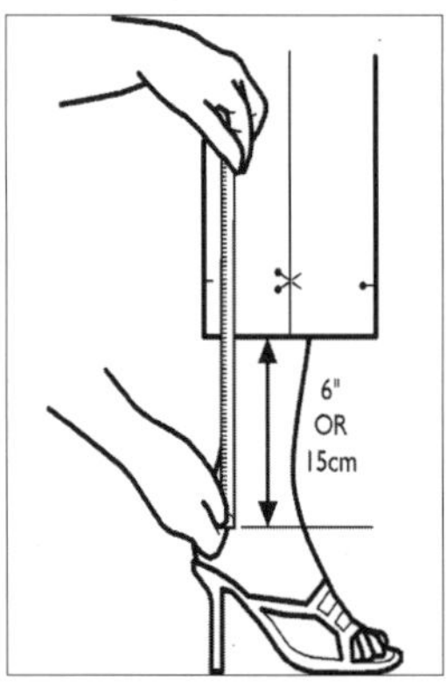

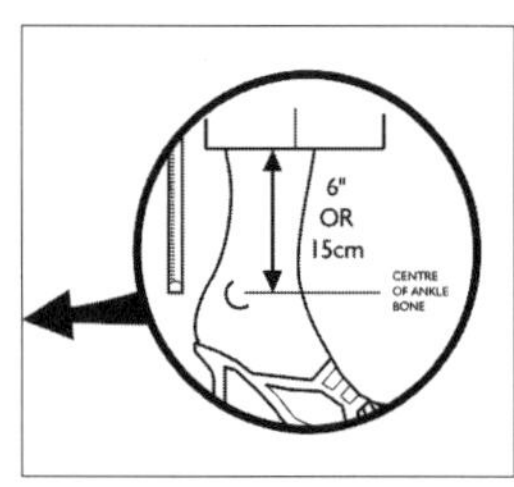

Step 4 - Place two pins in a cross at the outside seam. If there is a lot of fabric folded under, then place another pin above the crossed pins to keep the fabric up there.

Step 5 - Move around to the inside leg seam and place a pin to hold the fabric up.

Step 6 - Place a pin at the front of the pants.

Step 7 - Place a pin at the back of the pants.

Step 8 - Proceed to Taking Up Technique page 32 - 39.

Capri length

The ankle length is similar to how sailors in the old days wore their pants. It was called 'Half mast' back then. The calf is almost covered by the new hemline.

Only the ankle is exposed, so it looks great if you have a slim ankle.

This length looks great on people who are of average height or taller.

Step 1 - Place the beginning of your tape measure over the centre of the ankle.

Step 2 - Measure up 3" (7.5 cm) from the centre of the ankle working up the leg towards the knee.   Place a pin at this measurement.

Step 3 - Fold the excess fabric up into the pants on the outside seam.

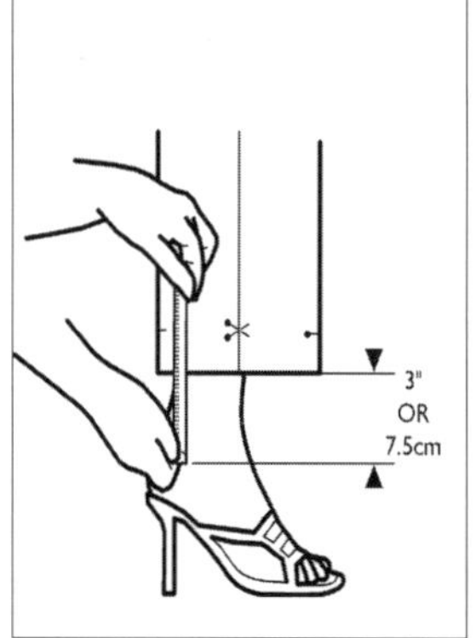

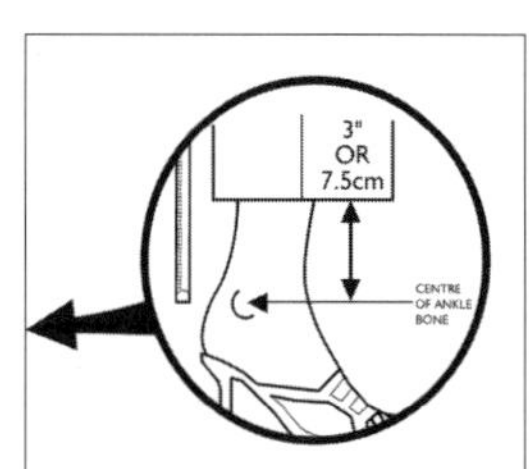

Step 4 - Place two pins in a cross at the outside seam. If there is a lot of fabric folded under, then place another pin above the crossed pins to keep the fabric up there.

Step 5 - Move around to the inside leg seam and place a pin to hold the fabric up.

Step 6 - Place a pin at the front of the pants.

Step 7 - Place a pin at the back of the pants.

Step 8 - Proceed to Taking Up Technique page 32 - 39.

Ankle length

The short length focuses more on the shoe than the leg.

Step 1 - Place the beginning of your tape measure over the centre of the ankle.

Step 2 - Measure up 1" (2.5 cm) from the centre of the ankle working up the leg towards the knee.   Place a pin at this measurement.

Step 3 - Fold the excess fabric up into the pants on the outside seam. The new hem line should be at the 1" or 2.5 cm length as per illustration.

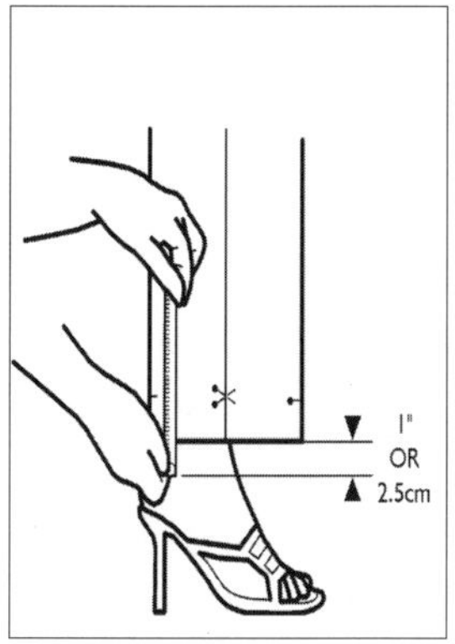
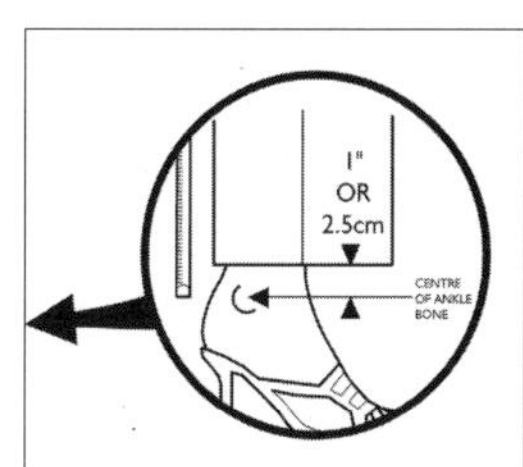

Step 4 - Place two pins in a cross at the outside seam. If there is a lot of fabric folded under, then place another pin above the crossed pins to keep the fabric up there.

Step 5 - Move around to the inside leg seam and place a pin to hold the fabric up.

Step 6 - Place a pin at the front of the pants.

Step 7 - Place a pin at the back of the pants.

Step 8 - Proceed to Taking Up Technique page 32 - 39.

False hem – let down

A lot a people buy pants, only to find they are too short, or they shrink when washed.

Tall people can also find it difficult to buy pants that are long enough.

To work out whether a hem can be lowered and whether it will look alright, try on the pants and put the shoes on that you want to wear with them.

Step 1 - Measure the amount of the hem allowance on the inside of the hem. Measure from the fold to the over locking and/or tape around the hem. Write this amount on a piece of paper.

Step 2 - Have the person stand side on to a mirror.

Step 3 - Put the tape measure on the existing fold line at the amount you wrote down on the piece of paper. For example if the amount is 1 ¼", then put the tape at 1 ¼" on the existing hemline with the tape facing down.

Step 5 - Let the balance of the tape measure drop down towards the floor.

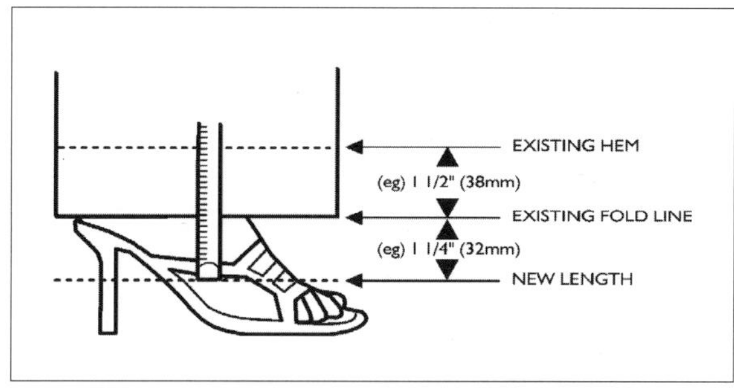

Step 6 - Where the tape finishes will be the finished length.

See over the page for types of pants a tall person can buy and/or options they can use to make pants longer.

Ideas for tall people

There are a number of ways to cheat when it comes to lengthening pants for tall people.

1. Pants with 3" (8cm) hems

Some designers create large hems on their pants. The largest I have seen is around 3 1/2" or 9 cm. This means that the hem can be let down to the maximum, with a false hem put on, or you can lower it the amount needed and still have a small hem allowance.

Please note that where pants are tapered or flared at the bottom, the original hem will need to be adjusted at the seam.

The reason for this is that the seams will have been tapered in, so that the hem will sit correctly.

When the hem is lowered, the seams will have to be opened out, so the flare will continue outwards.

If the seams can not be opened out, you will have to re taper the pants from the knee down to the new hem length.

If the pants are box style, then you should be able to lower the hem without opening or closing seams.

2. Pants with cuffs

Pants with cuffs are great for tall people.

The cuffs can be taken off completely. When you unpick the cuffed section, you will find a lot of extra length. You may even have to cut some off, because some cuffs have up to 4" extra, and sometimes even more than that.

Just like pants with large hems, if the pants are tapers or flared, the side seams will have to be re adjusted so that the fall of the pants is accurate. If the pants are box style, then you will not have to worry about tapering in or out.

Remember to keep the hem allowance before you cut anything off the hem.

See Preparing pants for more information.

3. Extensions can be added to hem lengths

You can add any type of fabric, or leather to the bottom of pants.

Lace looks great on casual pants or stretch pants.

If you do use lace or a different colour fabric, you could also add the same fabric or lace to other areas of the pants for design effect.

For example if the pants have pockets, you could sew some lace or fabric on to the top of the pockets.

You could applique the lace or fabric onto sections of the pants like the knee area.

Lower the hem, and add the extension on to the bottom. Make sure to taper the hem in or out depending on the style.

Legs different lengths

If you have ever had a pair of pants altered, and one leg is longer than the other, or if you are helping someone to shorten a pair of pants, and that person says to you that they went to an alteration shop once and the pants came back with one leg longer than the other, use this as a sign that maybe you should check their legs.

Alteration shops can and do make mistakes.

However, I have also found that some people are not aware that they have one leg longer than the other. If a person has had a leg broken, or an accident involving a hip, then it is possible that one leg is longer than the other.

Mothers have been known to rest their infant children on their hips. I used to rest my son on my right hip, and I now have one leg longer than the other by 1/2" or 1 cm.

All human beings have one side of their body different to the other. Some differences are great and some are small.

Follow this technique if you are not sure about your leg lengths.

Step 1 - Pin the right leg, using the knuckle technique. Make sure you place the cross on the outside seam.

Step 2 - Ask the person if they are happy with the length.

Step 3 - Ask the person to stand very still because you are going to measure the hem from the floor to the new length and you need them to stay still for this.

Step 4 - If the person is facing a mirror, I ask them to look into their own eyes. Alternatively, you can run your finger very lightly down their spine and say, "please keep your spine straight".

Step 5 - Kneel behind the right leg.

Step 6 - Place the tape measure on the floor next to the double pin on the right leg.

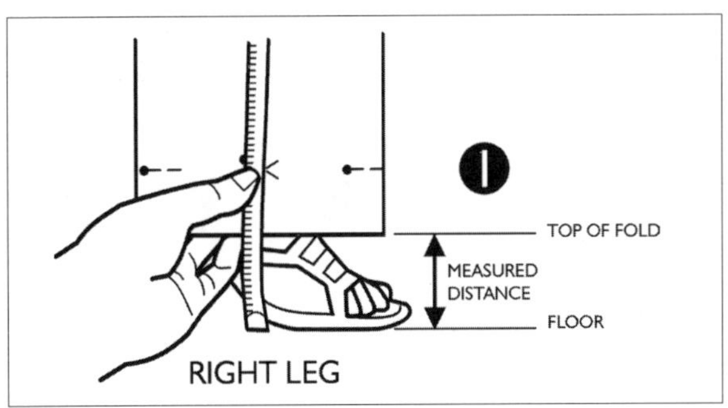

Step 7 - Note the measurement from the floor to the top of the new fold.

Step 8 - Move around to the left leg.

Step 9 - Fold the fabric up so it is the same amount as the right side.

Step 10 - Let's say it measured 2" from the floor to the new fold on the right leg.

Step 11 - Make the left leg 2" from the floor to the new fold.

Conclusion

You are trying to have the finished length on both pant legs measuring the same distance from the floor to the new hem length.

Whether the pants are 2"/5 cm from the floor or 1/2"/1 cm from the floor, you are going to make sure that both pants lengths are the same amount from the floor.

I had the situation where a person brings in a pair of pants that are tight on the thigh area, and because of this the lengths are different from one leg to the other. This is because they have one thigh thicker than the other. Follow this procedure for the tight pants only.

Pants

Taking Up

Mistakes people make

*"Pants cost money,
and guessing the length
could cost you even more"*

Introduction

Everyone has heard a horror story about a clothing alteration that went wrong.

> Pant hem cut too short
> Pants came back with one leg shorter
> Hem is puckered
> Hem is crooked

The only reason that a clothing alteration will end up a disaster is if the alteration was completed without any procedure being followed.

This happens all the time, because unfortunately, THERE ARE NO STANDARDS in the clothing alteration industry.

I have seen many different methods of determining the length of a pair of pants in my years working in the clothing alteration industry. I would like to share, what I believe, are some of the mistakes people make to work out the length on a pair of pants.

Folding hem outwards

When the fabric is folded out, your attention is drawn to the excess fabric on the outside of the pant leg, rather than looking at the finished length of the pants on the shoes or boots.

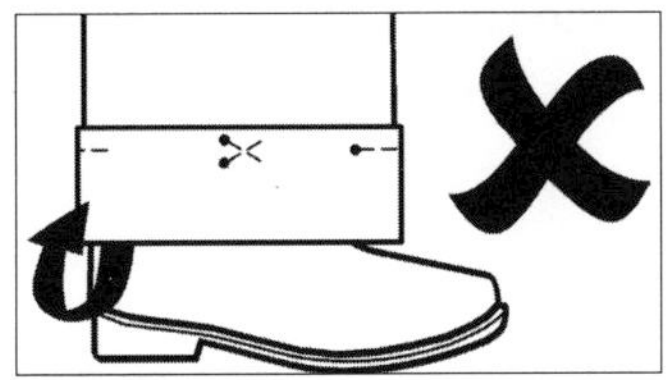

More often than not when the fabric is folded out the pants will be too short. I can only assume that this is because they are not looking at the finished length.

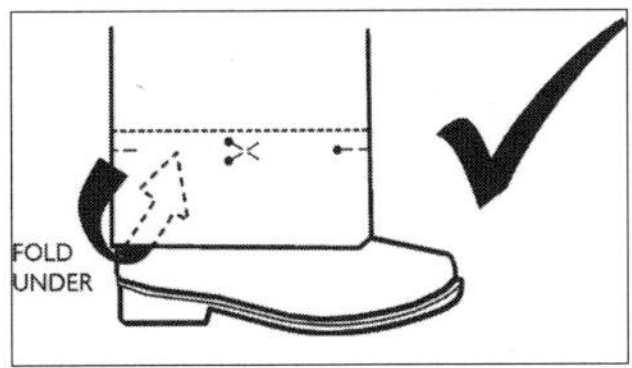

Holding hem up with staples

Staples are not designed to be placed into fabric. The staples are noticeable, and they can cause damage to the fabric. Particularly micro fibre. The holes are very noticeable. If you are going to buy a pair of pants, take the time to have a professional hem put on the pants.

Wearing a belt

Some pants have belts and some do not. If a pair of pants has belt loops, and the person is likely to use a belt, then I would recommend using the belt at the fitting.

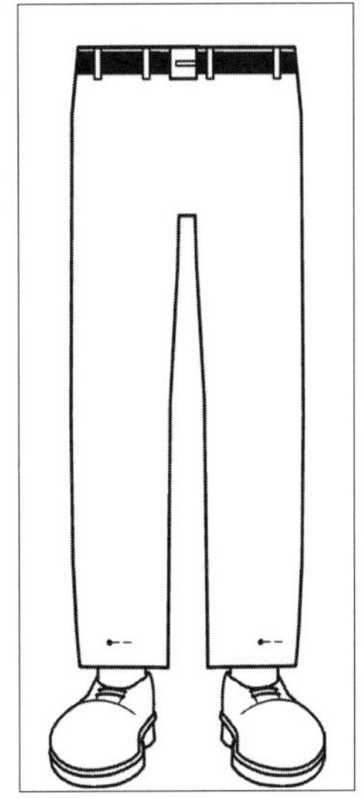
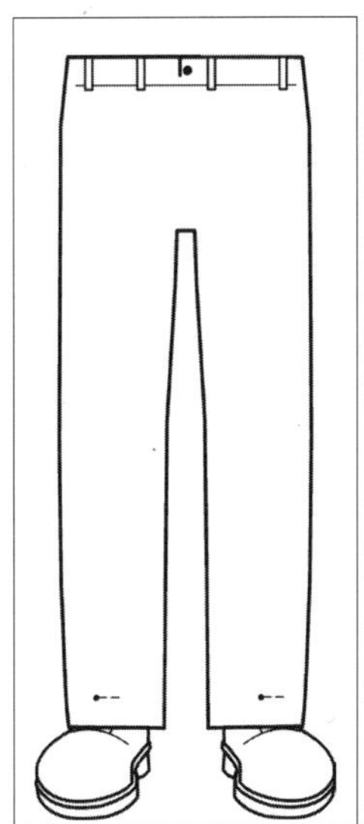

When a belt is secured at the waist or hip, it can raise the pant leg by up to 1" or 2.5 cm.

If a belt is likely to be worn, but the person does not have one available at the time of pinning, ask him/her to place their hands on either side of pants at the waist (if waist pants) or hips (if hipsters).

Ask the person to use a little pressure when doing this, in the same way that a belt will tighten when done up.

Holding pants against body and guessing the length

Do not hold pants in front of your body and guess the length. It does not work, because of the following reasons.

* The pants may sit differently at waist or hip.

* The crotch may be longer.

* The width at the base/hem may be wider.

* The pants will not hang at the right length, because they are not on your body.

Try this test - Hold pants against your body and guess the length. Write down the outside leg measurement.

Now put the pants on and pin correctly. Measure the outside leg, and look at the difference between the two.

As you can now see, there are a number of reasons why you shouldn't use one pair of pants as a guide for another pair of pants new length.

Having said all that. If you have a new pair of pants, and they are identical to a pair you already have, then by all means, go for it, and use the outside or inside leg as a guide.

Marking pants with pen

Do not mark the hem length with a biro or permanent marking pen.

You will be surprised how many people do this, and they do not just mark one leg, they mark both legs.

If the legs are marked at different lengths by mistake, the mark may show when the hem is taken up.

Measuring inside-leg of pants that person is wearing

I have had men come in and want me to measure the inside leg of a pair of pants that they are wearing. Now I am a confident "out there" sort of a person, but I really do not want to go measuring up into some man's crotch.

Get the measurement when the pants are off.

I have the convenience of a fitting room, which I get the person to go into, take the pants off, then I will measure the inside leg, if that is what they want. Usually I will try to talk them out of that technique and get them to try on the new pants they have brought in for alteration.

Pinning without shoes

Some people think that the only way to work out the length on pants is to stand in bare feet and fold the new hem up so it touches the floor.

I do not agree with this method. The reason I do not agree is because this only works if the pants are wide at the base of the leg.

Some pant legs are very narrow, and if you use this technique, when you put your shoes on, you will find that the pants will bunch at the base of the leg like in the illustration.

Only use this technique for pants with a wide base.

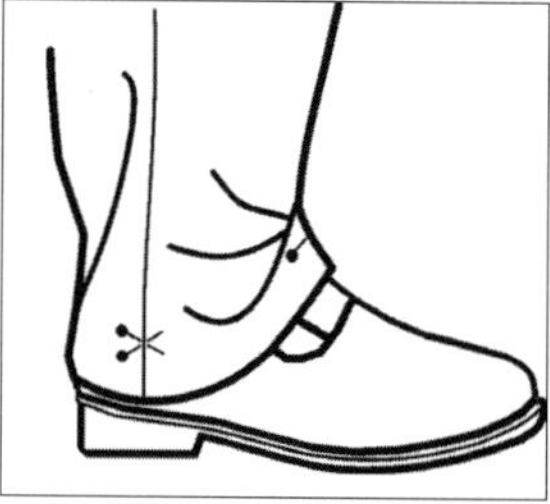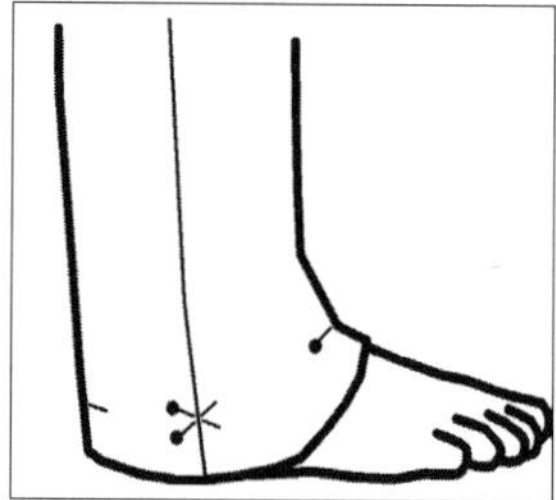

You can see from the two illustrations that when shoes are put on the pants pucker at the ankle.

Using another pair of pants as guide for length

Do not use an old pair of pants to work out the length for a new pair of pants. There are a number of reasons for this.

1. The most common error is measuring the outside leg measurement (measurement from the top of the band to the hem) from an old pair of pants and using this measurement for a new pair of pants.

Some people use the inside-leg measurement instead of the outside leg, but both techniques could mean disaster.

Here's why - The following illustration shows the crotch on one pair of pants versus the crotch on another pair of pants.

Notice that one crotch is longer than the other. This means the pants will sit differently on the body. A longer crotch on one pair of pants will mean the inside leg measurement will be shorter than a pair of pants with a shorter crotch measurement.

The only time this would not be true is if the person pulled the pants up higher on the waist or hips. But this rarely happens. Most people wear their pants at the same position on the waist or hips, and let the crotch hang down.

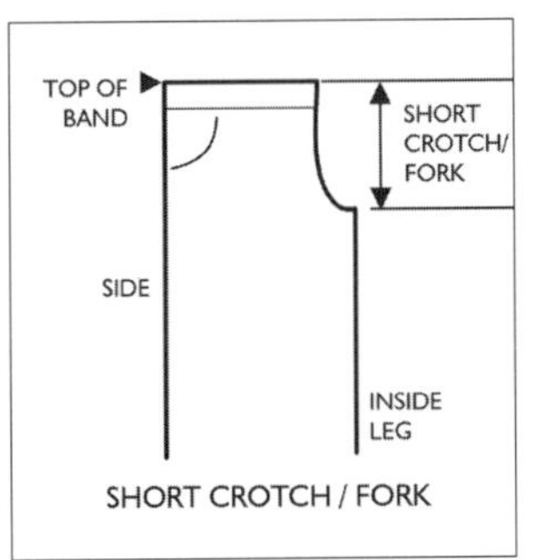

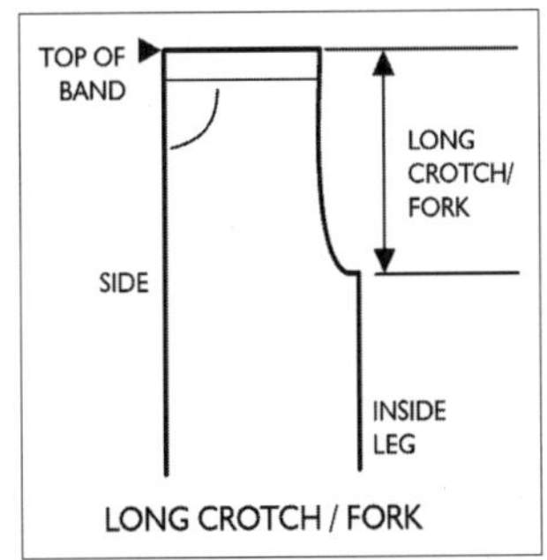

2. The measurement around the waist band will also determine where the pants will sit on the body.

If the pants are too big at the waist they may sit lower (if the person doesn't wear a belt). If pants are tighter at the waist they may sit higher, which makes the length shorter.

Have you ever put on weight, and found that your pants seem to have shrunk? It's because they have got tighter at the waist, and maybe the hip and thigh area, which makes the pants shorter.

3. The width at the base of pants are not always the same. A wider base will sit lower over the shoe than a narrow base.

Using iron on hemming tape

This tape can be very handy when you are pushed for time, and want to wear the pants immediately.

The problem for someone like me, is that the tape is very sticky and when I un peel the tape off the old hem, it may have stuck to the fabric. That means when I use my machines to over lock or put a blind hem on, the needles can get coated in the sticky substance, and could cause my machine some damage.

Using only one pin

From the illustration, you can see that the finished length at the back of the pants is different from the finished length at the front.

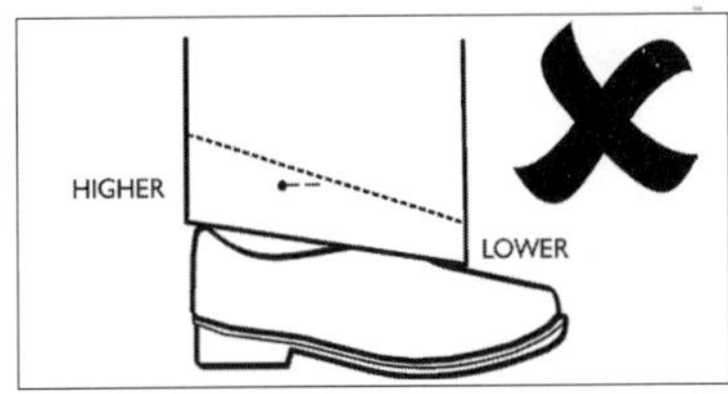

Which length will you use? I get a lot of people bring in pants that have been pinned in this way.

I always use the outside seam as my reference point (explained later) but in this case, the pants would be in between the front and the back.

What if these pants are from an expensive suit?

Wearing joggers instead of dress shoes for fitting

One of my pet hates is people coming in wearing joggers, and in their hands is a pair of good dress or suit pants that needs the hem taken up.

Joggers are totally different from dress shoes. If you look at a pair of joggers you will notice that they generally have a raised front section which is similar in height to the back section, which means the foot is sitting flat in the shoe.

If you look at most dress shoes, you will notice that the heel forces the foot into a downward position.

I find men are the worst culprits at not bringing in dress shoes to wear at the fitting to determine the new length for their pants.

All of this makes a major difference to the finished length on a pair of good dress pants.

Wearing the wrong shoes at a fitting

How often would you like to wear a pair of pants with different heeled shoes? I cover this point further on in the book, however just a quick note here.

If you want to wear low heeled shoes and high heeled shoes with your pants. Try on with the low heeled shoes and pin as long as possible. Then try on the high heeled shoes.

If you think the pants are still too short with the high heeled shoes, then you have to decide whether you will forgo wearing them with low heeled shoes.

If you only try on with low heeled shoes, and get the pants altered to that length, you may find them too short for high heeled shoes.

Conclusion

You may get away with some of these mistakes, and not have anything go wrong, but the day will come when you use one of these techniques only to find that the garment is not altered to the length you wanted.

Who are you going to blame?

If the person performing the alteration did not write down your requested measurements on a docket then you could blame them if the pants are too short or too long after the alteration.

However, there is a way to ensure that garments are not ruined. All it takes is for you to understand what you want, and transfer that knowledge to the person who is going to alter your clothes.

There must be a reference point that everyone understands. If there is no reference point, then it will always be your word against theirs.

The bottom line here is that if the pants or garment is altered incorrectly, you will never wear it and that means you have wasted money on buying the garment and on the cost of the alteration.

I guarantee my workmanship. If a mistake is made, (mistakes can happen) I replace the garment. That is how confident I feel about my technique.

Pants

Taking Up Technique

Pinning

*"Always pin the right leg, because
approximately 1 in 100 pants
will have one leg longer than the other,
which means you always know,
the right leg
is the correct measurement"*

The Knuckle Technique

By using this technique you will always pin the pants to the length the person wants, and the person wearing the pants will be able to see what you are doing and decide if they want the length shorter or longer.

I call this technique "The Knuckle Technique".

Before we begin, I need to explain a very important point.

I ALWAYS pin the right leg.

The reason I pin the right leg is because the manufacturer could make the pants with one leg longer than the other. By knowing that the right leg is the correct length, you will always be able to make an adjustment if you find one leg longer than the other. The right leg is the one you pinned, therefore you can now make the left leg the same.

Ask the person if the pants are secure on the waist or hips.

If a belt is usually worn, then the person should put a belt on BEFORE you do any pinning.

Make sure they have the shoes they want to wear with these pants. If the person wants to wear both low shoes and high shoes, get them to put the low shoes on first.

Kneel directly behind the right leg, because you are going to pin the right leg length.

If you kneel off to the side, you may twist your spine. By kneeling behind the right leg, you are in control of the fabric.

Your right hand should be positioned on the outside of the right pant leg.

Step 1

Fold the excess fabric up and inside the pant leg.

Try to have the same amount folded up and under.

If you have folded too high, there is a simple way of getting the fabric back to the position you want.

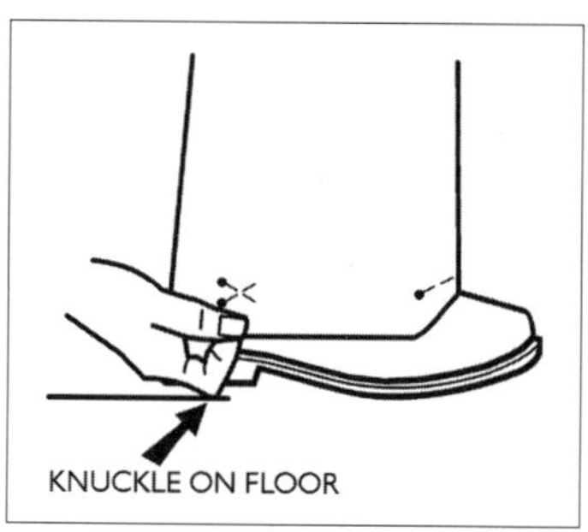

I find that licking my fingers gives me more control over the fabric.

Therefore if you have folded the excess fabric up too high, try licking your fingers and roll the fabric back down to the length you want.

Get the length you want at the outside leg seam first.

Place your index finger knuckle on the ground under the outside leg seam and place the edge of the fold (finished length) in between your thumb and index finger.

Place two pins crossed on the outside seam.

Step 2

Move your hands to the inside seam.

I place my right hand around the front of the pants and my left hand coming around the back of the pants.

Place your knuckle on the ground at the outside seam, and remembering where the hem finished in your fingers on the outside leg, roll the fabric up or down to the same position on the inside leg.

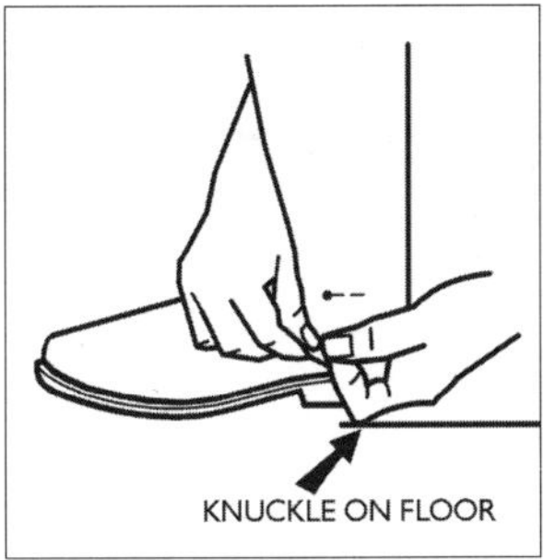

You may need to lick your fingers again when doing this so that you can roll the fabric up and down.

Look to see if it is the same as the outside leg. You don't have to be too accurate here, because the outside pin is the one that the length will be taken from.

Place the pin across the inside leg centre seam of the pants.

Step 3

Pull the fabric taut at the front, pulling from side to side.

Place a pin at the front of the pants.

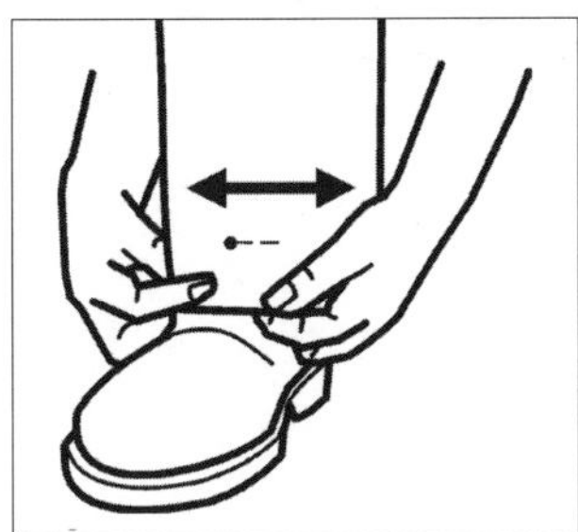

Step 4

Now pull the fabric taut at the back and place a pin at the back of the pants.

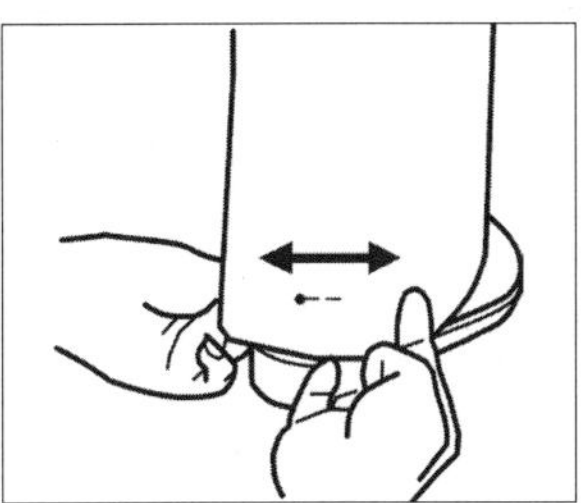

Conclusion

The length of the pants will be determined by -

1. The width at the base of the pants.
2. The heel height of the shoes.
3. The persons preference for long length.
4. The persons preference for mid length.
5. The persons preference for short length.

By following this technique, the person who is having the pants shortened will be able to see what the finished length will be.

Remember that if the person wants to wear the pants with low heeled and high heeled shoes, you should pin to the low heeled shoes first, then have the person try on the high heeled shoes to see if they are happy with the overall length.

Take your time. Find your pinning accuracy first. It will take a little bit of getting used to, but once you have this down pat, you will wonder why you didn't pin like this before.

Happy pinning

P.S. I use a kneeling pad, which is made of rubber and is comfortable to kneel on. The floor can be very hard on the knees.

Pants

Taking Up Technique

Writing down Measurements

"Arrow up = amount folded under

Arrow down = hem allowance

Always cut on the bottom line"

Writing down measurements

The first process of pinning the pants hem is now completed.

The next step is to measure the amount that you folded under and pinned into position.

This is the amount that you pushed up towards the persons knees.

To measure this amount you need to fold this excess fabric out so you can measure the amount you had folded under, but DO NOT TAKE THE PINS OUT. Leave the pins exactly where they are.

Place the beginning of the tape measure on the new folded hem line. In the illustration it shows the new folded hem line is at the top, sitting in the palm of the hand.

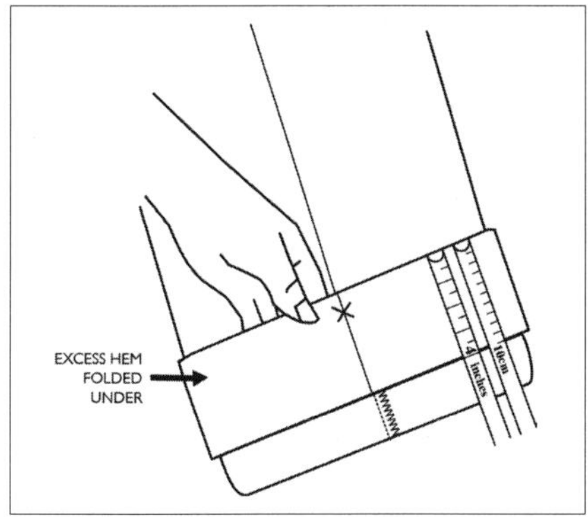

The pant leg is not inside out. The pants are the right way out, and the only part of the pants folded out is the amount that was folded under.

I am going to say for this example, that these pants are 4" or 10 cm too long.

The original hem line (before pinning) is where the tape measure shows 4".

The section below the hem line is the inside of the pants. It shows the inside seam and the over locking on the edge of the seam.

Try this yourself, by taking a pair of pants, folding 4" under, pin then pull the amount you folded under out.

The next step is to write down the amount that was folded under. In this case it would mean the pants are being taken up 4" or 10 cm.

The two notes below are of a ladies pair of pants and a man's pair of pants. This is how I would write down my measurements.

The hem is going up 4" or 10 cm.

I place an arrow going up with 4" or 10 cm beside it.

The next step is to write down the hem allowance. Mistakes are made when the hem is cut at the amount folded up, without making an allowance for a hem allowance.

I have a standard hem allowance for ladies and men's dress pants.

Ladies hem allowance = 1 1/2" or 4 cm
Men's hem allowance = 2" or 5 cm

I have provided a list of hem allowances under H - Helpful Hints & Tips page 219.

Copy and use for writing down your measurements.

Pants

Taking Up Technique

Preparing

*"Check the leg lengths
before you cut."*

*"The right and left leg
must be the same length."*

Checking

Before you mark and cut the pants, you need to do some final checks.

Check 1

Before you take out the pins, measure from the top of the band to the bottom of the new hem length, running your tape measure all the way down the outside leg seam.

Make sure the two side seams at the top of the pants are matching at the top.

The hip area may need to be flattened out as you work from the top of the band to the bottom of the hem.

You are going to do this if you would like to record the outside leg measurement for a particular style of pants. Some people buy the same brand and size all the time, so if you register the outside leg measurement, you will not have to try the pants on again.

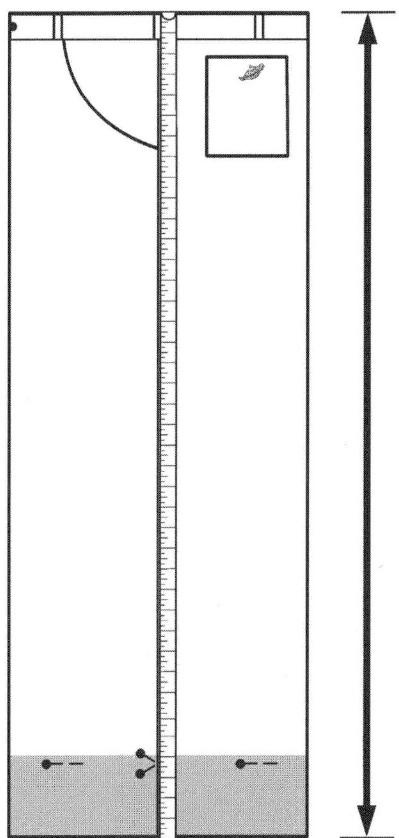

Check 2

Take the pins out.

Your next step is to check to make sure the pant legs are the same length.

As previously discussed, manufacturers can make a mistake with leg lengths, and occassionally you may come across a pair of pants with one leg longer than the other.

I use two checks for this :-

1. Fold the two side seams together. Place the two sides of the band together and run your hand down the two side seams, all the way to the hem. Check to see the lengths are the same. If the fabric is a stretch fabric, you may find it easier to lay it out on the table as per the second way of checking.

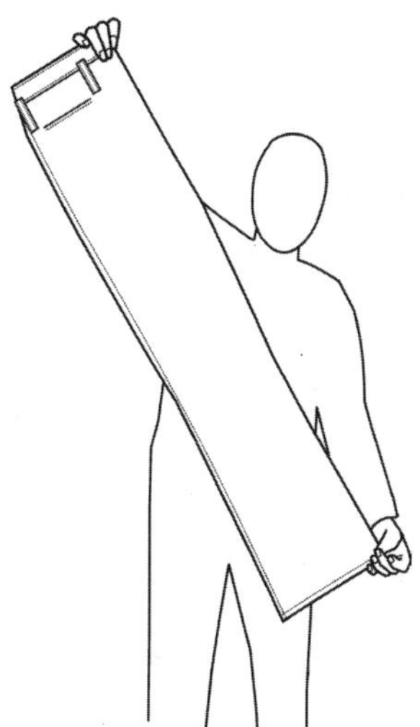

2. Lay the pants on the table with the two side seams together.

Check to see that the legs are the same length.

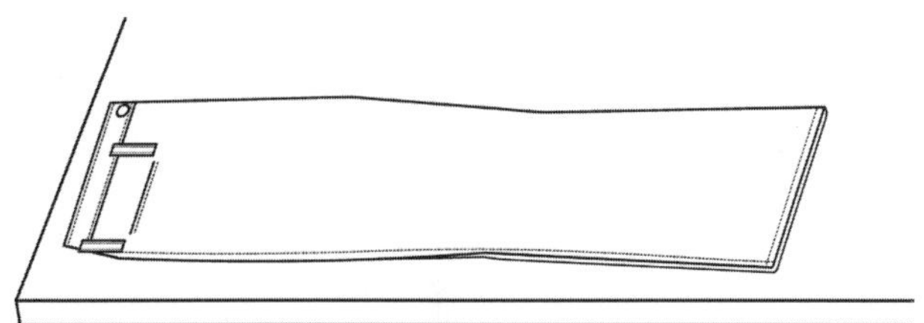

Marking

If you have to unpick a hem before marking, refer to the section at the back of the book on Tips and Helpful Hints. For How to Unpick a Blind Hem see page 211.

Step 1

Lay pants flat on table with the front of the pants facing upwards.

Have legs side by side.

The side seams should be at the edges of the folded pants.

If there is a crease in the pants it should be in the middle.

Step 2

You are going to place chalk marks in three positions on the front of the pants, and three positions on the back.

The first position is next to the inside leg seam - approximately 1 1/2" or 3 1/2 cm from the side seam.

The second position is in the centre of the leg.

The third position is on the right hand side next to the outside seam - 1 1/2" or 3 1/2 cm from the side seam.

The illustration is marking ladies pants with a 1 1/2" hem allowance.

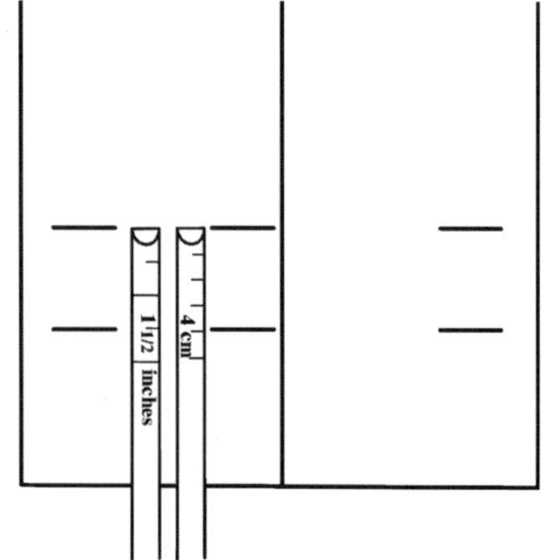

The following illustration is of a pair of men's pants being marked with a 2" hem allowance.

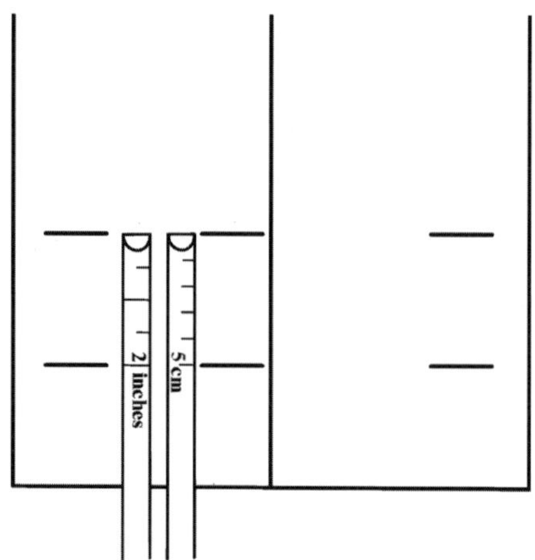

Cutting

All pants are cut the same. Once you have marked the pants, you are ready to cut.

Cut on the bottom line.

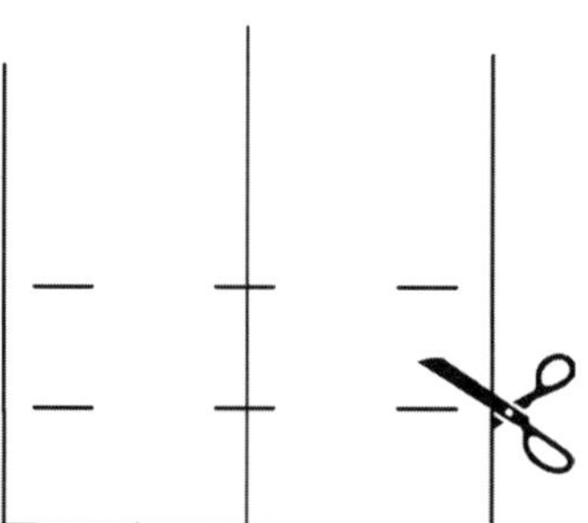

I always remember the saying - "The bottom line is...." If you remember "The bottom line" you will never make a mistake.

Place a nick in the fabric and cut around the pants so that the original hem is still in tact. You must cut around the pant leg, do not cut the pant leg with the front and back folded together.

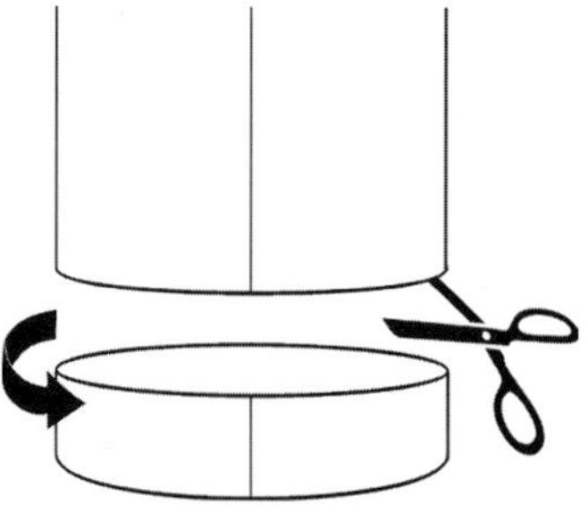

If you make a mistake, you can re-attach the hem as a false hem, or use it for other pants.

Pants

Taking Up Technique

Sewing

*"If you don't have an over locker,
sew a nice satin ribbon over
the cut raw edge, then hand stitch."*

Sewing

Tapered pants

If the pants are slightly tapered, the new hem allowance will not fit up into the pants without bunching and puckering.

Releasing side seams

Step 1 - To find out whether you need to open out the seams, fold the new hem allowance up and see if the hem allowance will fit into the new pant length.

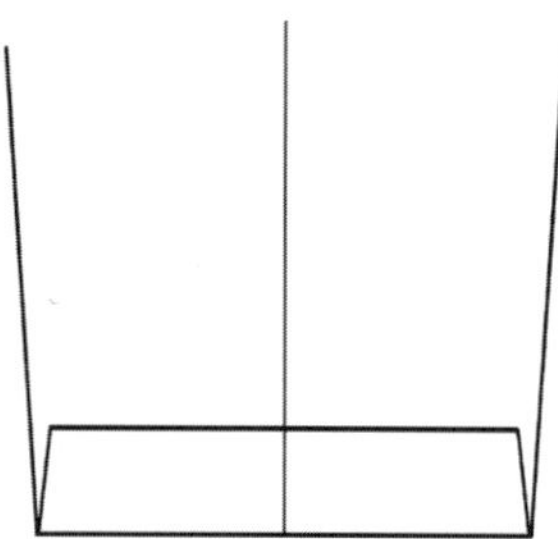

You can see from the above illustration that the section folded up does not fit back into the pants. You will need to open out the side seam from the new hem line to the end of the hem allowance.

Step 2 - If the seam is not top stitched, begin with the inside leg. Sew a seam from the new hemline (see the dotted line) to the edge of the over locking. Unpick the old seam.

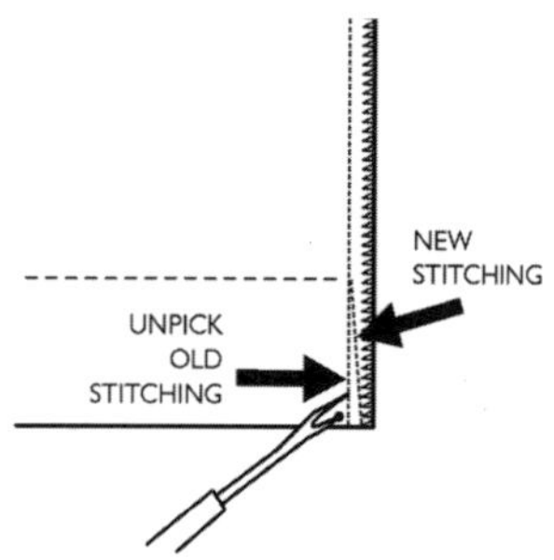

Repeat Step 1 to see it the new hem allowance fits into the new pant length. If it still does not fit, then **Repeat Step 2** on the outside leg.

Whether you over lock the raw cut edge or sew on ribbon, the fabric will be pulled in slightly by the over locking or ribbon, so I usually have just a tiny bit more than the exact fold up to the fabric.

Flared pants

The opposite situation will happen if the pants are flared.

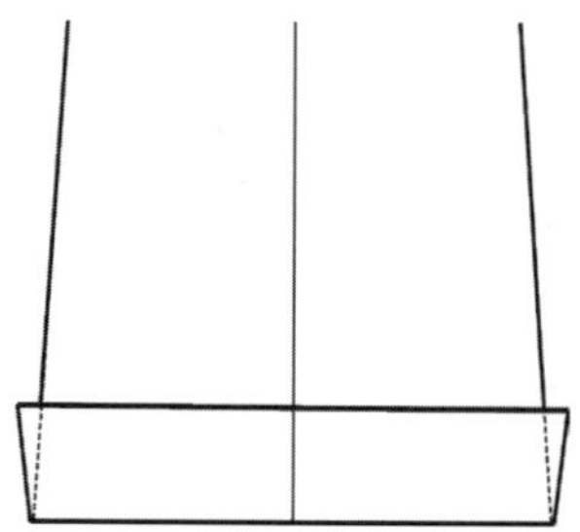

Step 1 - Fold the hem allowance up. If the pants are too flared the new hem allowance will be too wide for the pants.

Step 2 - Depending on the width of the flare, you may only need to taper in the inside leg.

Begin sewing from the new hem line (dotted line on illustration) and sew away from the original seam. This will close the side seam so that the new hem allowance will fit.

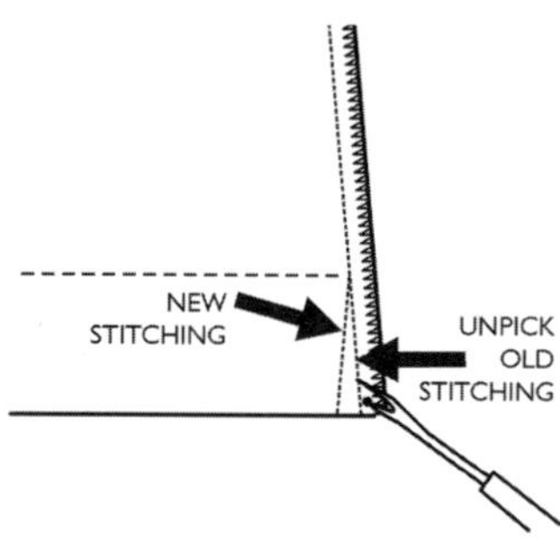

Repeat Step 1 to see if the hem fits into the new hem length. It is doesn't then **Repeat Step 2** on the outside leg.

If side seams are over locked together, you will not need to unpick the old seam stitch, but if the side seams not over locked together, unpick the old seam stitch and open the seams flat.

The pants should look like the illustration when the new hem allowance is folded up.

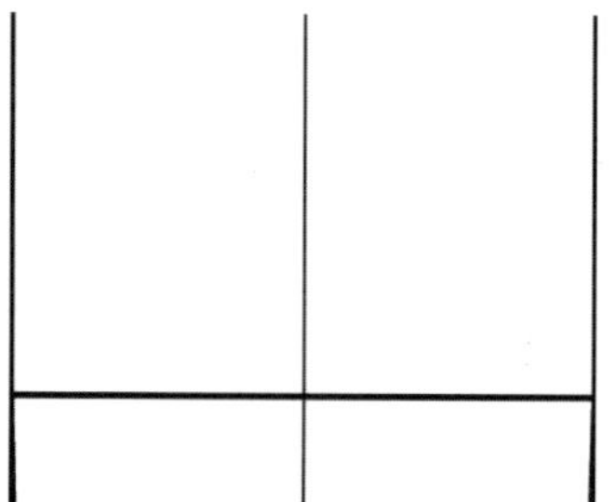

You are now ready to over lock or sew on some nice satin ribbon.

If you have an over locker, over lock the raw edge.

As an alternative, satin ribbon can look nice sewn over the top of the cut raw edge of the fabric. The ribbon should be no more than 1/2" or 1 cm wide.

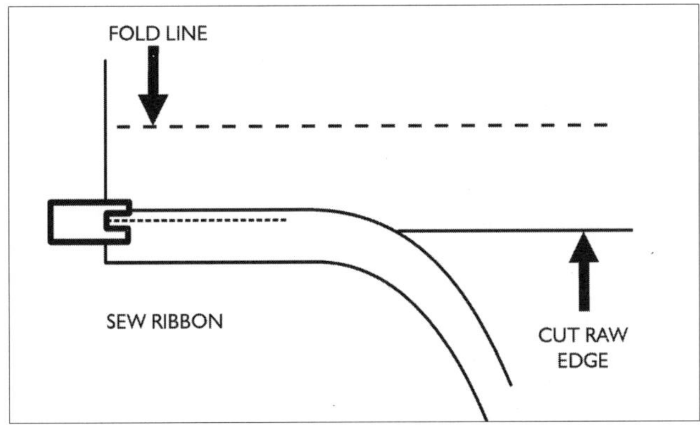

Some world-renowned designers use this technique rather than over locking.

Hand stitch around the hem using a slip stitch or your favourite hand stitch. When you place the needle into the outer fabric of the pants, try to only catch one or two threads. This way you end up with a blind hem that is not seen from the other side.

The only fabric that is difficult to achieve a blind hem with both hand stitch and a blind hemming machine is micro fibre. The reason being that the fabric is such a close weaved fabric that it is also impossible to take up one or two stitches without going through to the other side.

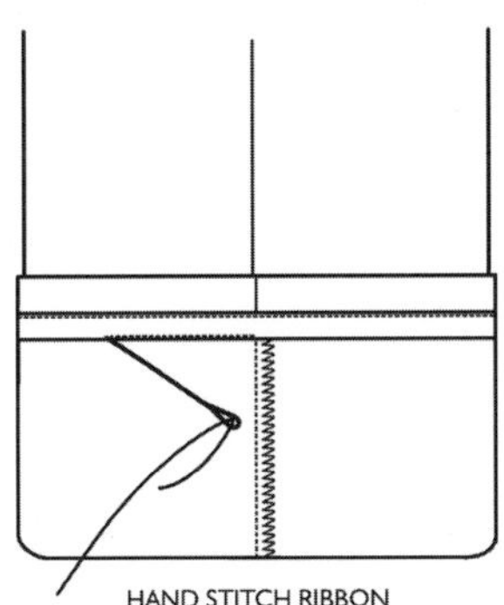

Pants that are very tapered

If the pants are very tapered, you have two choices.

Step 1. Fold the hem allowance up so that you can see how much you need to taper the pants. Place a chalk mark on the inside seam at the amount you need to take in.

Taper the pants in beginning from the knee and sewing down the inside leg coming in towards the chalk mark.

Now from the hem line come out to the over locking.

Step 2. Leave a small gap in the front and/or back of the centre front or centre back seam. This is definitely cheating, but it will save you a lot of hassle.

The illustration shows the gap. Do not hand stitch this section.

Pin your side seams so that they are even, and the gap is at the fold in the centre front or centre back of the pants.

Most pants have a crease down the front and back. This is exactly where I leave the gap.

When the pants are turned out, you will not notice that the hem does not fit.

Begin sewing either side of the centre front or centre back crease, and finish on the opposite side.

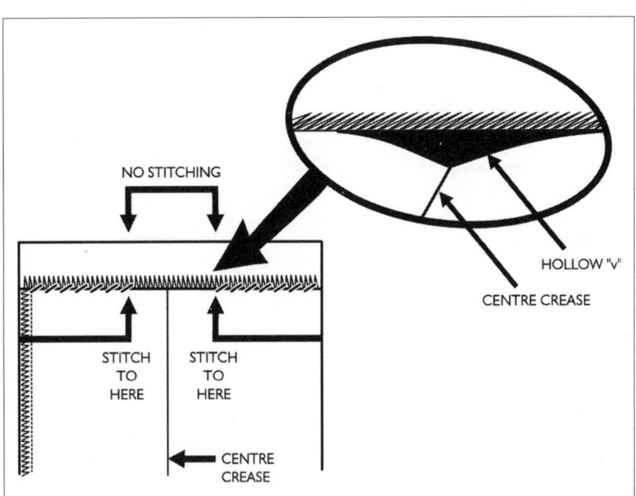

Pants

Taking Up

Ladies & Men's Dress Pants Hems

"Always put a good sized hem on dress pants."

Dress Pants

My definition of dress pants is "Pants that have a blind hem." You can't see any stitching at the hem.

Suit pants and good dress pants are the most common to have a blind hem.

Some manufacturers put a small hem on pants. I prefer to use 1 1/2" for ladies and 2" for men. The reason is a good sized hem adds weight to the bottom of the pants, letting them fall better.

The other reason is if a mistake is made, or the pants shrink, you have a good sized hem to lower.

Pin hem as per page 29.

Ladies Dress Pants

A 1 1/2" hem on ladies dress pant hems should look like this illustration. I have shown both tape measures for you, because some people work on imperial and some work on metric.

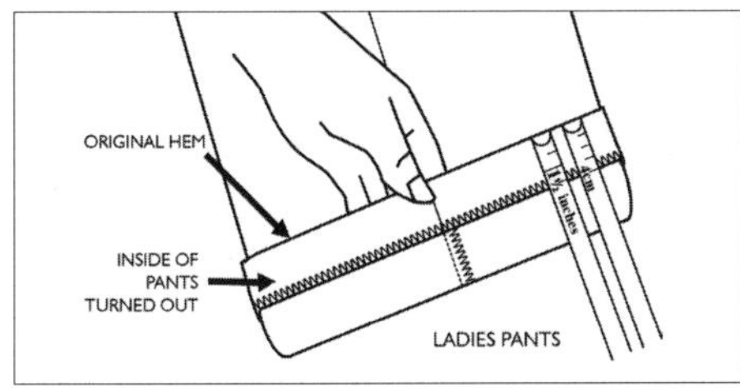

Step 1 - Measure the amount you have folded under.

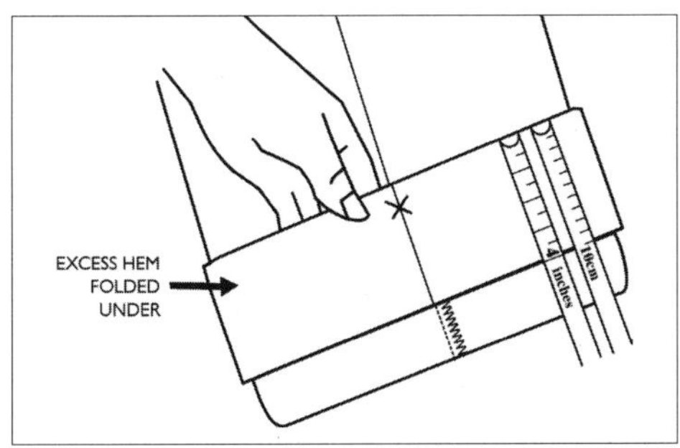

Step 2 - Write this amount down on your paper with an arrow up for amount you folded under and an arrow down for the amount of hem allowance.

I have put an X where you would put the amount the pants are being shortened.

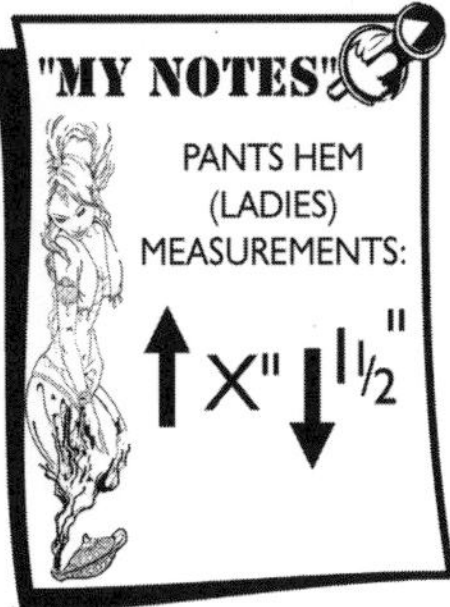

Step 3 - Take pins out of hem.

Step 4 - Check leg lengths are correct from Manufacturer. See page 35.

Step 5 - Mark pants as follows -

1. Place the tape measure over the pants hem with the amount folded under on the original hem line. See next paragraph for example.

In the illustration we are shortening the pants by 4" / 10 cm. Place the tape measure over the existing hem length with the 4" / 10 cm mark of the tape measure at the original hem.

2. Place the first chalk mark at the tip of the tape measure, at the side of the top, not above.

3. Move down the tape and place another chalk mark beside the 1 1/2"" or 4 cm mark on the tape measure. This is the hem allowance.

4. Repeat this process on the opposite leg, then turn the pants over and repeat the same process on the back of the pant legs.

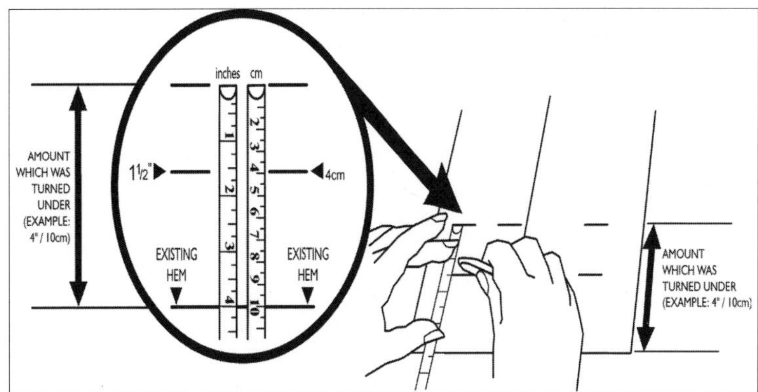

Step 5 - Cut pants as per page 36.

Step 6 - Sew pants as per pages 37-39.

Men's Dress Pants

As discussed earlier, I prefer to put a 2" hem on men's pants.

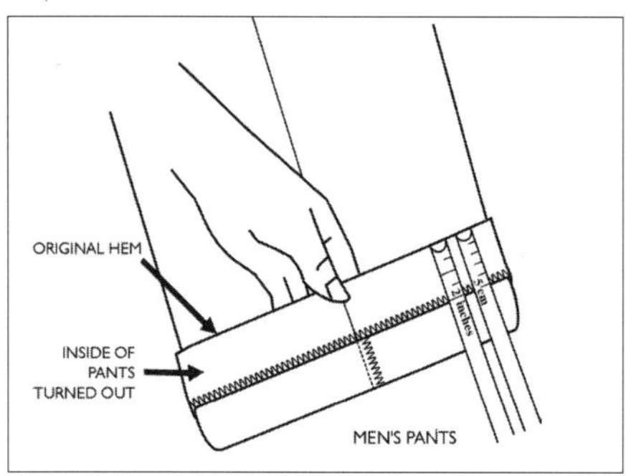

The original hem allowance should look like the following illustration.

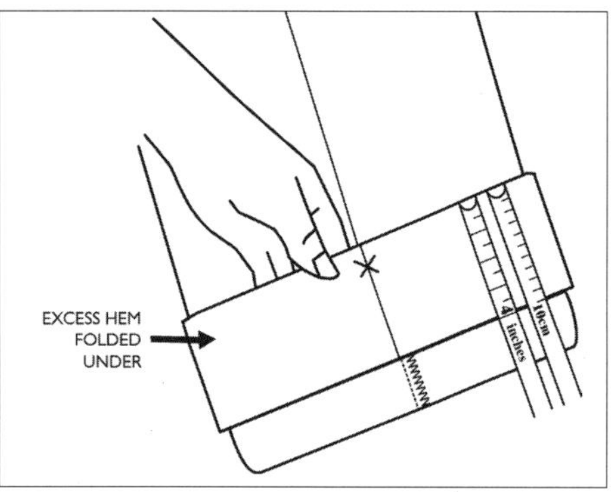

Step 1 - Measure the amount you have folded under.

Step 2 - Write this amount down on your paper showing an arrow up for the amount you folded under and an arrow down for the amount of hem allowance.

I have put an X on "My Notes" but this will be the amount you are taking the pants up by.

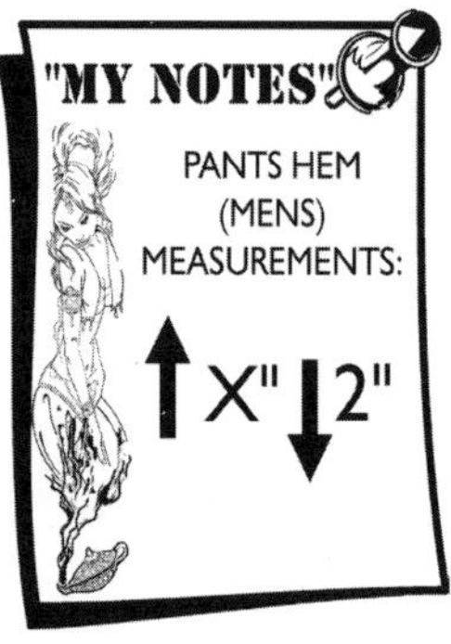

Step 3 - Take pins out of hem.

Step 4 - Check leg lengths are correct from Manufacturer. See page 35.

Step 5 - Mark pants as follows -

1. Place the tape measure over the pants hem with the amount folded under on the original hem line. See next paragraph for example.

In the illustration we are shortening the pants by 4" /10 cm. Place the tape measure over the existing hem length with the 4" / 10 cm mark of the tape measure at the original hem.

2. Place the first chalk mark at the tip of the tape measure, but at the side of the top, not above the tape.

3. Move down the tape and place another chalk mark beside the 2" or 5 cm mark on the tape measure. This is the hem allowance.

4. Repeat this process on the opposite leg, then turn the pants over and repeat the same process on the back of the pant legs.

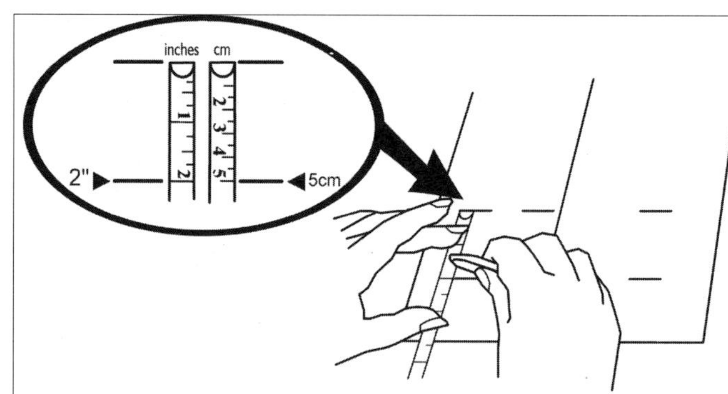

Step 6 - Cut pants as per page 36.

Step 7 - Sew pants as per pages 37-39.

Casual Pants

Taking up

Hem

"Casual pants could be Cargo pants, tracksuit pants or any pant with a machine stitched hem."

Procedure

Casual pants usually have a larger hem allowance than jeans, and most casual pant hems are what I call 'Turn twice'.

When a hem is turn twice, there will need to be an additional turn up. Usually that turn up is an additional 1/2" (1 cm). Some examples are -

1" + 1/2"	(2.5 + 1 cm)
1 1/2" + 1/2"	(3.5 + 1 cm)
2" + 1/2"	(5 + 1 cm)

I have come across larger hems. The rule of thumb is usually to repeat the hem allowance that is on the pants you are shortening.

I am assuming you have pinned the casual pants as per page 29.

Step 1 - Measure amount pinned and write down the measurements on a piece of paper. Place the arrow going up with the amount pinned under, and an arrow down for the existing hem allowance. If it is a turn twice, then put another arrow for the amount turned under which will be 1/2" or 1.5 cm.

For the "My notes" illustrations I have assumed that the hem allowance is 1/1/4" (3 cm).

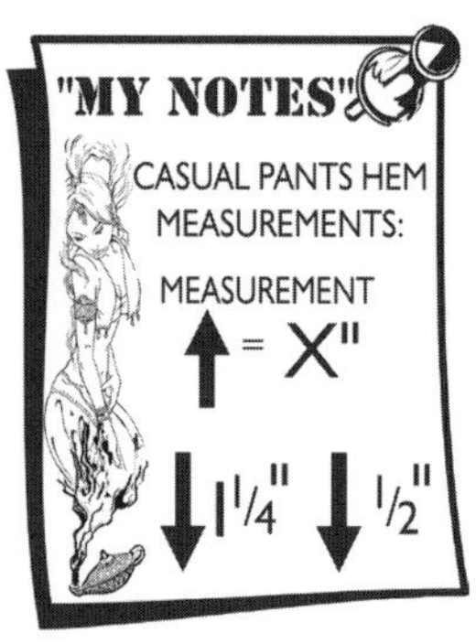

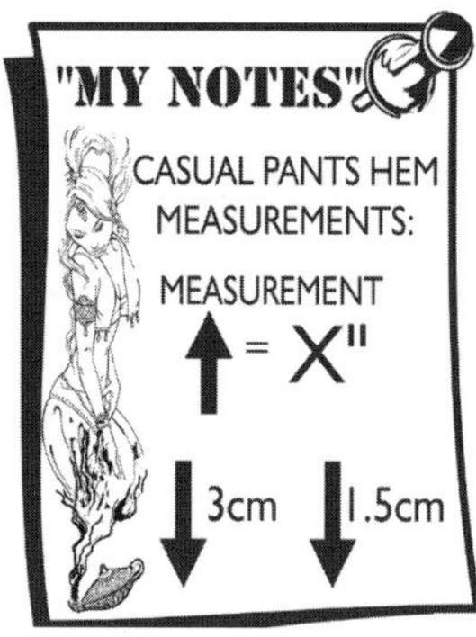

Step 2 - Take pins out.

Step 3 - Check legs are same length as per page 30.

Step 4 - Place the tape measure over the casual pant hem.

The position of the tape measure is important.

In the illustration we are shortening the pants by 4"/10 cm. Therefore place the tape measure over the existing hem length with the 4"/10 cm mark of the tape measure at the original hem.

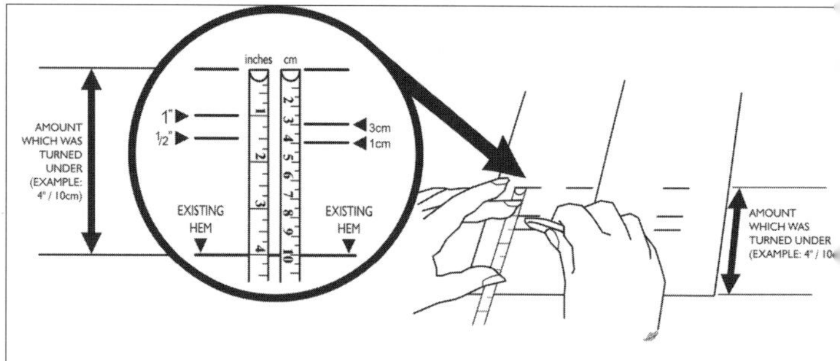

Step 5 - Beginning on the left hand side of the pants, place the first chalk mark beside the top of the tape measure, then move down 1 1/4" or 2.5 cm and place another mark, then move down the tape measure again and place a chalk mark at the 1 3/4" or 4.5 cm mark **(which is 1/2" below the 1 1/4" mark).**

Step 5 - Repeat Step 4 but place the marks in the centre of the pants.

Step 6 - Repeat Step 4 but place the marks on the right hand side of the pants.

If the original hem allowance is in the way of where you are going to cut, then you must unpick the original stitching on the hem. (see Slicing a jeans hem - Helpful Hints & Tips)

Step 7 - Repeat on the opposite leg and then the backs of the pant legs.

Step 8 - Cut the pants on the bottom line as per page 36.

Step 9 - Check to see that the pants will fit up into the new hem allowance as per page 38.

Step 10 - If the pants will not fit into the new hem allowance, then you need to open out the seams.

You will notice that on the following illustration, the procedure for opening out the seams is a little different from dress pants. The reason

for this is because of the extra hem allowance of 1/2".

Begin the let out process at the new fold line, and sew a seam out to the over locking at the edge but this should be 1 1/4" or 3 cm long. When you reach that length, sew straight down to the edge of the over locking at the bottom of the hem.

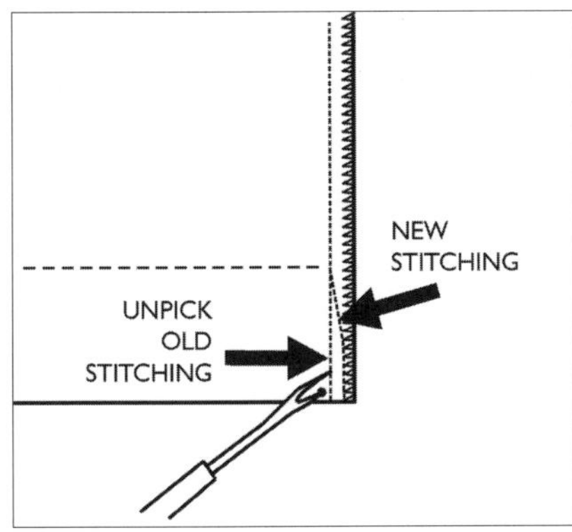

In Casual pants you can copy the same process for jeans, and sew topside, or you can turn the pants inside out and sew inside out.

This is the only time I prefer to turn the pants inside out and sew inside out.

The reason being that some casual pants have a very large hem allowance. It could be 1 + 1/2 or it could be 1 1/2 + 1/2, or 2 + 1/2 or even 3 + 1/2. You may have worked out by now that all of these are in inches. Convert to metric for those of you who use metric.

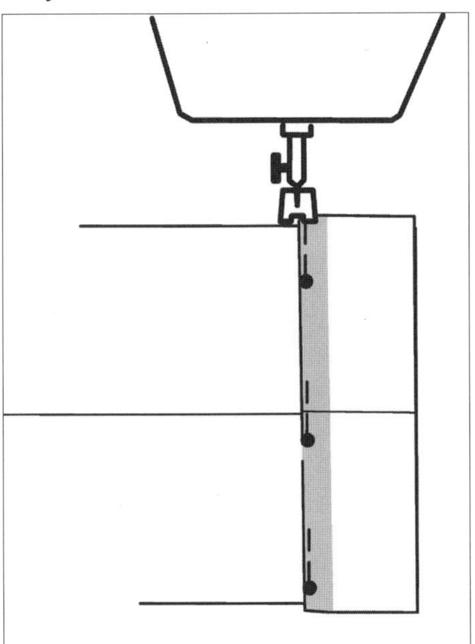

Conclusion

A lot of casual pants have a double stitched hem. In this instance do your first row of stitching on the very edge of the fabric with the 1/2 turned under, then begin the second row using the sewing machine foot as a guide so that your stitching is exactly the same distance apart all the way around the seam.

I use the button hole foot when I do this because my button hole foot is clear, and that means I can see the stitching.

I line up my first row of stitching on the centre of the arm of the sewing machine foot and I concentrate on keeping the stitching in the same position all the way around.

You will come across casual pants with a hem that has been over locked and machine stitched.

The same rules will apply here as for a blind hem, except instead of hand stitching you can machine stitch.

Pants

Taking In Technique

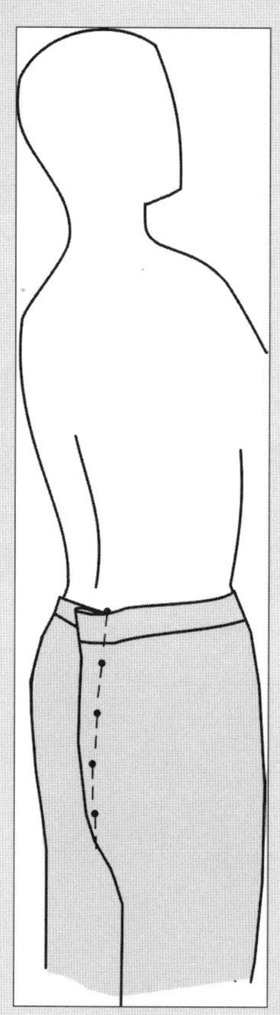

"Taking in the back on a pair of pants
is sometimes the best option
if you have lost weight."

Introduction

When a garment is being taken in, it is extremely important to follow the contour of the human body, and to pin with accuracy.

With hemming we talked about the importance of pinning all the way around the hem accurately, and we used the analogy of "Where I pin is where I sew".

The same principle applies to Taking In a garment. Your pins become your temporary seams. If you pin a garment accurately to the contour of the body, or to the effect that is required, and you take the garment in at the exact position of those pins, then it stands to reason that the finished, altered garment should be 100% accurate.

Some people like their clothes to be snug and others prefer them slightly loose. So whether you are pinning for yourself or for someone else, be sure to have the communication lines open and know what the person wants.

Just to recap the pins become the most important aspect of this part of the alteration. The reason for this will become clear as you read on, however for now I would like to show you the difference between pinning correctly and pinning incorrectly.

The illustration on the left shows the pins in no particular order.

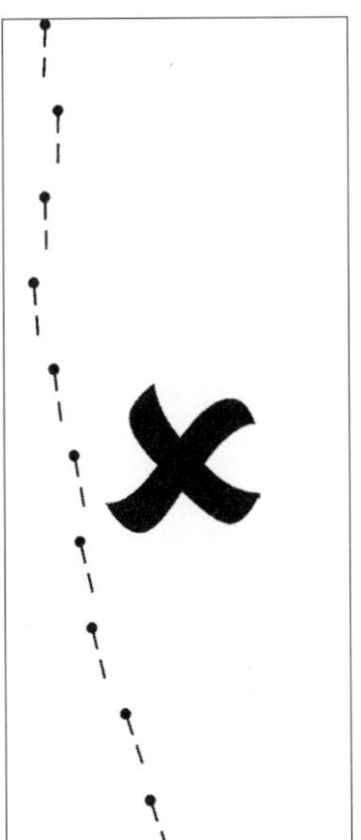

The illustration on the right shows the pins following one after the other.

When taking a garment in, always pin with the garment right side out (not inside out). The reason for this is if you wear the garment inside out, the seams will stick out and the seams will draw your attention away from the pins.

Another reason is with the seams sticking out, the garment will look bigger than it is.

By having the garment on the right way, you will only see the amount being pinned, and not the additional seams.

The illustration on the left shows a pair of pants that have been pinned in a slap dash (incorrect) manner.

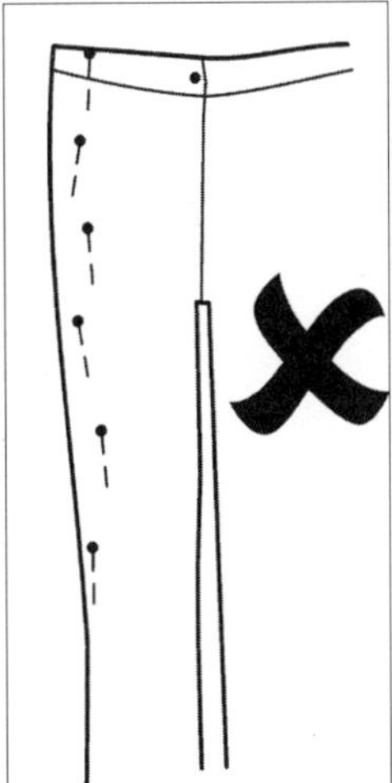
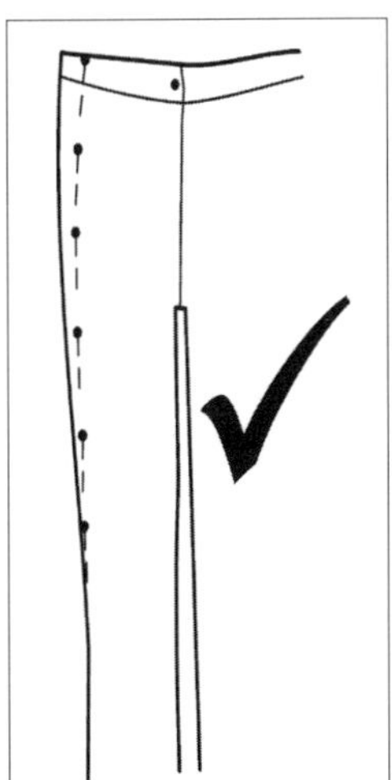

The illustration on the right shows the correct way to pin.

You may think people wouldn't do this, but I have had many garments brought into my shop which has been pinned like this, and I have been asked to take the pants in as per the pinning. Impossible to do.

Which pin is the reference point?

So just to clarify again, the pins should be used like a seam. Think of the pins as your temporary seam. You wouldn't sew a seam like this so why pin like this?

Pants

Taking in Technique

Pinning

*"Always pin with garment
on right side out."*

"Never pin inside out."

I am using the example of taking in the back of a pair of pants to explain my Taking In Technique.

However, please note that this could be any type of taking in, from taking in the back on a pair of pants, taking in the sides of a jacket or coat, or taking in the sides of a top. Even taking in a garment with a zip. It covers all alterations.

Let's say you purchased some pants, and whilst the thigh area is great, the waist and part of the hip area is too big .

You could take in both sides, however before I pin the sides I pin the centre back because 99% of the time, if the amount is not great, taking in the back works well.

Step 1 - Begin by taking hold of the fabric at the centre back seam, making sure you have the centre back seam in the middle. Your fingers should be taking up all the excess fabric away from the body. Your index finger and thumb are the anchor points for the position of the first pin.

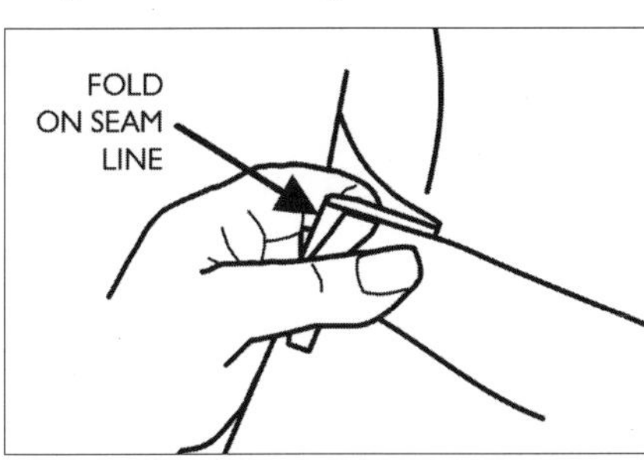

Step 2 - Use a large hat pin and push the pin through from one side to the other, beginning at the top of the band. When the pin is half way through, turn the pin into a downward position and then push it back through the band to the other side.

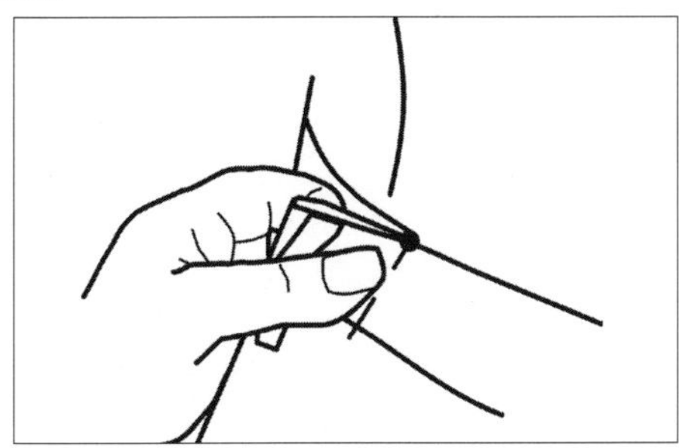

Step 3 - Take hold of the fabric below the band, and place a second pin underneath the first pin, pinning the two sides together on the body of the pants.

Step 4 - Take hold of the excess fabric below the second pin, and using your thumb and index finger pinch the fabric together. Place a pin in this exact spot.

Step 5 - Follow Step 4 until all excess fabric at the centre back is gone. Stop pinning BEFORE you move into the crotch area.

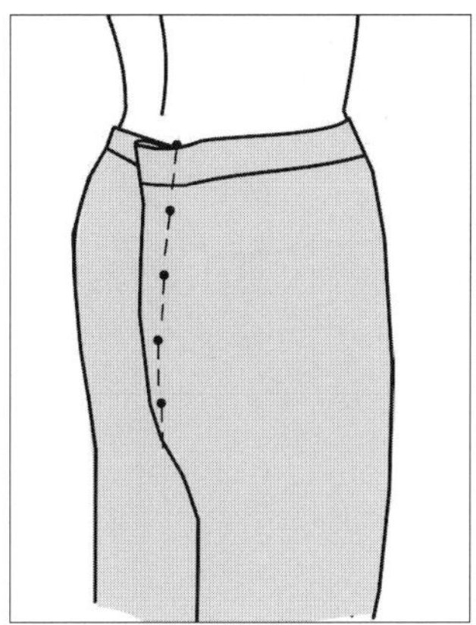

Note that on the illustration, the pins are following one another from the beginning to the end.

In this illustration I have pinned down from the centre back down 10" in imperial and 25.5 centimetres in metric.

A lot of people think that 1" = 2.5 cm, but it is not exactly 2.5 cm. The point is if you are using metric try to get as close as possible, and if you are using imperial, stay within the 1/8th of an inch area.

There will be times when the pants are too big from the top of the band through and into the crotch. When this happens, pin down to around 10" or 25.5 cm (as above), but leave your last pin where it feels comfortable on the person.

Do not pin into the crotch. You don't want to harm the person, and you can taper into the crotch from the last pin position, without any problems at all.

For this exercise however, I am working on the above illustration with the pins tapering out and finishing at 10" or 25.5 cm down.
There are going to be times when you are not going to be able to get through the thickness of the band.

Taking pressure off band

To help you take the pressure off the band and so you can push the pin through, ask the person wearing the pants to place their hands on the band at the sides and push the fabric back towards you.

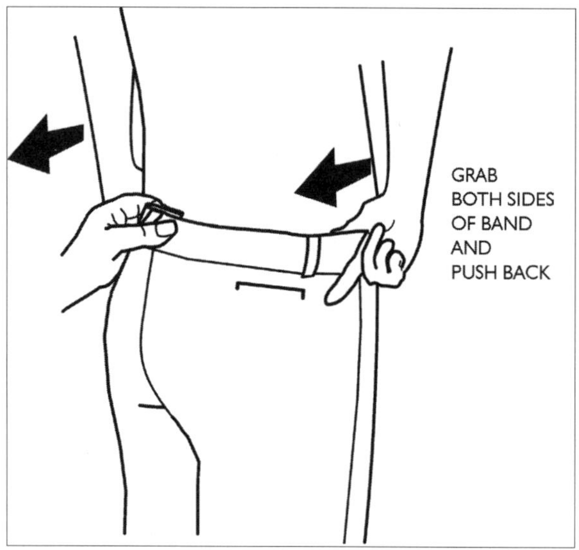

If this still doesn't work because the band is too thick, try the next option.

Pinning each side of band

Follow Step 1 on page 49 to determine the amount to be Taken In.

Now place a pin in front of your thumb on the right hand side, but only pinning through the single section of band. Place another pin in front of your index finger on the left hand side pinning through the single section of band on that side

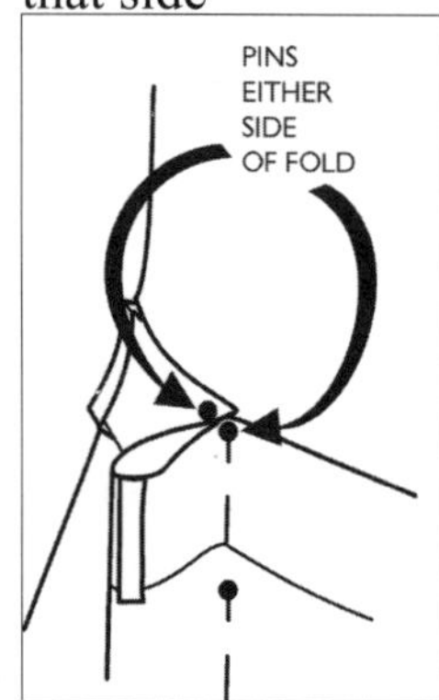

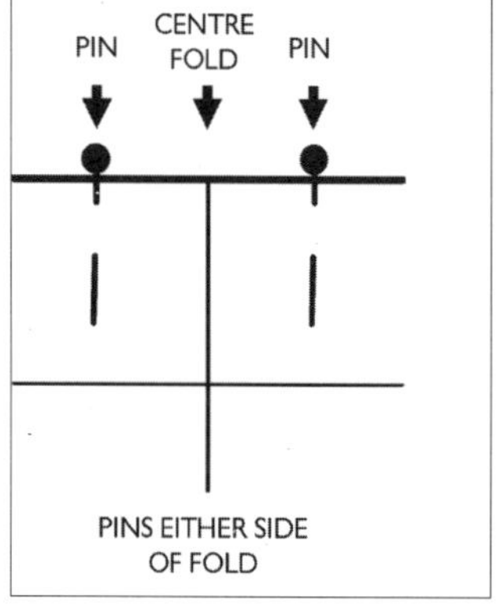

Conclusion

Pin to the contour of the body, or pin so that you take away the excess fabric that is no longer needed.

Some people like their garments to fit their body snugly and others like it a little loose.

When you insert the pin for the first time into the garment, put the pin where you think, but let the person know that you will adjust the pins if he/she feels the garment is too tight or too loose.

Remember that at the end of the day it is how the person feels in the garment, not what you think.

Get the pinning correct, and the garment will be perfect.

If you are taking in a garment from the top of the band or facing, then you are probably taking hold of a reasonable amount of fabric.

As you pin down the body you will either pin all the way to the end of the garment, or you will taper off to seam.

If you taper off to seam it is extremely important that your pins taper in gradually, and your last pin should be on the edge of the seam.

If you come in too fast, when you sew the garment you will create what I call a duck tail effect. The fabric will pucker out and you will not be happy with the result.

In the following Section we will be Writing Down our Measurements.

I am still using the previous example of Taking In a back seam on pants.

Pants

Taking in Technique

Writing down measurements

"Think of yourself as a carpenter, except you are working with fabric."

Writing down measurements

The world is divided on imperial measure and metric. Because I intend for this book to sell internationally, I have provided a section on both Imperial and Metric.

My preferred way of measuring is with Inches. There is a reason for this. I always buy the tape measure which has the one inch broken down into 1/8th of an inch segments.

When I take a garment UP or IN, I move up and down or in and out by 1/8th of an inch.

There are eight (8) 1/8th segments in one inch.

It probably has something to do with my age, but I find it easier to see a 1/8th of an inch movement when marking.

Also I find that the accuracy with the 1/8th of an inch is a lot higher than using metric.

I have provided a section at the back of the book on Imperial & Metric Explained to help you.

Now let's discuss Metric.

On the opposite side of any tape measure you will find metric. So one side is imperial and one side is metric.

The measurements in metric are broken down into one millimetre. There are ten millimetres in a centimetre.

A centimetre is a little bit less than 1/2 and inch.

On a metric tape, they provide you with the full 10 millimetre marks, with a larger mark at the half way point for half a centimetre.

If you have ever used a tailors pencil, the tip of the pencil is bigger than a normal lead pencil. When you are marking the inside of a garment, you will be using a tailors pencil. It is almost (not completely) but almost impossible to be accurate with millimetres with a tailors pencil.

If you were going to just work in half centimetre segments, you would not get the accuracy.

So I use the imperial because it gives me the accuracy I need.

It's up to you. As I said before I have provided a section on how to understand Imperial and Metric at the back of the book.

Inches

Step 1 - The example we are going to use is the same as the previous illustration of taking in a pair of pants through the centre back seam.

Step 2 - Lay the garment on your work table with the back section that you pinned facing you. Have the pin heads on the top side.

A kitchen table or dining table works well for a prepare table.

Step 3 - Draw an outline of the garment and/or the section you are working on, onto a piece of paper.   For this example I have drawn the back of a pair of pants with the band at the top, and a line which represents the centre back seam.

Step 4 - You are going to transfer the measurement of the pins from the garment to your paper.

Step 5 - Your reference points will be the measurements from the top of the band, the bottom of the band, and every 2" from the bottom of the band down the seam of the garment to the last pin on the edge of the seam.

Step 6 - To show what I mean, I have provided an illustration showing a tape measure down the side seam beginning at the bottom of the band.

If you have two tape measures it would be helpful, however this illustration shows what I mean about taking down the measurement on the side seam.

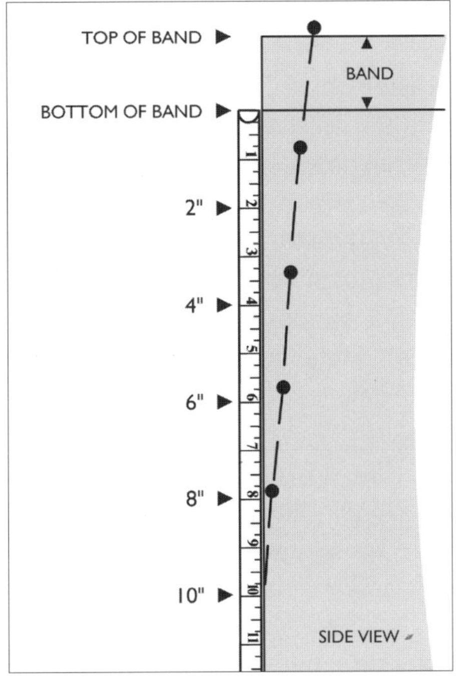

Step 7 - Measure at the top of the band from the pin to the fold or edge of the fabric. On the illustration this measurement is 1". Write down on your drawing - top of the band = 1".

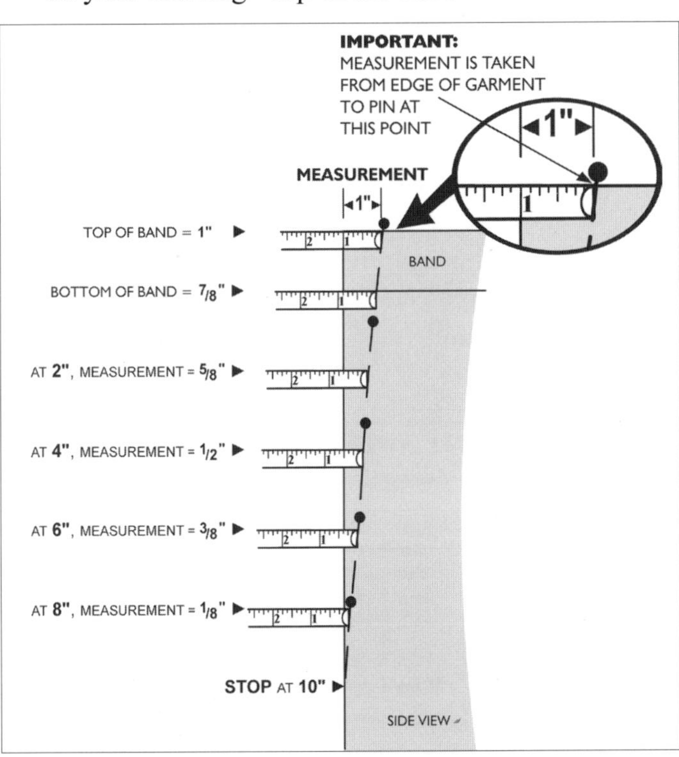

Step 8 - Measure at bottom of the band from the pin to the fold or edge of the fabric. On the illustration this measurement is 7/8". Write down on your drawing-bottom of the band =7/8".

Step 9 - Measure down 2" from the bottom of the band. On the illustration this measurement is 5/8". Write down on your drawing - 2" = 5/8".

Step 10 - Measure down 4" from the bottom of the band. On the illustration this measurement is 1/2". Write down on your drawing - 4" = 1/2".

Step 11 - Measure down 6" from the bottom of the band. On the illustration this measurement is 3/8". Write down on your drawing - 6" = 3/8".

Step 12 - Measure down 8" from the bottom of the band. On the illustration this measurement is 1/8". Write down on your drawing - 8" = 1/8".

Step 13 - At 10" the edge of the pin is against the side of the seam. On your piece of paper write down - 10" = Stop.

Writing down the exact measurements from the pins is critical to your alteration.

Finally, notice how the measurements on this piece of paper match the measurements of the pins all the way down the seam in the above illustration.

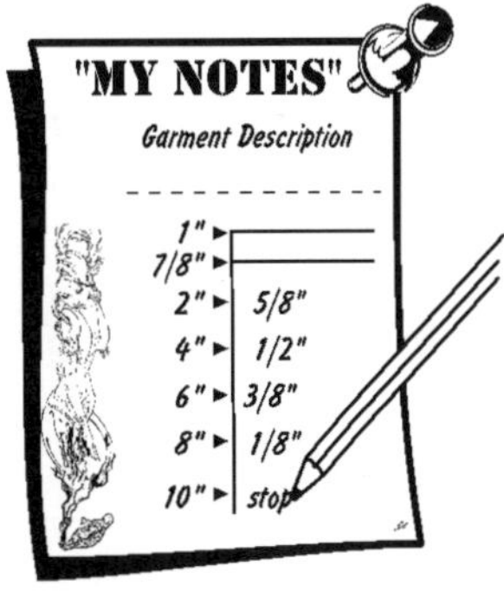

Conclusion

No matter what you are taking in, use the same principle. Pin accurately, measure the pins from a reference point on the garment, write down the measurements at those reference points. I find 2" is a good gap in between amounts.

Metric

Follow the same procedure on page 52 for Inches, up to and including Step 6.

The tape measure down the centre back seam in this instance is in metric

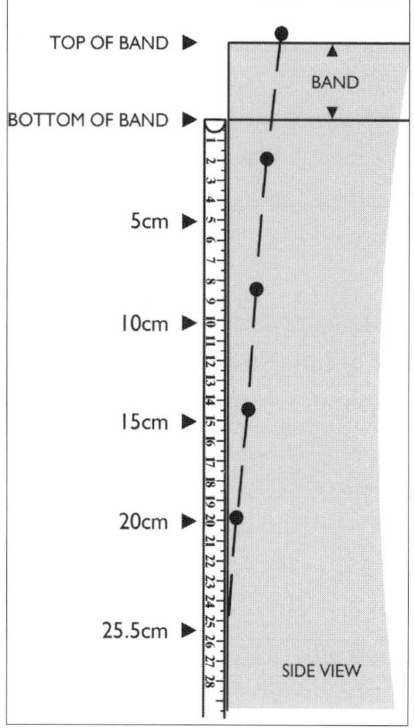

Step 7 - Measure at the top of the band from the pin to the fold or edge of the fabric. On the illustration this measurement is 2.5 cm. Write down on your drawing - top of the band = 2.5 cm.

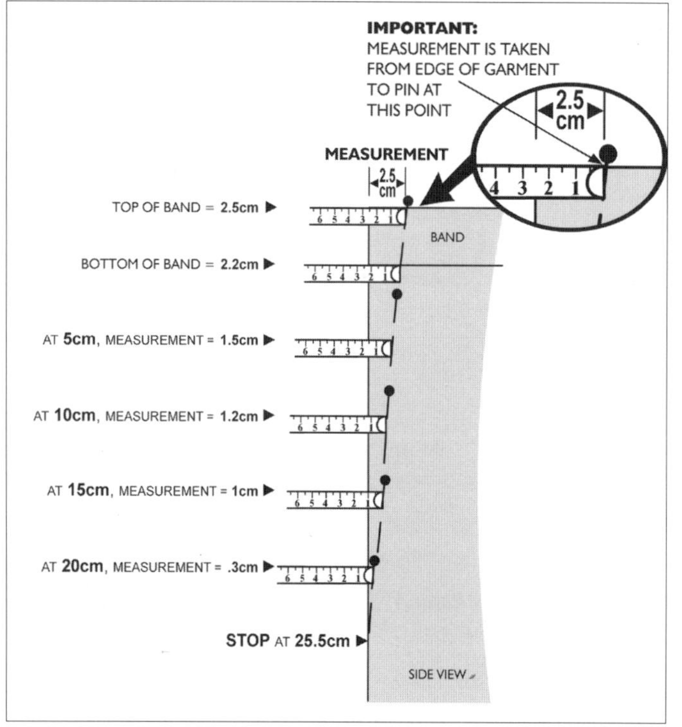

Step 8 - Measure at the bottom of the band from the pin to the fold or edge of the fabric. On the illustration this measurement is 2.2 cm. Write down on your drawing - bottom of the band = 2.2 cm.

Step 9 - Measure down 5 cm from the bottom of the band. On the illustration this measurement is 1.5 cm. Write down on your drawing - 5 cm = 1.5 cm.

Step 10 - Measure down 10 cm from the bottom of the band. On the illustration this measurement is 1.2 cm. Write down on your drawing - 10 cm = 1.2 cm.

Step 11 - Measure down 15 cm from the bottom of the band. On the illustration this measurement is 1 cm. Write down on your drawing - 15 cm = 1 cm.

Step 12 - Measure down 20 cm from the bottom of the band. On the illustration this measurement is .3 cm. Write down on your drawing - 20 cm = .3 cm .

Step 13 - At 25.5 cm the edge of the pin is against the side of the seam. On your piece of paper write down - 25.5 cm = Stop.

Writing down the exact measurements from the pins is critical to your alteration.

Notice how the measurements on this piece of paper should match the measurements in the above illustration.

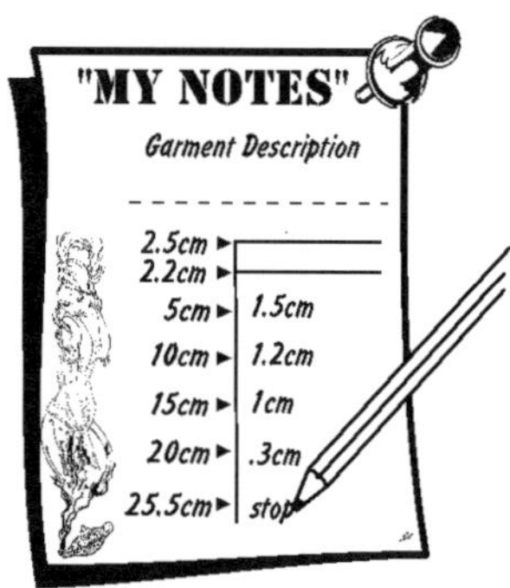

Pants

Taking in Technique

Preparing

*"When making a garment
you work forward
at each stage."*

*"When you are altering a garment
you work backward - reversing the process."*

*"When the adjustment is made
you work forward to reassemble."*

Preparing

You should now have all your measurements written down on a piece of paper. You are now ready for the next stage.

Step 1 - Take the pins out of the garment.

You have two options the way you alter the back of the pants.

Option 1 - Take band off

This is the most time consuming option.

Take the band off beginning at the button end of the band. Not the end with the button hole.

Usually a band is sewn to the body of the garment first, then folded over and sewn down by stitching in the ditch, or on edge of band.

Begin unpicking the back of the band (if this is the last seam sewn), and I would unpick to about 6" or 15 cm past the centre back seam.

Then unpick the front of the waist band to about 3" or 7.5 cm past the centre back seam. Leave the band hanging and proceed as per Step 5, which is marking the body of the garment.

When you have completed marking the body of the garment, complete the section on Placing dots for take in amount page 58 - 59, then sewing page 60 - 62.

Now pin the band back on but work backwards. I want you to sew into the fold of the waist band which means you have to pin it backwards. Begin pinning at the centre back section with the band facing you, all the way back to the button section. Make sure you have the band firm, because you are going to sew from the button end back to the centre back seam, and you do not want it to pucker.

When you have that done, shorten the band at the button end, and sew the waist band down.

Sew the button back on.

Option 2 - Undo band at Take In point

This is the quickest and is the option I use.

Unpick the band three times the amount you are taking the back in.

For this exercise we are taking in the back by 1" or 2.5 cm from the centre back seam. This means we are taking it in a total of 2" or 5 cm because we had the centre back seam folded.

Therefore you should unpick the first section by 6" or 15 cm in total. To clarify this you will unpick the band 3" or 7.5cm EACH SIDE OF THE CENTRE BACK SEAM. This gives you room to fold the band back and sew it.

Look at the pants and determine what was the last seam sewn, because this is the first seam you unpick.

Usually a band is attached to the body of the garment, then folded over and sewn down stitching in the ditch, or stitched on waist band.

This means you will begin unpicking this last seam first. I always unpick this seam a little bit more than the seam that is attached to the body of the garment.

Before you unpick the band from the body of the garment, I want you to place a nick in the band above the centre back seam.

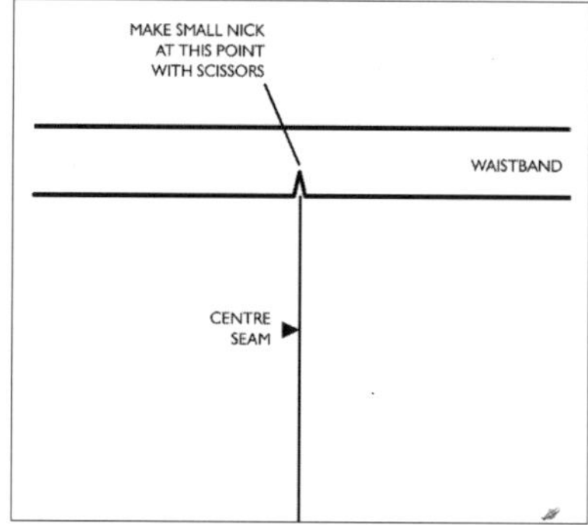

The final step with the second choice is to unpick the band from the body of the garment. And if the pants are being taken in 1" from the centre back seam, then I would unpick this section about 2" or 5 cm each side of the centre back seam, which is 4" total or 10 cm total.

Special Note:

One of the major mistakes people make when altering a garment is to unpick the original side or back seam.

Once this seam is unpicked you have absolutely NO REFERENCE POINT to work with.

Everything you do when altering a garment is based on having reference points to work from.

When you are taking in the side or back of a garment, the original seam is the reference point.

When you are pinning the garment, you had the side seam or back seam folded with the seam in the middle. And when you measured from the side to the pin, this was really from the original seam to the pin.

I can not say that it would be 100% of the time that I would not unpick a seam, but it would be 99.9% of the time.

Everything is based upon how a garment is made, and there are occasionally times when the manufacturer has created a master piece which is difficult to alter.

However, 99.9% of the time do not unpick side seams or back seams until after you sew the new seam.

Placing Dots Band

Step 2 - Fold the waistband back on itself. The section that you nicked with the scissors is your new centre back seam on the band.

Your fold must be even.

This means you need to make sure that when the band is re sewn, all the folds including the top of the band will be joined so that it does not look like it has been altered, other than the fact that it has a centre back seam, which it probably didn't have before.

Step 3 - Place your pins through the centre fold, and the front and back folds at the bottom of the band.

You will notice on the illustration that the waist band has been folded out, which means the centre is actually the top of the band.

The two outside pins are pinned on the original seams which attaches the band to the body of the garment.

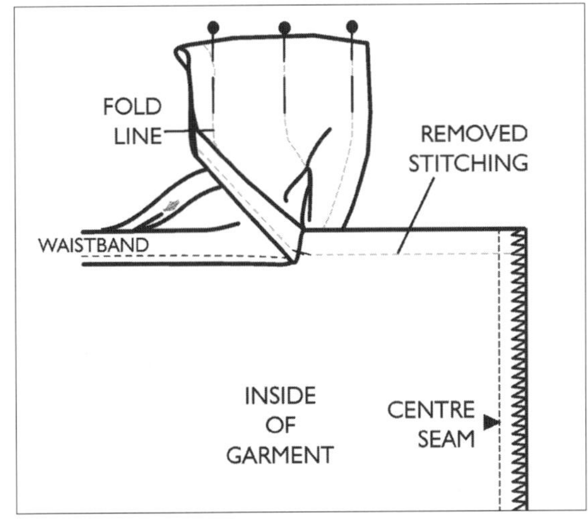

Step 4 - Place your tape measure on the bottom front fold and place a dot for the measurement at the bottom of the band.

In this case it is 7/8" or 2 cm.

Then move your tape measure to the centre fold line, which is the top of the band and place a dot for that measurement which in this case is 1" or 2.5 cm.

Now move to the last fold line and place a dot the same measurement as the first dot, which is 7/8" or 2 cm. This is the bottom of the band.

Imperial

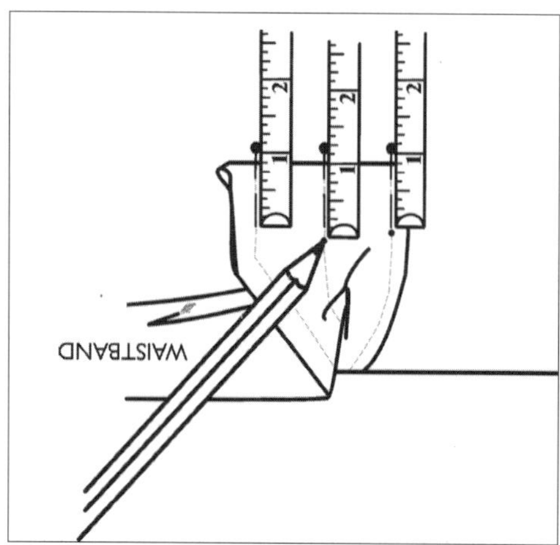

The metric illustration is the same as the imperial but the tape measure is obviously in metric.

Metric

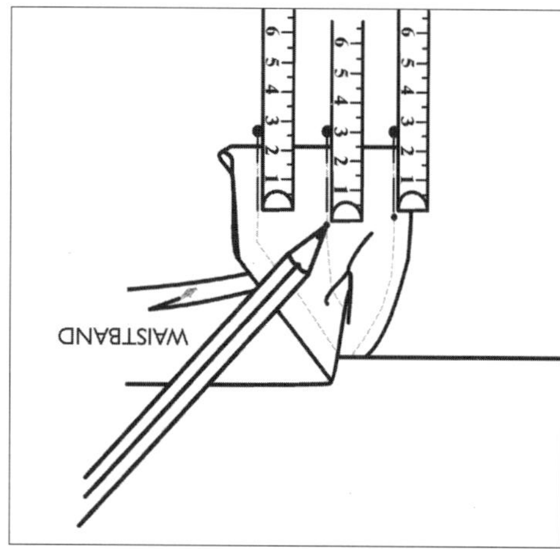

Unpicking the band area may seem like a longer process than unpicking the whole band, however when you get better at it you will become quicker, and this is truly a faster way.

Placing dots body of garment

Before we place the dots down the centre back seam, I would like to mention the importance of marking the garment so that the side you are placing the dots, is the side you will be sewing on the machine.

Imagine yourself sitting at your sewing machine and sewing something. You do not want all the bulk of the fabric on the right hand side of the machine. You want the bulk to be on the left.

This means that if you were taking in the sides of a garment, you have to prepare the right side one way and the left side the opposite way.

I try to sew from the top down the side or back seam to the finished position.

If in doubt, imagine that you are sitting at your sewing machine sewing the garment. This way you will ensure you mark each side in the correct way.

You are now ready to mark the body of the garment.

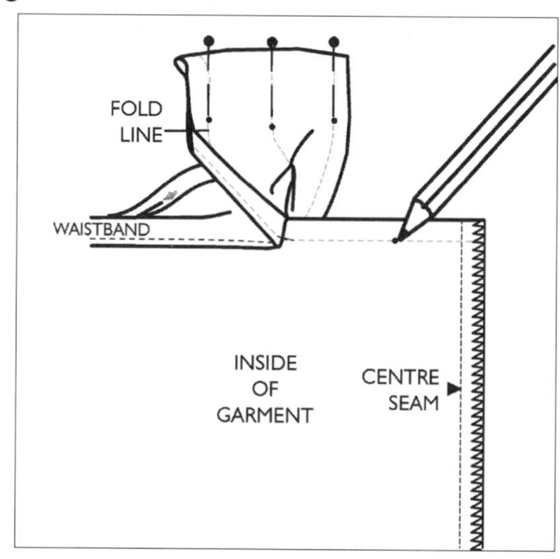

Step 5 - Measure in 7/8" or 2 cm from the original seam line (centre back seam) and place a dot on the stitch line that the band was attached to.

This measurement must be the same measurement as the bottom of the band.

The reason for this is because when you sew the band back onto the body of the garment, the amount that you took the band in, must be the same amount that you take the top of the body of the garment in.

If you do not have these two positions taken in the same amount, then the band will not fit back onto the body of the garment.

Step 6 - Measure down every 2" / 5 cm and place a dot as per the original measure.

Step 7 - Place dots all the way down the garment in the same position as on your piece of paper.

Imperial

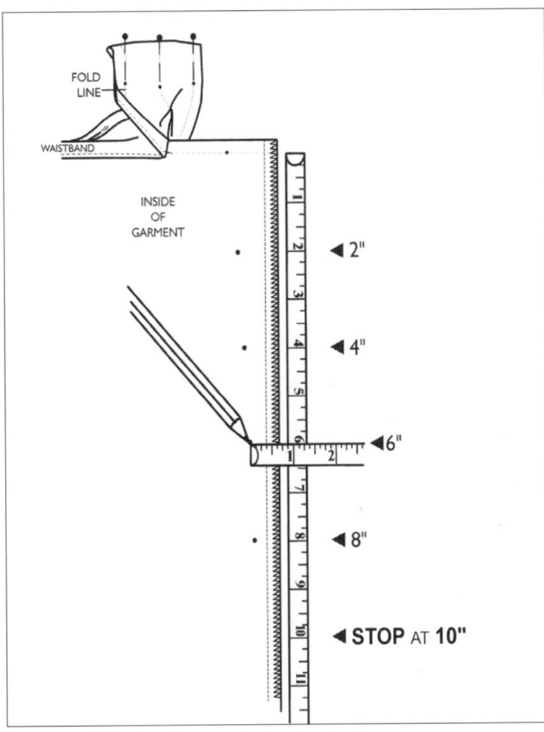

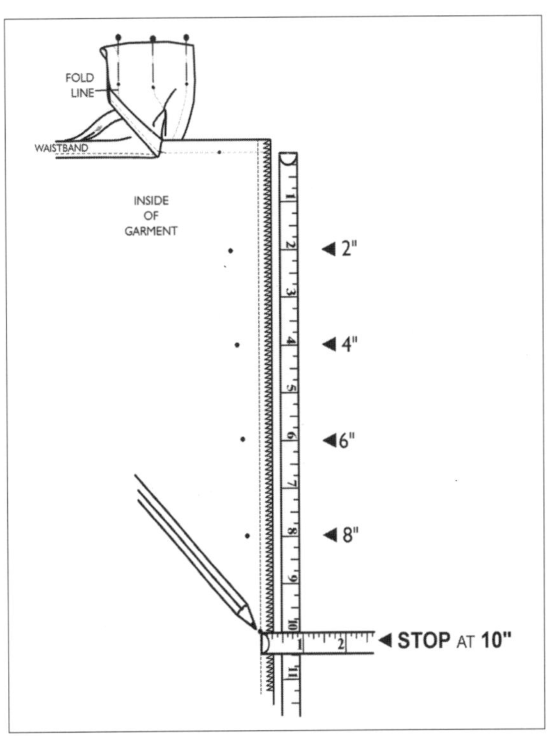

Metric

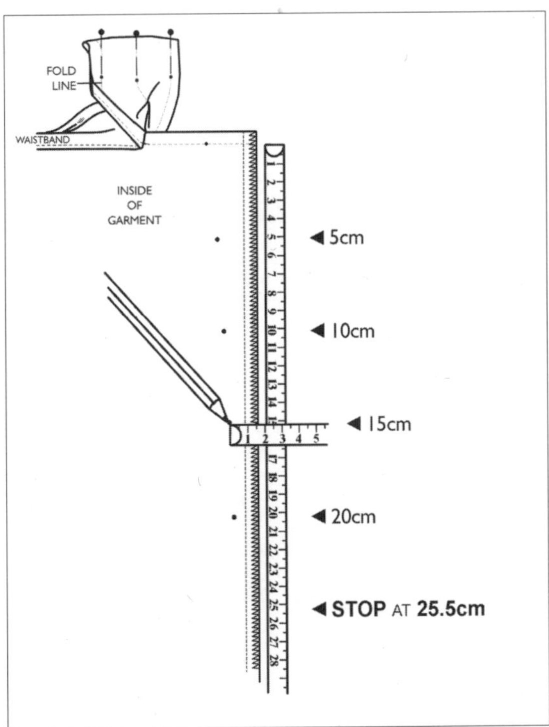

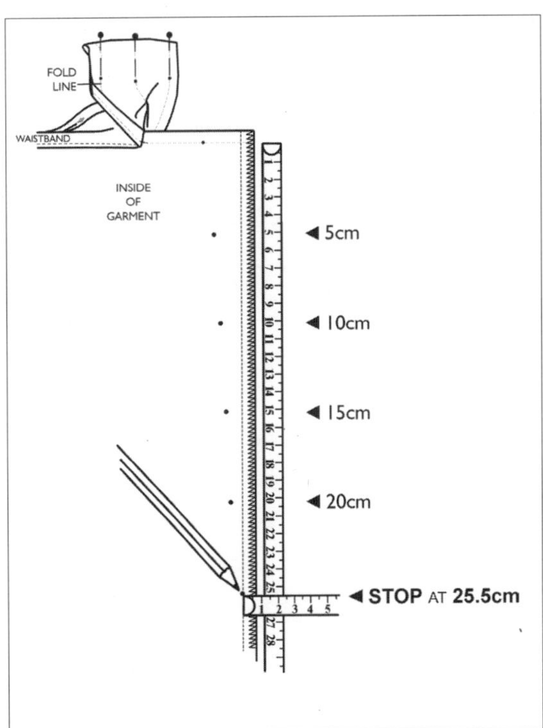

Pants

Taking in Technique

Sewing

"Use your iron."

"Turn the garment inside out and place over the bottom of the ironing board."

"Use your iron to press your seams flat."

"Pin your garment together whilst on the ironing board."

Sewing the garment

Step 1 - I find it easier to sew the band first because I need to have some room with the band folded back on itself.

If you sew the body of the garment first, you will have less manoeuvrability with the band.

Step 2 - Sew through the dots.

Note - When you are sewing a band, where the centre is a different measurement from the top and bottom, it is important to begin sewing on the edge of the fabric in the EXACT position of the dot on the fold line.

This means you are sewing straight from the edge to the first dot. Now turn towards the second dot in the centre.

When you reach the dot in the centre, you will turn the fabric and sew on a slight angle back to the dot on the opposite side.

When you reach this dot you will have the fabric straight and you will sew straight to the edge of the fabric. This is extremely important, because if you sew on an angle to the edge, your band will not fit back on properly.

Step 3 - It is now time to sew the body of the garment.

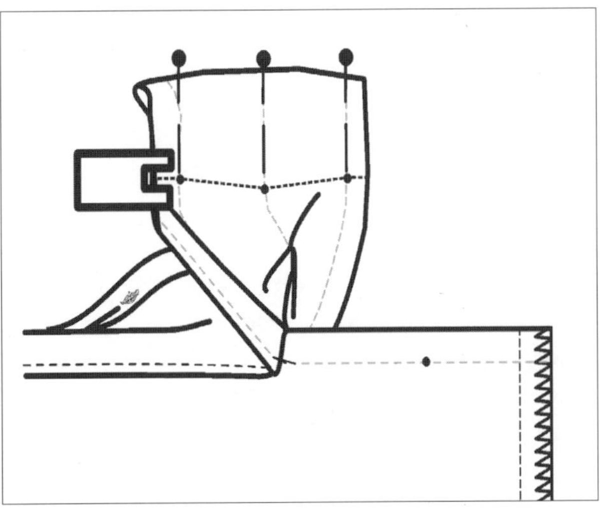

Step 4 - Cut the excess off the band and open out the seams so they are sitting flat on either side of the new seam.

Step 5 - Sew down the body of the garment beginning at the top of the garment.

Follow the same procedure as the band, which means sew straight down from the edge to the old stitch line. Once you reach the stitch line, begin to sew down to the second dot.

Continue to sew down following the dots until you reach the last dot which should be positoned on the original seam. It is extremely important that your seams must flow. When you are finishing into a seam, taper in slowly. If you come off too quickly you will end up with a duck tail effect. That means you end up with a lump sticking out on the right side of the fabric.

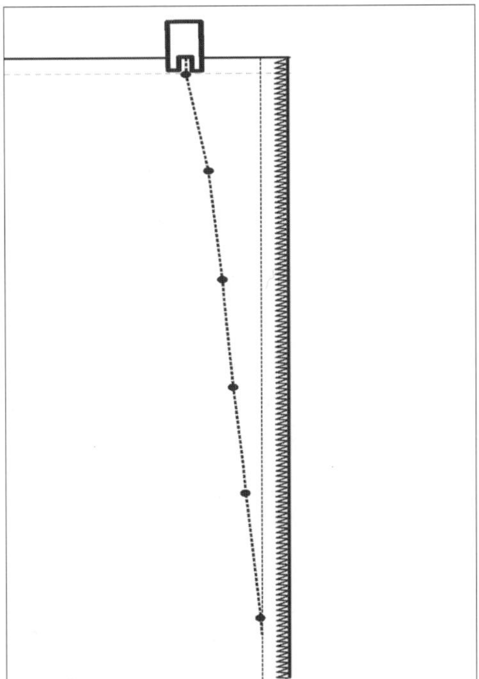

Step 6 - Over lock the excess fabric off or cut the excess off and fold some ribbon and sew it over the cut edge for neatness.

Step 7 - Use your ironing board and lay the garment over the end, inside out, and iron the seams flat. Check to see that the band will fit back on to the body. Iron the band with the body in the position it is to be sewn.

Step 8 - Sew the band back on working backwards as discussed previously. Make sure you sew in the original positions. Don't create new stitch lines, use the old ones and sew over the top of these old stitch lines.

Conclusion

You have now seen my technique for taking in a garment. I am proud to say that it works 100% every time.

I had a team of seamstresses working for me, and we all followed the same technique. This mean that one person could be pinning a garment, another preparing the garment, and finally someone else could be sewing the garment.

We all followed the same process, which meant we achieved an extremely high success rate.

People came from near and far to have us alter their clothes. They knew that we worked for a 100% professional finish.

You may be asking yourself the following question.............

How do others do clothing alterations?

There are many different techniques for altering clothes. The most common form of altering is after pinning the garment, turn it inside out and place a chalk mark close to or where the pin is in the fabric.

Sometimes this will work, but other times it won't. Well not with accuracy.

A lot of clothing alterations have been a bit of hit and miss. Take it in a little bit, then try it on and see if it fits. Then take it in a little bit more.

I believe that the reason there have been so many stories of garments being ruined is because the person performing the alteration was not following a technique. If the person was following a technique, then there should be no reason for a garment to be ruined.

So let's go over the Taking In Technique one more time. Remember this applies to all garments that are being Taken In.

1.   Use your pins as if they are your new seam. This means pin the garment on the body as if this is the final fitting. Make sure that the garment is not too loose or too tight. Make sure the pins follow one another, so that you are creating that imitation seam.

2.   Draw an outline of the garment, and write down the measurements on your piece of paper.

3.   Look at the garment and work out what the last thing was that was sewn on the garment. Now work backwards and unpick the last seam, working up to the seam holding the garment together.

Remember - DO NOT UNPICK SIDE SEAMS OR BACK SEAMS.

You are only unpicking waist bands, facings, or in the case of garments that are lined, you are separating the lining from the outer at the point that you are going to take in - i.e. above the side seam or back seam.

4.   Place your dots at critical reference points. On the band, place dots at the beginning of the fold stitch line, in the centre, and on the opposite fold stitch line.

5.   Place dots down the body of the garment, making sure the top of the garment is the same measurement as the fold stitch line of the band.

6.   Cut off any excess fabric. Over lock or sew folded ribbon over the top of the cut edge.

7.   Place the garment over the end of the ironing board inside out. Iron the seams open on the band, and check to see it fits back onto the body of the garment.

8.   Sew the garment back together, using the same stitch lines, so that you will not notice it has been altered.

Pants

Taking in

"Use the Taking In Technique on all of the following clothing alterations."

Introduction

I have covered both ladies and men's pants in this section, because at the end of the day, the types of alterations when taking in are similar.

There are some pants that are slightly different, it would be impossible to cater to every scenario.

When writing down your measurements, you could photocopy the relevant page, and use the illustration provided to put your measurements on.

I have listed below the areas I have covered for Taking In Pants for ladies and men.

Pants too big

Take in back – no zip

Take in back – with zip

Take in front – no zip

Take in back suit pants

Take in sides - waist to hips

Take in sides - waist to hem

Take in sides - hips

Take in sides - hips to hem

Take in sides - hips to hem with pockets

Taper pant legs in – Permanently pressed pants

Taper leg in – Excess fabric on inside leg

Taper leg in – Excess fabric on outside leg

Take up crotch/fork

Take up crotch/fork and back leg

Pockets sticking out – pin down

Pants too big

If a pair of pants are too big, your first choice should be to pin the centre back first.

If you find that the sides move around too far, then you should consider taking in the sides, however, the back should be the first choice.

Let us look at what happens when you pin the back.

I find it better to have the person stand in front of a mirror.

Take the excess fabric in your thumb and forefinger (with the centre back seam in the middle) at the back of the pants.

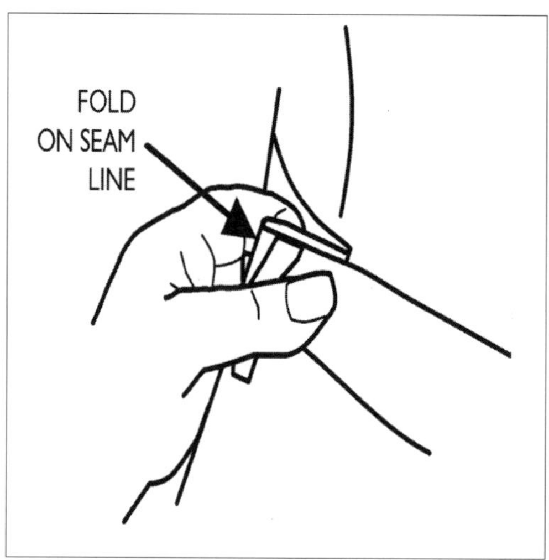

Option 1 - Take in back

If the side seams do not come around to the back, then the garment can be altered from the back. (See Take in back)

Option 2 - Take in sides

If the side seams come around the back too far, then the sides need to be taken in rather than the back. (See Take in sides)

Option 3 - Take in front

If the front section still sticks out, then you need to pin the sides or the front. (See Take in front)

Take in back

Although I have covered this alteration in the example, I have repeated it here because there are some other areas I need you to consider.

Step 1 - Take hold of the fabric at the back of the pants with the centre back seam in the middle of the fold as per first illustration.

Using your thumb and first finger, make the pants firm on the waist by pressing the two sides of the band together - excess fabric is between your thumb and first finger as per illustration.

Step 2 - Look at the amount you have between your thumb and first finger.

You are now ready to pin the back. Ask the person to take a deep breath to help take pressure off the band.

IMPORTANT - Ask the person to stand straight, and that they MUST NOT bend in any way, because the pin could snap with too much pressure.

Step 3 - Place a large hatpin through the band. Same amount you had in Step 2.

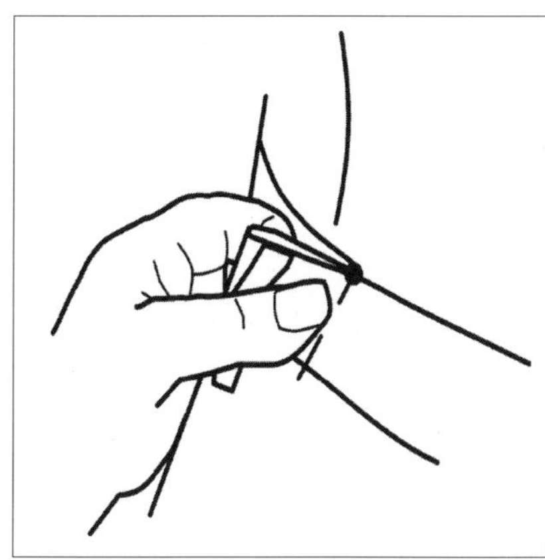

There are four ways to pin the back of pants.

Option 1 - Normally when you place a pin into fabric that is not very thick, you will have the pin in a downward position and will push the pin in and across to the opposite side of the fabric; then push it back through the fabric to the same side the pin entered the fabric.

Option 2 - If the band is thick, you may find it difficult to take a hold of the excess fabric and pin all at the same time. So you need help.

Ask the person wearing the pants to place their hands on the side seams and have them push the band back towards you.

This will take the pressure off the band for you to put the pin through the band.

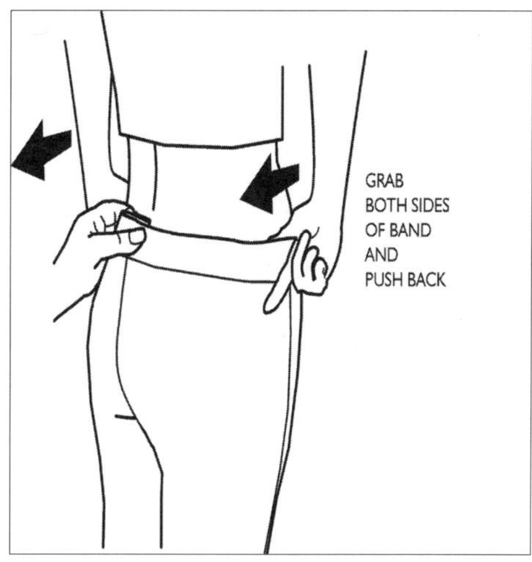

Option 3 - If you have a third person, you can ask them to stand in front of the person being pinned, and ask them to take a hold of the band on both sides of the waist. Ask them to push the band in the direction of the person pinning, who should be standing behind the person being pinned.

Option 4 - Place a pin on either side of the band at the position where you would have placed the pin.

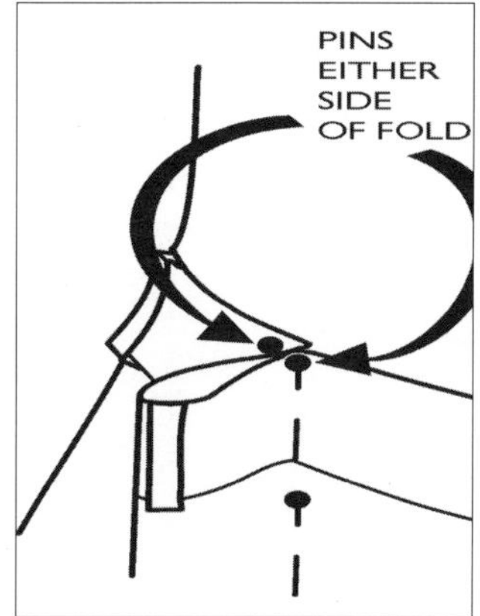

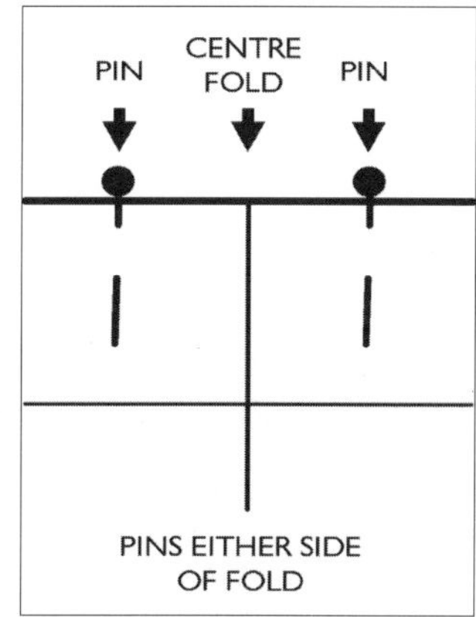

Ask the person if the amount taken in feels comfortable. Is it too loose, too tight or just right? Explain you have more to pin, you are just determining the top section at the moment.

Step 4 - Take hold of the fabric below the first pin. Make sure the seam is in the middle. Press your fingers together pushing as far against the body as possible, so that the fabric is firm.

Step 5 - Place a pin underneath the first pin in the same position as your fingers, making sure the pin is pointing straight down.

Ensure that it is neither too tight nor too loose on the person.

Step 6 - Place the pins all the way down the bottom using the same technique with your fingers determining the amount to be pinned.

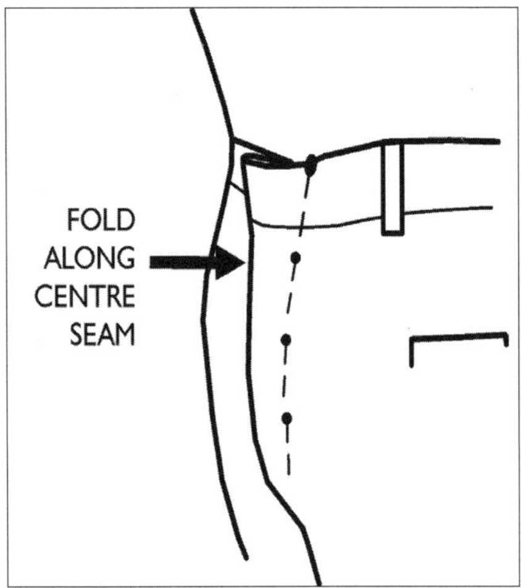

Step 7 - In the above illustration, I have stopped pinning before the crotch area. My last pin is still in from the centre back seam, but stops before going under the bottom. Everyone's bottoms are different shapes. I never pin into a crotch.

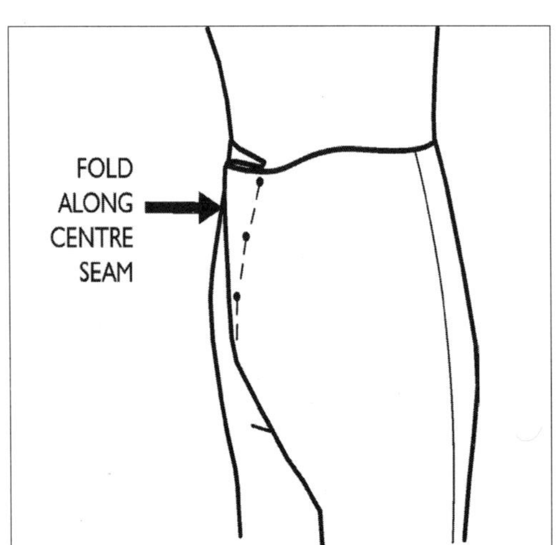

The previous illustration is of a person who needs the waist area taken in, but the bottom is more rounded and therefore fills out the bottom area.

Whatever the persons body type, your pins should take up the excess fabric over the bottom, and should be pinned in such a way that the person can see exactly what it would look like with the excess fabric taken off.

Step 8 - Turn the person sideways and show them how you have pinned the pants.

Step 9 - Ask if they are happy with the pinning.

Step 10 - If you have pinned as far as possible down the back seam, and there is excess fabric below the pin, explain that when the pants are altered, the seam will be taken into the crotch area.

Step 11 - If you find that the back leg seems to have a lot of excess fabric, AND the crotch is hanging low, refer to the section of Take In back leg, or Take Up Crotch/fork.

Step 12 - Tell the person to get changed if they are happy, however tell them NOT TO BEND, as this could cause the pins to snap and jab into the body.

Ask them to undo the zip and DROP the pants onto the floor.

Explain that if you have pinned the under garments, to call out and you will help take the pins out.

Step 13 - Prepare the garment as per my Taking In Technique page 51-62.

Take in back - with zip

Pinning pants with a zip in the back is slightly different from pinning without a zip.

The same process applies as pinning without a zip, until you come to the final stages of pinning. However, let us start at the beginning so that there is no confusion.

Pinning

Step 1 - . Take hold of the fabric at the back of the pants with the zip in the middle of the fold.

Step 2 - Determine where you think it will be secure on the person by using your thumb and first finger to make the pants firm on the waist.

Step 3 - Look at the amount you have between your thumb and first finger and place a pin into this section, making sure the pinhead is at the top and the sharp end of the pin is facing down.

Step 4 - Take hold of the excess fabric below the first pin, and place a pin underneath in the same position as your fingers.

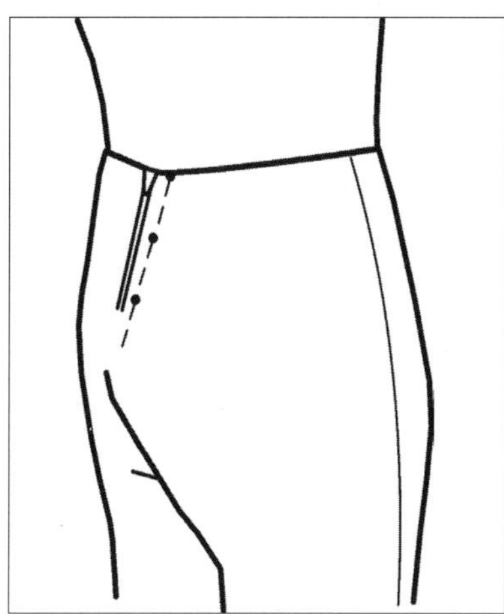

Pin should be facing down, and the pants should feel secure..

Step 5 - Follow this procedure all the way to the end of the back however stop pinning before you move into the inside bottom area.

Everyone's bottoms are different shapes, but you should never pin into the bottom area. Your last pin will show the person that they should taper into the crotch from this point.

Step 6 - Turn the person sideways and show them how you have pinned the pants. Ask if they are happy with the pinning.

Step 7 - If the person has a larger bottom, you will pin coming out until the fabric is firm.

The pins should follow one another coming out to the seam gradually.

For the person to get out of the pants, proceed with the following procedure.

Step 8 - Place a pin over the top of the original pin on one side only. I usually do the right hand side.

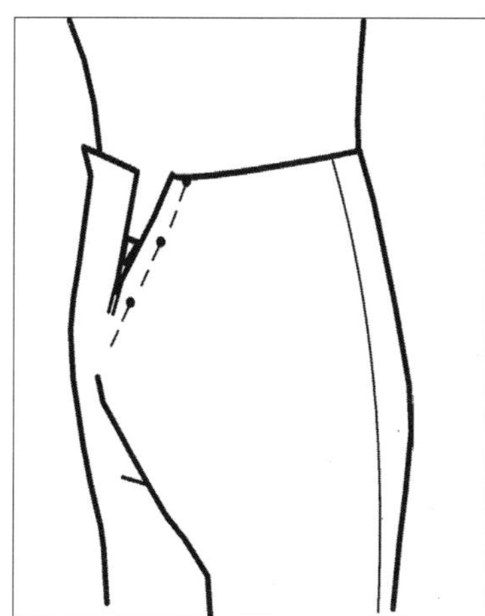

 The position of this pin is directly over the top of the original pin, but only pierces the fabric on the right hand side.

The pin does not go through to the fabric on the opposite side.

Step 9 - Continue doing this all the way down to the bottom of the zip.

You should be able to slide the pins out that you put in originally, thereby freeing the customer to undo the zip.

The pins on the right side show how much to take in.

Preparing

Step 1 - Use the same procedure on page 51 for writing down measurements.

Step 2 - Do the zip up and fold the pants at the zip so you are only looking at the side with the pins.

Step 3 - Draw an outline of the pants, and measure the position of the pin at the top of the pants, measuring from the pin to the edge of the zip.

Step 4 - Measure down every 2" taking a measurement until you come to the last pin.

ALWAYS take a measurement at the bottom of the zip.

Step 5 - If the last pin is against the seam, then say Stop, but if the last pin is not on the edge of the seam, then just put this last measurement down on the paper, and right next to it TTC This means Through to Crotch.

Step 6 - Take the zip out of the pants.

When you unpick the zip, you will notice at the top that the facing or lining will be sewn onto the zipper. Look at how this is attached.

When you unpick at the very top, there may be under stitching along the band to about 1" from the zip.

If you do not unpick the under stitching, when you bag the corner (see page 144 Splits for example on bagging corners) and sew across the top stitch line, the under stitching will get in your way, and your seam will not sit flat.

I prefer to use an invisible zip when taking in.

When you are taking a garment in with a zip, you are more than likely going to change the seam position. It may be that the fabric goes on the bias. An invisible zip works well in this situation.

Step 8 - Unpick the zip and lining or facing, and place the dots on the outside of the garment.

So this means if your back seam is coming in 1" at the top, you will put a dot at 1" on BOTH SIDES at the top on the right side of the fabric.

Do not make a dark dot.

It should be so that you can see it, but not dark enough that others will notice it after it is altered.

Step 9 - Mark all the way down to the bottom of the zip area.

If you are putting an invisible zip in, then unpick a little of the centre back seam - about 1" only.

Step 10 - Turn the garment inside out and place a dot for the bottom of the zip measurement.

Step 11 - Now place any other measurements using dots from the bottom of the zip to the last measurement you have.

Sewing

Step 1 - Turn your garment inside out, and start sewing from the BOTTOM OF THE ZIP sewing down towards the hem.

Step 2 - Now unpick the original seam next to the new seam you have just sewn.

Step 3 - Place the garment over your ironing board (inside out). Iron the new zip section back at the dots. You should have dots on both sides.

Step 4 - Cut or over lock the excess fabric off. I leave about 5/8" for my seam allowance.

Step 5 - If you have never put an invisible zip in before, Lay the zip (right side facing up), into the zip opening on the garment. This way you can see which side is attached to the fabric.

Now undo the zip and pin the right side of the zip to the right side of the fabric opening.

The plastic knob at the top of the zip should be about 1/8" below the original stitch line.

I use my ordinary zipper foot, with the needle moved across into a position next to the zip itself.   I use my fingernails to pull the zip back so that I can sew next to the zipper.

You must not sew on the teeth of the zip.

If you do then the zip will not work. If you do find that you sew the teeth of the zip as you are sewing, just reverse back, then continue forward again, and unpick the mistake later.

Step 6 - Sew to the end of the zipper. You will not be able to sew all the way to the end.

Step 7 - Close the zipper.

Step 8 - Pin the left side of the zipper to the left side of the fabric opening, beginning at the bottom of the zip, making sure you line up the two sides of the fabric so that the fabric sits flat.

If you pin one side higher the other you will end up with a pucker at the bottom of the zip.

Step 9 - Move up to the top of the zip and pin the top section together, making sure you have the plastic knob the same measurement from the original stitching as the opposite side.

Step 10 - Place a pin in the middle easing zip in.

Step 11 - Sew from bottom of zip to top.

Note - Place the needle into the zip and fabric, BEFORE you take pin out, so zip doesn't move.

Step 12 - If there is no lining or facing, take your zipper foot off and use your normal machine foot. Stitch down the edge of zip attaching the fabric to the zip. Re attach the waist band.

Step 13 - If there is lining or facing, you should attach these to the side of the zipper using your sewing machine. Some people hand stitch. Get used to using your sewing machine because this is the professional way of sewing.

Step 14 - Place the right sides of the facing or lining to the zipper flap. Pin through the original stitch line of the facing or lining, with the pin piercing the middle section of the zip. (The middle is between the zipper on one side and the edge of the fabric of the zip)

Step 15 - When you sew the lining or facing on to the edge of the zipper (right sides together) you will notice that, the lining or facing is smaller than the outer. This is correct. You want the facing or lining to be less than the zipper section.

Step 16 - Fold the zipper section back on itself. The facing or lining will now sit flat.

Step 17 - Sew across the top in the original stitch line.

Step 18 - Turn the fabric back the right way.

When you sew the opposite side at the top, make sure that you have the top sections the same amount from the top of the zip to the top of the fabric. If you don't get it right the first time, you may have to re sew this section a few times till you get it correct.

Take in front – no zip

The only time you will take in the centre front seam of a pair of pants is if the back section from the side seams to the back fits the person, but from the side seams to the front, there is excess fabric.

Fold the fabric with the centre front seam in the middle.

Take hold fabric between your fingers, and look to see that the side seams are actually sitting on the side of the body. If the side seams move around to the front when you do this then you should not take in the front.

If the side seams stay at the side, then you will need to take in the front.

Depending on how large the pants are, the take in amount could be from the top of the waist all the way through to the crotch, or from below the band to the crotch.

If it is the later, you will notice a lot of fabric bunching around the crotch.

Pinning

Step 1 - Take hold of the fabric at the front of the pants with the front centre seam in the middle of the fold.

Step 2 - Determine where you think it will be secure on the person by using your thumb and first finger to make the pants firm on the waist.

Step 3 - Look at the amount you have between your thumb and first finger.

Step 4 - Ask the person to take a deep breath to help take pressure off the band.

Step 5 - Place a pin through the band making sure the knob of the pin is at the top and the sharp point of the pin is facing down.

Step 6 - Sometimes you will find you need to push the pin across from one side to the other in a horizontal fashion, rather than in a vertical or downward motion.

Take the pressure off the band by taking extra fabric in the fingers, then move the pin into the downward position, pinning back through the pants to the same side the pin entered the fabric.

Step 7 - Ask the person if the amount taken in feels comfortable. Is it too loose, too tight or just right? Explain you have more to pin, you are just determining the top section at the moment.

Step 8 - Take hold of the fabric below the first pin. Make sure the seam is in the middle. Press your fingers together pushing as far against the body as possible, so that the fabric is firm.

Step 9 - Place a pin underneath the first pin in the same position as your fingers, making sure the pin is pointing straight down.

Ensure that it is neither too tight nor too loose on the person.

Step 10 - Place the pins all the way down the front using the same technique with your fingers determining the amount to be pinned.

Step 11 - Stop pinning before you move into the crotch area.

Step 12 - Turn the person sideways and show them how you have pinned the pants.

Step 13 - Ask if they are happy with the pinning.

If there is excess fabric at the crotch area, explain that when the pants are altered, the seam will be taken into the crotch area.

If you are only pinning the top section of the pants, because the person has a tummy or the pants are only loose at the top, then you need to make sure that the pins follow one another coming out to the outside seam gradually, showing the exact position you will stop sewing.

Step 14 - Follow the Take In Technique pages 51 - 62.

Take in back – suit pants

Most men's suit pants, and some women's dress pants have a section at the centre back with excess fabric. This is where suit pants should be taken in if the pants are too big.

The pants can be constructed at the back in a number of ways, however there are two styles that are more readily used than others.

Option 1 - Excess fabric exposed at the centre back up to and including the waist band.

Option 2 - Excess fabric exposed at the centre back but balance of fabric is encased in waist band.

Pinning

Follow the same procedure for pinning the back of pants, including writing down measurements.

Option 1

This is by far the easiest method.

Step 1 - Unpick any belt loops in the way.

Step 2 - Turn the pants inside out.

Step 3 - To open out this seam, you only need unpick the bar tack holding the sides down.

Step 4 - Place your tape measure at the edge of the centre back seam and measure in from the seam the amount that you have down on your paper for Top of the Band. Place a dot at this position.

Step 5 - Move down to the bottom of the band and place a dot at this measurement.

Step 6 - Move down every 2" from the bottom of the band and place dots as per your written down measurements.

> **SPECIAL NOTE:** Do not unpick the original seam UNTIL you have sewn the new seam. Remember you need a reference point to work from.

Step 7 - Sew the new seam beginning at the top, and making sure you line up the waist band, so that when you turn the garment in the right way, the bands will match.

Step 8 - Unpick the old seam.

Step 9 - Iron the seam out flat on your ironing board. (Garment is still inside out)

Step 10 - If the back of the pants sits correctly, sew the second row of stitching over the top of the first, which will reinforce the seam.

Step 11 - If the excess fabric at the back seam becomes too great, over lock the excess off or cut away the excess, leaving about 2" or more for future needs.

Step 12 - Place a ribbon over the frayed end and stitch into place.

Step 13 - Tack the top section of the back down. I usually hand stitch from the bottom of the band to the top of the band.

Step 14 - Sew belt loops back on as follows:-

Step 1

Lay the belt look over the waist band, so that only 1/8" or 2 mm is below the bottom of the band.

The stitching must be facing up.

Stitch across the bottom of the belt loop close to the edge.

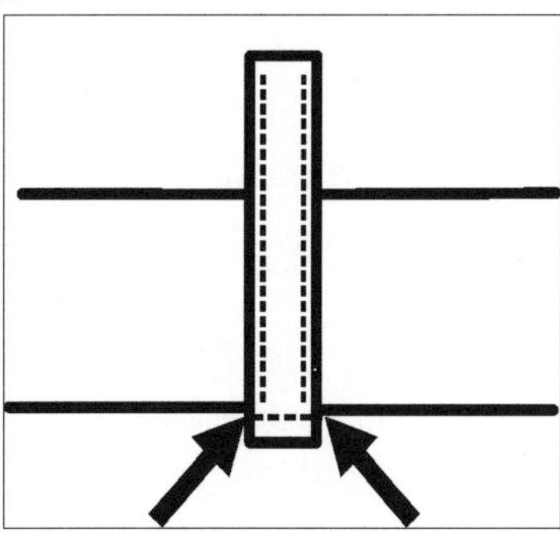

Step 2

Fold the belt loop down, and stitch across the bottom, making sure that the cut edge is encased inside the fold.

Step 3

Fold belt loop back up and stitch across the top.

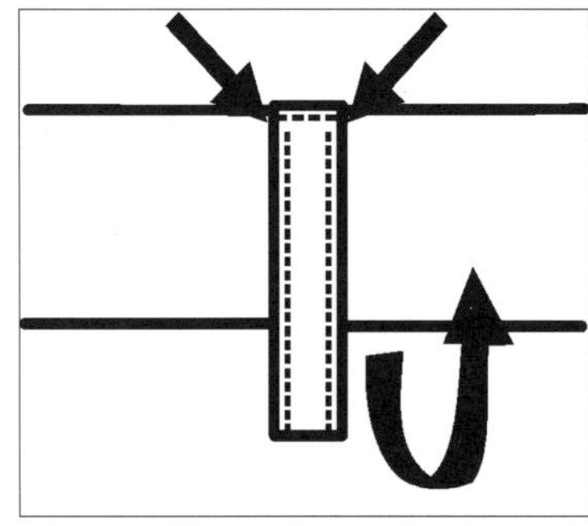

Option 2

This method is a little more complicated. The band has to be unpicked to expose the excess fabric in the band.

Step 1 - Unpick any belt loops. If the pants are being taken in a lot, then you may have to unpick the belt loop from the band. This means you MUST re sew that seam on the inside once you have the pants unpicked.

Step 2 - Turn the pants inside out.

Step 3 - Place your quick unpick into the stitching at the back of the band. I usually unpick at least 2" either side of the amount it is being taken in. This means you can open out the back section and sew with ease.

When the band is unpicked, the back of the band will fold up. This means that when you place your dots, the top of the band dot will actually

be in the middle. You really need to have a pair of pants open in front of you to understand what I am saying.

Step 4 - Measure the top section (this is the bottom of the band turned up) and place the dot at the measurement for the bottom of the band at this point.

The top and the bottom sections of the band, MUST be the same measurement.

The centre of the band will be the measurement at the top of the band on your piece of paper.

Step 5 - Place the rest of your measurement dots down the centre back seam.

Always sew your new seam BEFORE you unpick the old seam.

Step 6 - After you have sewn the new seam, unpick the old. I sew one seam only, then I unpick the old seam and check to see it sits correctly.

Step 7 - Place over the ironing board, and iron seams flat . (Pants are still inside out)

Step 8 - Fold the band back down and check that it fits perfectly back into place. If it does not fit perfectly then make an adjustment until it does. Once you have done a few pairs of pants, you will get the hang of it all.

Step 9 - If it all sits ok, then sew a second seam over the top of the first. I always sew two rows of stitching on a back seam to reinforce.

Step 10 - If there is too much excess fabric, cut off the excess and over lock or zig zag the edge or sew some ribbon folded over onto raw edge.

Step 11 - Most suit pants have white or cream on the inside, which means you will have to put this different colour in your bobbin, so that when you sew the band down, the cotton is the same colour as the under side.

Step 12 - Try to stitch into the join between the band and the body of the garment. This is called "stitch in the ditch". Sew belt loops on.

Take in sides - waist to hips

I take in the sides on a pair of pants if the person has lost a lot of weight, or if the person has a small waist and hips, but has thicker thighs.

To work out whether you will take in the sides, or the centre back seam, take hold of the excess fabric at the centre back.

If the sides seams do not move around to the back take in the back. If the side seams do move to the back, then you should proceed to take in the sides.

There is also another way to determine if the side should be taken in.

Let us say that you pinned the back of the pants. You think everything is ok, but when you look at the front of the pants, you will find that the front section is very loose.

This looseness would be around the centre front seam. This is due to the "cut" of the fabric. In this case, I would look at taking in the sides and or the front.

Kneel in front of the person with the person facing the mirror, so they can watch you.

Pinning

Step 1 - Ask the person to keep their spine straight. I always ask them to look directly into their own eyes in the mirror. This ensures they will stand up straight.

Step 2 - Take a section of fabric between your fingers on either side of the pants. Look at what you think the amount is and pin one side.

Step 3 - Pin the opposite side so the pants are firm on the waist or hips. (If it is 1" (2 ½ cm) make sure you have 1" either side)

Step 4 - Have the pin facing down.

Step 5 - Ask the person if this feels secure.

Step 6 - Place a second pin beneath the first on either side. This means asking the person to turn and face the opposite direction – give them a landmark i.e. please face the wall or please face the door etc.

Step 7 - Continue pinning down the side over the hips with the pins following one after the other.

Step 8 - You should pin no more than 2 or 3 pins one side then turn the person and pin the other side the same. This will mean that you are pinning the same amount on each side.

Step 9 - Taper pins in towards the outside seam and stop so the last pin is on the outside seam.

Step 10 - Stand behind the person and using your hands and the section of your arms below the elbow and pull the fabric back so that they can see how much will be taken off.

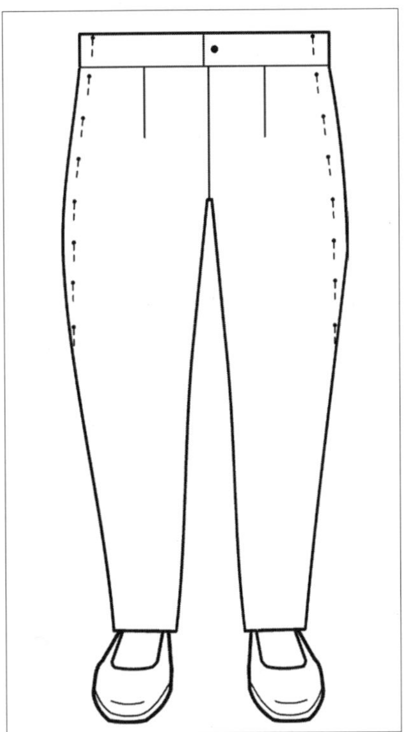

Step 11 - Use Taking In Technique page 51 - 62.

Make sure when you put the garment back together after taking in, that the seams are facing towards the back section of the pants if the seams are over locked together, or if the seams are separate make sure they sit flat. Use your iron to achieve this before re sewing.

Take in sides - waist to hem

This situation usually occurs when someone has purchased a pair of pants one size too large.

Before you go to the trouble of pinning the sides, pin the centre back seam to see if that fixes the problem. If it does not and the pants are still too big all over, then you need to pin the side starting at the top of the band.

Pinning

Step 1 - Kneel in front of the person with the person facing the mirror, so they can see what you are doing

Step 2 - Ask the person to keep their spine straight. I always ask them to look directly into their own eyes in the mirror. This ensures they will stand up straight.

Step 3 - Take a section of fabric between your fingers on either side of the pants. Look at what you think the amount is and pin one side.

Step 4 - Pin the opposite side so the pants are firm on the waist or hips. (If it is 1" (2 ½ cm) make sure you have 1" either side)

Step 5 - Have the pin facing down.

Step 6 - Ask the person if this feels secure.

Step 7 - Place a second pin beneath the first on either side.

This means asking the person to turn and face the opposite direction – give them a landmark. i.e. "Please face the wall or please face the door".

Step 8 - Continue pinning down the side over the hips with pins following one after the other.

Step 9 - You should pin no more than 2 or 3 pins one side then turn the person and pin the other side the same. This will mean that you are pinning the same amount on each side. Pin all the

way to the hem.

Step 10 - Stand behind the person and using your hands and the lower section of your arms, pull the fabric back so that they can see how much will be taken off.

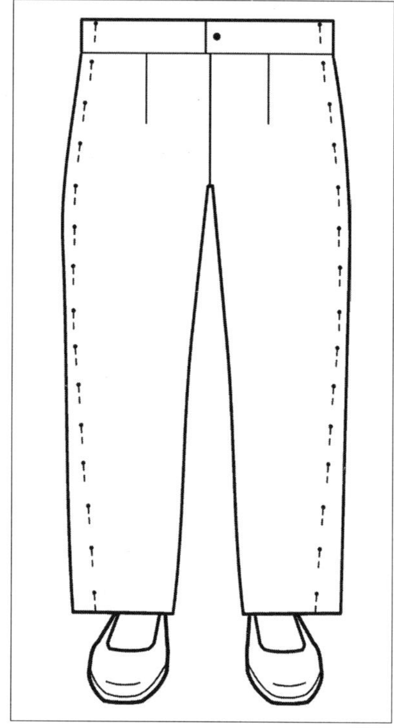

Step 11 - If the pants have pleats, you need to pin the sides to see if the pleats pull to the side.

Step 12 - If the pleats pull to the side, you may want to reconsider taking in the back.

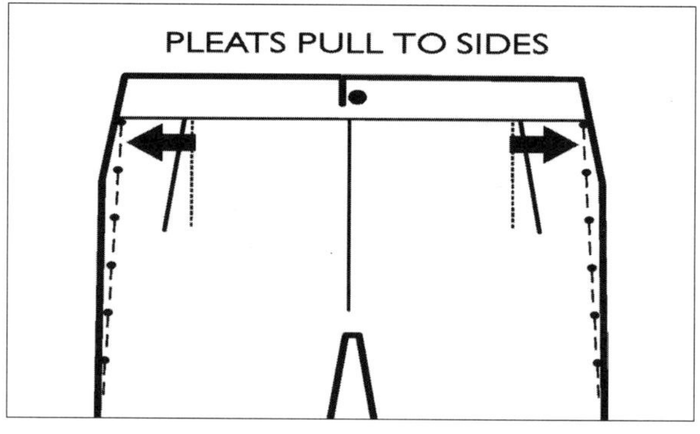

Step 13 - Use Take In Technique page 51 - 62.

Always undo the hem at least 2" either side in addition to the amount the garment is being taken in.

Make sure when you put the garment back together after taking in, that the seams are facing towards the back section of the pants.

Take in sides - hips

Some pants fit perfectly at the waist and the leg, but have this Jodhpur effect over the hips. It looks like you have riding pants on.

It is always best to pin both sides to ensure that the amount pinned is accurate.

You must always try to pin the same amount on both sides, and you need to begin pinning at the same position and stop pinning at the same position.

Some people have one hip bigger than the other. If this is the case, when you pin make a mental note that the sides are different, so that when it is prepared for alteration both sides will be taken is as per the pins.

Because I use an invoice book, I always write on the invoice "Sides Different".

Pinning

Step 1 - Kneel in front of the person with the person facing the mirror, so they can see what you are doing.

Step 2 - Ask the person to keep their spine straight. I always ask them to look directly into their own eyes in the mirror. This ensures they will stand up straight.

Step 3 - Looking directly at the hip area, you will notice where the fabric is sitting hard against the body, and where it is too loose.

Step 4 - Place the pin on the very edge of fabric with the top of the pin hard against the seam, and the bottom of pin about 1/8" in towards the body.

Step 5 - Press your fingers against the person's body and place the second pin against the body in the downward position just under the first pin.

Step 6 - Press your fingers against the person's body and place the third pin against the body in the downward position just under second pin.

Step 7 - Turn the person around and have them face in the opposite direction and pin as per the first side. Sometimes I find it easier to place my hands on the person's hips and turn them in the direction I want them to face.

Step 8 - Follow this process until the pins are in line with the outer seam of the leg.

Step 9 - Continue to pin down the hips until the pins are in line with the seam on the outside of the leg section.

Step 10 - Make sure, when you are pinning that the two sides are pinned the same amount. For example if one side is 1" (2 ½ cm) make sure you have 1" other side. Ask the person if this feels secure.

Step 11 - Make sure that the pins gradually come out to the edge of the seam.

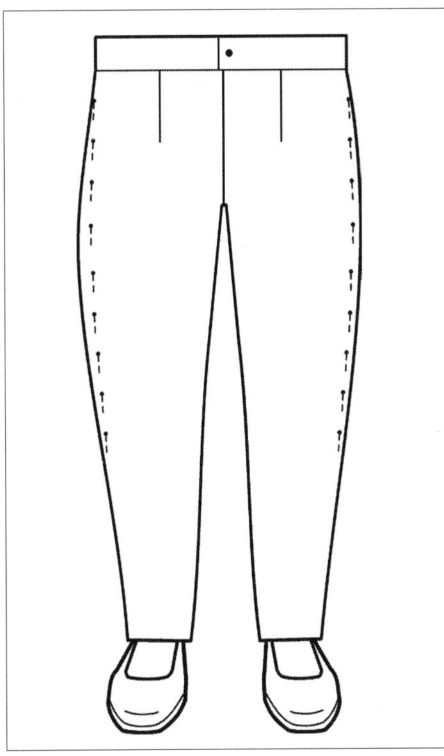

Step 12 - Use Take In Technique page 51 - 62.

You may not have to unpick the band, if you are going to begin sewing about 2" below the band.

If the pins are at the bottom of the band, I would suggest you unpick the band, so you can get the sewing machine foot in close enough.

Take in sides - hips to hem

Because our bodies are all different, you may find a pair of pants that fit you on the waist, but the hips, thigh or legs are too big.

Some of us prefer the comfort of a waist that fits, and would rather alter the hip and thigh area than search for a perfect fitting pair of pants.

This means you need to pin from the hip to the hem.

Pinning

Step 1 - Kneel in front of the person with the person facing the mirror, so they can see what you are doing.

Step 2 - Ask the person to keep their spine straight.

I always ask them to look directly into their own eyes in the mirror. This ensures they will stand up straight.

Step 3 - The waist will be fine in this situation, but from just below the waist there will be excess fabric.

Step 4 - Begin to pin at the point where the fabric becomes loose.

Place a pin on the very edge of the fabric with the top of the pin hard against the seam, and the bottom of the pin about 1/8" in towards the body.

Step 5 - Press your fingers against the person's body and place the second pin against the body in the downward position just under the first pin.

Step 6 - Press your fingers against the person's body and place the third pin against the body in the downward position just under the second pin.

Step 7 - Turn the person around and have them face in the opposite direction and pin the exact

same amount as the first side. I find it easier to place my hands on the person's hips and turn them in the direction I want them to face.

Step 8 - Continue to pin down the hips.

Step 9 - Make sure, when you are pinning that the two sides are pinned the same amount. For example if one side is 1" (2 ½ cm) make sure you have 1" other side.

Step 10 - Pin all the way down to the hem.

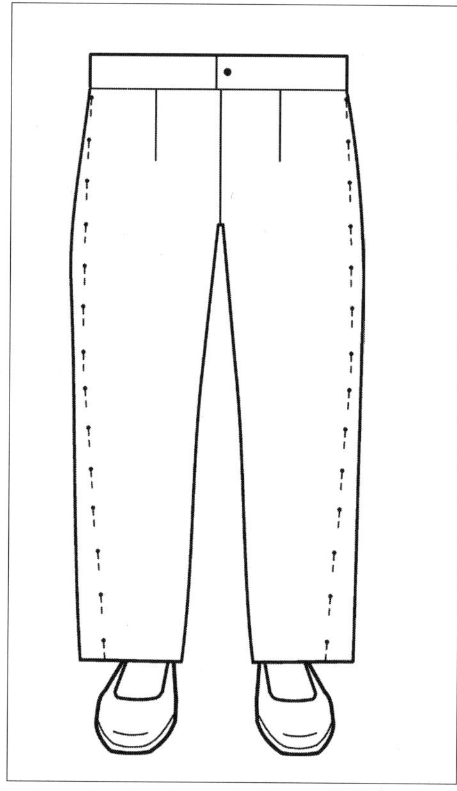

Step 11 - Use Take In Technique page 51 - 62.

Always undo hems and sew through to the very end of the fabric for a professional finish.

Take in sides - hips to hem with pockets

If pants have pockets on the sides, you need to consider taking in at the back instead of the sides. There are two types of side pockets.

No 1 - Pockets down side seam

This type of pocket is set into the side seam. This means that taking the pants in at the sides will mean losing the pockets all together.

The band will have to be unpicked so that the pockets can be detached from the band.

No 2 - Pockets on an angle

This style of pocket is on an angle to the side seam. Taking in the sides too much can mean that the person will not be able to put their hand in their pocket.

If this is the case, consider taking in at the back.

If you are not sure pin the side seam and see if the person can use the pockets.

Pinning

Step 1 - Kneel in front of the person with the person facing the mirror, so they can see what you are doing.

Step 2 - Ask the person to keep their spine straight. I always ask them to look directly into their own eyes in the mirror. This ensures they will stand up straight.

Step 3 - I place my first pin about 1 ½" or 4 cm below the band. This pin is right on the edge of the fabric at the top and slightly in at the bottom.

Step 4 - The second pin is directly underneath the first pin but coming in towards the zipper area.

Step 5 - Ask the person to turn and face the opposite direction and place the first pin on the opposite side. Then place the second pin under the first.

Step 6 - Your third pin should be around the bottom of the pocket. I would not pin in more than say ½" or 1 cm at this point.

Step 7 - If you do pin more than this the person may not be able to use the pocket. However if the pants are very loose, then you may have to pin further in.

Step 8 - Ask the person if they can put their hands in their pockets being very careful of the pins.

Step 9 - If they can use their pockets, then continue to pin the excess fabric.

Step 10 - Pin through to the hem placing a few pins at a time on each side and turning the person back and forth to pin accurately.

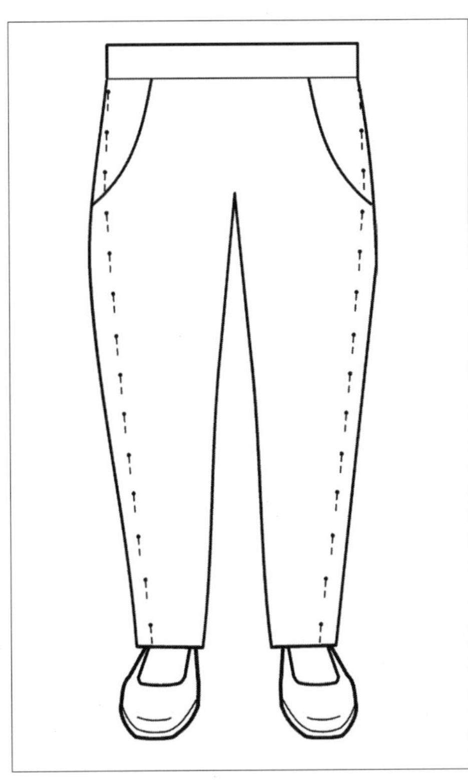

Step 11 - Use Take In Technique page 51 - 62.

Always undo hems and sew through to the very end of the fabric for a professional finish.

Taper legs in – Permanently Pressed

Permanently pressed pants need to be taken in from the inside and outside leg.

The amount needs to be the same from inside and outside leg; otherwise, the permanently pressed line will be out of alignment when ironing.

Note it can be difficult and/or impossible to iron out a permanently pressed front and back seam.

Pinning

Step 1 - Always take in equal amounts on both sides of permanently pressed pants.

Usually when a person wants the leg taken in, it is because the pants are too wide.

Step 2 - Begin pinning at the point on the body where the pants are becoming baggy.

This could be from the knee, the thigh or hip.

Step 3 - Place a pin in the edge of the fabric with the pin facing down.

Step 4 - Place the second pin underneath the first and move down the leg gradually taking in the amount that the person wants taken off the pants.

Step 5 - Pin all the way down to the bottom of the pants.

Step 6 - Begin pinning the inside leg, starting at about 6" or 15 cm from the crotch.

Do not place this pin on the edge of the seam.

This pin should be the same amount in from the edge as the pin on the opposite outside leg.

Step 7 - Place the second pin under the first, but the same amount in as the pin on the outside leg.

Step 8 - Continue pinning down the inside leg,

making sure that the amount you are pinning is the same as the outside leg. When you have finished pinning the inside leg, check to see that the amount is the same on both sides.

In most cases with the sides coming in, the pants may have to be taken up because the leg will bunch around the ankle. Make sure the person has the shoes on that they will be wearing with the pants.

Step 9 - Being careful of the pins, fold the excess hem amount up and into the pants.

Step 10 - Use the knuckle technique, or if the hem is high off the ground, then just get the outside seam amount correct first, then pin the inside leg, and then the front and back.

If the you are taking in a lot at the sides, and are not sure about the length, I would recommend that you take in the sides first, then have a fitting for the new hem length.

Step 11 - Use Take In Technique page 51 - 62.

Always undo hems and sew through to the very end of the fabric for a professional finish.

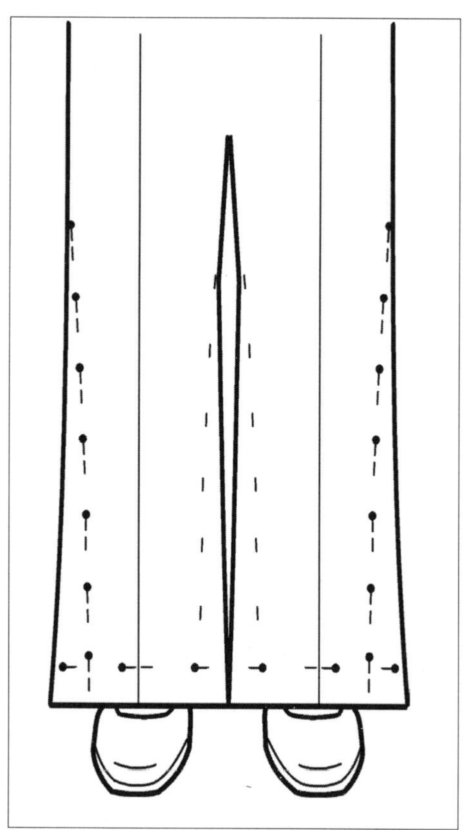

Taper legs in - Excess fabric on inside leg

If you find that your pants feel baggy, but you are not quite sure what is wrong, stand in front of a mirror, with shoes on, and have a look at where the excess fabric is sitting.

If all the fabric is at the inside leg, and the pants are resting against your outside leg, then you will know that this is where you should be pinning.

You will probably need someone to help you to pin the inside leg.

Depending on the persons body shape, I may pin all the way up into the crotch, or I may pin up to the knee area.

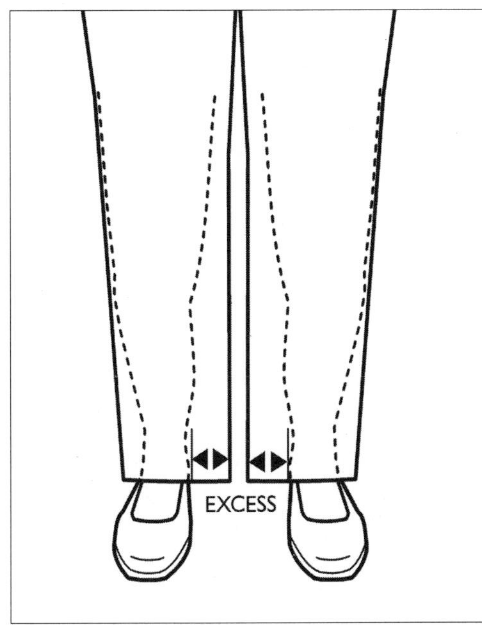

Pinning

Step 1 - You can begin pinning the inside leg anywhere from 6" or 15 cm from the crotch or further down depending on where the excess fabric is on the pant legs.

Step 2 - Place the second pin underneath the first pin moving down the inside leg, but the pin will be in towards the leg more.

Step 3 - Place a pin at the bottom of the hem about 1" or 2.5 cm to 1 ¼" to 3 cm in towards the ankle.

The amount to pin in at the bottom of the hem will be determined by the person's preference for the width at the base of the hem.

Step 4 - Go back to the second pin on the inside leg, and gradually pin down the inside leg until you meet the pin at the base of the hem.

Step 5 - I would not recommend that you pin all the way up to the crotch, even if the excess fabric is all the way to the crotch. Finish pinning by the inside thigh.

When altering, you will be able to use your imagine and draw a line from the finished pin to the crotch.

Step 6 - Ask the person to turn and face the opposite direction so that you can pin the other leg. (It's easier for them to move than for you to move)

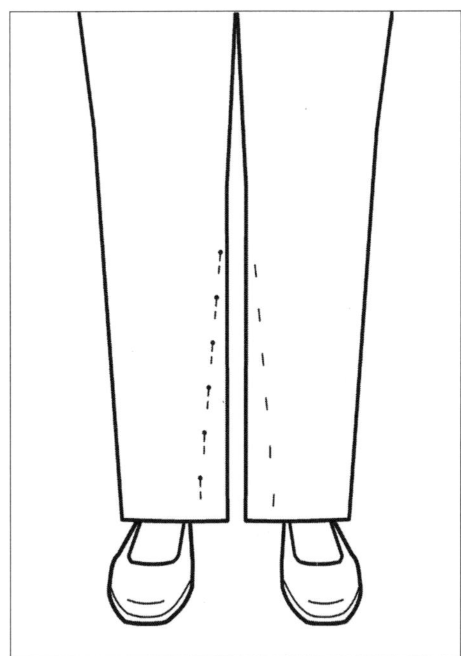

Step 7 - The hem may need to be taken up depending on the amount taken in at the bottom of the pants.

Step 8 - Use Take In Technique page 51 - 62.

Always undo hems and sew through to the very end of the fabric for a professional finish.

Taper legs in - Excess fabric on outside leg

In this scenario, the pants feel baggy, but when you stand in front of the mirror, with your shoes on, all the excess fabric is on the outside of the pant leg. You can tell if this is the case, because the inside seam will be resting against the inside leg.

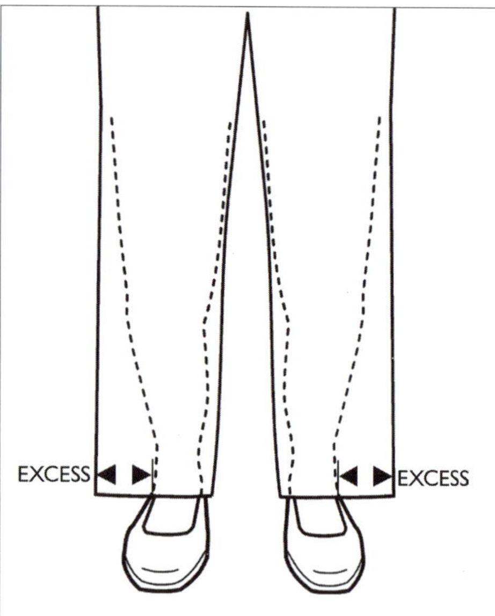

You will need help to pin the excess fabric on the outside leg.

Pinning

Step 1 - Kneel in front of the person.

Step 2 - Place a pin at the thigh area on the very edge of the seam.

Step 3 - Place the second pin below the first moving further into the fabric.

Step 4 - The amount to pin in at the bottom of the hem will be determined by the person's preference for the width at the base of the hem. I find that this amount is usually around 1'or 2.5 cm to 1 ¼" or 3 cm.

Step 5 - Now fill in with the pins moving gradually down to the hem.

Step 6 - Ask the person to turn and face the opposite direction so that you can pin the other leg. (It's easier for them to move than for you to move)

Step 7 - The hem may need to be taken up depending on the desired length.

Step 8 - The narrower the pants the higher the hem will need to be.

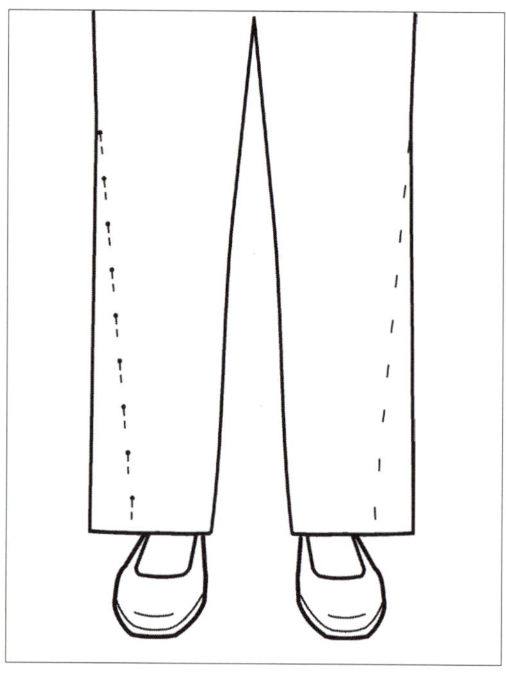

Step 8 - Use Take In Technique page 51 - 62.

Always undo hems and sew through to the very end of the fabric for a professional finish.

Take in back leg & crotch/fork

In this section we only going to look at what to do when the back of pants are baggy.

Usually in this situation, the front of the pants are resting on the persons thighs, and could not be taken in.

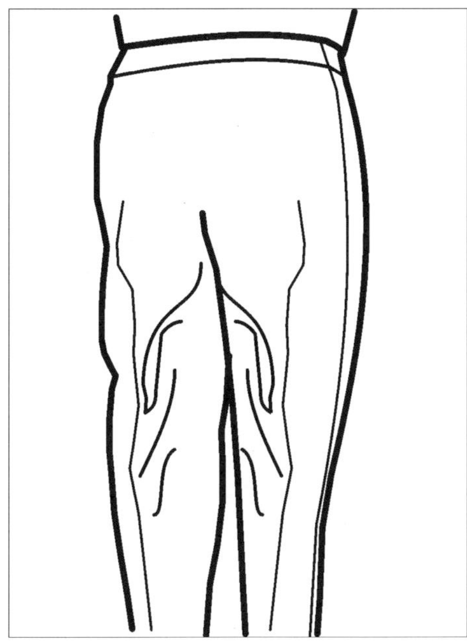

Therefore you can not take in the front panel at all.

I usually explain to my clients that the back panel of the pants is too big. Whether this happened because of a mistake by the manufacturer, or whether the person in question has a smaller bottom than most, the positive is that it can be fixed.

Because it is a strange way to pin on the person, I find it better to explain what I am going to do.

For example, I say, "The pants need to be unpicked from around the knee area up to the crotch". I face the client and show them with my hands starting from the knees and coming up to the crotch.

I explain that I will move the back section across and rejoin it to the front section. I will then cut away the excess fabric in the back section.

To do this type of clothing alteration, the crotch must be hanging down too low and there must be sufficient fabric in the thigh area.

If the thigh area is too tight, you cannot do this type of alteration. Usually there is sufficient fabric in the thigh area, because it is too baggy to start with.

Proceed as follows:-

Step 1 - Place hand over the centre back seam and grab hold of the excess fabric.

If the person is standing in front of a mirror, they will notice that the crotch area has just risen.

Step 2 - Place a pin across the pants as per illustration.

Step 3 - Take hold of the excess fabric at the back of the thigh area.

Step 4 - Ask the person to check and see that they have enough fabric in the crotch area (about ¾" or 2 cm).

Step 5 - Pin down the thigh. The amount that you pin down the thigh is the same amount that you have pinned across the back seam. Your first pin should be alongside the pin that is across the back seam.

Step 6 - Place another pin below the first moving down the centre section of the pants.

Step 7 - Continue to pin down the leg until the

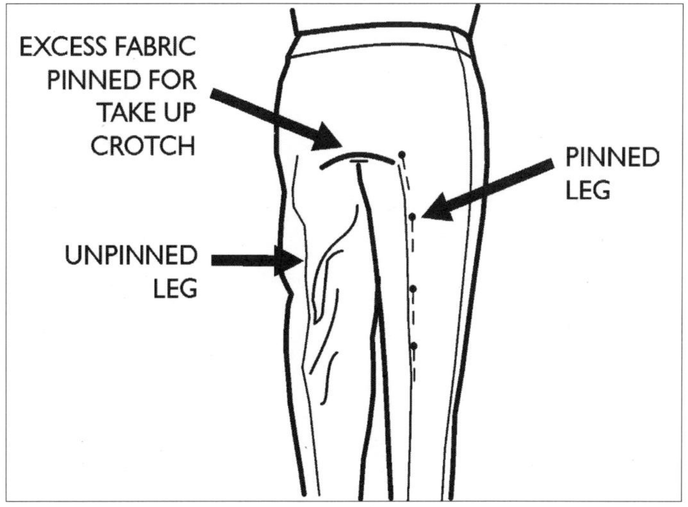

excess fabric has been taken up into the pinned area. (Usually I finish around the knee area)

Step 8 - Write down the amount you have pinned at the back seam. Measure from the fold to the pin.

Step 9 - Turn the garment inside out and unpick the inside-leg from the crotch down 15" towards the knee area. Clean old cotton stitches away.

Step 10 - Place a dot on the back leg only at the crotch. The dot should be the measurement you have written down and should be this distance from the original stitch line in.

Step 11 - Pin the front seam to the dot. Have the front section on the top and the back leg underneath. Place the pin through the seam on the front leg. I want you to re sew the leg together at the exact same position of the original front seam.

Do this on both sides. This means on one leg you will sew up from the knee and the other leg you will sew down from the crotch, because you are sewing into the original stitch line of the front leg.

Do not force the fabric. The front panel will be different from the back panel, but you can adjust at the crotch.

Step 12 - Cut off the excess fabric from the back leg. Over lock it if possible, or at least zig zag so the fabric does not fray.

When you join the front and back seams together, you may find that you have to reshape the front crotch seam. Make sure that you sew the seam with a gradual taper to the zip so that the seam sits correctly.

Take in crotch/fork

You may buy a pair of pants that has a very low crotch/fork, or you may loose weight, and when your tummy becomes smaller, your pants will hang lower in the crotch/fork.

The crotch can be raised if the thigh area is not too tight. If the pants are tight at the thigh area then you should not do this alteration to the pants.

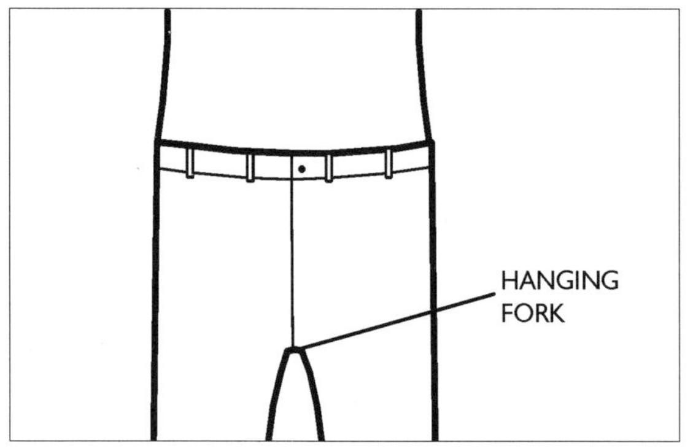

The illustration shows the fork hanging low on a pair of pants.

Step 1 - Pinch the center back seam at about 5" down from the band.

Pinch the fabric ACROSS the centre back seam until you have about 5/8" or 1.5 cm of fabric pinched in your fingers.

Step 2 - Place a pin ACROSS the seam pinning the desired amount you have in your fingers.

The pin will be going across the bottom from left to right as per illustration.

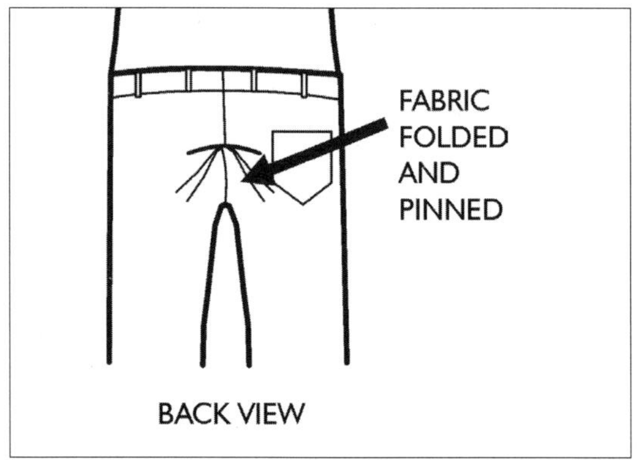

When you pin ACROSS, the person will notice that the fabric, which is hanging low in the crotch, is no longer there.

You must make sure that the crotch is not too tight. The last thing you want to happen is for the fabric to be very tight under the crotch.

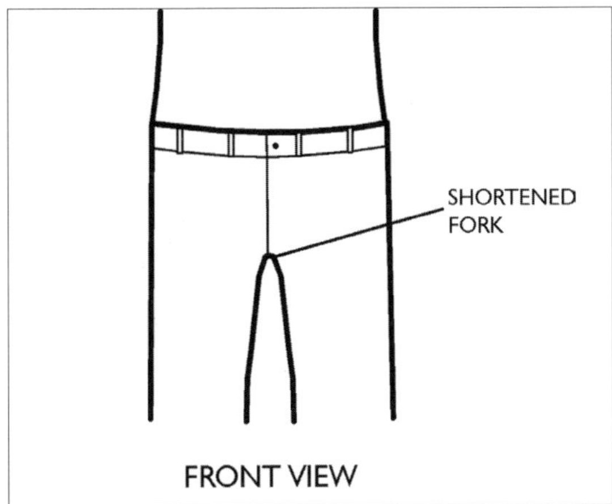

Sometimes I will take the pin out, and allow the fabric to drop back down, then re pin again to show the difference.

You must make sure that the crotch is not too tight.

To check this you need to ask the person to see if they can grab hold of about ¾" or 2 cm of fabric in the crotch area.

Explain to the person that when the crotch is taken up, the inner leg will also be taken up. This means that the thigh area will become tighter.

If the pants are tight around the thigh area, you cannot alter the crotch. In most cases if the crotch is low, then the pants are generally too big around the thigh any way.

The crotch must be altered before any other alterations are done to the sides. The reason for this is that the thigh area will become tighter.

Because of the way I pin the crotch, it does not show how much it will alter the sides by taking in the inside leg. Therefore alter the crotch first, and then have a second fitting for the sides.

You may find that once the crotch is altered, the sides have been taken in enough, and are fitting comfortably.

Step 3 - Measure the amount that you have

pinned at the back and write down on a piece of paper. This is the amount you are going to take out of the crotch.

Step 4 - Turn the pants inside out.

Step 5 - Unpick the centre back and centre front seams at the crotch.

Step 6 - Fold the inside leg seams together, making sure to allow the fabric to fall where it wants to fall.

The front panel will probably be lower than the back panel. Do not force it. Let it be this way.

Step 7 - Place the tip of the tape measure on the inside seam, and place a dot at the measurement you pinned the crotch.

Some pants have the inside leg seam running straight through from hem to hem, and other pants have the centre front and centre back seam running through the inside leg seam.

If the seam is straight through, you will have to check that the back section and the front section will be the same amount. If it isn't then you may have to take in the back section a little so it fits into the front section.

If the front and back seam run through the inside leg seam, you will have to unpick the centre front and centre back seam at the crotch, so that you can take in the inside leg seam.

You may have to reshape the front slightly to allow for the loss of fabric in the leg area. To help you with this, try pinning from the knee area up to the crotch. That will ensure that the fabric is not twisted at the crotch.

Step 8 - Sew from the knee area to the crotch on both sides. Measure down 15" and start sewing from here.

Step 9 - Over lock off the excess, and rejoin the front and back centre seams.

Pockets sticking out – pin down

Have you ever bought a pair of pants only to find that the pockets stick out?

I have one particular customer that brings her pants straight to me to sew down the pockets before she even wears them.

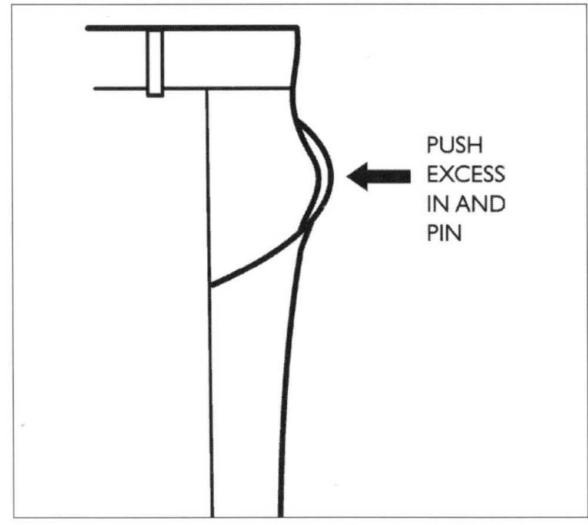

The pockets should be pinned on the person, so that you get the right amount of fabric pinned into the pocket. Stitch the pocket flat by sewing as close as possible to the edge of the pocket.

Step 1 - Pin the pocket on the person.

Step 2 - Make sure that the top of the pocket is sitting flat. Ask the person to push the excess fabric into the pocket.

Step 3 - Pin all the way around the pocket.

Make sure all the pins are going in the same direction.

Step 5 - Sew the pocket down, sewing the seam close to the edge of the pocket.

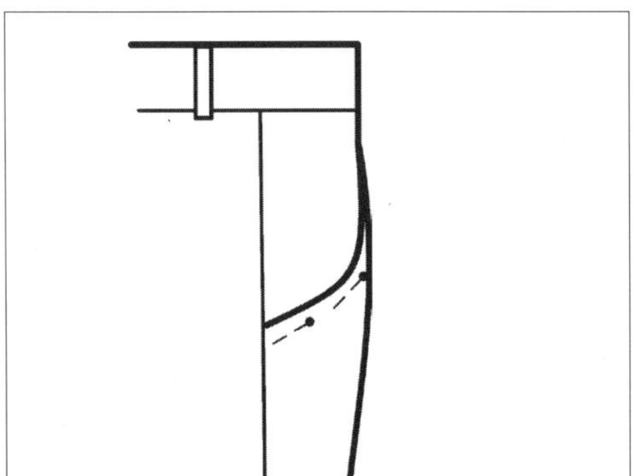

Conclusion

You may find that I have repeated myself in sections on Taking In Pants. I apologise for that, however, it has been done intentionally.

The reason for that is because I felt you may want to go to a particular type of alteration, and just refer to that alteration only.

I have asked you to refer back to the Taking In Technique at times which can only reinforce in your mind how to Take In a garment.

I have also spoken as if you are helping someone, or that someone is helping you.

It is almost impossible to pin yourself accurately when taking in a garment.

Always refer back to the Taking In Technique if you get stuck, and always look at how the garment was constructed in the first place to help you put it all back together.

Mobile phones have cameras now, so if you feel unsure, take a picture of it. It just might jog your memory and help you put it all back together.

Pants

Letting out

"Dress pants can be released
by taking the band off and
releasing at pleats or darts."

"Suit pants can be released
by using the excess fabric
at the centre back seam."

Pants too tight – Extension in waist

Putting on weight can cause problems with some suits, pants and skirts.

I have many women come in with a pair of pants (that belong to a suit), and the pants are too small.   The hip area is fine, but the waist is too tight.

Step 1 - Measure the person's waist. Write this measurement down on a piece of paper. (Make sure they are not holding their breath)

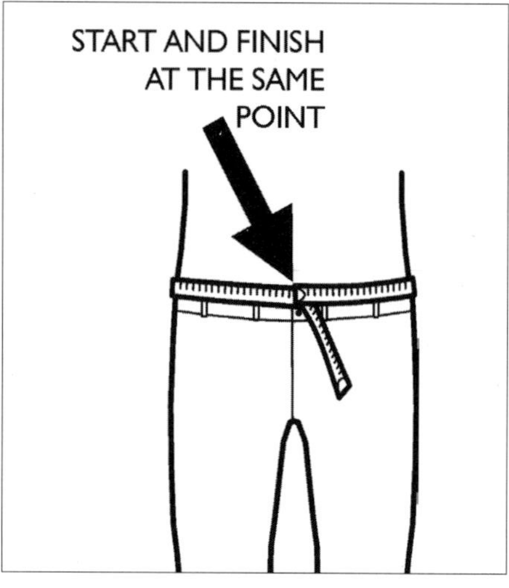

Step 2 - Measure the pants by closing the zip and do up any button or hook and bar. Place the beginning of your tape measure on the edge of the band.

Carefully measure around the band until you come back to where you started.

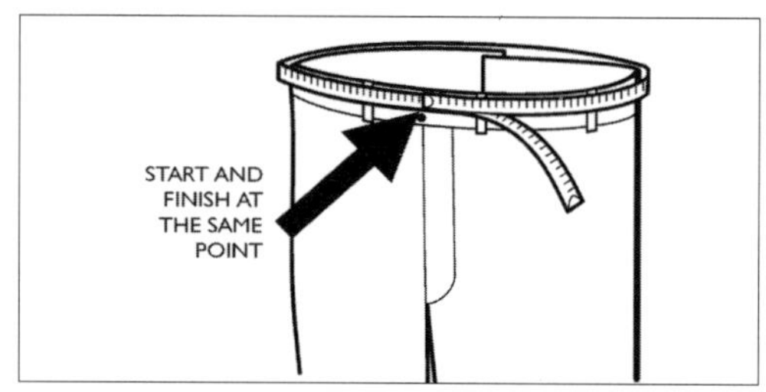

Step 3 - Work out the difference between the person's waist measurement and the measurement around the pants.

Step 4 - You now need to work out if there is enough fabric in the pants darts or pleats to extend the waist for the person.

Step 5 - Poke the tape measure into a pleat and measure the amount of the pleat. You must make sure you push the tape measure up hard against the inside seam.

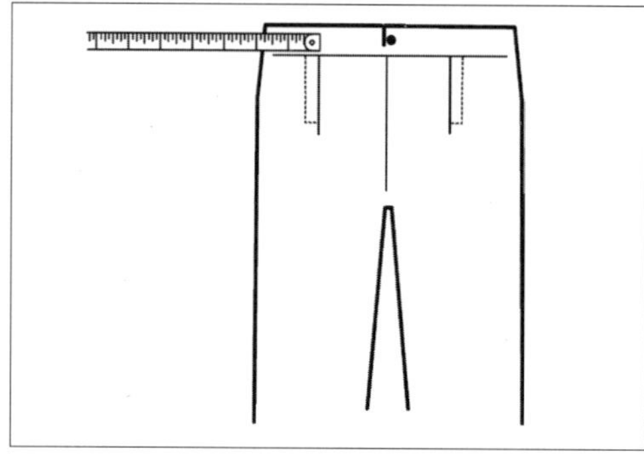

Let us say that the measurement is ½" or 1 cm. You now know you have 1" or 2 cm in total, because the fabric is folded over on itself.

Step 6 - If you have two pleats, then you know that you have 2" or 4 cm excess fabric in the band once the band is taken off and the pleats are released.

If you have four pleats then you can work out how much is there and use the amount you need.

Step 7 - If the pants have darts, then measure the amount of the dart at the top next to the band.

Because the fabric is folded over, you should double the amount. Most pants have four darts in the garment.

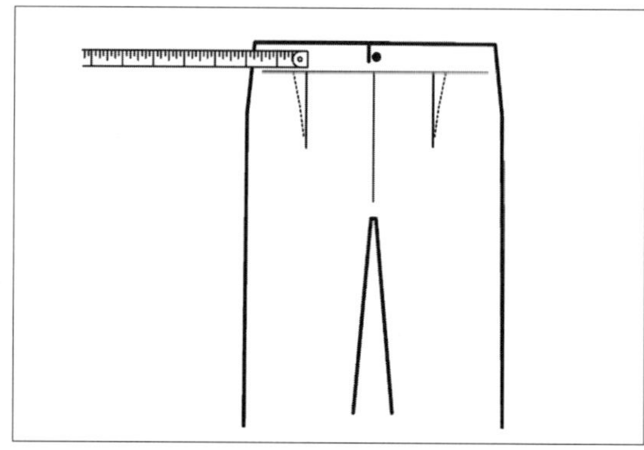

Step 8 - Work out how much extra you will have when you release the pleats or darts, and do your maths against the person's waist measurement. If you have enough to continue then proceed as follows.

Sewing

Step 1 - I take the band off beginning at the button (not the buttonhole end) and unpick up to the pleat next to the buttonhole.

Do not take the band off completely

Step 2 - Release the pleats/darts the amount needed.

Some darts have a burn hole in it from the manufacturer, so if this is the case, make the pleat or dart as small as possible, so that you do not see the burn hole.

Step 3 - Pin the band back on. Place the pins through the band.

This means the band is facing you.   The pins will be pointing towards the button.

The reason for this is that you want to sew into the old fold line on the waistband. This will ensure you sew over the original stitch line.

Step 4 - The extension will go on the button end. Either match the fabric as best as possible or try finding some fabric within the garment.

Places to find fabric are

1. Take off one pocket
2. If pants shortened, use off cut
3. Use the fabric at the back of the waistband, and replace with fabric a similar colour. Make sure to leave enough room for seam allowance. Don't cut on the fold line.

Step 5 - Cut your new extension to the same measurements as the existing band. i.e. width of the band and the length required.

With the length I tend to allow an extra amount just in case the person wants to let it out again later.

Step 6 - I prefer to iron some interfacing on to the new extension so that it is as firm as the original band.

Step 7 - Attach the extension to the waist band.

Step 8 - Iron seams flat.

Step 9 - Iron new fold into band so that the two waistbands are identical for seam allowance and the width of the band to the fold at the top.

Step 10 - Continue to pin the band onto the balance of the garment.

Step 11 - Measure around the waist band to make sure you have the correct measurement.

When you release pleats or darts, you will have unpicked some stay stitching, and the garment may have stretched a little.

Step 12 - If the measurement is correct, begin to sew the waistband.

I am assuming that this waist band is like most waist bands, and that the front of the band is sewn on first.

IF THIS IS THE CASE. you must begin stitching from the BUTTON end sewing back to the buttonhole end.

If the opposite is true, then you will be sewing from the buttonhole end to the button.

The bottom line - Sew into the original stitch line with the waist band facing up.

This means it is very important to pin the band on firmly, so that you do not end up with bunching when you reach the original seam near the buttonhole.

I usually have a fitting to make sure I have the correct amount.

It is at this point that I measure where the button will be sewn on.

Positioning a button

1. Pin the two bands together at a position that the person is happy with.

For the person to take the garment off you need to take the pin out that is holding the waist band together.

2. Place a pin at the end of the band which is on top, but pin through the band underneath, which means the pin is resting against the top waist band.

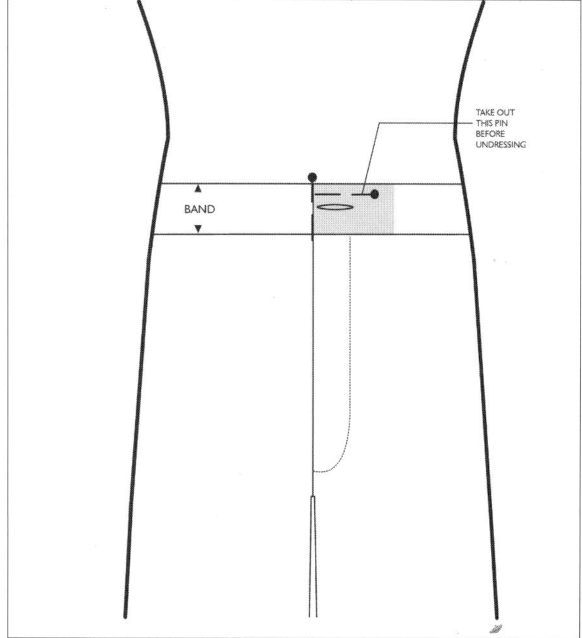

Before you can finish the waist band you need to put a dot for the position of the button.

3. To determine the exact location of the button, place the top waist band at the edge of the pin. Now place your tailors pencil through the buttonhole putting a dot for the position of the button.

You can now finish the band.

Step 13 - Fold the end of the band and iron flat.

Step 14 - Turn the band inside out, so that the top of the band is folded back on itself.

Step 15 - Sew down the fold line.

Step 16 - Turn the band back the right way, and use a point turner or tweezers to push out the top corner of the band.

Step 17 - Stitch in the ditch or sew the band on the way it was originally.

Sew your button on.

Here are some examples of how to sew on a button. These are also provided at the back of the book for easy reference.

1. Using a self threading needle.

Purchase from any shop selling needles.

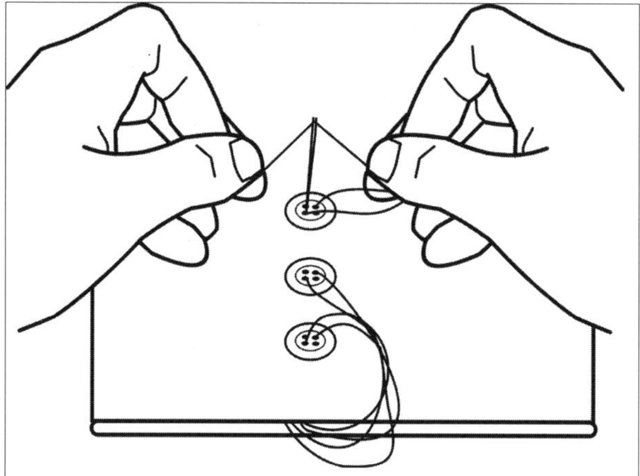

2. Fast method using a normal needle with a large eye.

Pull the cotton out from the spool to arms length, then pull another length the same. This means you have a very long length of cotton.

Fold it in half. Wet the ends and snip ends clean.

Thread through the eye of the needle as a double thread. You will now have four threads on the needle. Knot off the end and sew the button on. You only need to go through the eye of the needle twice and lock off.

3. Sew button on with sewing machine.

Change dials to zag zag (around 3) and have straight stitch on O (zero). Place button underneath foot of machine and lower foot onto button. Turn wheel by hand until you have position right, then sew a few times.

Use a needle to sew thread from front to back and sew a knot.

Release back – Suit pants

Most suit pants have a section at the centre back with excess fabric. This section can be released which will make the pants bigger.

There is no need for a person to try the pants on if they are too tight. To work out how much needs to be released do the following steps.

Step 1 - Measure the person's waist.

Have the beginning of the tape at the front, and take the tape around the persons waist, coming back to the beginning of the tape measure.

Ask the person to let their breath out. Usually a person will hold their breath when you begin to measure, which means they are holding their stomach in.

Write this measurement down on a piece of paper.

Step 2 - Your next step is to measure the pants.

This will allow you to determine how much you need to release at the back of the pants, and to see if there is enough fabric at the back to get the amount required for the person.

Step 3 - Close the zip on the pants.

Step 4 - Do up the button or hook and bar.

Step 5 - Place the beginning of your tape measure on the edge of the band

Step 6 - Carefully measure around the band until you come back to where you started.

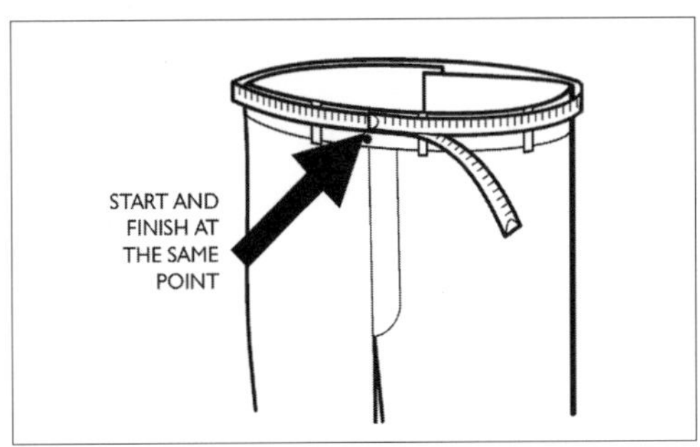

Step 7 - Now calculate the amount of the person's waist, less the measurement around the waistband. The difference is the amount that needs to be released from the back seam.

Step 8 - Take a look at the centre back seam of the pants. Measure the amount of excess fabric in the back of the pants just below the band.

You only need to allow a very small seam, so you can get most of what you need from there.

Men's suit pants are constructed in a number of ways, however there are two ways that are more readily used than others.

Option 1 - The first, and the easiest is where the centre back seam is open all the way from the band to the crotch. Proceed as follows -

Step 9 - Turn the pants inside out.

Step 10 - Unpick any belt loops that are in the way.

To open out this seam, you only need unpick the bar tack holding the sides down.

Step 11 - Place your tape measure at the edge of the centre back seam and measure out towards the edge of the fabric.

Step 12 - Place a dot at this new measurement.

Note - If the person wants 2", then you would measure out 1", because the fabric is doubled. When it is let out in full there will be 2".

SPECIAL NOTE: Do not unpick the original seam UNTIL you have sewn the new seam. Remember you need a reference point to work from.

Step 13 - Sew down at your new measurement.

Step 14 - Unpick the old seam.

Step 15 - Iron seams flat.

Step 16 - Sew over top of the first seam to reinforce the seam.

Step 17 - Tack the top section of the back down. I usually hand stitch from the bottom of the band to the top of the band.

Option 2 - The second style of back seam has the band folded over, which means you will not know how much is inside the band until you unpick it. Sometimes there is more, and sometimes there is less. Proceed as follows -

Step 9 - Turn the pants inside out.

Step 10 - Place your quick unpick into the seam holding the band down at the back of the band. I usually unpick at least 2" either side of the amount I need. This means you can open out the back section and sew with ease.

The back section will open out so that the bottom of the band will be at the top.

Step 11 - Measure the centre section, which is the top of the band.

Step 12 - Measure the top section (this is the bottom of the band turned up) and the bottom section of the band.

The top and the bottom sections of the band, MUST be the same measurement. The centre or top of the band can be a different measurement.

For example let's say that you can release 2" at the top of the band and 1 ½" at the bottom of the band. That means you need to place a dot at 1 ½" at the top when the band is folded out, 2" at

the centre and 1 ½" at the bottom of the band.

Step 13 - Always sew your new seam BEFORE you unpick the old seam.

Step 14 - After you have sewn your new seam, unpick the old. I sew one seam only, then I unpick the old seam and check to see that it sits correctly.

Step 15 - With the pants still turned inside out, place them over the ironing board, and iron the seams flat.

Step 16 - Fold the band back down and check that it fits perfectly back into place. If it does not fit perfectly then make an adjustment until it does. Once you have done a few pairs of pants, you will get the hang of it all.

Step 17 - If it all sits ok, then sew a second seam over the top of the first. I always sew two rows of stitching on a back seam to reinforce.

Step 18 - Most suit pants have white or cream on the inside, which means you will have to put this different colour in your bobbin, so that when you sew the band down, the cotton is the same colour as the under side.

Step 19 - Try to stitch into the join between the band and the body of the garment. This is called "stitch in the ditch".

Step 20 - Sew belt loops back on. See page 71 - 72.

Pants

Replacing zip

"Replacing a zip after pants are made is different from sewing a zip in as you are making pants."

Introduction

I have had people come in to my shop who have tried to take a zip out and replace the zip, only they don't undo the flap area, and they try to sew the zip in without preparing the garment correctly.

The result is that the job looks terrible, and the zip will not last the distance. If you want to do something, then do it right the first time.

This is a Step-by-Step procedure which explains how to unpick the old zip and replace with a new one.

I would just like to make a comment here. I have some elderly men come in and ask me to replace the nylon zip with a metal zip in their lightweight pants.

I really do not believe that a metal zip will last any longer than a nylon one.

To my way of thinking, a metal zip is for heavy fabrics like denim or moleskin. Nylon zips are for fabrics like cotton, linen and wools.

So replace your nylon zip with another nylon zip and have fun sewing.

Here is a tip for saving your zips.

It doesn't matter if they are metal or nylon. the same rule applies.

BEFORE WASHING PANTS - DO THE ZIP UP COMPLETELY AND DO UP THE BUTTON TO ENSURE THE ZIP DOES NOT COME UNDONE.

If you leave a zip open, when the pants are being washed, the open zip could get caught on something and the zip will break.

I always do up my zips, and I have only replaced one zip in a pair of my own pants in over 20 years.................

What you will need

New zip – Measure the old zip. Place your tape measure at the top of the zip where the metal piece is located. Measure down to the bottom of the zip where the other metal piece is located. This is the size of the zip.

Zips usually come in standard sizes. The most common size is 7" or 18 cm, for suit pants, but occasionally you will come across a suit pant that has a 8" or 20 cm zip in it.

If you have a longer zip and want to cut, it down to size just cut a section off one side of the zip at the very bottom. Make the piece about 1 ¼" or 2.5 cm long and ½" or 1.5 cm wide.

Sew this piece across the zip at the length you want the zip to be. Make sure you stitch it securely on either side of the teeth.

Cut the excess zip away up to the edge of the fabric cover.

You can sew a piece of bias binding across the bottom before you cut the excess off or you could use a piece of fabric. Whatever way you decide, do not try just stitching across the bottom and cutting the excess off. Without some type of fabric there, the zip will break.

Zipper foot – All sewing machines come with different types of sewing feet. The zipper foot is the one that looks like it is cut in half down the middle. All sewing machines have manuals with them, so if you are not sure, consult the manual.

Standard needle – Having the right needle will make a big difference to your sewing. The most common to use for cotton or woollen fabric is an 80/12, however I personally like to use a 75/12 – Stretch needle for most of my sewing. It seems to give a better finish.

Cotton – You need a reel of cotton the same colour as the pants. Have a look at the fabric colour under the flap. If it is the same colour as the pants, then you only need one bobbin in the colour of the pants, but if the colour underneath

is white or cream, then you need a second bobbin in this colour.

Quick unpick - I use a good quality quick unpick. There is a brand called Clover. It has a brown handle. I find this style easy to use; however, there are many brands on the market for you to choose.

Some people prefer to unpick with a pair of nippers. They are like scissors but small. I also know a woman who unpicks using a razor blade. She is very quick. Find the style you prefer.

Before we go into the steps to replace a zip in suit pants or dress pants, you need to know that women's pants are different from men's pants. It is a bit like the buttonhole difference.

I remember which side a women's buttonhole goes when I say, "Women are always right." This means that the buttonhole for a woman goes on the right hand side, and the men's goes on the left.

With pants, the zips are usually put in differently. The women's pants have the flap section on the right, and the men's pants have the flap section on the left.

I have had two illustrations done to show the difference.

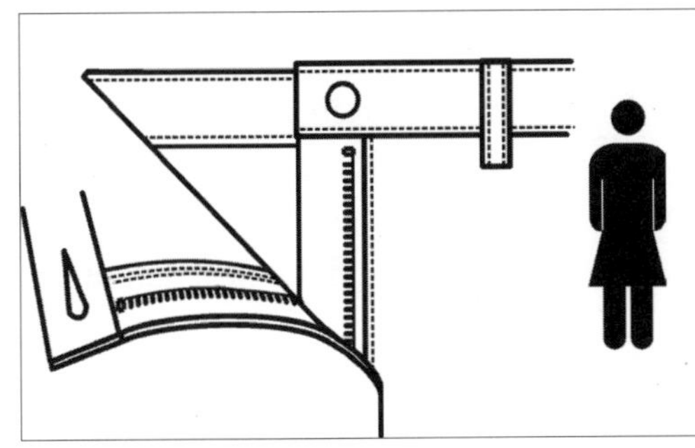

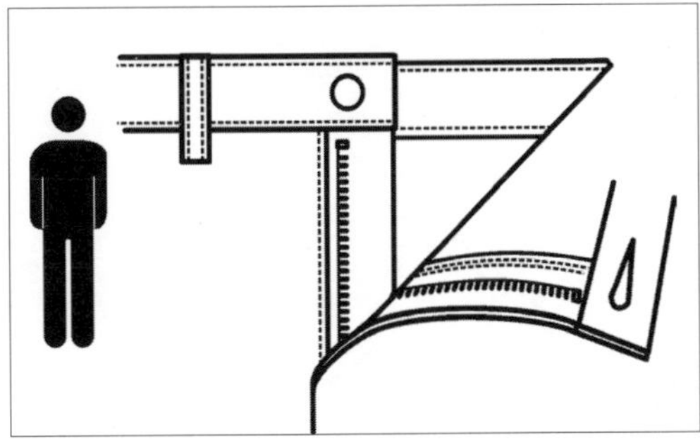

Step By Step Instructions

Before you start, you might like to consider having a second pair of pants along side, so you can refer to them if necessary.

Step 1 – You need to release the zip from the waist band.

Unpick one stitch on the waistband and insert finger as far as possible, and give a little push to open the waistband.

Now unpick another stitch and push your finger into the waistband to open a little more.

Only unpick enough to get the zip out. DO NOT UNPICK THE BAND FROM THE BODY OF THE GARMENT.

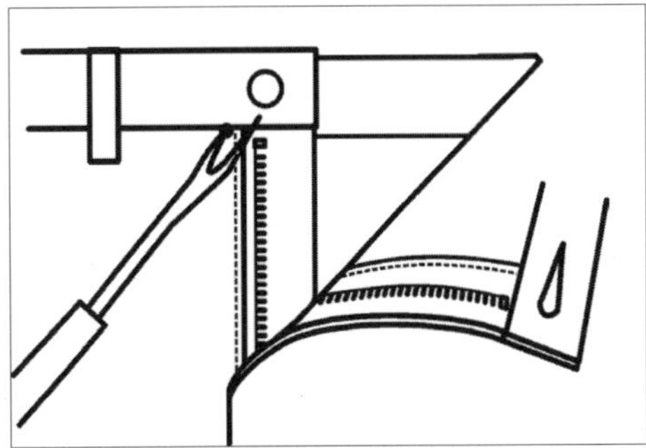

I find once I have the waistband opened a little I can insert the quick unpick and slice across the waistband.

Be careful when slicing. If this is your first time, unpick slowly.

Step 2 – Unpick the zip from fabric insert side. You may find it easier to slide the quick unpick in between the zip and the fabric and slice.

You must be very careful not to cut the fabric.

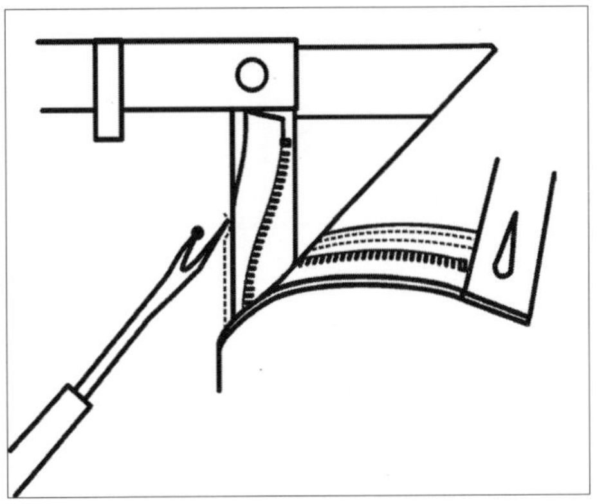

Step 3 – Unpick the zig zag stitch which is located at the bottom of the fly facings (joins fabric insert to flap side).

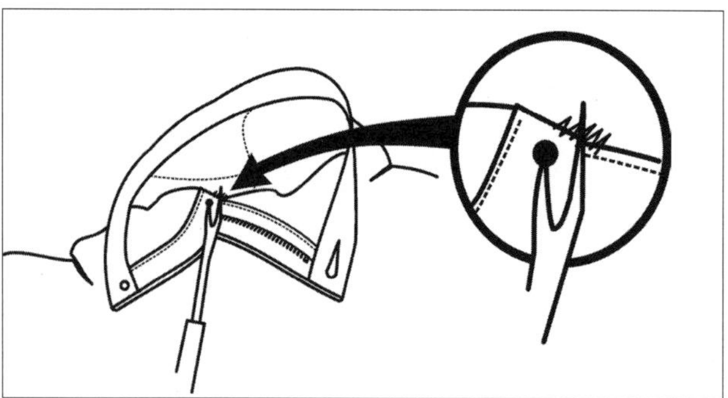

Step 4 – Unpick the zip and release the zip from the fabric insert section completely.

The zip should be unpicked completely on this side and the fabric insert should be released at the bottom.

Some suit pants have the fabric insert attached at the crotch area. You do not have to unpick this particular section, because usually the manufacturer has not attached for about one inch from the bottom of the zip to the reattached section.

Even if you have the zip released, if the fabric insert is still attached to the seam at the zip area, it will make fitting the zip harder if not released.

Some manufacturers over lock the zip and fabric insert together, which means that you will have to undo the over locking.

I would suggest that you either re over lock the fabric insert or zigzag the edges or cover with bias binding to stop the fabric from fraying.

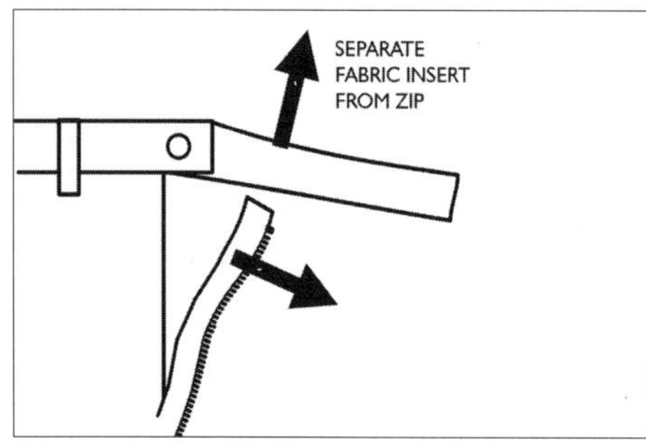

Step 5 – Unpick the zip from flap side, beginning from the bottom of the zip and working up towards the band.

On some pants, if the cotton is not too thick, I will grab hold of the zip at the bottom and give little jerk movements and RIP the zip out. This can only be done if the cotton is not too thick.

If you are unsure use the quick unpick.

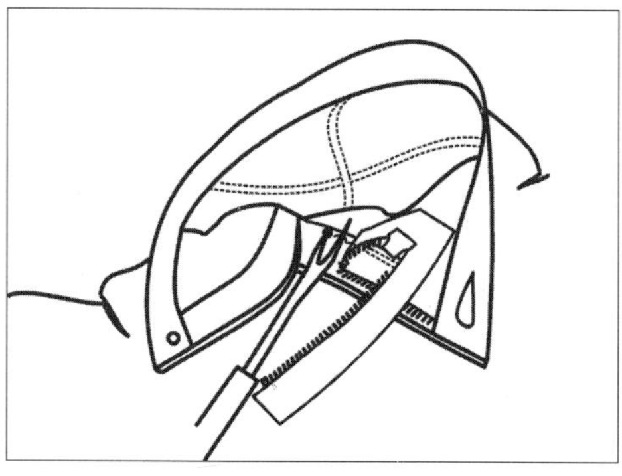

Step 6 – Insert quick unpick into the stitching in the waist band.

Nick one stitch and give a little pull to open the waist band area. You need to unpick just enough stitches to release the zip from band.

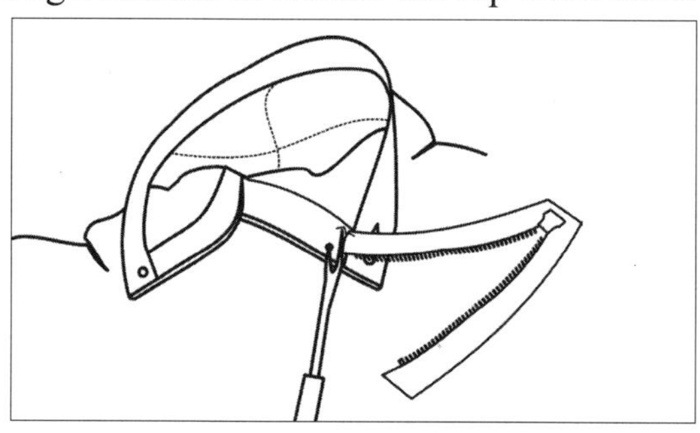

Now that you have the zip released, unpick a little bit further so that you have the flap released.

Step 7 - Now unpick stitching holding flap side to outer fabric. This stitching begins at the top of the waist band and goes down and curves in to the centre front seam. This is where a lot of people make their mistake. They don't unpick the flap.

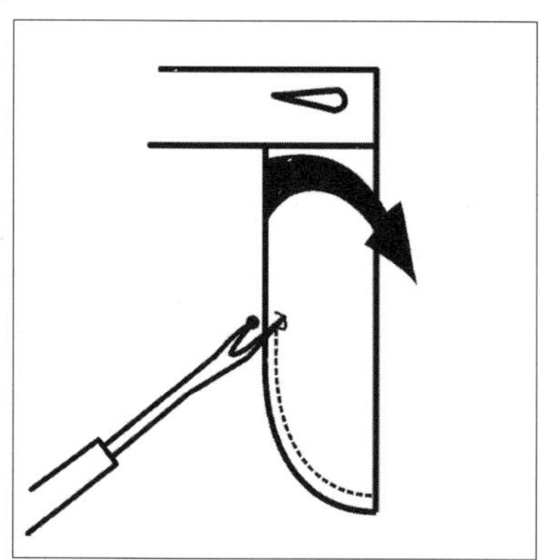

Step 8 – Pick off all the excess cotton in the seams that you have unpicked.

In particular you need to remove the old un-picked stitching on the front of the pants.

I call this removing the fluffy bits. It was a standing joke in the shops, that I was very fin-icky about removing all the old cotton threads before you begin sewing again.

You are now ready to put the zip in.

Step 9 – Insert the zip between the outer fabric and the fabric insert.

I find it easier to use a pair of tweezers to insert the zip because the tweezers give you more control over the zip.

Make sure you have the top metal piece of the zip about 1/8" or 3 mm below the original stitch line.

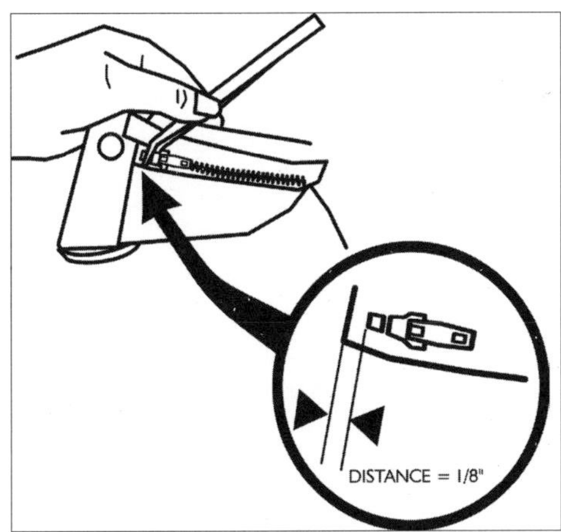

Step 10   Pin zip in place beginning with the first pin at the top, second pin following and then a third pin at the bottom.

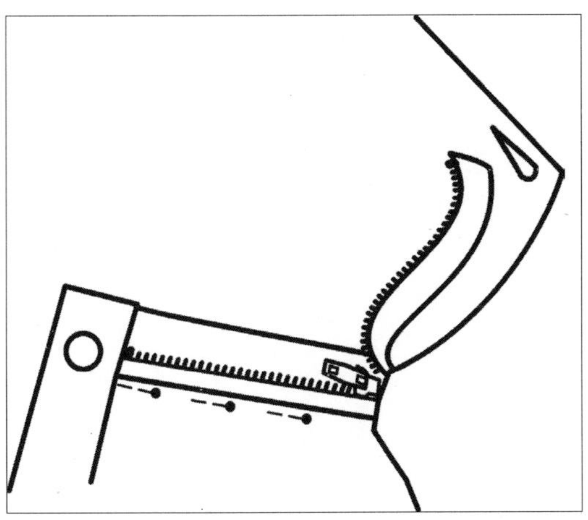

Step 11 – To ensure that the zip is pinned back in the original position, check the back side to see if the pins are in the original stitch line.

Re-adjust pins until they are in the original seam line at the back of the insert, and are still pinned correctly at the front in the original stitch line.

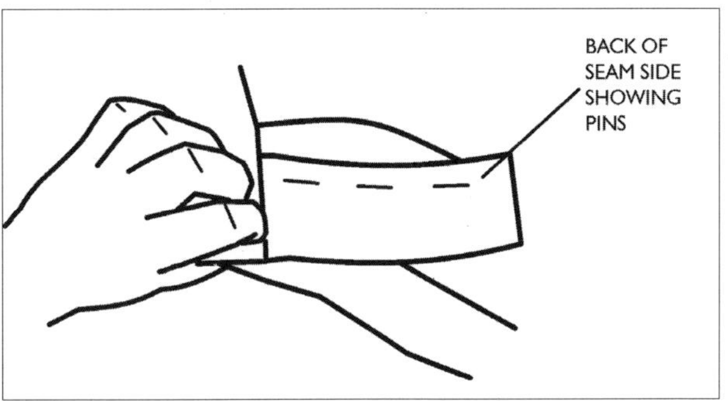

Step 12 – Put the cotton on the machine that is the same colour as the pants.

If the fabric at the back of the zip is white or crèam, place this colour bobbin in your ma-chine.

Sew zip into fabric insert side.

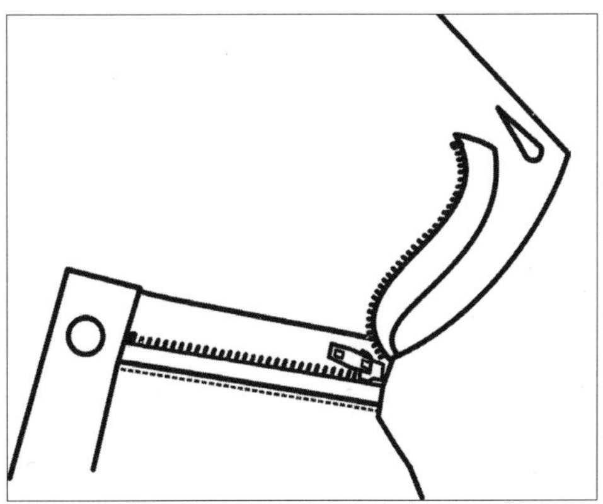

Step 13 – Do zipper up. This is important. If you do not do the zipper up, you will not set the zipper in correctly.

Pin bottom of zip to flap side only. Do not pin to the outer fabric, just pin onto the flap side.

Make sure that the two sides are even at the bot-tom of the zip. If you have one side uneven, the zip will not sit correctly.

Now pin the top of the zip making sure you have the top of the zip 1/8" or 3 mm below the original stitch line.

If zip is over 15 cm long place a pin in between the top and bottom pin.

You may find that you have to ease the zip in the middle section. In this case place a pin in the centre to hold the zip in place.

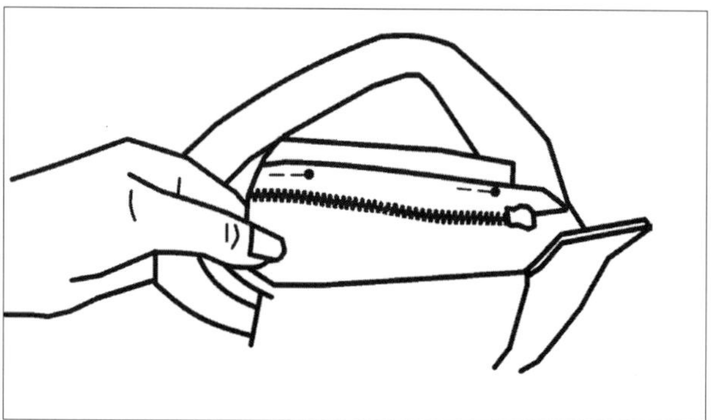

Step 14 – Turn the garment in the correct way, and make sure that the waistband lines up.

If the waistband does not line up, then you have the zip pinned incorrectly on the flap side.

Re pin the zip until the waistbands meet.

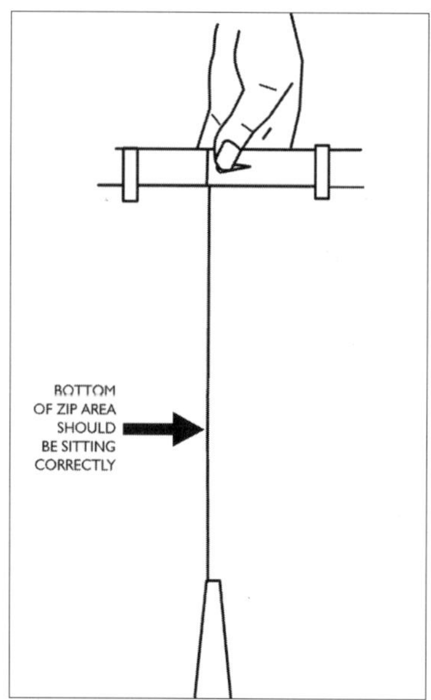

Step 15 – Change bobbin to same colour as pants.

Undo the zip. Make sure the zip clip is sitting flat and not sticking up. If it is sticking up it will get in your way.

Before you take your pins out you must secure the zip in the position it is now, so you should lower the needle into the position you are going to sew, and then take your pin out.

Sew zip onto flap area by sewing a row of stitching from the bottom of the zip to the top of the zip.

The seam should be in the middle between the side of the zip and the teeth of the zip.

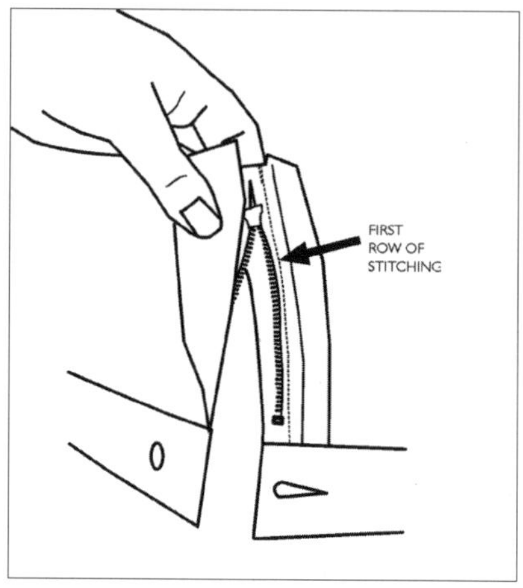

Step 16 – Sew a second row of stitching on the very edge of the zip beginning from the bottom of the zip to the top of the zip.

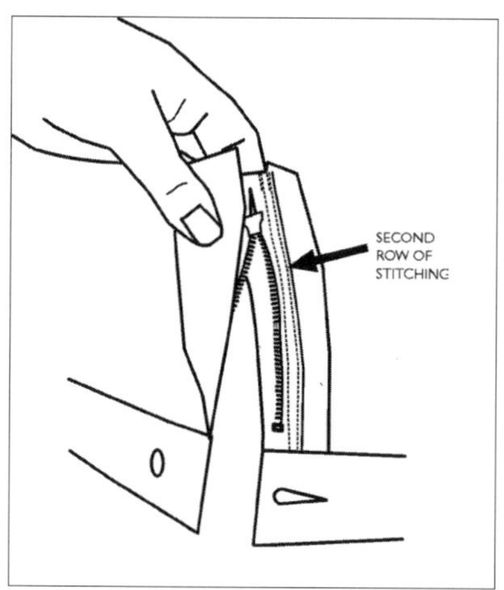

Step 17 – Open zip. When you sew the flap back on to the outer fabric, you need to ensure you sew into the original stitch line.

Fold the flap down flat and sew the first row of stitching beginning at the top of the band coming down towards the crotch of the pants.

As you curve in towards the centre front seam, you must follow the original curve line.

You can actually sew in as far as possible WITHOUT stitching the fabric insert side.

In this illustration I have stopped about 1" from the centre seam. Depending on how the jeans are made, sometimes you will have to stop as per the illustration, and other times, you may be able to stitch up close to the centre seam.

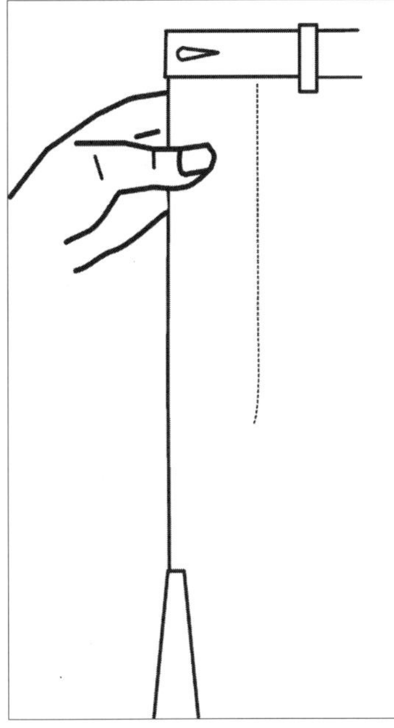

If you are doing this for the first time, you might find it easier to pin the flap down.

Place the pins so that the head of the pin is on your left, and make sure the flap is sitting flat.

Please note that the fabric insert side is NOT pinned with the flap side. It should be folded out of the way. If the zip is undone (which it should be) then it is easy to have the fabric insert out of the way.

Step 18 – Change bobbin to same colour as underneath.

If it is white or cream underneath then change to this colour.

To complete this section, the fabric insert side should now be folded across and should be underneath the flap side.

Make sure the sections underneath are sitting flat.

Now sew the curve area from 3 to 4, and then stitch from 3 to 2 only.

To cover the join you can do a small zig zag at the join, or if you are careful, just stitch over the end of the seam you are meeting and do a small bar tack back and forward.

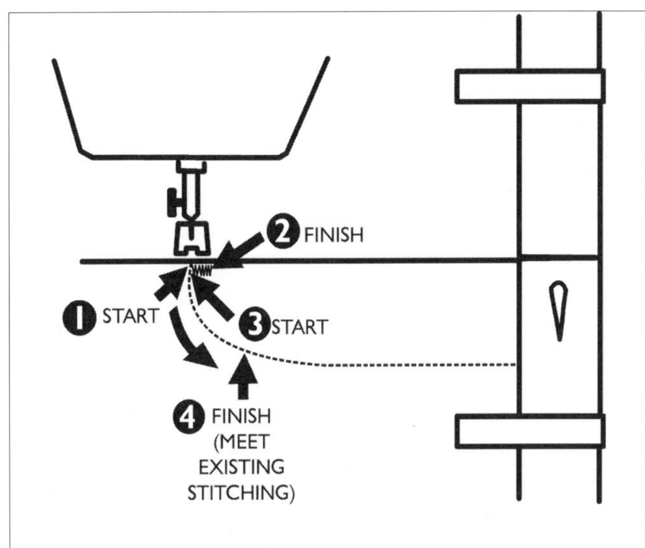

Step 19 – Insert zip and fabric into band.

Sew across band. If there is no stitching on the band, Sew from the belt loop to the edge of the band.

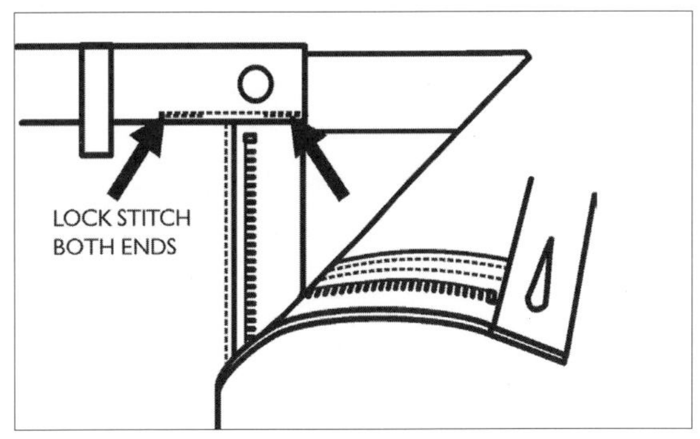

Normally people where belts, so the stitching will not be seen.

Some pants have bars or buttons that stop you getting into the inside of the band. If you can get inside then sew the band back on to the body of the garment, then stitch in the ditch to sew the band to the body of the garment.

Step 20 - Insert flap back into band and sew back together. Lock both ends.

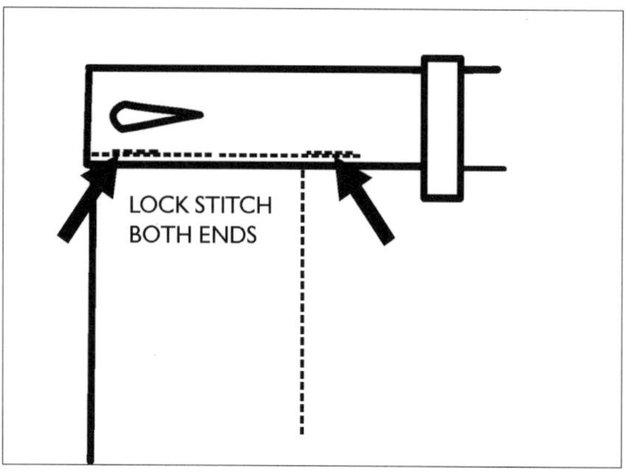

If you can get inside the band, then sew it the same as described in Step 19.

Congratulations - Zip replaced in suit pants.

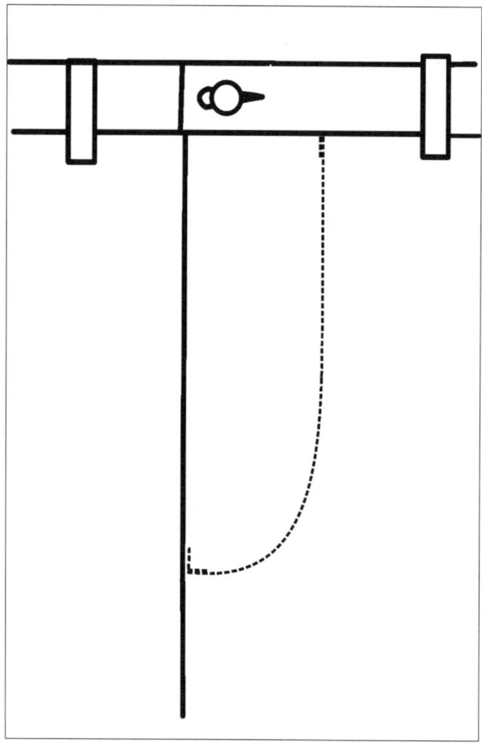

Conclusion

As I stated in the beginning, replacing a zipper in a pair of pants is very different from making a pair of pants and putting the zip in as the garment is being made.

I have provided you with illustrations on a basic suit pant zip.

It would be impossible for me to provide you with all of the possibilities for replacing a zip.

Some manufacturers can change the style, and that may affect how the zip is to be replaced.

One final point. When replacing a zip, always make sure that the pants have been washed before you begin working on them. You will be working in the crotch area, and for health reasons it is better to wash the jeans first.

Happy sewing

Jeans

Taking Up _with the_

Jean Genie

"You don't need an industrial sewing machine to create a professional jean hem."

Introduction

The magical Jean Genie has been supplied with this book to help you sew professional jean hems every time.

I developed the Jean Genie because I had so many people come into my shops with their jeans or their family members jeans, saying they couldn't take up the jeans on their domestic sewing machine.

For the first eight years doing clothing alterations, we only used domestic sewing machines, but we had help when it came to sewing over the thick seams at the sides.

In fact one of the shops would go over to one of the major jean outlets and collect the jeans every day, and we returned them with a professional jean hem sewn on our domestic sewing machines.

But its not just the jean genie that makes the hem look professional. There are a few other little tricks of the trade that you need to follow.

Before we get into sewing the jeans, let's begin with writing down your measurements.

I am assuming that you have followed the process for pinning the jeans as per Taking Up Technique page 32 - 39.

You may think that there is only one type of jean hem. Unfortunately that is not true. There are a number of different types of hems on jeans.

Most jeans have a standard 5/8" + 5/8" (1.5 + 1.5 cm) hem allowance. The Jean Genie has been designed with the measurement in mind.

However, some designers put smaller hem allowances. I have seen some that are as small as 1/4" + 1/4" (.5 + .5 cm).

There are also jeans that have larger hem allowances, much like casual pants.

Writing down measurements

Measure the amount folded under with your Jean Genie as per illustration A.

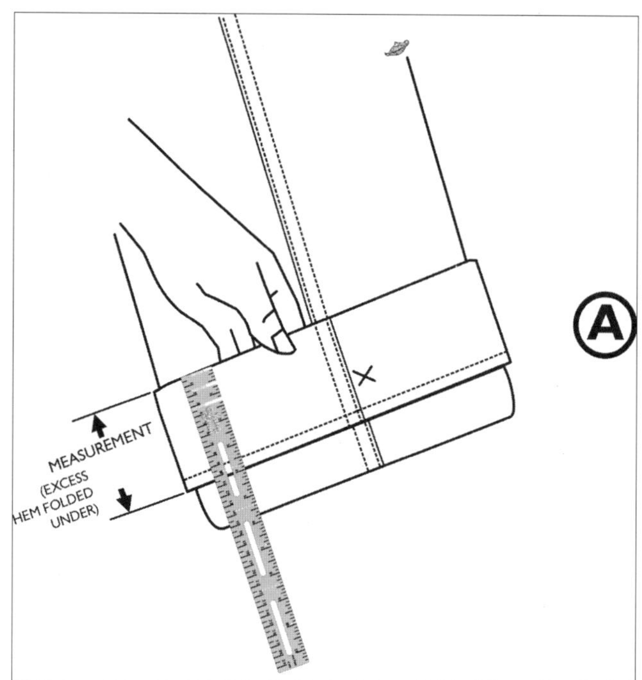

For those of you who are going to sew a normal jean hem I have provided you with "My Notes" based on the standard jean hem allowance.

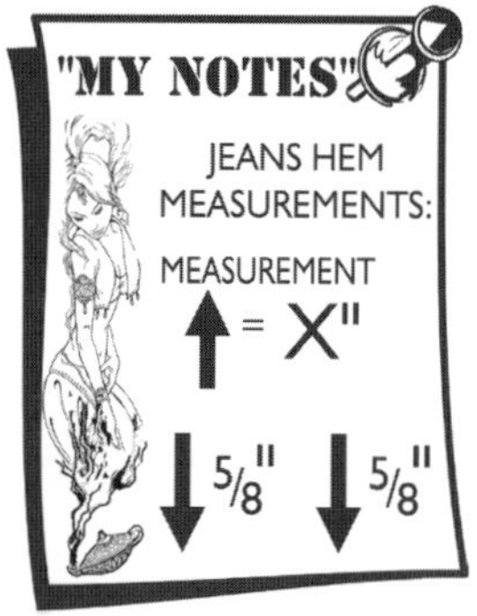

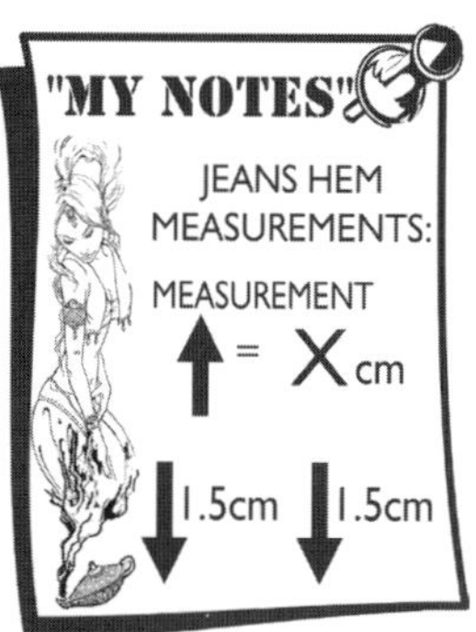

Whilst the majority of jean hems are as per the above, there are some that are a little bigger at 3/4" + 3/4" or 2 cm + 2 cm.

I have had customers who prefer I repeat exactly what is on the hem, so in this case I do what they ask.

Hint - I have a set of samples 6" x 6" of all the different types of hems I can do. They are pinned together at my front counter. That way I can show the customer exactly what the new hem will look like from the samples.

Preparing Jeans with the Jean Genie

Step 1 - Take the pins out and check to see that the legs are the same length as per page 34 - 36.

Step 2 - Lay the jeans on the table with the front legs facing up, sides seams at the sides.

Step 3 - Place the Jean Genie over the jean hem, with the measurement from A being the position of the ruler at the original hem line. Begin on the left leg and in about 2" from the side as per illustration B.

Step 4 - Place a chalk mark into the nick at the top of the Jean Genie marked "Hem Line".

Step 5 - Move down to the second nick on the Jean Genie marked "Fold Line" and place a chalk mark in the nick.

Step 4 - Move down to the third nick on the Jean Genie marked "Cut Line" and place a chalk mark in the nick. This is the hem allowance.

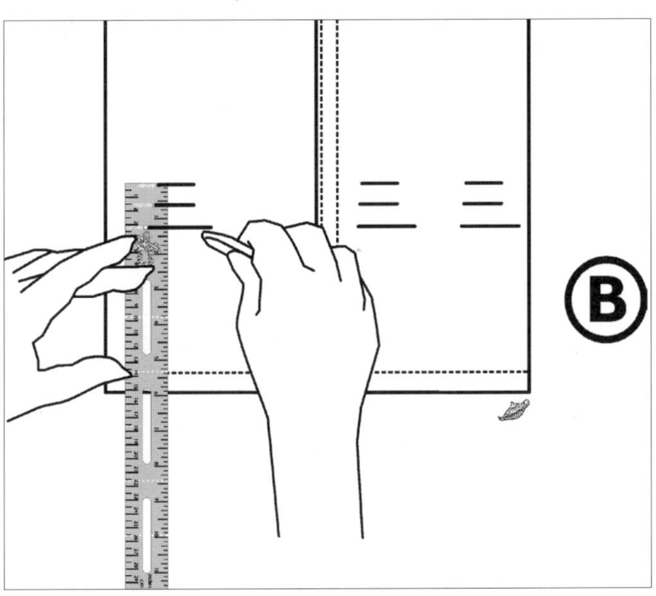

Step 5 - Cut on the bottom chalk line.

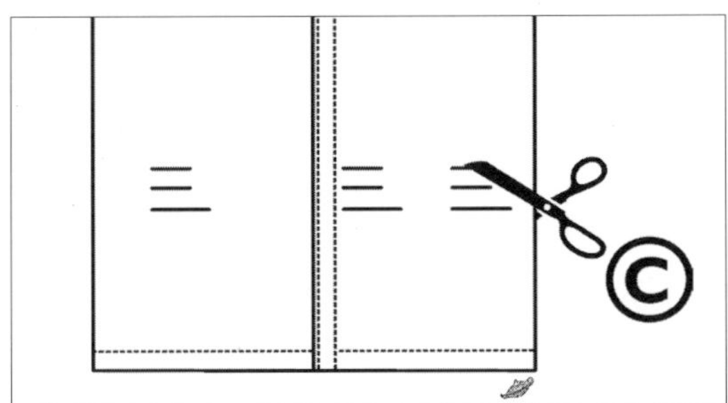

Sewing Jeans with the Jean Genie

I would have made at least a million dollars if I had received a dollar for every person who said they couldn't sew a jeans hem on their domestic sewing machine.

I use a domestic sewing machine for all jean hems. I have never used a industrial sewing machine in any of my shops to sew a jeans hem.

How do you sew a professional jean hem on your domestic sewing machine?

First thing you need to do is find two cottons that when they are lain side by side, become a close match to the colour of the cotton on the jeans.

For example - The standard orange/kharki colour on most jeans can be achieved by using one cotton that is orange, and the second cotton which is kharki.

Lay these cottons together, and you will have a great jean cotton colour.

Manufacturers are using many different cotton colours, so you will have to get a little creative here.

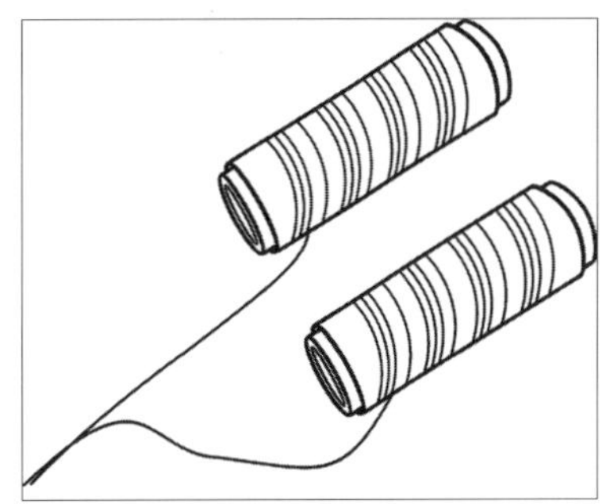

There are many different colours used now on jeans, from beige, black, red, and many different shades of orange.

Attach the two cottons you have chosen onto the machine, threading the two threads together at the top all the way through to the needle.

All domestic sewing machines since 1975 have the ability for two cottons to be threaded from the top down and into the needle.

Insert your jeans needle, and thread the two cottons into the needle.

The eye of this needle is larger than a smaller type of needle, so it should accommodate easily.

I use tweezers to thread my machines.

I snip the cotton so the ends are "clean", then I wet the ends and thread with the tweezers into the size 90/14 Jean Needle.

Special Note - DO NOT turn jeans inside out.

You are sewing what I call topside, which means you turn the hem under.

Step 1 - Beginning with the inside leg, turn the fabric over to the first chalk mark.

Step 2 - Turn the fabric over to the second chalk mark.

To hold in place put a pin into the folded hem, but not at the thick centre seam.

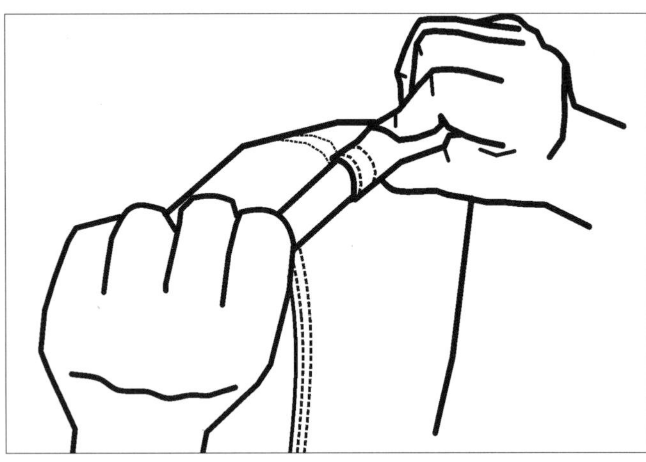

As you get more experienced at sewing jeans hems this way, you will not have to put pins in the hem.

Because I have sewn thousands of jeans hems, I just fold and begin sewing in front of the thick seam of the inside leg.

Your pins should be placed so that as you sew, you will pull the pins out towards you.

If the seam is very thick, you can try giving the thick seam a few tapes with a hammer. (clean hammer of course).

Hammering the thick seam will make it easier to sew over the thick section.

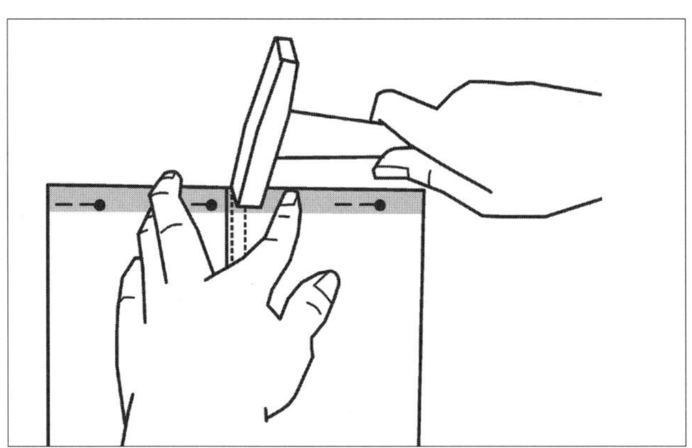

If you are not sure about the hammering (I don't use one), just try using the jean genie first, then if its really too thick, use the hammer.

Step 3 - Begin sewing at the inside leg.

The reason you do this is because the seam join will be on the inside leg, rather than the outside leg.

Place the folded hem under your sewing machine foot. The back of the sewing machine foot should be just touching the inside leg seam as per the illustration.

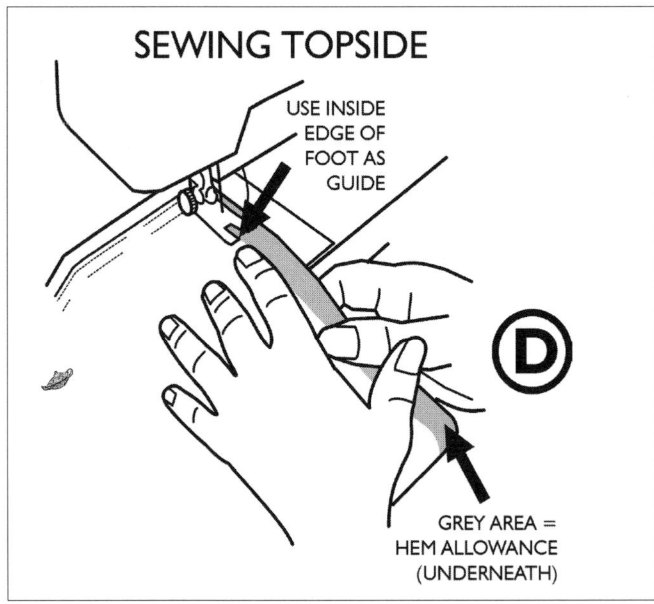

The left side of the sewing machine foot should be over the top edge of the hem underneath.

If you look carefully, you will see the indent from the hem underneath. Have a look where your sewing machine foot is in relation to the folded hem underneath.

For example I place my machine foot so that the inside of the foot on the left hand side is over the edge of the hem allowance underneath.

This means I sew on the edge of the hem allowance every time. But your sewing machine foot might be slightly different to mine, so experiment until you get it right.

Step 4 - Sew along the hem until you come to the first side seam.

If you started sewing in front of the inside leg seam, then the next side seam you come to will be the outside leg seam. Sew up to this side seam, until the front of the foot is touching the thick seam.

You are now ready to use the Jean Genie

JG-1.   Lower needle into fabric.
JG-2.   Raise the foot.
JG-3.   Fold the Jean Genie at the fold lines. The white sections should be pulled out.
JG-4.   Push the Jean Genie in underneath the foot. Make sure you push it up to the edge of the thick seam. Lower foot.

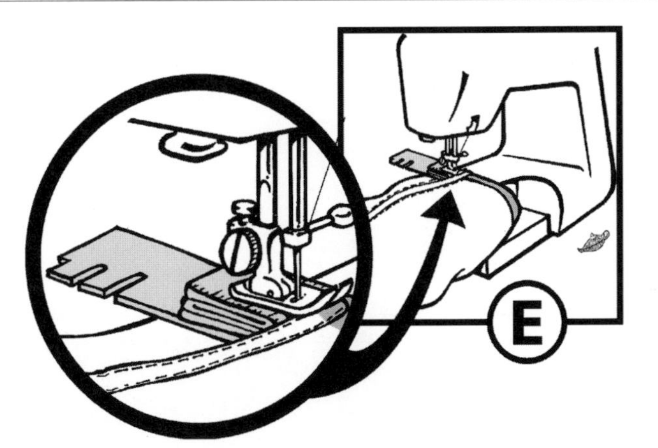

JG-5.   Sew up to the centre of the side seam. If the seam is extremely thick you may have to work the needle across by turning the balance wheel by hand.
JG-6.   Lower the needle into the fabric at the centre of the side seam.

JG-7.   Raise the foot.
JG-8.   Take the Jean Genie out from the back of the foot and place it at the front of the foot in front of the side seam.
JG-9.   Lower foot. Sew into the groove of the Jean Genie until the back of the sewing machine foot has cleared the thick seam.

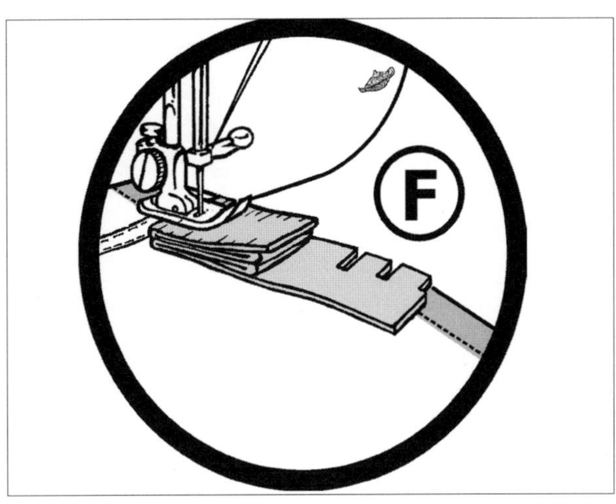

Step 5 - Remove the Jean Genie and sew along the seam until you come to the next thick seam.

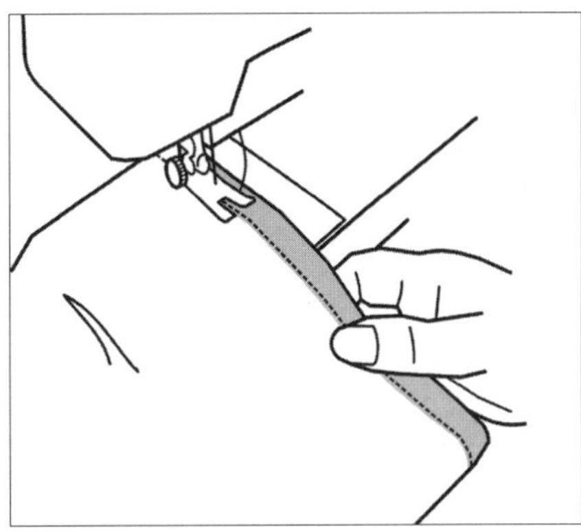

Step 6 - Repeat JG-1 to JG-9.

Step 7 - Sew over the top of your original seam and lock off reversing back and forward.

Special Note

If you ever find that the stitching is mangled underneath, it is because you have NOT LOWERED THE FOOT before you began to sew with the Jean Genie. You must always lower the foot when sewing over the Jean Genie.

Enjoy sewing a professional jean hem with the Jean Genie.

Jeans
Taking Up

Original Finish

"Keep the frayed feature on your jeans hem."

Introduction

When shortening jeans most people think they will loose the frayed look because they do not know how to put it back on.

There are a number of ways to do this, and some are easier than others. My technique for Original Finish (European Finish) is to put the frayed section back on so that it almost looks the same as it did before it was altered. And I don't just mean on the outside. I want the inside to look good as well.

These illustrations were difficult to do, because of the nature of the alteration, however I hope that you can follow it, and perhaps as a thought, you should try this with an old pair of jeans first, before you cut into the expensive designer jeans.

Pinning

Step 1 - Pin the frayed section up as per pinning technique.

I have included two illustrations of what it will look like with low and medium heeled shoes.

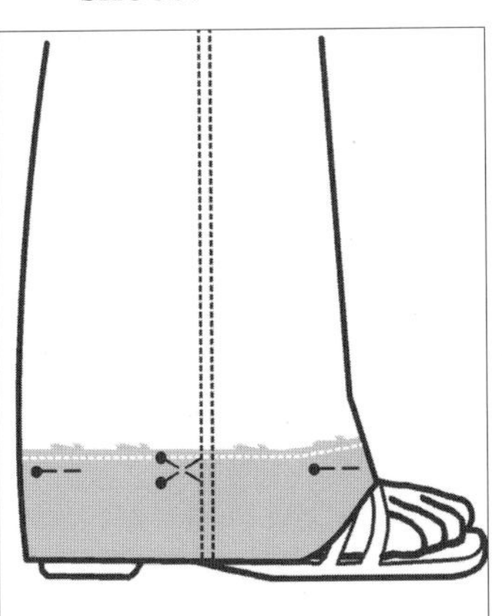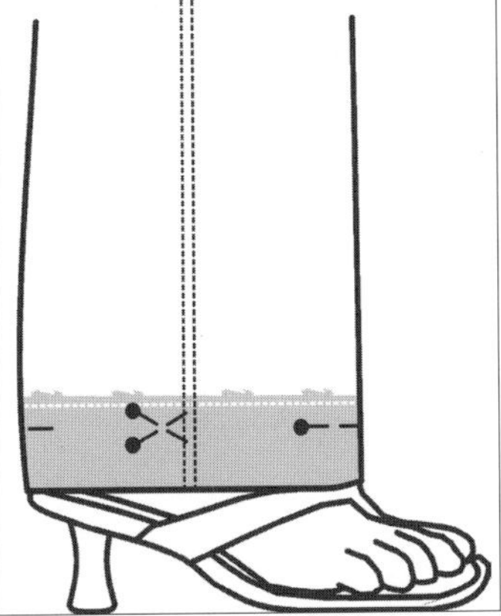

Step 2 - Measure the amount that you have folded under and write this down on a piece of paper.

This is one of the few times you will not be using arrows on your paper. Do not write down a hem allowance. Your hem allowance is the original finish which you will put back on.

Preparing

Step 3 - Check to see if the legs are the same length.

Step 4 - Unpick the original stitching on the hem. You can use a quick unpick or you can use the slicing technique.

I use the quick unpick, and I slice along the seam from the inside.

To do this you need to practice on old jeans that you are going to throw away, because if you are not careful, you can cut the fabric, and you don't want to do that. remove all bits of cotton.

Using a quick unpick

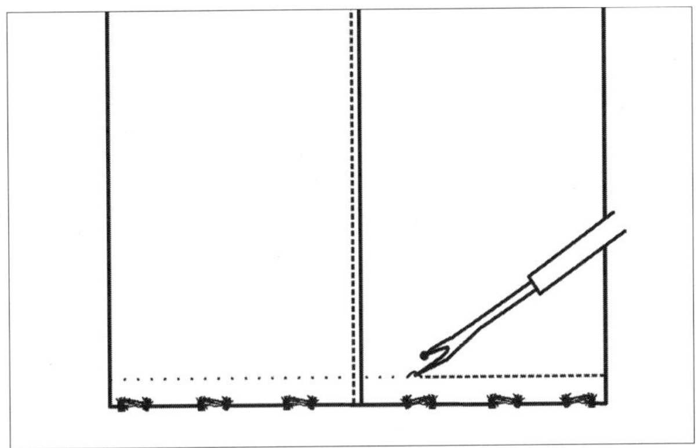

Slicing hem with a Stanley blade.

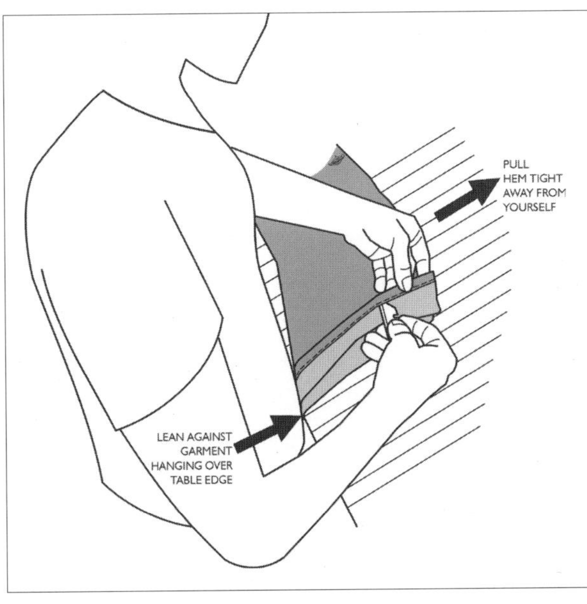

The procedure you are about to follow will mean that the finished length of the jeans will be exactly as per the amount you folded when you pinned the jeans.

Step 5 – Place the tape measure with the ½" or 1.5 cm on the dotted line where the original hem was before you unpicked it.

Place a chalk mark at the top of the tape measure.

Do this in three places on the jeans.

This means you are placing chalk marks ½" or 1.5 cm above the original seam.

On the left hand side
In the middle
On the right hand side

Repeat the process on the second leg, then turn the jeans over and mark the same on the opposite side of the leg.

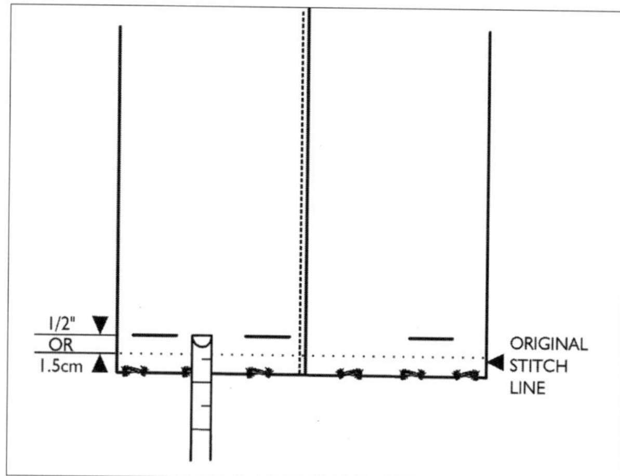

Step 6 - Place the tape measure over the original hem at the EXACT amount that you have to take the jeans up.

So if the jeans are going up 4" or 10 cm – then the number 4" or 10 cm should be at the fold of the original frayed hem, and the tape measure should be going up the jean leg with the numbers going to zero on the tape measure.

Place a chalk mark at the top of the tape

measure in the same three positions as you did at the bottom of the hem.

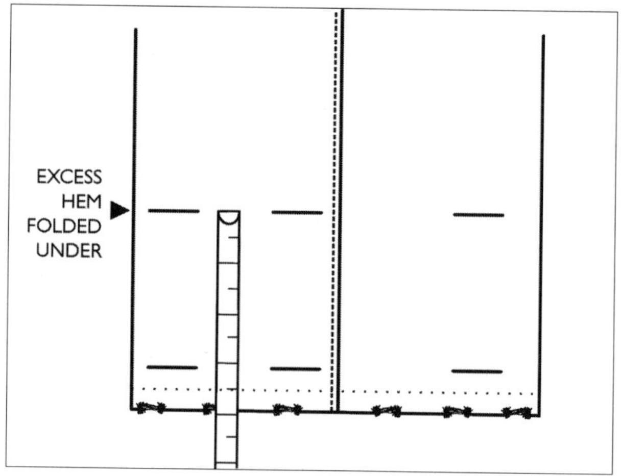

You are now ready to cut.

Do NOT cut UP to the chalk mark

This illustration is an example of how you should cut all the way around the hem.

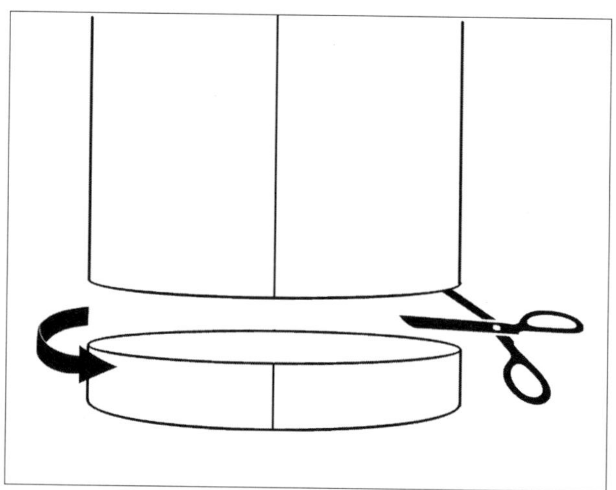

Step 7 - Nick the side of the jeans on the BOTTOM chalk line then cut all the way around.

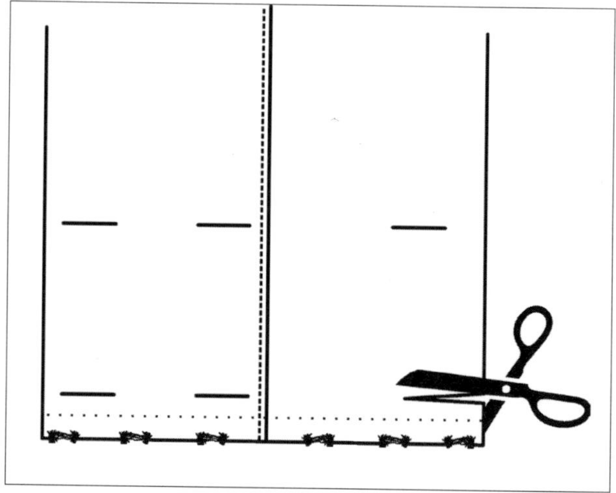

Step 8 – Now cut on the top chalk mark nicking at the side and cutting around the jean leg.

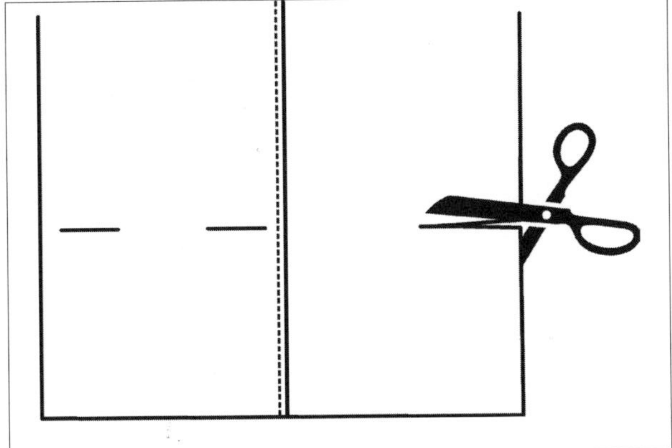

You are now ready to attach the original hem back on to the jean leg.

Jeans usually have the inside leg seam top stitched and the outside seam does not have top stitching.

For the purpose of this procedure, I will assume that this is the case with your jeans.

What you must do is re attach the top stitched side to the same top stitched side.

If both sides were top stitched then BEFORE you cut, place a pin on the seam above the top chalk mark, and a pin on the bottom that is going to cut off. This way you will know which side seams should be matched together.

Step 9 - Slide the original hem back onto the leg of the jeans. Right sides must be together.

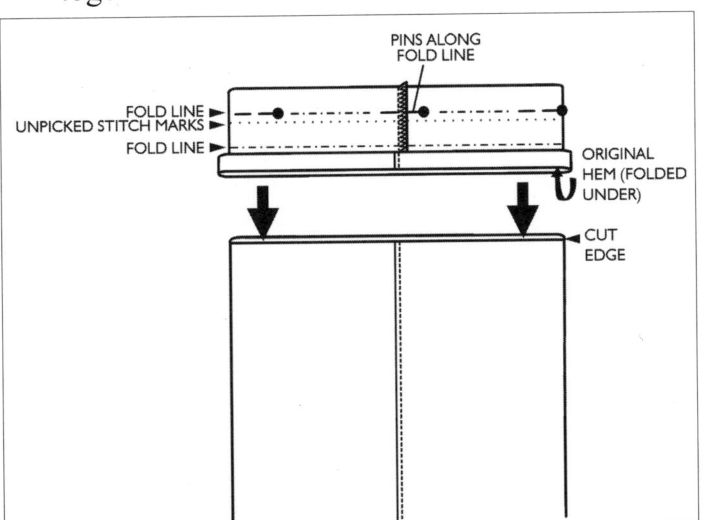

In the illustration for Step 9, I have shown the original hem above the jeans, BEFORE it is placed over the jean leg.

Step 10 – Pin the original hem to the jean leg section beginning with the seam that is top stitched.

Place your pin into the original folded section of the jeans just below the original seam stitching that you unpicked.

There should be a faded section just below the original seam stitching. This is where you pin.

You must line up the seam with the top stitching exactly on both the piece being sewn back on and the leg of the jeans. If you don't do this it will be very noticeable.

Once you have the top stitched seams matching pin around to within 3" of the opposite side seam.

Come back around to the side seam you pinned first, and begin pinning around in the opposite direction to the opposite side seam.

If the jeans are Box Jeans, then the piece will fit in perfectly. If the jeans are flared or tapered, you will have to make an adjustment on the piece.

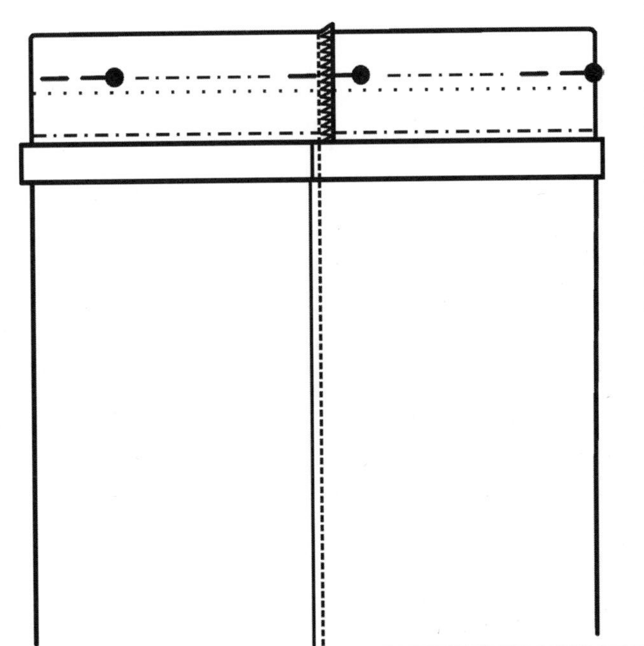

This is why you pin the top stitched side first. You don't want to have to undo any top stitching on the cut off piece. It is easier to take in or let out the side seam without top stitching.

If there is any excess fabric at the seam without top stitching now is the time to make the adjustment.

Step 11 - Pin the excess fabric.

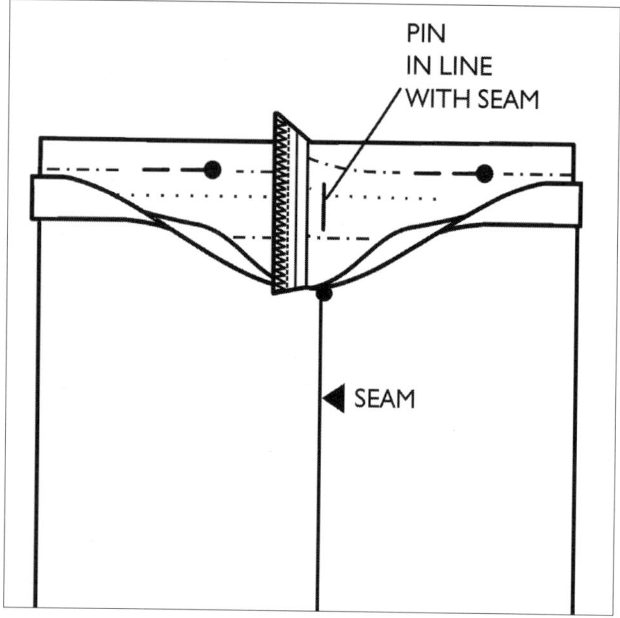

Sewing

Step 12 - Take in the seam as shown on the illustration. Use cotton the colour of the denim on the outside, not orange. Use a 90/14 jean needle.

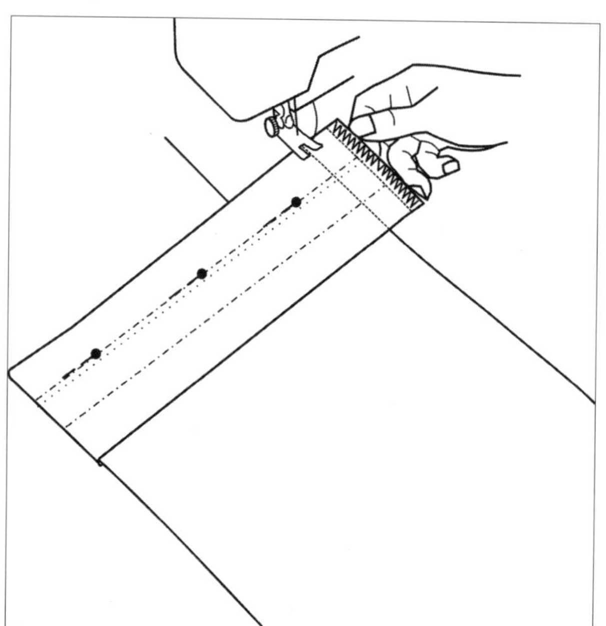

Step 13 – Cut off the excess fabric and open out seam.

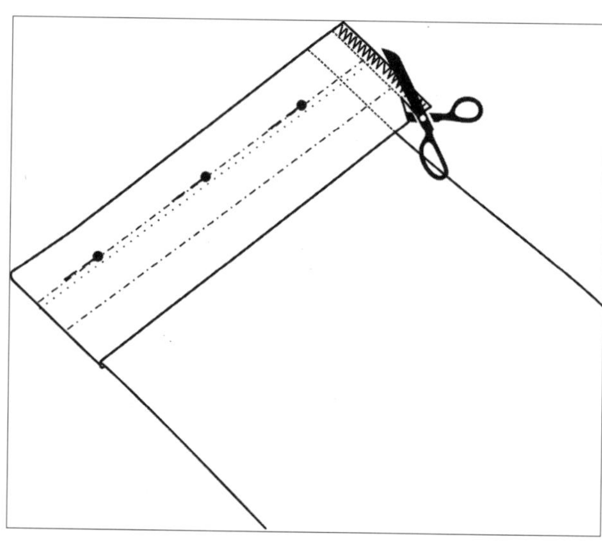

Step 14 - You are now ready to sew your original jeans hem.

To create a professional finish, use two cottons in your domestic sewing machine.

You don't always have to try to match the cotton colour with the same two colours. I find it works better if I match two different colours together.

For example. The cotton that is used on a lot of jeans is an orange/kharki colour. The colour orange would be too bright and the colour kharki would be too green. However if you put a jean orange (not bright) with a kharki, the colour will be perfect for some cottons used on jeans.

If you are sewing black jeans, use two black cottons. It looks better than one cotton.

Attach the two cottons onto the machine, threading the two threads together on the machine and down into the needle.

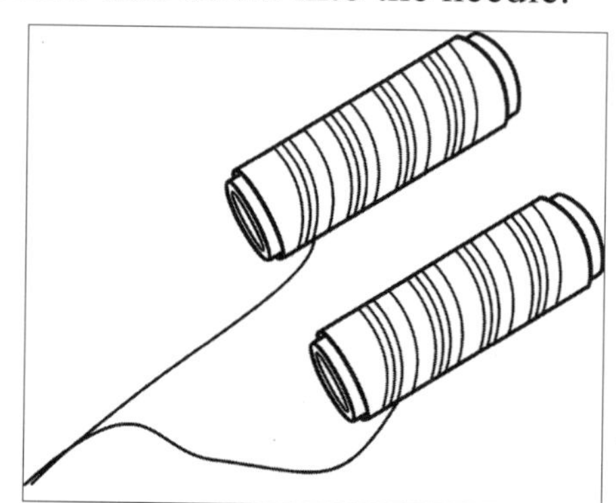

Just to confirm you should have a 90/14 Jeans needle inserted.

Thread the two cottons into the needle. The eye of this needle is larger than a smaller type of needle, so it should accommodate the two threads easily.

If you have difficulty, try using some tweezers to push through the eye of the needle.

Lick the two threads together, then snip with your nippers or scissors, then thread with the tweezers.

Step 15 - Sew the original hem back on by stitching into the old fold line just BELOW the original seam that is represented on this illustration with dots.

I find that if I place the sewing machine foot over the original stitch line and sew into the folded section or frayed section, then you will have the piece sewn on perfectly.

My reference point on my sewing machine foot is the inside edge on the left hand side of the foot.

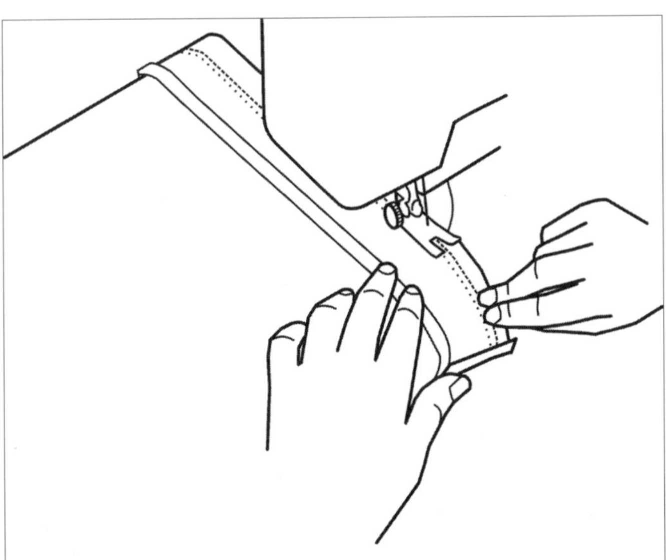

If you find that the side seams are too thick, then use the Jean Genie to help you over the thick seams. Refer to page 102 E and F.

Step 16 – Fold the hem back over to the inside of the jeans.

Cover the seam you have just sewn with the section from the original hem.

This means that you should only now see the original hem back onto the bottom section of the jeans.

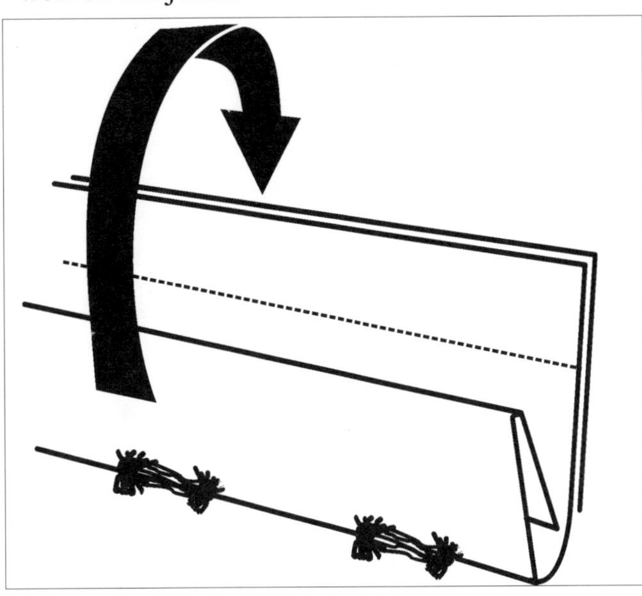

Step 17 – Pin the hem into place making sure you pin through from the front of the jeans to the inside, and that you pin through to the attached hem on the opposite side.

The pin should be in the exact position you want the seam to be.

If you do not pin into the hem at the back you may miss sewing through that section of the original hem at the back of the jeans, and the back section will fall down.

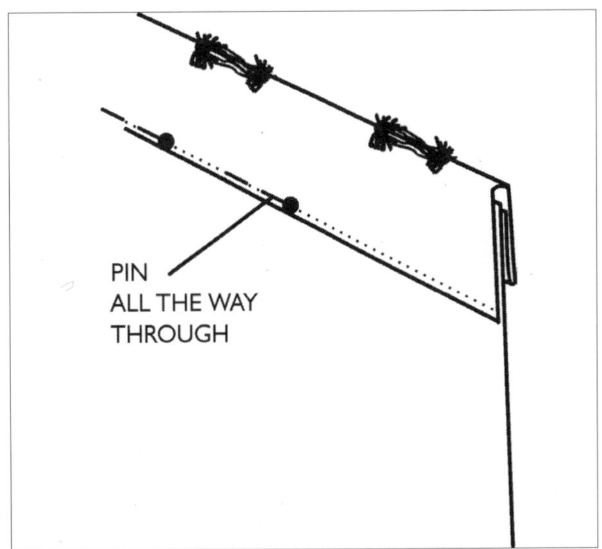

Step 18 – Sew all the way around the hem stitching into the original seam. This is called sewing Topside.

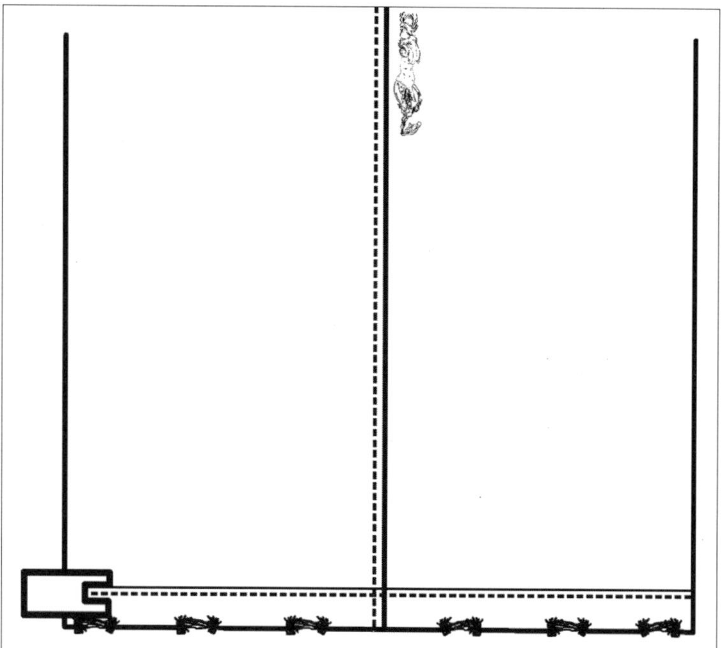

If you have difficulty with the thickness, try using a clean hammer to tap the thick seams before you sew.

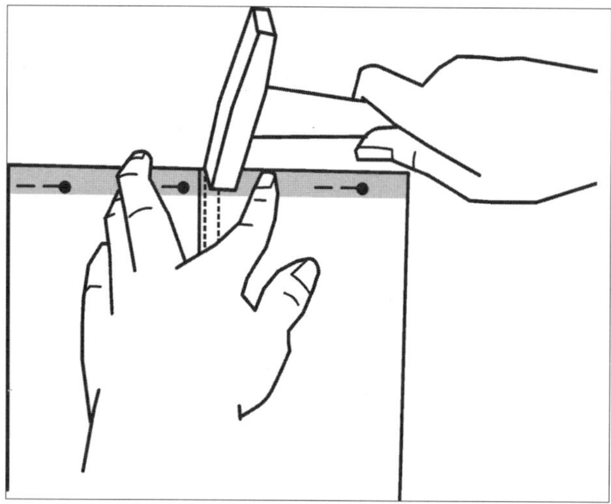

Then use the Jean Genie. You may not need to use a hammer if the fabric is not too thick. It really depends on the thickness of the denim.

Sewing topside

I call this sewing topside, and when you perfect this way of sewing, you will never have a hem that is puckered and twisted.

I thought I would provide you with an illustration so that you can see what I mean.

Use this technique when sewing almost all your hems, except on Casual Pants, which is why I provided you with that section.

Place your sewing machine foot in front of the thick seam, so it is on the flat denim not on the thick seam. Have the edge of the foot over the top of the edge of the hem underneath. If you look carefully, you will see the indent from the hem underneath.

Stitch into the original seam.

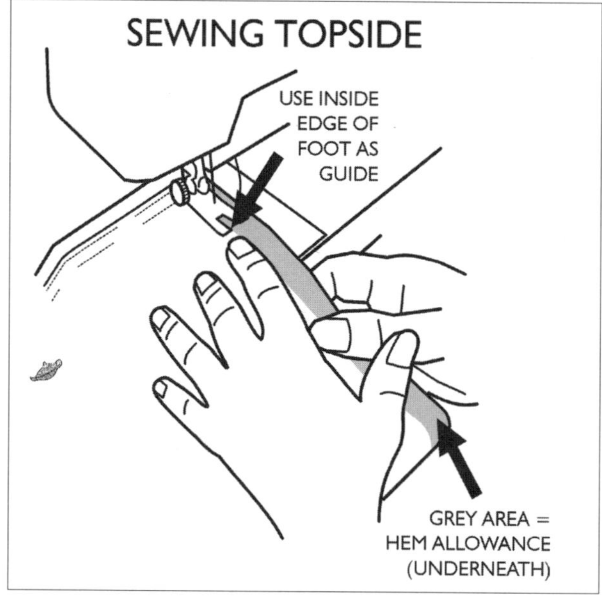

Conclusion

Putting the frayed hem back on a pair of jeans is not as difficult as you may have once thought.

There are some situations where it may not be possible to do this, and one of those situations is where the person has worn the jeans while the jeans are too long. This means the back of the jeans may have worn away. You do need all the fabric to be in tact to sew the original hem back on.

If the hem is worn away, I would just over lock to the longest point, and turn the hem over. But I would use two threads in the machine so that the hem still looks like a jeans hem.

Jeans

Taking In

*"Does the back of your jeans
(at the waist band)
stick out?"*

*"There's an easy solution for
people with sway backs."*

Introduction

I have written a separate section on jeans, because the process of altering jeans is different to altering normal dress pants.

Some casual pants could come under this section, if the pants have been top stitched at the seams, and in particular down the centre back seam.

There are two options when taking in the back of jeans.

Option 1 - Waist only

This is where the waist only is too big. Because of the curved nature of the female body, the waist on jeans can be too big, yet the hip area fits perfectly.

Wearing a belt does help, but it also tends to bag the fabric, and it is not a flattering look to have the waist all bunched up.

Option 2 - Take In Centre Back Seam

If a pair of jeans is too big, I would always look at taking in the centre back, before I went to the trouble of taking in the sides.

The reason for this is that the side seams usually have studs at the pocket, and sometimes they have a fob pocket inserted into the pocket, which could get in the way.

Use the same technique here as you do for Taking In a pair of pants. Pin the back centre seam, and if the side seams do not come around to the back, then you can take in the centre back seam.

If the sides move around to the back then you need to consider taking in the side seams.

If you do decide to take in the sides, refer to Take in Sides of normal pants. The only difference will be removing the stud and unpicking the Top Stitching down the side seam beside the pocket as you prepare the jeans for sewing.

Take in band only

I have not had this situation happen too often with men, however I do have it happen a lot with women.

The reason I believe this happens is because of the shape of the female body. Our waists are usually smaller than our hips, and we have sway backs.

This all adds up to a pair of jeans fitting beautifully at the hip area, but way to baggy at the waist.

There is a simple solution, because it is only the band and a small amount around the baske of the jeans. The baske is the section below the waist band at the back.

Pinning

Step 1 - Check to see that it is only the waist.

I have provided an illustration to show what I mean.

In this illustration I have taken hold of the belt loop at the back and pulled back on the jeans.

Only the waist band section is too big. The rest of the jeans are sitting nicely on the bottom area.

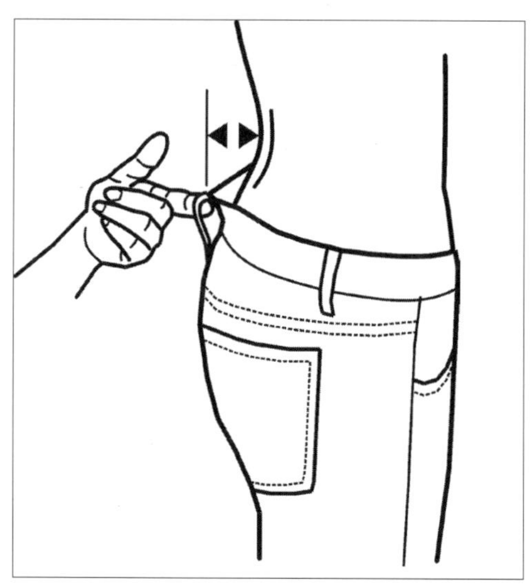

Looking at it from another angle, you can see the bottom of the jeans fit well.

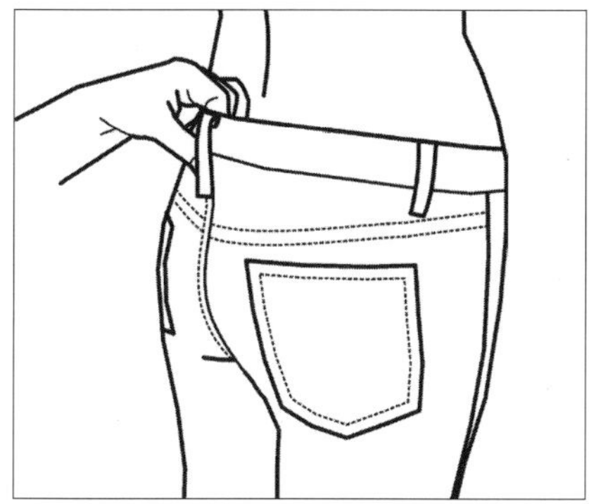

Step 2 - Using your thumb and index finger take a hold of the excess fabric

The band on jeans can be quite thick, so you need to use a large hat pin or a long pin.

Step 3 - Place the pin through the band the same amount that you held with your thumb and index finger.

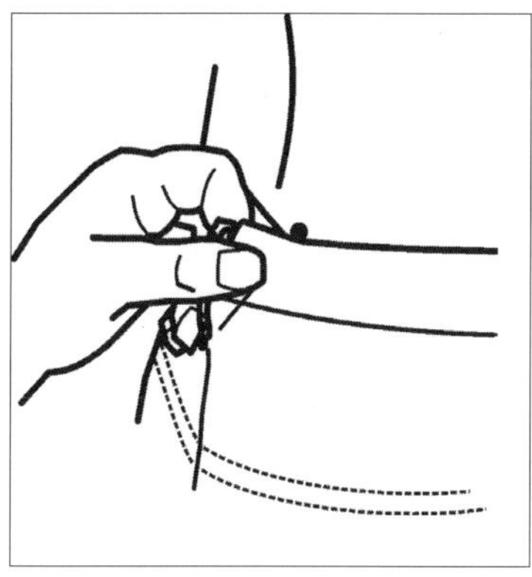

Step 4 - The top of the pin should be quite a way into the band, whilst the bottom of the pin should only have a small amount of fabric in it.

The most you would want to have at the bottom of the pin would be about 1" or 2.5 cm.

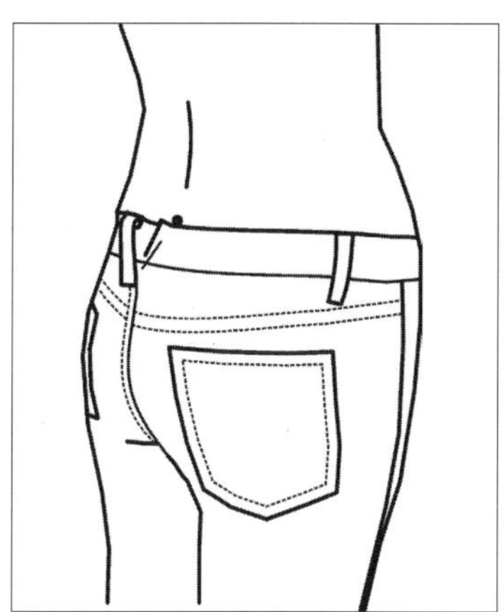

Preparing

Step 1 - Draw your outline of a centre back seam.

Step 2 - Write down the amount that is pinned at the top of the band, and the amount that is pinned at the bottom of the band. See Taking In Technique on page 47.

Step 3 - Take the belt loop or loops off.

Step 4 - Place a nick in the band above the centre back seam.

Step 5 - Unpick the band about 6" or 15 cm either side from the centre back.

Most jeans are sewn with an unraveller at the base of the band. see how to unpick an unraveller on page 208 - 209.

If the leather label is in the way, you may have to unpick that as well. You can sew it back on later, using a leather needle (100/12), and sew in a big stitch.

Step 6 - Pin two darts in the baske section on either side of the centre back seam.

The amount of these darts is half the amount that was pinned at the bottom of the band.

I usually have these darts about 2" or 5 cm each side of the centre back seam.

The darts should finish at the top of the two seams running vertical above the pockets. This means you should pin down to the baske and not below it, because these seams would be too thick to sew a dart in.

Step 8 - The waist band on jeans can be constructed in two ways.

Option 1. The band is in two separate pieces and the front and back of the band are top stitched together.

Option 2. The band is one piece that is folded over to create the front and back of the band.

Option 1 - Both sections of the band need to be pinned into place. You must make sure you have these two folded and pinned in the same position.

Place a dot at the top of the band for the amount being taken in at the top.

Place a dot at the bottom of the band for the amount being taken in at the bottom of the band.

Option 2 - Place the nick in the centre, and fold the waist band back on itself as per Preparing Pants on page 53.

Pin the band into position making sure to line up the centre fold, and the folds at the bottom of the band on both top and bottom.

Place a dot beside the top and bottom of the band for the measurement at the bottom of the band.

Place a dot beside the centre fold for the amount that is being taken in at the top of the band.

Make sure you have unpicked enough on the band, so that you can turn the band inside out.

Step 9 - Sew the band together.

Step 10 - Cut off excess leaving about a 5/8" or 1.5 cm seam allowance.

Step 11 - Sew the darts.

Begin sewing from the raw edge straight down to the stitch line where you should have your first dot.

Then begin to sew at an angle across to the edge.

This should be a gradual taper, so that by the time you get to the end of the dart, you have a nicely tapered dart.

Step 12 - Iron dart with fabric going towards the centre back seam.

Step 13 - Iron the waist band with the seams flat

on each side of the band.

Step 14 - Use the iron to make sure that the band will sit back onto the body of the garment.

Step 15 - Sew the band back onto the body of the garment.

Step 16 - Sew label and belt loops back on.

I would like to show you another illustration that shows a pair of jeans that are just a little bit bigger than the alteration we have just discussed.

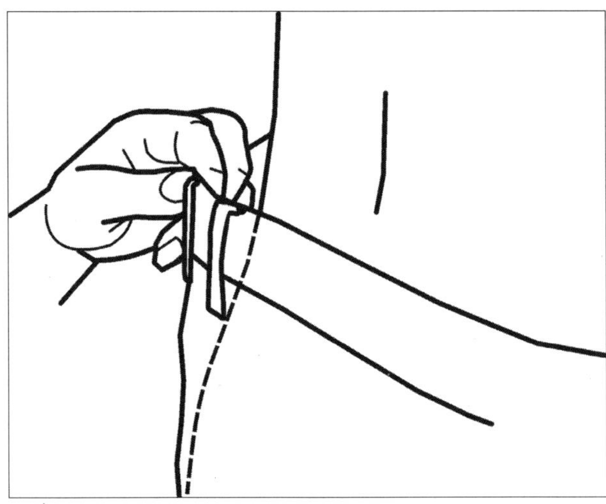

In this case you have two choice.

1. Take in band only with darts.

2 Take in through the centre back.

If it was my choice, I would take in through the centre back, even though it is a more complicated alteration, because I think the jeans would stick out below the baske, and that would not look good.

Any of these scenarios can cause a "V" in the centre back. This is caused by the amount you take in. If you take in a lot the "V" will be more pronounced.

Take in centre back

When jeans are too big from the band to the thigh, you might like to try just pinning the back section, but in this case you are pinning all the way down the bottom.

Usually it is difficult to take jeans in at the sides because of the pockets.

Another hindrance are the metal studs on the sides The metal studs can be taken out, however if the jeans are coming in a lot, then the person may not be able to get their hands in their pockets.

I have had many people come in thinking that their jeans needed to be taken in at the sides, only to find that taking in the centre back solves the problem, and the jeans look great.

This is because when you take in the centre back you automatically take in the hip area.

Pin the back first and see if it solves the problem. Nine times out of ten, it does take the jeans in enough.

Step 1 - If you have a full length mirror, ask the person to stand facing the mirror, and you should be standing behind the person.

Step 2 - Take hold of the excess fabric in the band, making sure you have folded it on the centre back seam.

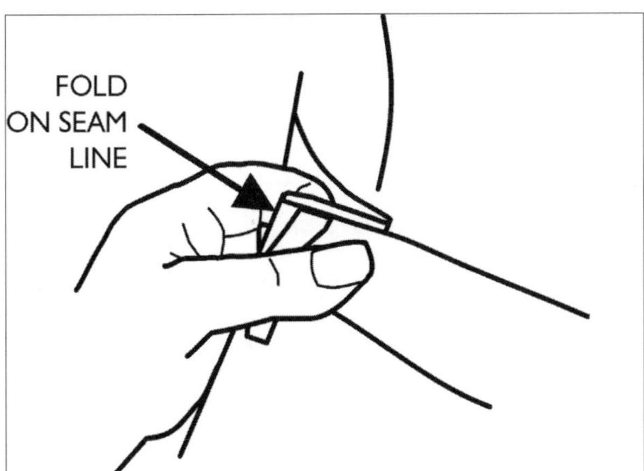

Step 3 - Place a pin in the excess fabric.

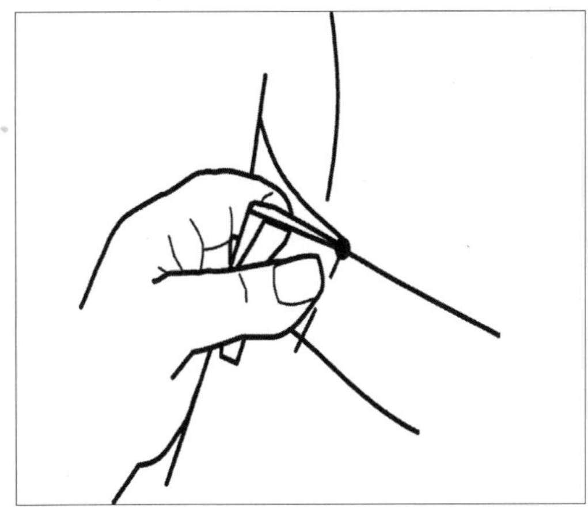

I would recommend using a large pin, preferably a hatpin.

The pin should go from the top of the band to the bottom of the band.

Step 4 - Place a second pin underneath the first pin. Make sure it takes up the excess fabric.

Your thumb and index finger should be pushing against the body so that you have pulled the pants tight on the person.

Step 5- Place a third pin underneath the second pin, again pulling the jeans tight so that they are sitting firm on the body.

Step 6 - Continue pinning like this all the way down to where the bottom curves under.

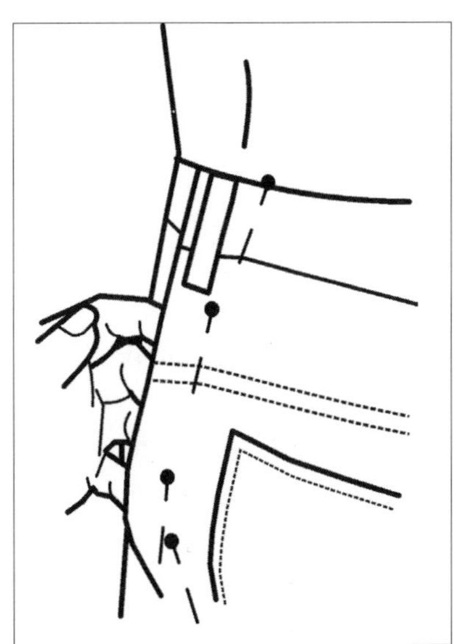

The shape of the person's bottom will determine where you finish pinning. If the person has a large bottom, then you will gradually move the pins out towards the seam, finishing where you can no longer grip any fabric for pinning.

If the jeans are too big all the way through to the crotch then your pins will be down the centre back as far as possible to pin.

Do not pin into the crotch. Stop pinning before the curve into the crotch.

By leaving your last pin at the curve of the bottom, you will automatically know that you need to curve the new back seam into the crotch.

Use the Taking in Technique for pants which begins on page 47. This covers how to draw your outline, and take down your measurements.

You could also refer to the previous section on Taking in the Waist on jeans which explains about how to prepare and sew the band.

When it comes to preparing the jeans there are a few points on double stitching I would like to cover.

There are two types of seams in jeans with double stitching.

Option 1 - Machine Stitched then over locked.

Option 2 - French Seam.

With Option 1, you will need to unpick the double stitching all the way through to the crotch. It could be an unraveller, or it could be normal stitching. No matter which one it is, only unpick the double stitching.

Do not unpick the seam which holds the two sides of the back panels together.

Follow the Taking in Technique for marking and sewing.

The only difference between jeans like this and normal dress pants taking in, is the fact that you have to undo the double stitching, and put it back on again when you put the garment back together.

Refer to the jeans section for hems which explains about using two threads and sewing top side.

If it is Option 2 - a French Seam, then you need to unpick the double stitching VERY CARE-FULLY and have your pins ready to re pin the centre back seam together in the exact same position it was in for the french seam.

Unpick the french seam all the way through to the crotch seam.

Do not attempt to put the french seam back on.

Once you have created your new centre back seam, cut the excess fabric off, and over lock, or zig zag, or place bias binding on the edges.

Conclusion

Taking in the back of jeans can be a difficult job, but can be very rewarding, because you are saving a pair of jeans that you probably love.

I have found that of all the clothes people have as favourites, jeans would have to be at the top of the list.

When you have moulded that special pair of jeans into a perfect fit, with frays and darns and the denim has faded to a light blue, how can you not rescue them.

You could get another 10 years out of your favourite jeans.

And even if they are not as bad as all that, I am sure you have worn them in enough to want to keep them for years to come.

Surely its worth all the hard work.

Band too thick to pin

Some jeans are made from thick denim. You may find it difficult to force the pin through the double thickness on the waist band. When this happens, you need to have help from the person who is being pinned.

Step 1 - Stand behind the person.

Step 2 - Ask the person to take of hold of the band on either side at the side seams.

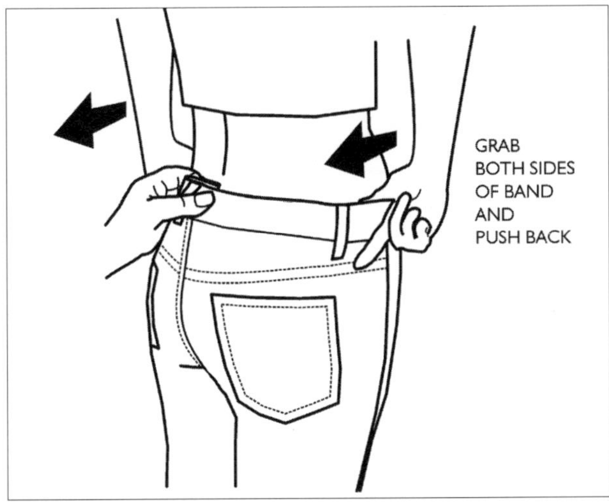

Step 3 - Ask her/him to push the band back towards you (towards the back) This will take the tension off the band, and may allow you to pin through the thick band.

If the band is too thick for the pins, then you can use your pins to mark the two sides of the band.

Place your fingers on the band as per the above illustration to determine the amount that is being taken in.

Place two pins on either side of the band, marking the exact amount of fabric you were trying to pin.

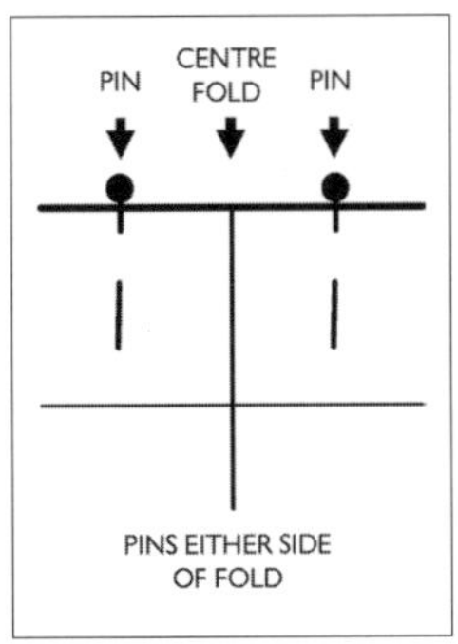

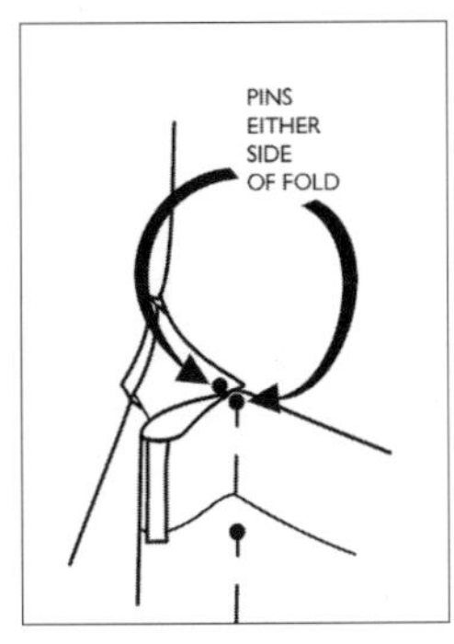

Lower the waist on jeans

If you do happen to buy a pair of jeans that are too high on the waist, it is a reasonably easy process to lower the waist an inch or two.

Step 1 - Take the band off.

Step 2 - Mark down from the stitch line that the band was sewn to.

The amount you mark down should be the same all the way around, unless you want the front lower than the back. If that is the case, then just proportion the amount on either side and at the back.

When you mark down for the amount you are lowering the jeans, then come back up towards the top and place another mark 1/2" or 1.2 cm above the first mark.

Step 3 - Undo zip. Cut on the top mark. Use normal scissors to cut through zip. Never use good tailoring scissors to cut things like zips.

Step 4 - Begin to pin your band back on working from the front around to the back. Stop just past the side seam.

Step 5 - Pin the opposite front section of the band back on working from the front to the back stopping at the sides.

Step 6 - Measure the balance of the band from side seam to side seam.

Step 7 - Measure the body of the jeans from side seam to side seam.

Step 8 - Create darts at the back beginning about 2" from the centre back seam. Use one or two darts each side of the back seam.

Step 9 - Pin the balance of the band back on.

Step 10 - Sew the band on using two threads in your sewing machine, sewing topside. Use Jean Genie over thick sections, and sewing over zip.

Jeans

Replacing zip

"Washing your jeans with the zip undone, can cause the zip to break."

"Always do zip and button up before washing."

Introduction

There seems to be a myth that domestic sewing machines cannot sew denim. Of all the alterations I do, the two most common that people believe they cannot perform on their domestic sewing machines involves denim.

The first type is a jeans hem. I have already cover that alteration type earlier. As I said then I only used domestic sewing machines in my clothing alteration shops.

The second type was replacing a jeans zip. I think that it was probably the same problem as the jeans hem. People believe that you need to use an industrial sewing machine to sew denim. This is simply not true. All you need is to learn some of the tricks of the trade, and you will be able to replace a jeans zip in no time at all.

What you will need

New zip – Measure the old zip. Place your tape measure at the top of the zip where the thick metal piece is located, and measure down to the bottom of the zip where the other thick metal piece is located. This is the size of the zip.

Zips usually come in standard sizes. The most common size is 7" or 18 cm. However, since the hipster jeans came in the zip size has become very small. This may mean you will have to cut a zip down to size.

To do this I cut a section off one side of the zip at the very bottom. Make the piece about 1 ¼" or 2.5 cm long and ½" or 1.5cm wide. Sew this piece across the zip at the length you want the zip to be. Make sure you stitch it securely on either side of the teeth. Cut the excess zip away up to the edge of the fabric cover. Fold the excess fabric under and sew. You can also just use a piece of bias binding or fabric.

Zipper foot – All sewing machines come with different types of sewing feet. The zipper foot is the one that looks like it is half the size of the normal sewing foot. All sewing machines have manuals with them, so if you are not sure, consult the manual.

Jeans needle – If you do not use the correct needle, you will not be able to sew denim. Needles come in size 90/14 or 100/16. I would suggest you purchase the 90/14. They work well for all types of denim.

Cotton – You need two reels of cotton. For your alteration to look professional, you need to use two cottons on your machine.

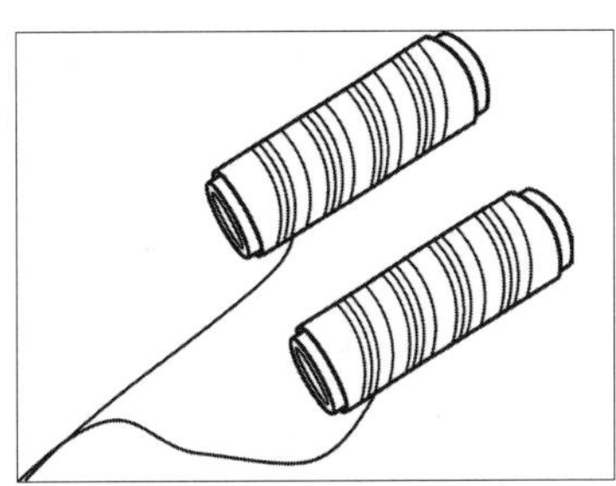

All sewing machines since 1975 have a position for a second reel of cotton. If you have an older machine, you can purchase a cotton holder that will sit at the back of your machine, where you can put a second reel of cotton on.

The next thing you need to do is match the thread colour of the jeans. The most common jean thread colour is orange; however, some orange thread can be too bright. I mix khaki cotton to orange cotton and I get the perfect colour. You will need to play around until you find the right combination.

If the colour is beige, you may have to mix beige with tan to give the right colour. Take your time doing this, so that you get it right.

Quick unpick - I use a good quality quick unpick. There is a brand called Clover. It has a brown handle. I find this style easy to use; however, there are many brands on the market for you to choose. Some people prefer to unpick with a pair of nippers. They are like scissors but small.

I also know a woman who unpicks using a razor blade. She is very quick. Find the style you prefer.

Nippers - Nippers come in a variety of shapes and sizes, and they are great for cutting threads.

Before we go into the steps to replace a jeans zip, you need to know that usually (not all the time) the zip on women's jeans is on the opposite side to men's jeans.

I have had two illustrations done to show you the difference.

The women's jeans have the fabric insert side on the left hand side below the button and the flap side on the right hand side under the buttonhole.

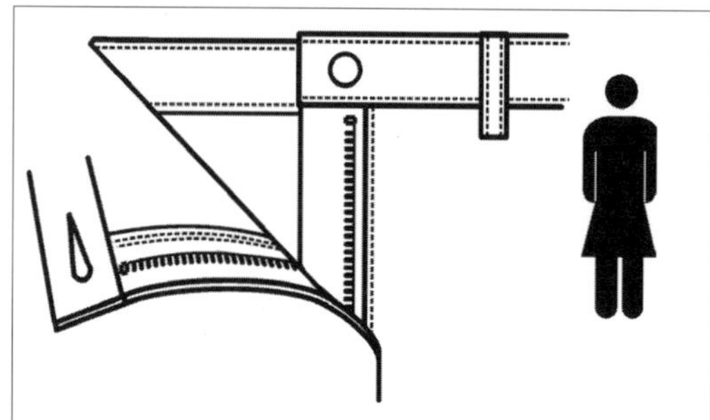

The men's zip has the fabric insert side is on the right hand side below the button and the flap is on the left below the buttonhole.

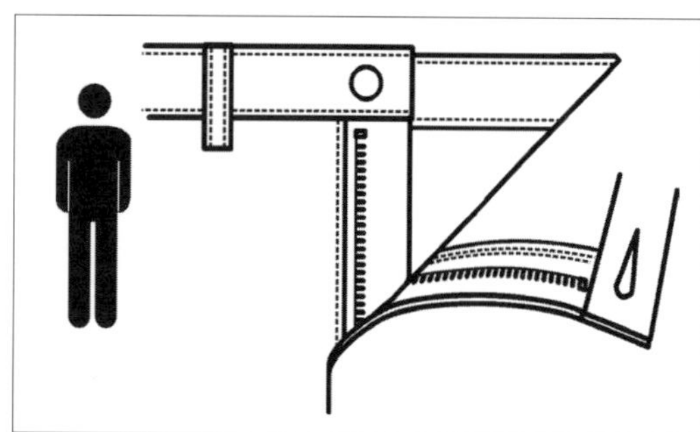

For the sake of these illustrations, I have used a men's pair of jeans to insert a zip.

Step-By-Step Instructions

I have tried to explain every step I do to replace a zip. This is the technique that I find works for me. It allows me to take the zip out, and replace it in a very short time frame, with the added bonus that the zip looks like it has not been replaced.

In other words the workmanship is professional. Over the years, I have tried to find ways to do clothing alterations that achieve two things.

First is the finish. I want the alteration to look as professional as possible. Attention to detail such as cotton colours is important.

Second, I want to complete the alteration in the shortest time possible without sacrificing workmanship.

Before you start, you might like to consider having a second pair of jeans along side, so you can refer to them if necessary.

Preparing

Step 1 – You need to release the zip from the waist band. Unpick one stitch on the waistband, insert your finger as far as possible, and give a little push to open the waistband. Now unpick another stitch and push you finger into the waistband to open a little more.

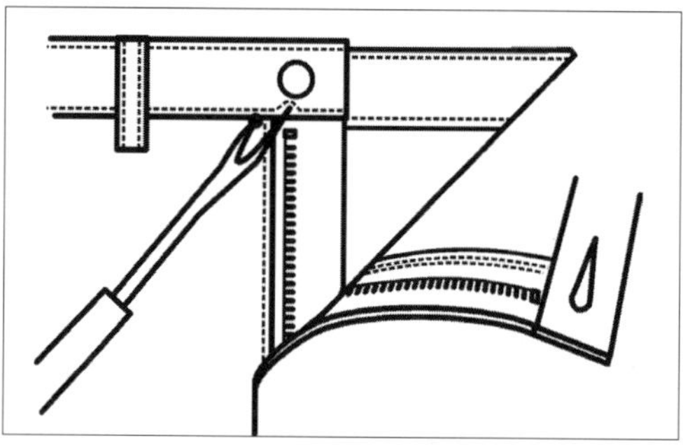

I find once I have the waistband opened a little I can insert the quick unpick and slice across the waistband.

Be careful when slicing, as you do not want to cut the fabric.

Step 2 – Unpick the zip from the fabric insert side. You may find it easier to slide the quick unpick in between the zip and the fabric and slice. However, you must be very careful not to cut the fabric.

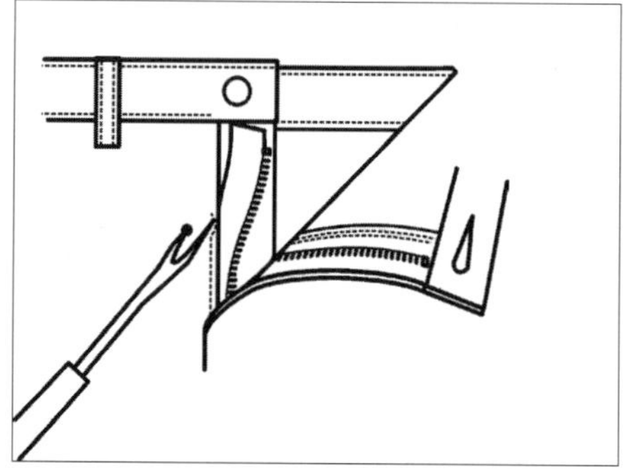

I actually rip the zip down once I have a good hold on the top of the zip. I do this in short, sharp movements.

I would recommend you only try this if there is one row of stitching, and after you have altered a few zips. I did not do it the first time I replaced a zip.

Step 3 – Unpick zig zag stitch which is located at the bottom of the fly facings. The facing joins the fabric insert to flap side.

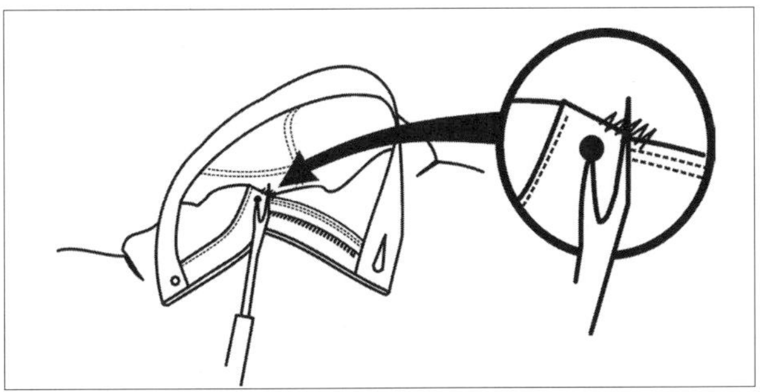

Step 4 – Unpick zip and release zip from fabric insert section completely. Note - do not detach fabric insert from the band.

The zip must be released from this side and the fabric insert should be completely released.

Even if you have the zip released, if the fabric insert is still attached to the seam in the crotch area you must release it. It will make your replacing of the zip easier if you do this.

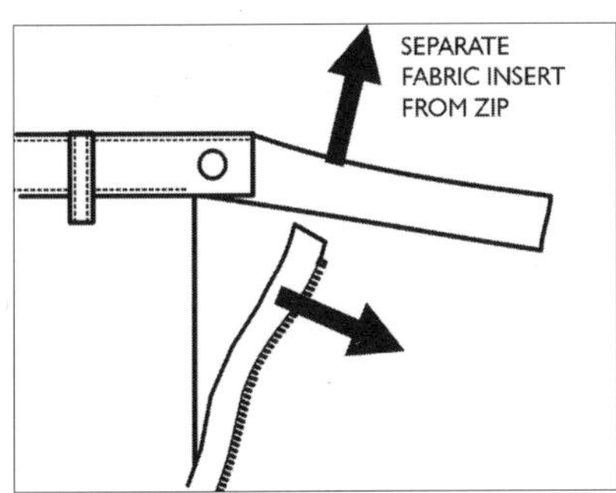

Some manufacturers over lock the zip and fabric insert together, which means that you will have to undo the over locking.

I would suggest that you either re over lock the fabric insert or zigzag the edges or cover with bias binding to stop the fabric from fraying.

Step 5 – Unpick the zip from flap side, beginning from the bottom of the zip and working up towards the band.

On some jeans, if the cotton is not too thick, I will grab hold of the zip at the bottom and give little jerk movements and rip the zip out. This can only be done if the cotton is not too thick, and the fabric is not too fragile – some old jeans can have a tendency to be weaker.

If you are unsure use the quick unpick.

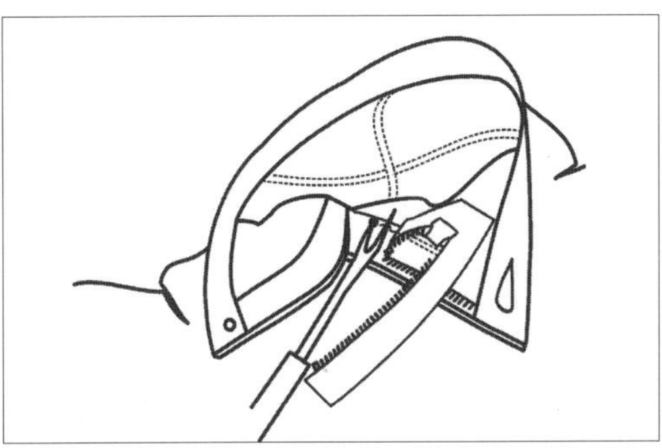

Step 6 – Insert the quick unpick into the stitching in the band. Nick one stitch and give a little pull to open the band area. Insert the quick unpick and nick another stitch. Work this way until you have undone enough stitches to release the zip from the band.

Unpick along the rest of the waistband until the flap section is released from the waistband.

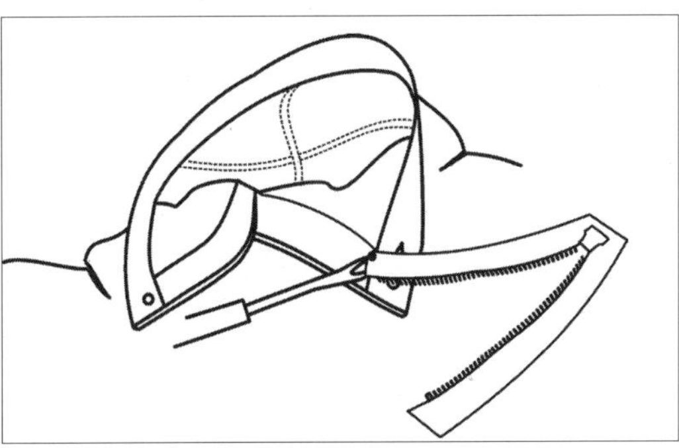

Step 7 – Now unpick stitching holding flap side to outer fabric. This stitching begins at the top of the waist band and goes down and curves in to the centre front seam.

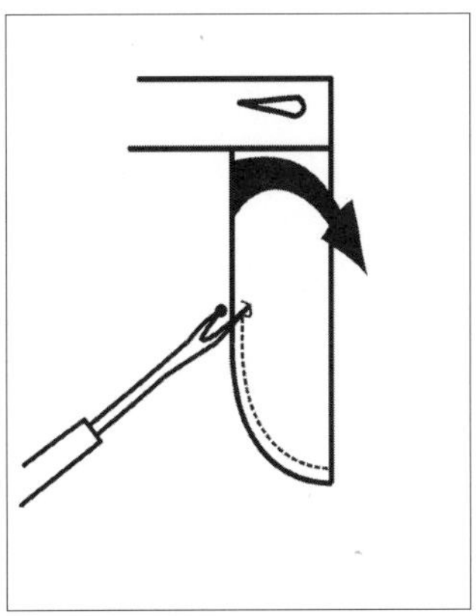

Step 8 – Pick off all the excess cotton in the seams that you have unpicked.

In particular you need to remove the old un-picked stitching on the double seams at the centre front.

The reason you do this is because you want to complete this job like a professional, and that means you take all the old seam threads off, so the garment is clean ready for the new zip.

You are now ready to put the zip in.

Sewing

Step 9 – Insert the zip between the outer fabric and the fabric insert.

I find it easier to use a pair of tweezers to insert the zip because the tweezers give you more control over the zip.

Make sure you have the top metal piece of the zip about 1/8" or 3 mm below the original stitch line.

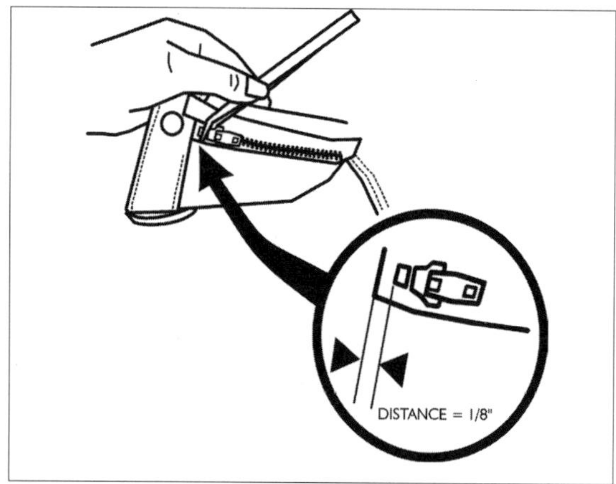

Step 10 - Pin the zip in place, beginning with the first pin at the top, second pin following and then a third pin at the bottom.

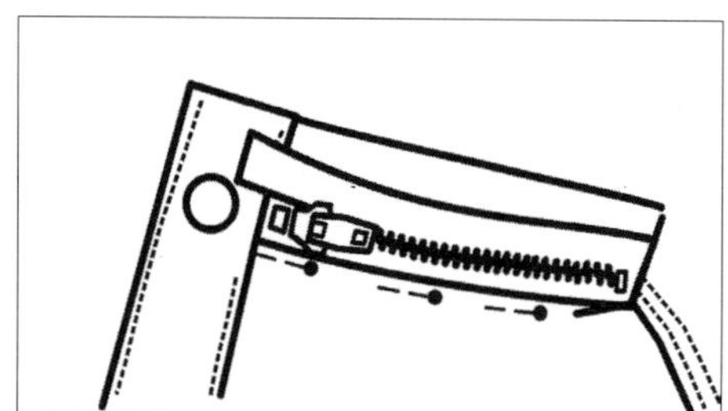

Step 11 – To ensure that the zip is pinned back in the original position, check the back side to see if the pins are in the original stitch line.

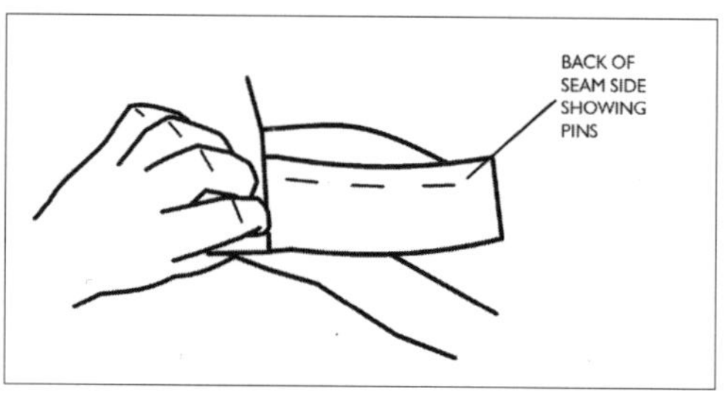

Readjust the pins until they are in the original seam line at the back of the insert, and are still pinned correctly at the front in the original stitch line.

Step 12 – Insert your jeans needle.

Attach the two cottons onto the machine, thread-ing the two threads together down and into the needle.

The eye of this jean needle is larger than a smaller type of needle, so it should accommo-date easily. I find using tweezers best.

I cut the ends of the cotton so they are even, then I lick the ends and using the tweezers, I insert into the needle.

Attach your zipper foot.

For men's pants, the zipper head should be on the left hand side.

For women it should be on the right. Refer to the first two illustrations, which show that women and men's zips are on different sides.

Sew zip into fabric insert side.

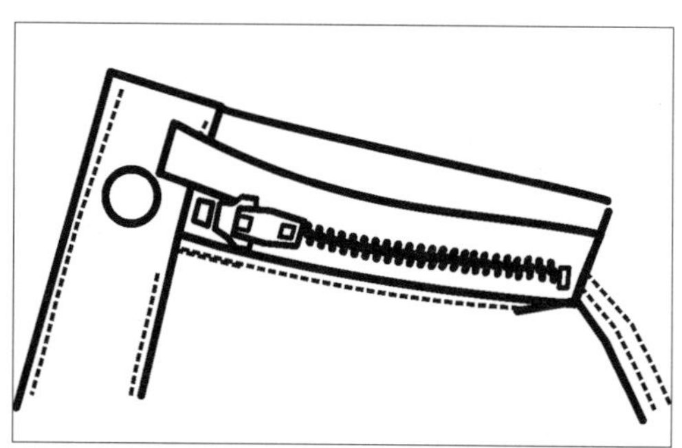

Step 13 – Do the zipper up.

Pin the bottom of the zip to the flap side only. Do not pin to the outer fabric, just pin onto the flap side.

Make sure that the two sides are even at the bottom of the zip. If you have one side uneven, the zip will not sit correctly.

Now pin the top of the zip making sure you have the top of the zip 1/8" or 3 mm below the original stitch line.

If the zip is over 15 cm long place a pin in between the top and bottom pin.

You may find that you have to ease the zip in the middle section. In this case place a pin in the centre to hold the zip in place. Note - Ease means forcing the fabric in the middle between the top and bottom section.

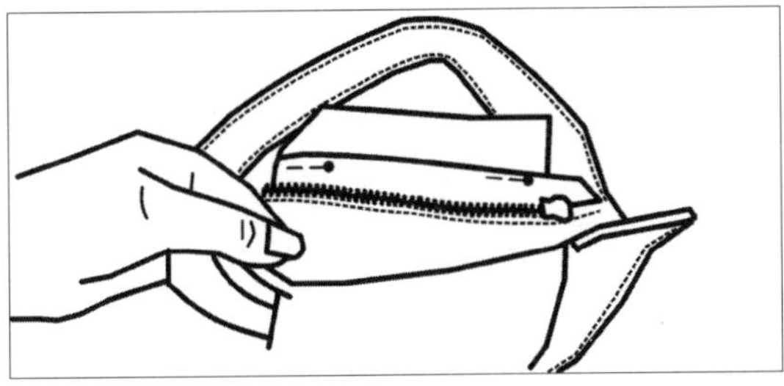

Step 14 – Turn the garment in the correct way, and make sure that the waistband lines up. If the waistband does not line up, then you have the zip pinned incorrectly on the flap side.

Re pin the zip until the waistbands, meet.

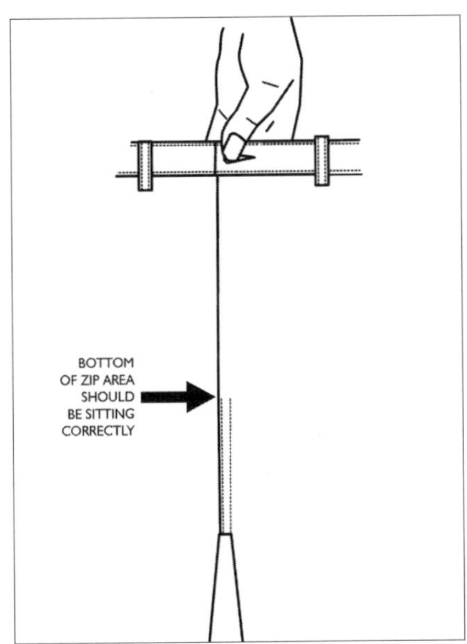

If you do not do this, and the waistband on either side is not lined up, the garment will be lopsided when you finish.

Step 15 – Undo zip. Make sure the zip clip is sitting flat and not sticking up. If it is sticking up it will get in your way.

Before you take your pins out you must secure the zip in the position it is now, so you should lower the needle into the position you are going to sew, and then take your pin out.

Sew the zip onto the flap area by sewing a row of stitching from the bottom of the zip to the top of the zip.

The seam should be in the middle between the side of the zip and the teeth of the zip.

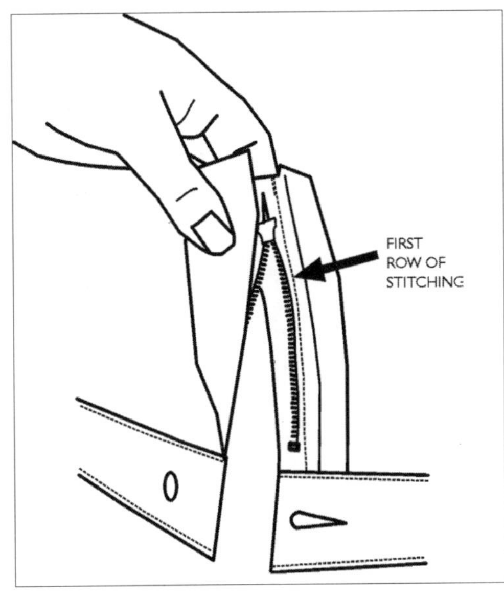

Step 16 – Sew a second row of stitching on the

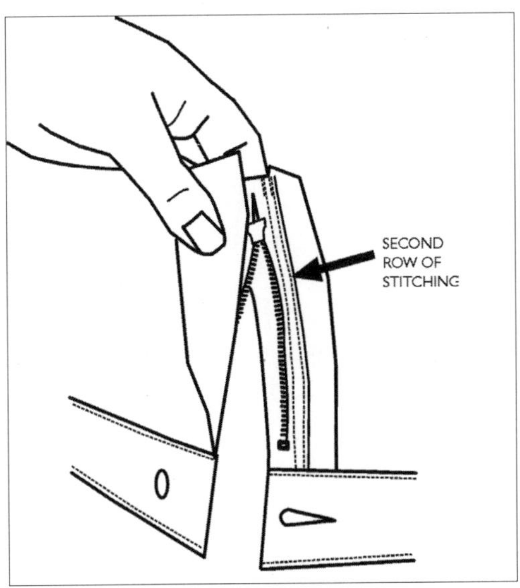

very edge of the zip beginning from the bottom of the zip to the top of the zip.

Step 17 – Your next step is to sew the flap back on to the outer fabric.

If you are doing this for the first time, I would recommend you pin the flap down to make sure it is sitting correctly.

Place the pins so that the head of the pin is on your left, and make sure the flap is sitting flat.

Sew into the original stitch line.

Sew the first row of stitching beginning at the top of the band coming down towards the crotch of the pants.

As you curve in towards the centre front seam, you must follow the original curve line.

You can actually sew in as far as possible WITHOUT stitching the fabric insert side.

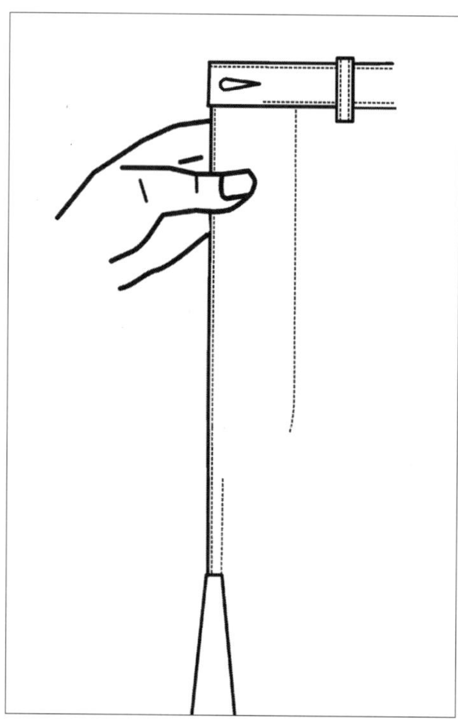

Step 18 – Sew the second row of stitching on the flap top side.

You usually have the benefit of the old stitch line to guide you, however if for some reason it is hard to see, make sure you line up your

sewing machine foot against the first row of stitching and sew exactly the same distance all the way down the front. If you are crooked here then it will not look professional.

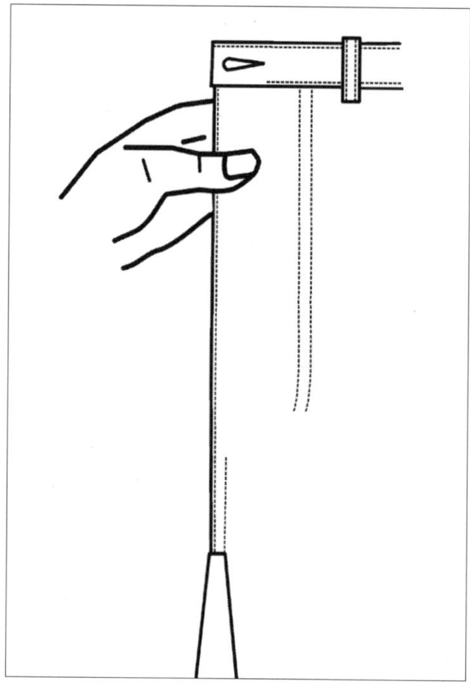

The following illustration is just showing that it would be best to pin the flap down at the bottom. The above two steps are only going to the curved area, or as close around the curved area as you can WITHOUT sewing the fabric insert on the opposite side.

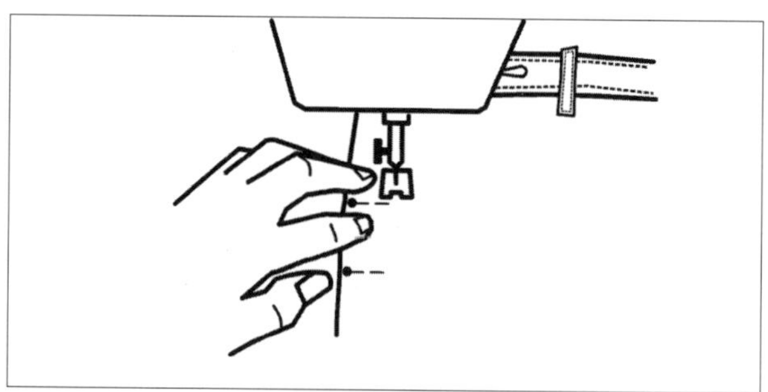

Step 19 – To complete this section, the fabric insert side should now be folded across and should be underneath the flap side.

Make sure that the sections underneath are sitting flat.

Place your zipper foot on the inside row of stitching on the front seam, beginning just below where you unpicked and sew up to just past the original stitch curve.

Repeat on the second double stitching on the front seam.

When you get to the top turn the fabric and stitch across to the first front seam and lock off.

Begin to finish the curve by starting on the edge and sewing around to meet your row that came down the seam.

Lock off.

Repeat the second row the same. To cover the join you can do a small zigzag over the top.

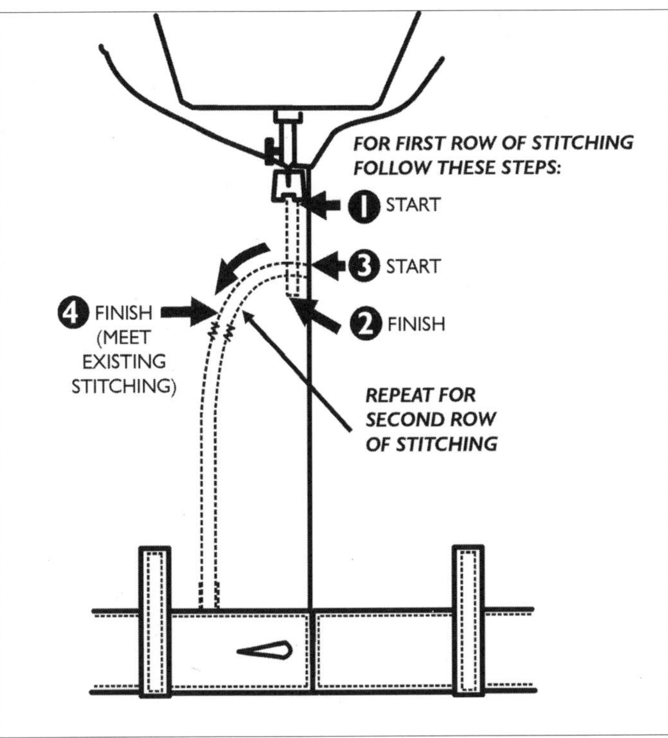

Step 20 – Insert the zip and fabric into the band. Sew across the band.

Make sure you lock the stitching both sides.

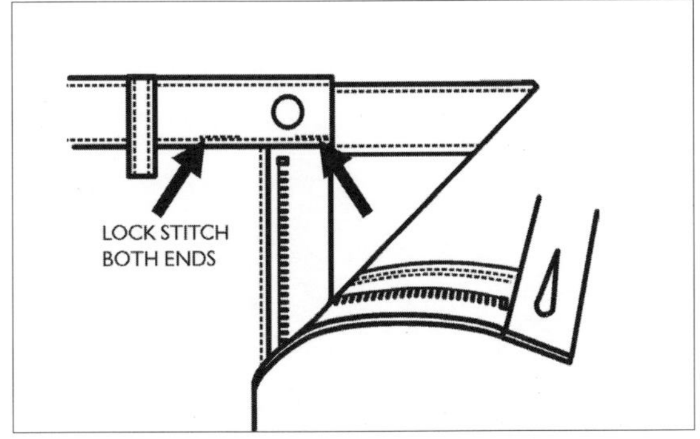

Step 21 - Insert flap back into the band and sew back together. Lock both ends.

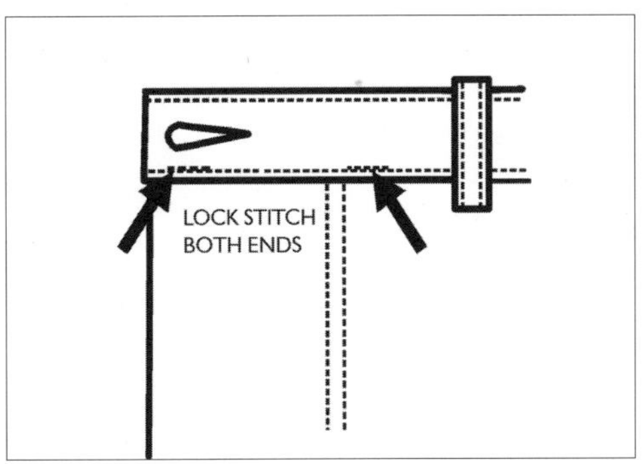

Step 22 – Finished zip. Congratulations you have now replaced a jean zip.

Replacing a jean stud

Jean studs can be purchased at a shop that sells fabric and haberdashery. (Haberdashery is the name for things like cottons, needles, and anything to do with sewing)

Usually you can get a packet of 6 or more.

The only comment I have is that usually when the jean stud comes out, it causes a large hole in the fabric.

When a stud is hammered into the fabric it causes a small hole, but when the stud is ripped out it will probably increase the size of the hole.

Cut a small piece of thick fabric and either stuff it in between the waist band, and sew backwards and forwards over this to lock it in, or unpick the bottom of the band if you can't stuff it in and slide the piece of fabric between the waist band and sew it into place.

When sewing back and forward, make sure you sew on the section that is not torn as well to lock it in.

Push the quick unpick into where the hole used to be, and make a small hole.

Place your new jean stud in the hole and hammer into place. Directions should be on the packet.

Dresses, Gowns & Skirts

Taking Up

"Getting sick of that long dress?"
"Why not turn it into a short dress?"

Introduction

I have included dresses, gowns and skirts in the same section because all of these garments have to be taken up certain lengths.

Whether it is short or long, the technique is still the same for each type of garment. Even some hems on skirts can be the same as on dresses.

Before we get into length of dresses, gowns and skirts, I would like to talk about garments that are cut on the bias and garments that are cut on the straight of the grain.

This is extremely important information for any dress or gown, because it will determine what you do and how you do it.

Straight of the grain versus bias cut fabric

The grain of the fabric is the direction in which the thread is woven to produce the fabric.

When a garment is cut out on the straight of the grain, it means that the garment is cut in the direction of the grain of the fabric. This means the fabric will not drop, and there is likely to be no stretch in the fabric.

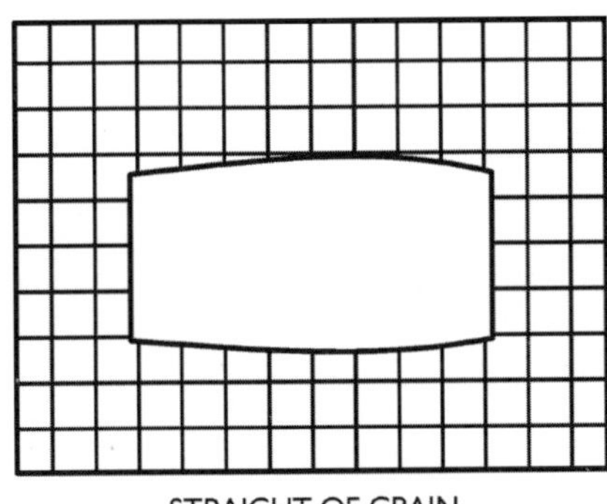

STRAIGHT OF GRAIN

RESULT

The bias of the fabric is where a garment is cut at a 45 degree angle on the fabric. The garment is then considered to be a bias cut garment.

Bias cut garments will drop at certain points on the garment where the bias section is exactly 45 degrees.

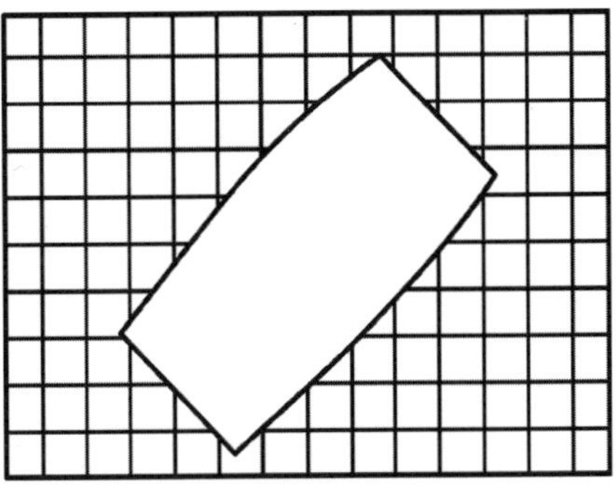

BIAS CUT

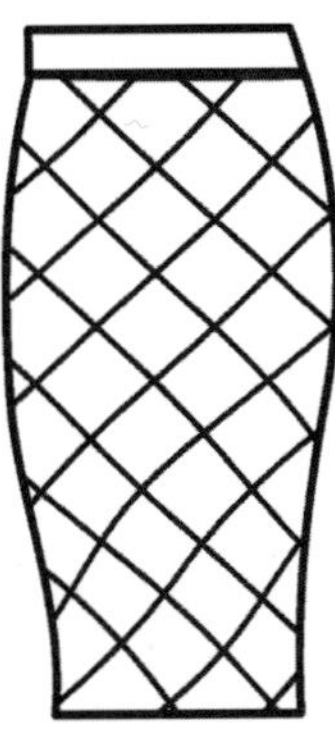

RESULT

You can test the straight of the grain and the stretch of the bias by cutting yourself a piece of fabric. Look at the direction of the weave.

Hold the fabric on the straight of the grain and give it a few short jerks. Try to snap the fabric by flicking your hands back and forth. You should notice that it doesn't move.

Now put the fabric on an angle and pull. The fabric will stretch.

When you are pinning a garment that is cut out on the bias, it will look a little different from one that you pin on the straight of the grain.

Garments cut on the bias will have a hem that is uneven, because the fabric has dropped at the bias section.

The longer a garment stays on a clothes hanger the more the bias section will drop.

I recommend to my clients to lay the garment in a drawer, rather than hanging on a clothes hanger.

I will sometimes put the garment in a plastic bag and hang on the clothes hanger on my racks. That way the garment will not drop any more whilst it is in my shop.

If you have a bias cut garment, I would recommend you use a chalk hem straightener.

A chalk hem straightener is like a ruler on a metal frame. The ruler is pointing up to the ceiling, and it has a small container with chalk attached to it. You can move the chalk container up and down the ruler.

Once you get the correct length that the person wants the garment to be, have the person stand very still. You move around the person, puffing on a puffer which in turn puts a chalk mark on the garment.

Later you can just cut below the chalk mark to allow for your hem, and you will have straightened the garment.

I use a chalk marker with women who have large busts, because usually a garment will be higher at the front than the back for them.

If you don't have a chalk hem straightener you can also measure from the floor up.

Work out the length that you want the garment to be by pinning the excess hem amount UNDER so that you are only looking at the new length the person wants.

Once you have determined this put a pin in the new hem fold, and unpin the rest of hem, so that the garment is hanging long again.

Have the person stand facing a mirror.

Make sure they have their spine as straight as possible and they look directly into their own eyes into the mirror.

Now using a tape measure put the beginning of the tape measure on the floor and measure up to the pin.

Note the measurement.

Now do the same every 6" around the garment putting a pin at the measurement position on the garment.

Care instructions for bias cut clothes

If a bias cut garment is not treated correctly, you can have the garment altered, only to find that after it's been hanging in the wardrobe for three months, the garment is gone totally out of shape again.

This is because the section that is cut on the bias will DROP, or stretch.

To stop this from happening I would recommend that you fold the garment carefully and lay it flat in a drawer.

Dresses, Gowns & Skirts

Taking Up

Hem Lengths

"Check to see if the hem on the dress or gown is straight before you alter it"

Hem not straight

Pinning

Pinning the hem up on a dress, gown or skirt can be challenging if the garment has a full skirt or is a floppy fabric.

Let us say that you have a garment and you want to take it up 5" or 12.5 cm. You would assume that you could just lay the garment out on a bench or table, mark up the required amount, allow for the hem, and cut.

WRONG………….

One of the biggest mistakes made with dress hems is the fact that the front, back and sides can be very different in the length.

The following illustration shows garment where the back of the dress is higher than the front.

Imagine if the dress or gown was touching the floor. You would not know that the back is shorter than the front.

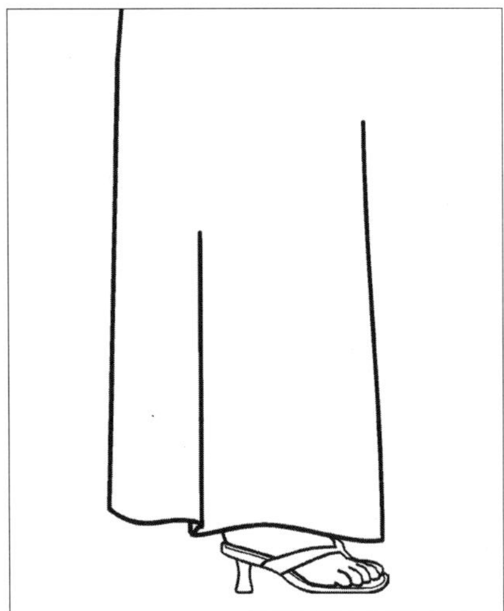

I have found that almost all dresses I have had to alter have had this problem.

The reasons can be.....

1. Dress is cut on the bias and it has dropped.
2. Manufacturer has cut hem crooked.
3. Person wearing the dress has a big bust.
4. Person wearing the dress has a big bottom.
5. Person does not stand up straight.

This could be shoulders hunched, hips out of alignment and other such problems. If one shoulder is lower than the other it will cause the hem to be crooked. This happens from carrying those heavy school bags on one shoulder.

The biggest mistake made when hemming a dress or gown is not checking to see if the hem is straight.

The only reason for this would be that the dress or gown is so long that it is hanging on the floor.

When a dress is being shortened, most people would work out what the amount is from the hem to their new length, and then if they are marking from the old hem, they would mark up the same amount all the way around the hem line.

I have had people bring me in a dress or gown, and say please take it up "X" amount.

The problem with this is that if the dress, gown or skirt has a crooked hem as per the illustration, then the person taking up the garment is going to take that crooked hem with them. And the person will get a garment back with the back shorter than the front. And no matter who is right or wrong, at the end of the day the person who did the clothing alteration is going to take the blame. And so she/he should, because at the end of the day, you expect a person in the clothing alteration industry to know what to do with a garment.

Have you ever had a garment shortened, only to find that the hem is crooked?

This section will explain how to straighten hems that are crooked.

Before we go into the how, I would like to stress the importance of wearing the correct shoes.

On page 14, I covered how a low heeled shoe places the foot at a different angle to a high heeled shoe.

Well shoes also make a difference when you are determining the length on a long dress or gown.

So before you work out the length, put the shoes on that you are going to wear with the garment. If the person does not have the shoes that they are going to wear with the dress, gown or skirt, then I would suggest they use a pair of shoes that is a similar height heel to the ones they will wear.

The length that a garment is worn now will depend on the person's preference and the style of the garment.

I have covered long gowns in a section further in the book, so for now we will look at shorter lengths.

I usually ask the person to pull the dress up to the length they would prefer.

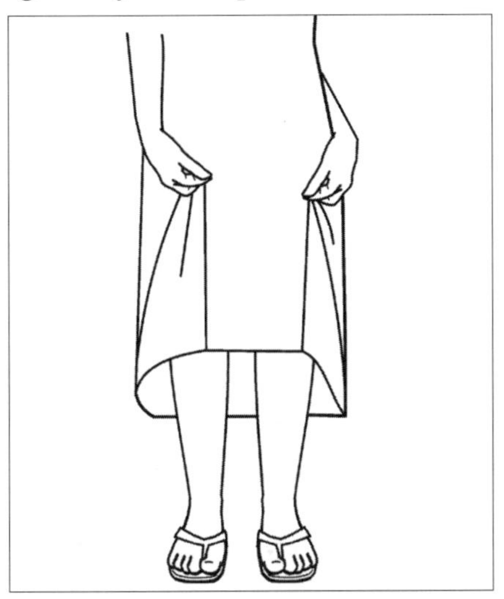

Even if you take time pinning different lengths, you will know by looking at the length whether it is right or not.

I usually kneel in front of the person and fold the fabric up to the length the person wants.

Measuring - floor to new hem length

Once you have determined the length, you should consider measuring all the way around, from the floor. If you have a chalk marker, then now would be the time to use it. However if you don't then this works just as well.

Always have at least four reference points. My reference points are -

1. Centre front
2. Left side seam
3. Centre back
4. Right side seam

If the dress is a full skirt, then I would measure every 6" or 15 cm around the hem and place crossed pins at each 6" position.

Measure from the floor to your new length. If the dress or gown is very flared, then use your reference points as above and probably a section in between these reference points.

Place your tape measure on the floor with the beginning of the tape measure touching the floor, and the measurements coming up towards the hem.

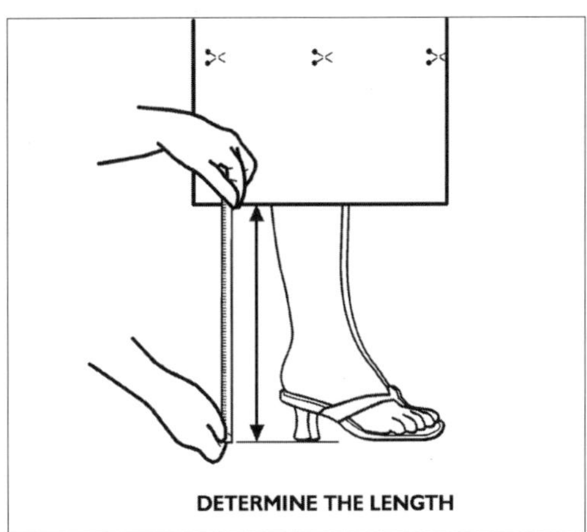

I always place two cross pins at each point that I have measured.

This means you will have crossed pins at the front, at the back and at the sides.

Refer to page 139 - 144 on how to Prepare a garment with a crooked hem.

Above the knee

This length should only be worn if you have reasonable knees. I don't mean to insult any-one, but I have seen women wear short dresses, and they have terrible knees, which means it does nothing for their overall appearance.

If you do have nice legs and knees, and like this length, always keep in mind the importance of pinning the back from the floor to the new length so that you are not surprised if the dress looks shorter than you thought.

I have often had women fold the hem up to where they want, and say go ahead with that length. Then I ask if they will just indulge me for a moment and I measure from the floor to the new hem length, then I go around the back of the garment, measure from the floor to the new hem length, and pin the back section up as well.

I then do the both sides, measuring from the floor to the new length.

Then I ask them to take a look at the back of the dress so they can see what the back will look like. Sometimes, the person will ask for the hem to come down just a little, because it appeared too short.

Step 1 - Ask the person to face the mirror.

Step 2 - Ask her to pull the dress up to show you where she feels she would like the hem to finish.

I do not expect her to turn the hem under, but rather that she just pulls the hem up to the length she wants.

Step 3 - Once you have seen where she wants the hem, kneel in front of her.

Step 4 - Fold the fabric up inside at the front, and place a double pin in the fabric to hold the fabric up.

Step 5 - Pin the fabric up either side of your first double pin.

Step 6 - Place your tape measure on the floor and measure up to the new fold line at the front. Remember this amount or write it down on a piece of paper.

Step 7 - Move around to the back and measure from the floor to the same amount as the front.

Step 8 - Put a pin in at this measurement, then fold the excess fabric up inside the skirt and secure with double pins.

Step 9 - Move to the right side and follow the previous step, measuring from the floor up to the new fold. Fold the excess fabric under and pin fold up with pins crossed.

Step 10 - Move to the left side and follow previous step. Fold the excess fabric under and place a double pin.

Step 11 - Now have the person stand side on to the mirror and see what she thinks of the length at the back.

Step 12 - If the garment has splits, check that the splits are not too high at the back or sides, or that the splits will become too small to leave on the garment. You need a minimum of 3" or 8 cm for a split.

Proceed to page 139 - 144 on Preparing and Sewing dresses, gowns and skirts.

On the knee

If you are going to choose this length, then the same principle applies as per Above the knee. You do need to have good legs and knees to wear clothes at this length.

Step 1 - Ask the person to face the mirror. Ask her to pull the dress/skirt up to show you where she feels she would like the hem to finish.

Step 2 - Once you have seen where she wants the hem, kneel in front of her and turn the fabric up inside the garment.

Step 3 - Place a double pin just above the fold line. Pin either side of the hem working around to both side seams.

Step 4 - Move behind her and fold the back of the dress/skirt fabric out of the way, so that she can see what the length will look like at the back.

Step 5 - When I pin on the knee, I try to have the finished length level with the curve of the knee. Above this point will move out to the thigh, and below this point will curve out to the calf.

Step 6 - Once she is happy with the length, measure from the floor up at the back and sides as per page 131.

Proceed to page 139 - 144 on Preparing and Sewing dresses, gowns and skirts.

Below the knee

This length suits anyone with curvy calf's. Even if your knees aren't that great, this length will still accentuate your nice legs and ankles.

This is a very feminine look.

Step 1 - Pin the hem up so that the fold of the new hem is at the base of the knee.

Step 2 - When you look in the mirror, the fold should cover the knee area by approximately 2".

Step 4 - Place a double pin just above the fold line.

Step 5 - Pin either side of the hem working around to both side areas.

Step 6 - Move behind her and fold the back of the skirt fabric out of the way, so that she can see what the length will look like in the mirror without fabric hanging.

Step 7 - Once she is happy with the length, you should measure from the floor up at the back and sides to ensure the dress will be straight.

Proceed to page 139 - 144 on Preparing and Sewing dresses, gowns and skirts.

Mid Calf

This is more an "After 5's" look. It could be a cocktail dress or it may be that you want a more conservative look .

A business woman might choose this length for a suit skirt. When you want people to take you seriously, you are better off wearing something a little longer, than marching in to a board room with a skirt with the hem above the knees.

Step 1 - Ask the person to stand still facing the mirror, with their spine straight.

Step 2 - Measure approximately 9" or 23 cm from the centre of the ankle to the new hem length.

When pinning mid calf, try to have the new length in the middle of the calf, so that the curve of the calf is now curving in towards the ankle.

Step 3 - Fold the fabric up inside the dress and place a double pin to hold the fabric in place.

Step 4 - When you are happy with the length, measure from the floor to the top of the fold at the front, then repeat for back and sides.

Proceed to page 139 - 144 on Preparing and Sewing dresses, gowns and skirts.

Above the ankle

This length is more for evening wear. Showing the ankle can be very flattering if you have shapely ankles.

Step 1 Try to have the fold so that when you look into the mirror, you can see the curvy shape of the ankle, before the leg widens into the calf.

Step 2 - Put the tape measure in the centre of the ankle and measure up 6" or 15 cm. Place a pin at this measurement on the fabric.

Step 3 - Fold the fabric up underneath and place a double pin to hold fabric in place. Move either side of this measurement and place pins to hold fabric up.

Step 4 - Measure from the floor to the new fold line where the double pins are.

Step 5 - Move around to the back and measure from the floor to the new length, placing double pins at this point.

Step 6 - Move around to the sides and do the same thing, measuring from the floor to the new fold.

Step 7 - If the dress is wide, then you need to pin with double pins every 6" around the garment.

Proceed to page 139 - 144 on Preparing and Sewing dresses, gowns and skirts.

Ankle length

This length is also more of an evening length. I would use this length if the person wanted to show off some really nice shoes.

You really can't see the leg at all, but it certainly does show of the shoes that a person is wearing.

Step 1 - The new hem should be just on the ankle.

Step 2 - Once you have the new hem length, measure from the floor all the way around at the front, back and side seams.

Step 3 - If the fabric is wide, then measure in between the front, back and sides and place double pins.

Proceed to page 139 - 144 on Preparing and Sewing dresses, gowns and skirts.

Evening gown length

All gowns should be straightened by pinning all the way around the hem – measuring from the floor up.

The only gowns that I have come across that do not need to be measured all the way around from the floor up are gowns that are slim lined gowns, where no panels are cut on the bias, and even then, you must always check that the back is not higher than the front.

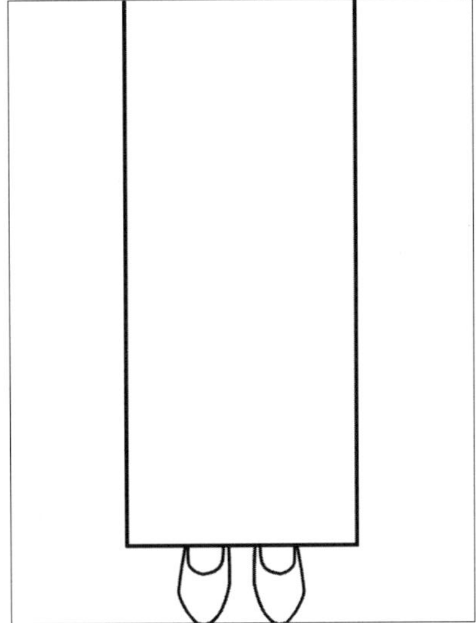

A gown made from a slinky fabric that is slim fitting will probably not need to be straightened either, however, if the person wearing the gown has a large bust, or a big bottom, then whether it was bias cut in the gown or not, you may have to straighten all the way around.

I can not stress enough that the person must have their spine straight and they must be looking directly into the mirror for you to get the hem length correct.

Step 1 - As a rule, I have found that pinning the new hem fold 1" or 2.5 cm from the floor is a good length.

Step 2 - At this length, you are not likely to catch your toe into the hem of the dress as you walk or dance.

Step 3 - The person should be wearing the shoes they are going to wear. The height of the heel is extremely important to the length of the gown, so you must ensure that the shoes that are going to be worn with the gown are the shoes that are on when the gown is pinned.

Step 4 - Kneel in front of the person and begin at the very front of the gown.

Step 5 - Place the end of your tape measure on the floor and fold the hem up so that the fold of the hem is 1" or 2.5 cm from the floor.

Step 6 - Place two pins in a cross position holding up the hem at the point where you measured 1" or 2.5 cm from the floor.

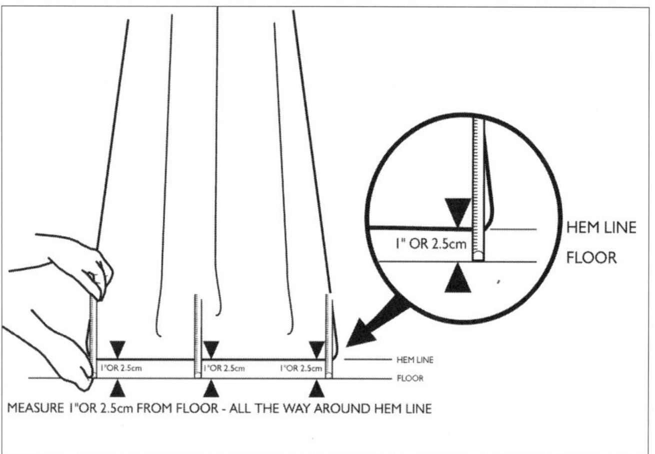

Step 7 - Move around the hem, pinning every 6" or 15 cm. Place two pins in a cross position at each interval. One of the most important points with the evening gown is to ensure you do pin all the way around, and in particular that you pin the back section only 1" from the ground.

Because 90% of evening gowns have the back shorter than the front you may find that the front needs to be taken up, but the back is even shorter than the new length you want the hem to be. You will therefore have to make the whole hem shorter, as per the back length.

Check the sides as well and make sure they are the same measurement as the front and back.

Step 8 - Ask her to put her right foot forward and see that she does not catch her shoe on the hem. The foot should clear the bottom of the gown.

Step 9 - When she walks, you should be able to see the shoe coming out from under the gown.

Step 10 - This length is great for gowns, but the person needs to understand that if they are walking up stairs or getting in and out of a car, they need to lift their hem.

Step 11 - I always show my customers how to take hold of the gown for walking up stairs. Most young women who are going to their first school formal or school prom do not know how to take a hold of the gown when walking up stairs.

Step 12 - Ask her to lean to the right, move her right hand down and grab hold of some fabric towards the back of the gown. She should then lift this fabric up and bring her hand to her side. Get her to practice a few times.

Step 13 - When the person has the gown off, have a look at the difference in the amount turned up from the front of the gown and the back of the gown.

Proceed to page 139 - 144 on Preparing Evening Gowns.

Gowns with trains

I have found that the perfect length for a gown is 1" or 2.5 cm from the floor at the front. Some people might like it a little longer, however if it is longer, then the hem will probably fray when it is worn for the first time.

At this length, you are not likely to catch your shoe into the hem of the gown as you walk or dance.

Gowns must always be taken up with shoes on.

The height of the heel is extremely important to the length of the gown, so you must ensure that the shoes that are going to be worn with the gown are the shoes that are on when the gown is pinned.

Step 1 - Kneel in front of the person and begin at the very front of the gown.

Step 2 - Place the end of your tape measure on the floor and fold the hem up so that the fold of the hem is 1" or 2.5 cm from the floor.

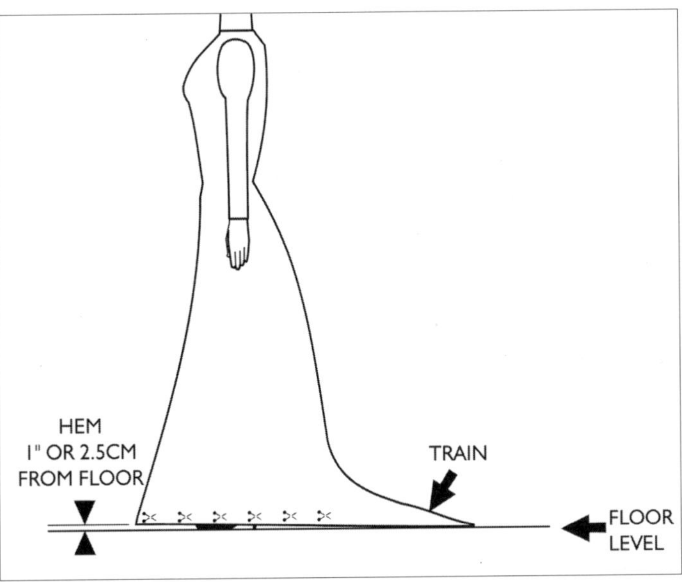

Step 3 - Place two pins in a cross position holding up the hem at the point where you measured 1" or 2.5 cm from the floor.

Step 4 - Move around the hem, pinning every 6" or 15 cm. Place two pins in a cross position at each interval.

Step 5 - Make sure the train is lain out behind the person.

Step 6 - As you pin around the garment, measuring from the floor up, you need to determine where you will stop measuring, and pin into the train.

Step 7 - I have found that when I am at the side seams of the gown, I have stopped measuring from the floor up, and have begun to pin into the train, so that the fabric flows properly.

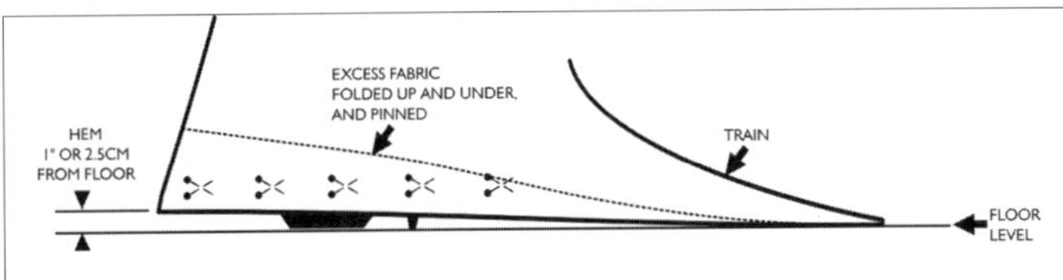

Step 8 - Once you have pinned both sides, ask her to put her right foot forward and see that she does not catch her shoe on the hem. The shoe should clear the bottom of the gown.

Step 9 - When she walks, you should be able to see the shoe coming out from under the gown.

Proceed to page 139 - 144 on Preparing Evening Gowns.

Bridesmaid gowns

Whenever you talk to a bride or bridesmaid about altering their gown, make sure you cover all the main points regarding the alteration.

Important Points

1. Try to have all the bridesmaids at the fitting at the same time. This way you can pin all the hems the same length for photos.

2. Everyone should have the shoes they are going to wear on the day at the fitting.

3. If a bra is going to be worn, then the bridesmaid should have it on at the fitting.

4. If corsets are going to be worn, they should be worn at the fitting.

5. Any other lingerie that is going to be worn should be worn at the fitting.

Talk to the bride if possible about the required length of the gowns.

If all the dresses are long, it is better to have the hem on all the gowns the same distance from the floor.

The photos will look more professional if the gowns are all the same length from the floor.

If this is the case, pin all the bridesmaids at the same time. I would have them all come in with everything that they are going to wear for the day.

If they cannot come in together measure one from the floor up and let them know what this amount is. The other bridesmaids can get their gowns altered the same distance from the floor. MUST DO – The gown must be pinned all the way around measuring from the floor up, because 9 times out of 10 the back will be shorter than the front.

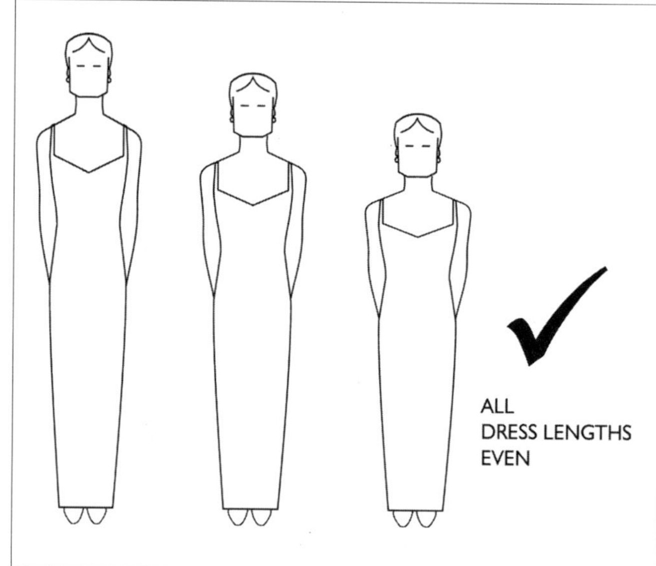

The only time you will not be able to have the bridesmaids with their hem lengths the same, is if you have a tall person whose gown is very short.

Refer to previous section on gowns for instructions on pinning the gowns.

Refer to page 139 - 144 on Preparing Evening Gowns.

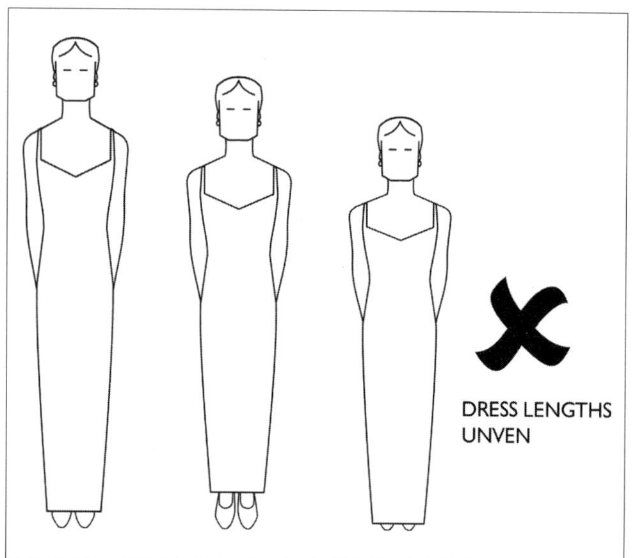

Dresses, Gowns & Skirts

Taking Up

Types of Hems

"The type of fabric will determine the type of hem you put on the garment"

Types of Hems

The first hem type is -

Blind hem

A blind hem is a hem that can not been seen on the right side of the fabric.

There are a number of ways of producing a blind hem.

1. Blind hemming machine

2. Use your blind hemming stitch on your domestic sewing machine

3. Hand stitch

I prefer to put a 1 1/2" or 4 cm hem allowance on dresses, gowns and skirts that are the classic straight or pencil style and/or slim lined (not flared) because it will give weight to the hem line.

Machine stitched hem

There are many different types of machine stitched hems.

Dresses, gowns and skirts usually don't have very large hems like pants, however I have seen a few that have very large hems.

Let's concentrate on the most common.

Hem Allowance - 1 1/4 " or 3 cm

If you have an over locker, then you would measure up the amount you are taking in the garment, and down 11/4 " or 3 cm.

I call this o/l m/s which means over lock and machine stitch.

If you are not going to use an over locker, then you need to do a turn twice. So your hem allowance will be 1 1/4" + 1/2" or 3 cm + 1 cm. I call this TT which means Turn Twice.

Hem allowance - 1" or 2.5 cm

This hem allowance is not far off the above, however you may come across this on some casual dresses and skirts.

You can also do a turn twice (TT) of 1" + 1/2" or 1.5 cm + 1 cm.

Hem allowance - 5/8" + 5/8"

This is a turn twice (TT). If you have covered the section on jean hems you will have seen this style of hem, because almost all jeans have this finish. Denim shirts would also be sewn this way or the next style.

Hem allowance - 1/2" or 1 cm

You would use this hem allowance for some dresses and skirts, particularly denim skirts, where you would over lock first then machine stitch topside.

The difference between over locking (O/L) a denim skirt and turn twice (TT) is that some denim is very thick, and if you don't want the skirt hem to stick out like cardboard, you should O/L only.

Hem allowance - 3/8" or 1 cm

This hem allowance is used a lot on a full skirt evening gown. However I would not do this hem on a chiffon or very light soft fabric. This is best suited to a satin or heavier weighted fabric.

The raw edge should be over locked (O/L) and I would sew topside, sewing into the middle of the over locking.

You can usually see the over locking from the right side. I would definitely not do a turn twice (TT) here.

If you don't have an over locker, then I would recommend you do all the cutting and preparing, and take the gown to a clothing alteration shop and ask them to over lock it for you. Then you can do the sewing.

Hem allowance - 1/4" + 1/4" or 3 mm+ 3 mm

This small hem can be sewn in a number of ways.

1. Cut the hem allowance at 1/2", which is your 1/4" + 1/4" doubled. This just saves you marking down 1/4" then down another 1/4".

Sew a row of stitching 1/4" in from the raw edge. This is the same as Stay Stitching.

What this does is give you a stitch line to follow, and it makes it easier to turn the fabric over twice, or turn twice (TT).

Use your finger to push the first 1/4" under, so you get the right hem allowance.

2. Cut the hem allowance at 1/2", which is double your 1/4" + 1/4".

Over lock the edge.

Note: Use only three threads on your over locker. Prepare your over locker as follows:-

Take the left hand needle out, so that only the needle in the right hand position is in.

Do not use the thread on the far left. Take the thread out of the machine.

You now have 3 threads only.

Over lock the edge with this thread.

Now turn twice (TT) use the over locking to help you get your small hem.

Hem allowance 1/8" + 1/8" 1.5 mm + 1.5 mm

Measure down 1/4" or 3 mm for hem allowance. You will now see what I mean about using metric versus imperial. I find it easy to mark down at the 1/4" mark on inches, rather than trying to find the 3 mm mark on metric.

Use any of the two techniques for 1/4" + 1/4", however you have one other option with this small hem.

Some domestic sewing machines have a rolled hem foot. It actually rolls the fabric in as you sew. It takes a little while to get used to it, but worth the while.

Instructions for use of this foot are in your sewing machine manual.

Rolled hem

There are two versions of a rolled hem.

1. Using a domestic over locker and converting to the rolled hem option

2. Using your domestic sewing machine using the zig zag stitch and sewing on the edge

My personal preference is No 1 using an over locker on rolled hem option.

You really do get a nice finish this way, but I have seen some gowns sewn with the No 2 option, and they have used fishing line in between which gives a good effect.

You sewn the fishing line in, as you zig zag.

Lining

I prefer to put a 1" or 2.5 cm hem allowance.

A lot of manufacturers will do what is called a turn twice, but generally I find that because lining is such a soft fabric usually, the hem twists.

One reason it twists is because they do not sew topside.

They sew with the wrong side facing them, and that means the hem will twist.

Try sewing lining topside.

You will find it very rarely twists, and if it does it's because you haven't open out the seams.

Writing down measurements

Get yourself a piece of paper and/or use something like My Notes below.

The first "My Notes" is on a garment with a 1 1/2" or 4 cm hem allowance.

The second "My Notes is of a garment with a TT or Turn Twice hem allowance of 1 1/4" + 1/2".

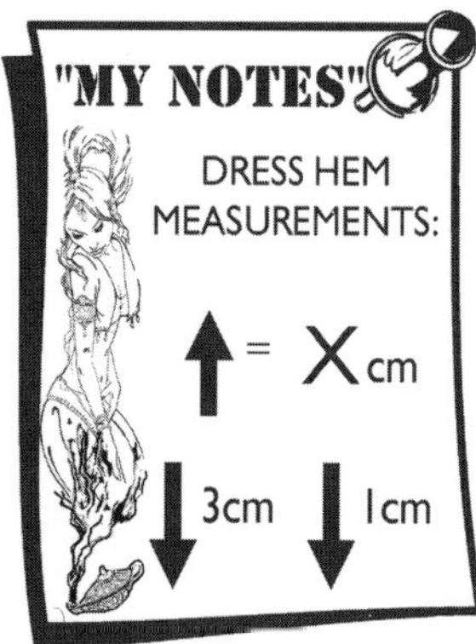

X = the amount you folded under and where you placed the cross pin.

The first example would be for a dress, gown or skirt that is going to have a blind hem with a 1 1/2" or 4 cm allowance.

The second example would be of a dress, gown or skirt that is going to be machine stitched and the additional 1/2" or 1 cm will be folded under the first hem allowance, so that there will be no cut edge or raw edge showing.

Preparing Technique

Preparing the hem on a dress is similar to preparing a hem on pants, except that you have more fabric.

Refer to the previous section on Hem Allowances before you proceed with this section, because you need to work out what hem allowance you are going to have on your garment.

If the hem needs to be straightened

If you have to straighten a hem, you will have placed crossed pins all the way around the hem.

Your next step is to place a pin into the new fold line at each position you have crossed pins.

This means the hem will drop down once you un pin the crossed pins.

Place a chalk mark over the top of each pin.

Mark down from chalk mark for new hem allowance.

If the hem is straight

Step 1 - Write down the amount of hem that you have folded under onto a piece of paper.

Write down the hem allowance you are going to have.

Step 2 - Place the tape measure over the original hem with the measurement you are going up at the edge of the original hem.

Step 3 - Place a chalk mark at the side of the top of the tape measure.

Step 4 - Place another chalk mark down 1 1/2" or 2.5 cm for the hem allowance.

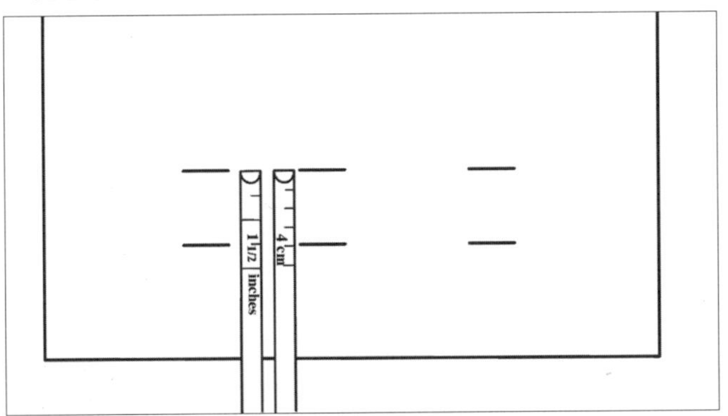

Note: In this example my hem allowance is 1 1/2", and that is all I am marking down, because I will over lock (O/L) after it is cut.

I am also including an illustration on a hem which is what I call a turn twice (TT).

This means that you are going up the amount pinned under, then coming down the first hem allowance, then down for the second hem under.

The illustration is a 1 1/4" + ½" hem allowance.

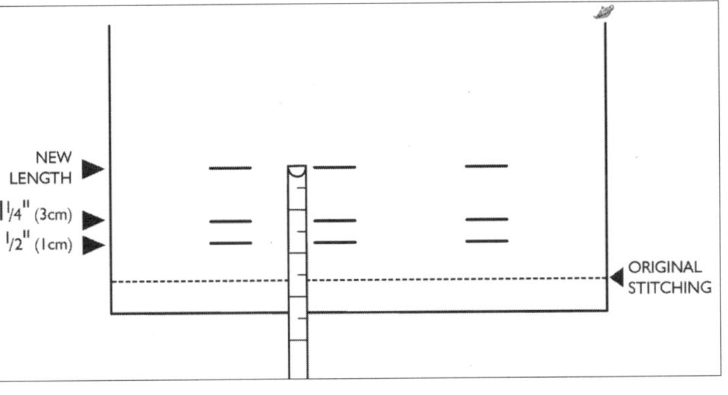

Step 5 - Always cut on the bottom chalk line, and always nick into the side of the garment, rather than cutting up from the hem. This gives you the option of lowering the hem or using the old hem as a false hem if you make a mistake.

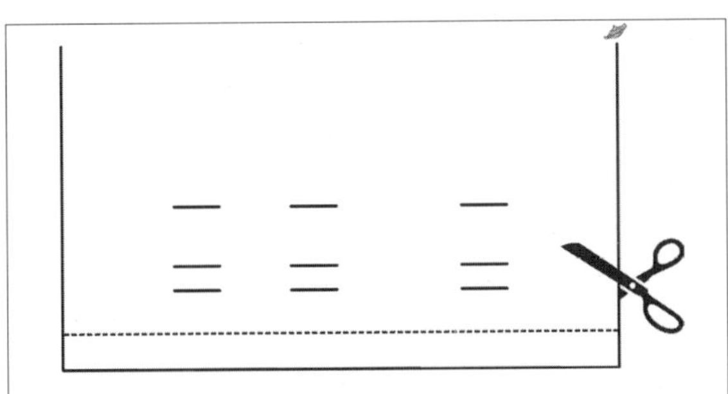

If the garment is not lined proceed to Sewing Outer Garment.

Sewing Outer garment

Keep the garment turned inside out and place it over the end of the ironing board.

Turn the hem up to the chalk line and iron the hem into place.

Make sure you line up the side seams and back seam if there is one.

Place a pin at the side seam and all the way around the garment as you iron.

Make sure you line up the splits, if there are any, so that when you bag the corners (see page 144 - Splits) the splits will be the same length.

When you have ironed up the hem, you will notice whether the new hem fits into the body of the fabric or not.

If the dress is flared at the hem, you need to take in the hem section on both side seams.

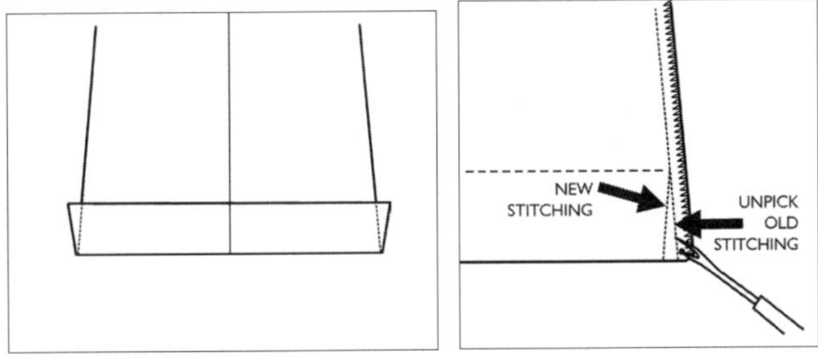

If the hem is too narrow and does not fit into the upper body of the garment, you need to open out the two side seams.

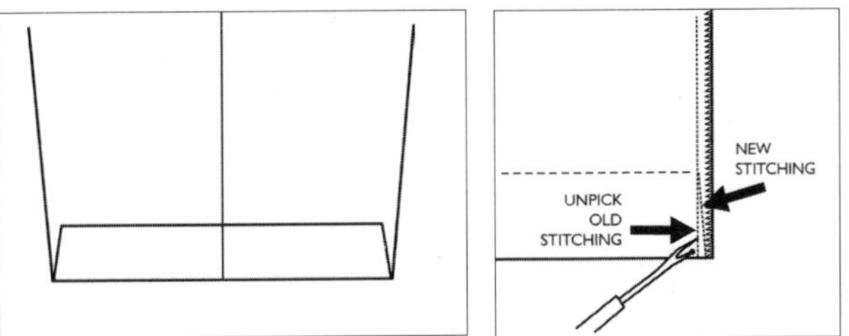

Check to see that after you have made the adjustment on the seams, the new hem allowance fits correctly.

You are now ready to over lock your hem. If you do not have an over locker, you can sew some ribbon onto the raw edge of the garment.

Stitch the ribbon over the raw edge, so that you cover the raw edge.

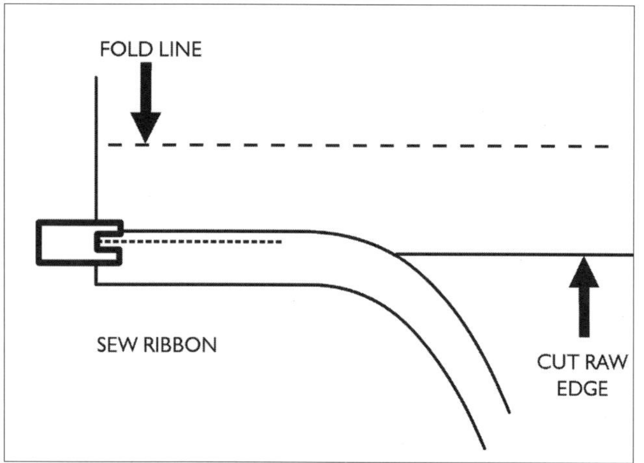

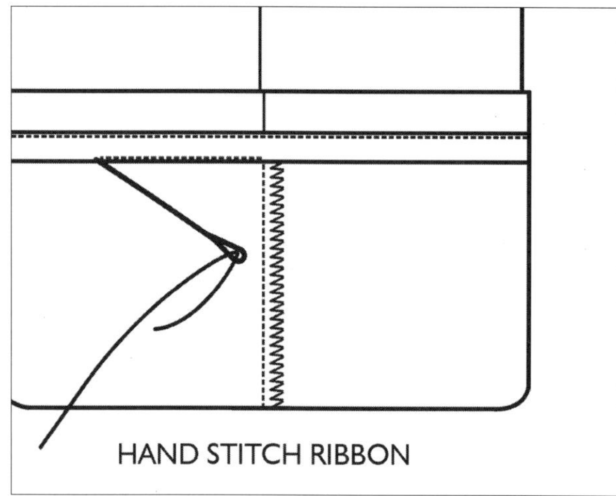

The small ribbon that is about 1/2" wide is good. A nice satin one would be even better. Lay the ribbon flat and sew with it covering the raw edge.

A slip stitch will do for the hand stitching. When you are catching some of the fabric from the body of the garment, only take one or two strands of the fabric.

A lot of people make the mistake of taking more than that, and then you can see the thread on the other side.

There are some great sewing books on the market which explain how to hand stitch, and how to use a machine. I am going to leave that area to them.

Splits

If there are splits, you need to bag the corners.

Explanation - Bagging the corners means that you turn the hem back on itself (right sides together) and sew along a predetermined hem line, then turn back to right side.

Step 1 - Turn the garment inside out and iron up the hem allowance. Make sure the splits are even.

Step 2 - Fold the right sides together.

Step 3 - Sew along the ironed fold line.

Step 4 - Turn the hem back and use a pair of tweezers or point turner to get a sharp edged finish.

Step 5 - Iron the bagged corner.

Step 6 - Place a pin through the over locking that comes down the side of the split, securing the hem at the same time.

Step 7 - Sew the two sections together using a straight stitch.

Lining

If the garment is lined, then you have a few ways that it will be constructed at the hem.

a.   The lining is separate to the outer fabric.
b.   The lining is attached to the split.
c.   The lining is attached to a side seam and is over locked in with the outer fabric.

a. Lining is separate to the outer fabric

After you have cut the outer fabric, turn the garment inside out and mark up lining on right side.

You will mark up the lining in the same way you marked up the outer section. I usually leave a 1" hem allowance on lining.

If you do not have an over locker, then you may

want to consider doing a ½" + ½" hem allowance, and just turn twice and sew the lining.

b. The lining is attached at the split

Step 1 - Mark up the outer fabric first.

Step 2 - Turn the garment inside out and mark up the lining.

Leave either a 1" hem allowance for a over locker or a ½" + ½" for turn twice.

Step 3 - Cut the outer fabric, and when you come to the split cut through the split and just nick into the lining a very small way.

Step 4 - Cut the lining on the bottom chalk line, nicking into the chalk line next to the split on the outer fabric. Cut all the way around the lining to the opposite side split.

Step 5 - Now unpick the section where the lining is attached to the outer fabric at the split. Doing it this way saves you time, and allows you to keep the fabric off cuts as a full piece, so if there is any mistake you can sew it back on.

One side of the split will be top stitched AFTER it was sewn onto the outer fabric.

Step 6 - Unpick the top stitching a little further than the first seam.

Step 7 - Unpick enough of the lining seam so that you have sufficient room to sew your hem allowance.

Step 8 - After you have sewn your hem on the lining, re attach to the outer fabric section at the split. Remember to re top stitch if it was done in the first place.

With the garment turned inside out, place over the ironing board and iron up the outer fabric following the same procedure as per (a).

c.   The lining is attached to a side seam

Complete your preparation the same as (b.) however when you are putting the garment back together, you will need to complete the hem on the middle section first.

Then re sew the side seam, joining the front and back sections together.

Cut all way around and copy original hem.

Conclusion

You may have noticed that the actual preparing and sewing of dresses, gowns and skirts is similar to pants. There are obviously different situations, but the over all effect is the same.

A blind hem is a blind hem whether it is on pants or dresses, and so on,

When lining is attached to a garment, it can be a little tricky to work out how to unpick it, shorten it, and put it all back together in the same way.

If you are not sure, only unpick one side and use the side that is not unpicked as a guide.

Some evening gowns have a panel which is attached over the body of the skirt. This will mean unpicking a side seam where the two panels are attached. You will then need to shorten one section at a time, and in some cases over lock and re attach a section before you can do the other section.

It would be absolutely impossible to cater to all the scenarios, however use your logic, and do one side at a time, so you have a guide.

Happy sewing

Dresses, Gowns & Skirts

Taking In

"We are all different shapes and sizes."

*"You may love the style and colour,
but it doesn't fit correctly."*

*"See how easy it could be to make the
alterations to suit your body shape."*

Introduction

The Taking in Technique has been covered in pages 51-62 under Pants Taking In. The technique for writing down measurements, marking etc will not change. What does change is the style and shape including the way the manufacturer has created the garment.

This section covers where you should pin for certain situations and why you should pin for certain situations.

Dresses and gowns will be covered first, then we will go into skirts.

Taking in

A dress or evening gown that is too big can be altered in a number of ways.

The way the garment is manufactured has to be taken into consideration as well as the shape of the persons body who is wearing the garment.

Option 1 - Take in sides of sleeveless garment

The front and back panels are too big. If the panels are the same front and back it should be a simple process to take in the sides.

Option 2 - Take in two back side seams

You would take this option, if the front panel is a different shape from the back panel at the sides, which means taking in at the sides would expose too much of the bust area.

Option 3 - Take in centre back seam

The back of the dress is too big compared to the front of the dress. The back panels have either been cut too big, or the person may have a large bust which takes up a lot of the front panel, leaving the back panels to look too big.

Option 4 - Take in the sides including sleeves

The dress is too big but it has sleeves. The sleeves must be taken in as well.

Option 5 - Creating darts

The dress or gown is too big, but it is mainly around the waist and hip section. Create darts in the front and/or back of the dress.

Option 6 - Take up straps

Dress feels too big, but by taking up the straps the dress is raised up higher on the body and solves the problem because it is now in proportion with the body. the bust area could have been too low, and once raised it fits the body.

Option 7 - Take up shoulders - sleeveless

Sleeveless dress is too big around the bust and neck area. Raise the shoulders.

Option 8 - Take up shoulders - with sleeves

Dress with sleeves is too big around the bust and neck area. Raise the shoulders from the neck to the sleeves.

Option 9 - Excess fabric around waist and chest area

Garment is loose at the top of the garment. This is caused by the dress being too tight over the hip area, which is causing the dress to ride up towards the bust area.

Option 10 - Breast enlargement cups

Bust area on cross over, halter neck or evening gown is too big and rather than taking in, the purchase of breast enlargement cups would fill out the fabric.

Which option is right for you?

Check the sides first by having the person stand in front of a full length mirror.

Step 1 - Stand behind the person and using your thumb and index fingers, pinch the excess fabric under the arms on both sides.

Does this cause the fabric to pull across the bust.?

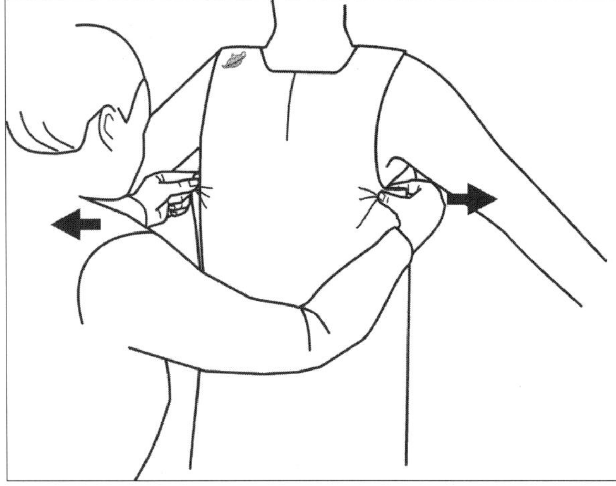

Step 2 - If it pulls on the bust area then you need to look at taking in one of the back sections.

This may be the two back side seams or the centre back.

Step 3 - Using both hands, grab hold of the centre back seam on the dress (if there is not one, just grab the centre back anyway), and take the excess fabric into your hands.

I usually position my hands one under the other.

Step 4 - By taking hold of the excess fabric in the back, you will see by looking in the mirror, if the garment fits the person without pulling on the bust.

If there is no centre back seam, you can create one.

Garment construction

If the dress is too big for the person, you need to look at how you are going to take in. There are two main types of front and back panels.

Front and back panels the same

In this situation, the panel at the front of the dress is similar to the panel at the back of the dress.

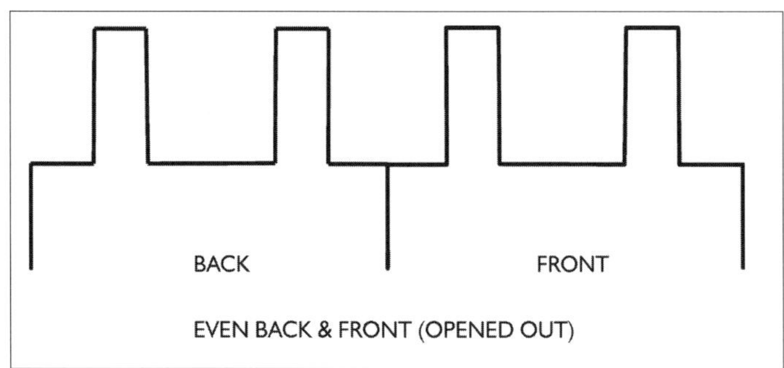

This means when you fold the dress at the side with the side seam in the center, the front panel and the back panel will be almost identical.

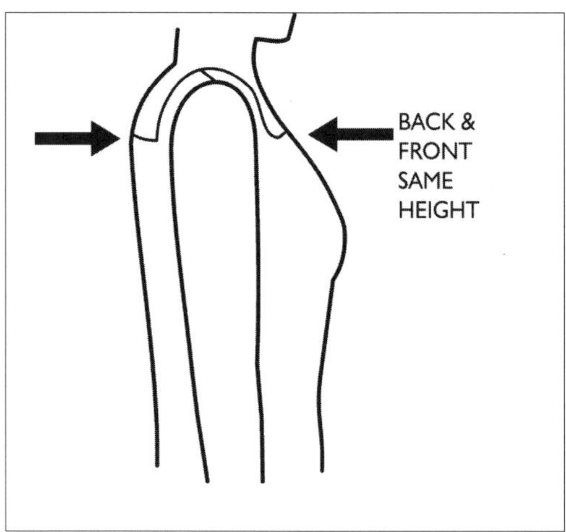

When the sides are taken in, the new seam will be near the old seam and the front and back will sit together easily.

Front and back panels different

In this situation, the front panel is shaped differently to the back panel.

The front is probably high and the back panel is probably dipping down with a zip at the back.

The illustration is for explanation purposes, and does not show the exact way a dress front and back would be cut.

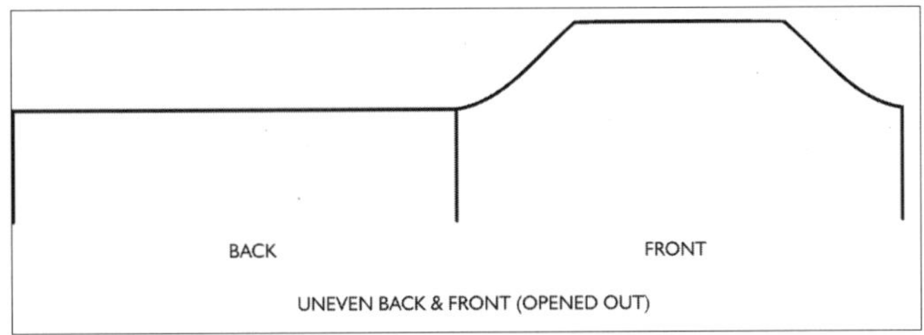

This means when the side seam is in the centre, the front and back panels will not be identical.

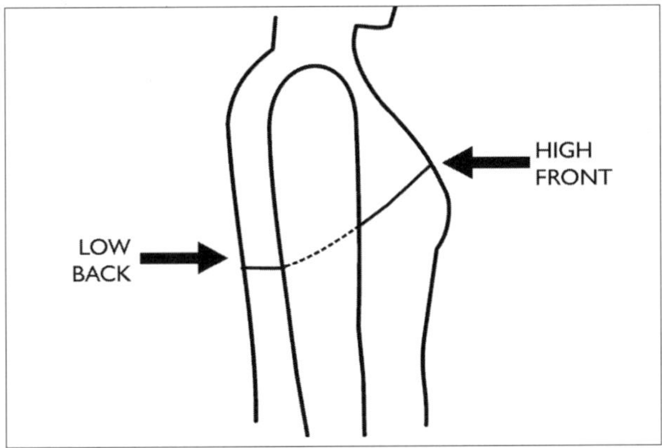

If you take in the side seams you will have to reshape the front panel, which will mean cutting away some of the fabric.

For a person with a big bust, this could mean more bust exposure. You will only know whether this will happen by pinning the garment on the person.

Taking in sides of dress

Option 1 – Take in sides of sleeveless garment

When you are taking a dress in to fit the persons body you need to pin the dress to the persons body shape. You need to imagine the shape of the person under the dress.

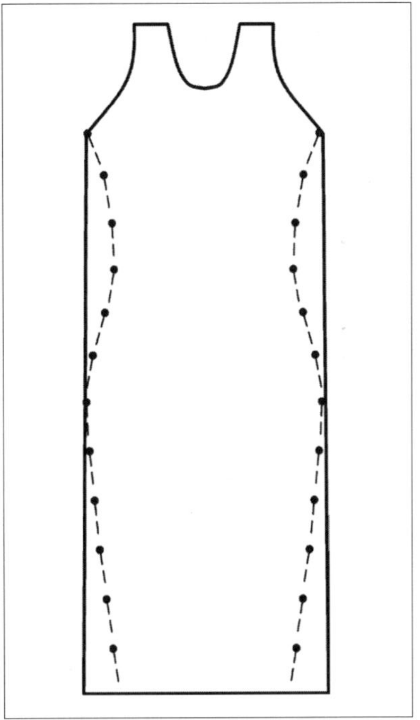

Some women like their dresses tight and others like their dresses a little looser.

The bottom line is that you need to pin the dress to the contours of the body whether you have the dress tight or loose.

1. Have the person stand in front of the mirror. Long mirrors are better, because you can see the overall effect.

2. Stand behind the person and take hold of the excess fabric under the arms using your thumb and index finger.

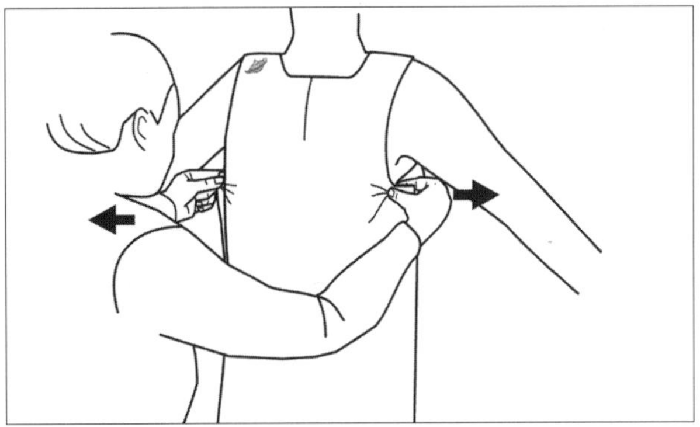

The excess amount of fabric means that when you take hold of the fabric between your thumb and index finger, the garment is firm on the person's body.

Just hold the excess and look in the mirror.

You can see that the garment will sit perfectly if it is pinned at the sides.

3. Ask the person to raise their arms slightly so you can see the amount that you have between your thumb and index finger.

4. If they raise their arms too high, you will not get a true indication of the amount needed to take in.

5. Place one or two pins into the excess fabric on the persons left hand side under the armhole. Have pin facing in the downward position.

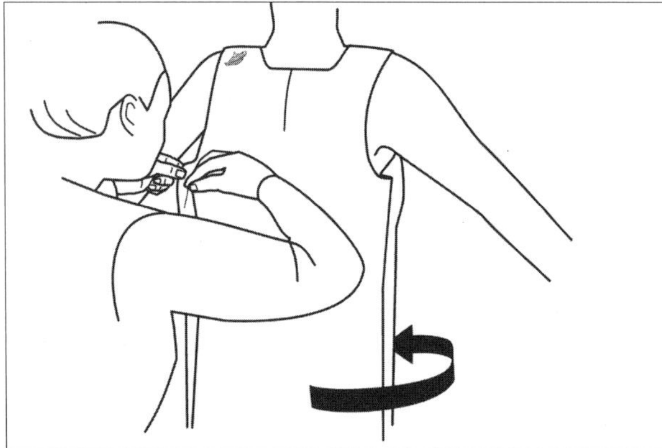

Note: Before you pin you need to make sure that the fabric is sitting where it should sit.

This may sound strange, but it is very important that you do not pull one side down to try to make the armholes meet.

One of the things my friend Carol always said was-

"Always let the fabric sit where it wants to sit"

Let me explain that. If you have two pieces of fabric. One piece of fabric is laying flat. You want the second piece of fabric to sit over the top of the first, but it doesn't seem to want to do that.

Because it has been cut differently or because it is sewn slightly differently, the fabric will not sit over the top of the first piece of fabric.

Your first option is to try and stretch the fabric so it will fit over the first. If you do this and sew these two pieces of fabric, one will look great and one will look pulled or stretched and out of place.

The bottom line is DO NOT FORCE FABRIC TO GO WHERE IT DOESN'T WANT TO GO. Let it move where it wants. This means you pin the same way. Don't force the fabric.

Back to pinning the sides.

6. Ask the person to turn and face you. Pin the excess fabric under the right hand side. The amount you pin should be the same amount you pinned on the left hand side.

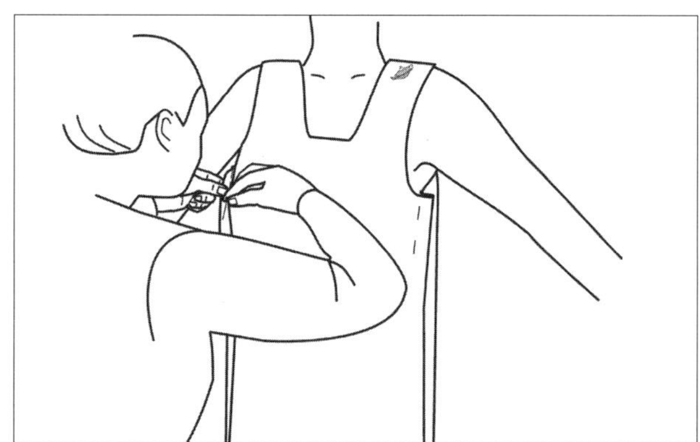

7. Now ask her to turn around with her back facing you. Pin her left hand side by placing the next pin underneath the last pin.

8. Your pins should be following the contour of the persons body.

9. Ask the person how the pinning feels under the arm and across the bust. The garment should not be too tight or too loose. It is important that the person feels comfortable with the pinning.

10. If you are pinning down over the hip area, you need to check to see if you need to leave a little room for movement.

The dress should be firm, but I usually check by grabbing the fabric on the hip area.

I like to have ½" or 1 cm folded in between my fingers.

11. Continue to pin both sides. Ask the person to move back and forth, so that you can stay in the same position. I usually place a few pins in one side, then I ask the person to turn and face in the opposite direction.

12. This allows you to stay in one position, with the person pirouetting front and back.

13. The pins should follow each other.

14. If you are only pinning down to the waist or before the waist, you must make sure you have the pins following one another just like a seam, and your last pin should be at the very edge of the fabric.

15. If you are pinning over the hip area, continue to pin with the pins fairly close together until you come to the thigh area.

16. You can then place the pins further apart.

17. If you are pinning through to the hem, I would suggest you continue to pin both sides so that the person can see exactly what the dress will look like when it is altered.

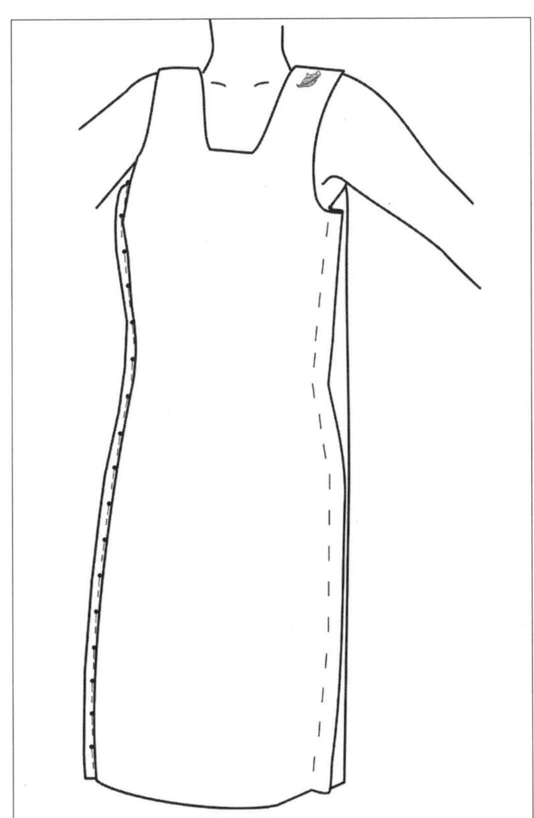

18.　　Use the Technique for Taking In when preparing the garment.

19.　　The dress will either be lined or have facing. Either way it should have under stitching which is a row of stitching on the inside of the garment which stitches the seam allowance to the wrong side. Unpick the under stitching about 1" more than the amount pinned on either side.

20.　　Always separate the facing and lining before altering, and always undo hems and sew through to the end, then re hem after the garment is taken in and the excess fabric over locked off.

Option 2 - Take in the back side seams

When you take the excess fabric under the arms and the two panels do not match, you may have to consider the back section. This will only occur if the two panels are very different, and reshaping will cause the front to be cut away too much.

This may sound drastic but if the front panel is cut away too much, it could expose too much of the breast.

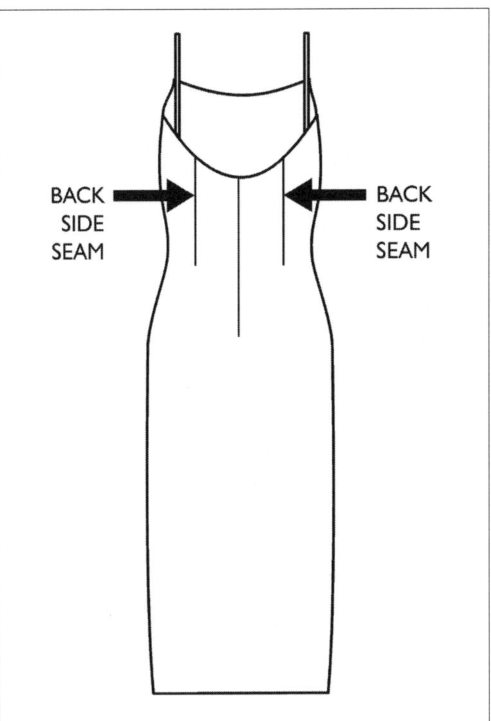

So switch your attention to the back of the dress.

At the back of the dress, there is usually a zip and in some cases, there are two side back seams.

In this option, we will look at pinning the two side back seams.

The two side back seams are on either side of the zip.

There may be a panel all the way to the hem, or there will be darts down to the waist. If there are darts to the waist and the dress needs to be taken in further than the waist, then skip this option and go to Option 3.

If the dress only needs to be taken in to the waist, then proceed with this option.

Step 1 - Have the person face a long length mirror.

Step 2 - Stand behind the person.

Step 3 - Take the excess fabric between thumb and index finger on the two side back seams.

The dress needs to be firm on the body.

Step 4 - Place a pin facing downwards in both seams the same amount that you had between your thumb and index finger.

Step 5 - Place a second pin under the third, and continue pinning down to the waist.

Step 6 - By the time you get to the waist you should have the last pin inserted right on the edge of the seam.

Step 7 - Turn the person side on to the mirror so they can see how the dress is fitting on her body.

Step 8 - Prepare this garment using the Technique for Taking In.

If the seams have boning, unpick the boning, take in as per the technique then sew the boning back on to the seam.

Option 3 - Take in centre back seam

Take a hold of the centre back section of the dress. There are going to be three options here.

Option A - Centre back seam without a zip
Option B - Centre back seam with a zip
Option C - No centre back seam - create one

Option A - Centre back seam without a zip

Make sure you have the centre back seam in the middle, and place pins beside the centre back seam.

The amount you pin in will be determined by how big the garment is on the person.

I find that by taking the excess fabric in between my fingers I can see how it changes the position on the person at the front, and this will affect the amount I pin down the centre back.

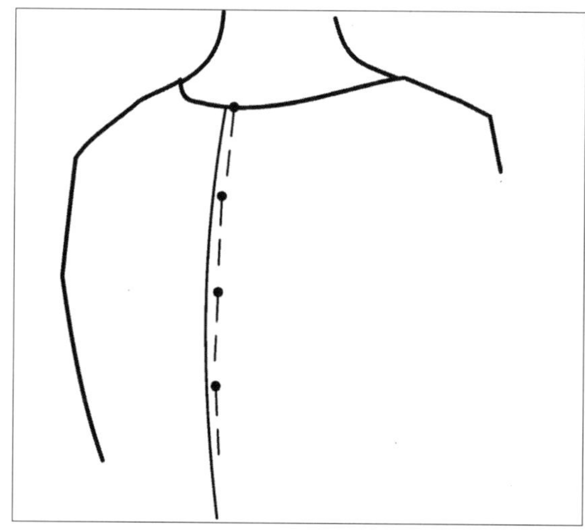

Once you are happy with the amount pinned, prepare and sew as per the Taking in Technique.

Option B - Centre back seam with a zip

When pinning the back of a dress with a zip, you need to pin the back as if the zip is not there.

Step 1 - Place the zip in the middle as if it is a

seam – THIS IS IMPORTANT.

Step 2 - Pin the back of the dress with the pins closely following one another.

Step 3 - Pin as far down the back of the dress as necessary.

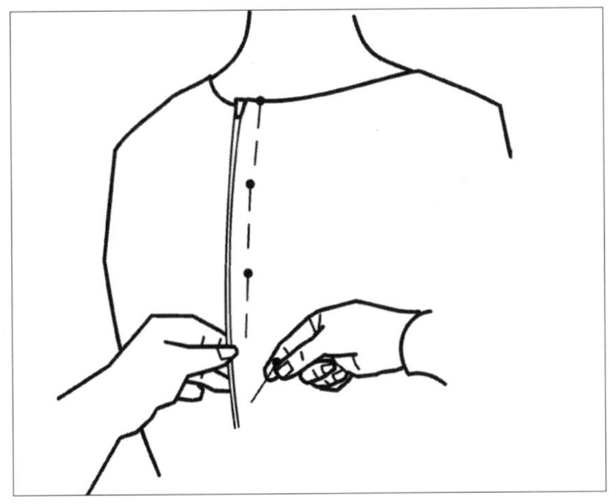

Step 4 - If you are pining through to the hem, then continue down to the hem area.

Step 5 - Note that once you pass the bottom/hip area, you can spread the pins out.

Step 6 - Turn the person so they are side on to the mirror and show them how the garment is pinned.

Step 7 - Once the person is happy with the fit you need to unpin the zip area so that she can get out of the dress.

Step 8 - Place a pin over the top of the original pin on the right hand side and pull the pin out that is through both sections of fabric.

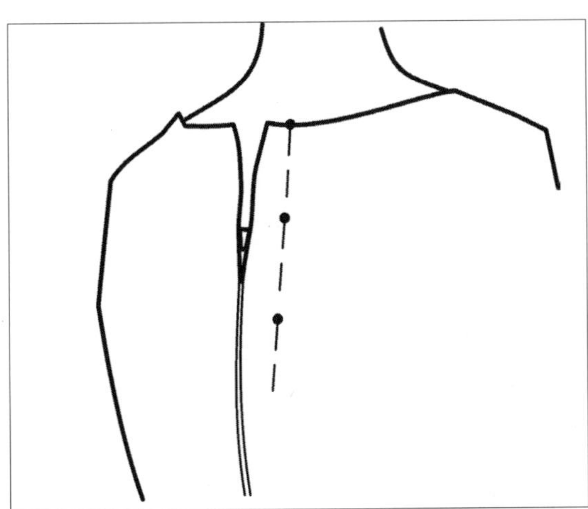

Step 9 - Continue doing this all the way down to the bottom of the zip.

Step 10 - The pins should be down one side of the zip area only.

Step 11 - All pins below the zip area should be left where they are.

Preparing zip in back

Step 1 - Write the pin measurements down on a piece of paper as per Technique for Taking In.

It is important to take the pin measurement at the end of the zip. All other measurements are every 2".

Step 2 - Unpick the zip and remove completely.

Step 3 - I always put an invisible zip back in when I am taking in the back of a garment like this.

The reason I do this is that when you take in the back section, the new zip will probably have sections where it will be on the bias.

A dress zip has a flap, which will twist if it is on the bias. An invisible zip will not twist on the bias.

Step 4 - Place the dots from the top of the garment on the outside side of the dress, on both sides of the opening.

For example if you were taking in the top at 1", then place a dot at the position 1" to right on the right hand side and 1" to the left on the left hand side.

Step 5 - Place your dots all the way down on the outside of the dress until you get to the end of the zip section.

Step 6 - Turn the garment inside out and place a dot on the wrong side of the garment next to the end of the zip.

Step 7 - When you have finished placing your dots, begin to sew, starting from the bottom of the zip following your dots to the finish.

Step 8 - Now unpick the original seam next to the new seam you have just sewn.

Step 9 - Place the garment over your ironing board (inside out), and iron the new zip section back at your dots.

Step 10 - Cut or over lock the excess fabric off, I leave about 5/8" for my seam allowance.

Step 11 - Insert your invisible zip. I use my ordinary zipper foot, with the needle moved across into a position next to the zip itself.

I use my fingernails to pull the zip back so that I can sew next to the zipper.

You must not sew ON THE ZIP.

If you do then the zip will not work.

If you do find that you catch the zip itself, then unpick and redo. Practice makes perfect.

Step 12 - Whether there is lining or facing, you should attach these to the side of the zipper using your sewing machine.

Some people hand stitch the facing or lining. Get used to using your sewing machine because this is the professional way of completing alterations.

step 13 - If you sew the lining or facing on to the edge of the zipper (right sides together) you will notice that the lining or facing is not sitting plush with the other.

This is correct. The lining or facing should not be flush because after you sew across the top in the original stitch line, you will pop the garment the right way, and the lining or facing will then sit flat.

Option C - No centre back seam - Create one

Try to find the centre of the back of the garment. You don't have to be exact here, because you will find the exact position when you are preparing the garment. What you are trying to achieve with the garment on the person is to find out how much you want to take the garment in at the back.

Step 1 - Place pins all the way down the back of the garment as if there is a centre back seam there. Follow the same procedure as Option 1 and Option 2.

Step 2 - When you are happy with the amount that has been pinned on the person, ask her to take the garment off. If she can not lift it over her head, then you will need to put a zip in.

In this case, you will need to write down the measurements with the pins in, then take the pins out for the person to get the garment off.

If the garment comes off over the head with ease, then you need to prepare as follows -

Step 3 - Write down the measurements from the centre fold to the pin. Follow the Taking in technique for writing down the measurements.

Step 4 - Take the pins out.

Step 5 - Turn the garment inside out and find the centre of the back panel. To do this you can either fold the garment in half and iron the centre fold into place. If this is too hard, then use your tape measure and measure from one side seam to the other side seam, then divide by 2 to find the centre, and measure in to this point and place a dot in that position.

Step 6 - Follow that process all the way down the centre back seam. I usually place pins down the back, so that I don't loose the new centre fold.

Step 7 - Place the dots as per the Taking in Technique in the position of the original pins.

Step 8 - Sew down through the dots.

Step 9 - You can either over lock the excess off as one seam, or cut the excess fabric off, but leave a small seam allowance. Over lock each side of the seam, or zig zag if you don't have an over locker.

> **Special Note. When taking in the back of a dress, you are usually taking it in from the top, however there are times when you will start sewing from just below the neck line. In this case please make sure you start at the very edge of the fold (centre) and come out very gradually, so that you don't end up with a pucker.**

Option 4 - Take in sides including sleeves

When a dress is too big and it has sleeves, you need to pin the sides and the sleeves to see if by pinning this way the dress will fit the body perfectly.

Always begin pinning under the arm first - pinning down the body, and then you will come back to the sleeves.

Step 1 - I prefer to have the person stand in front of the long length mirror.

Step 2 - Stand behind the person and put your hands into the armhole area.

Step 3 - Using your thumb and index finger, take a hold of the excess fabric under the arms. Look and see that it does not pull the fabric across the bust area.

Step 4 - Look at the amount you have in both your fingers, and put a pin in at this amount.

Step 5 - Make sure the pin is facing downwards with the knob of the pin in the armhole seam.

Step 6 - Place another pin underneath the first on both sides. Continue to pin down the dress take all the excess fabric into the pins.

Step 7 - The dress should be firm, but I usually check by grabbing the fabric on the hip area. I like to have about ½" or 1 cm folded in between my fingers.

Step 8 - If the pins are going to stop at the waist or hips, then you need to taper the pins out to the point where you are going to stop taking in.

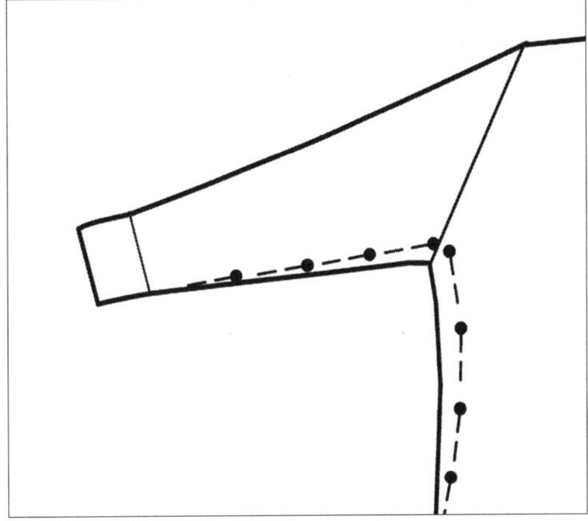

Step 9 - If the dress is being taken in through to the hem, then you need to pin both sides all the way to the hem.

Step 10 - Now you need to go back to the sleeve.

Step 11 - Place a pin after the pin under the armhole, but make sure the pin head is pointing towards the hand.

Step 12 - Continue pinning down the arm either to the point where you want to stop taking in.

Step 13 - If the sleeve is long, pin down and taper off either at the forearm if the sleeve is tight around the wrist, or pin to the end of the wrist.

Step 14 - Use the Technique for Taking In when preparing the garment.

Step 15 - Always unpick the sleeve from the body if it is sewn this way. I have seen people take in through a sleeve and they get lazy and sew straight through. Never cut corners when you are altering a garment.

Option 5 - Creating darts

Some dresses have no shape in them at all. The illustration shows a dress that has little shape to it before it is pinned.

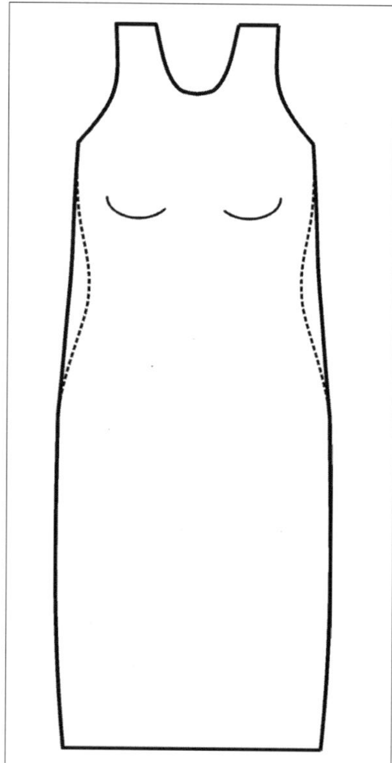

The first option to consider is taking in the sides of the dress, however if it pulls across the bust, then your next alternative is taking in the back.

If the garment is not too big at the back of the neck and shoulder area, and the hip area is fine, then you may want to consider putting darts in the dress.

There is a right and wrong way to pin and sew darts. Sewing darts takes a little bit of effort.

It is extremely important to begin at the edge of the fold and sew inwards in a gradual fashion.

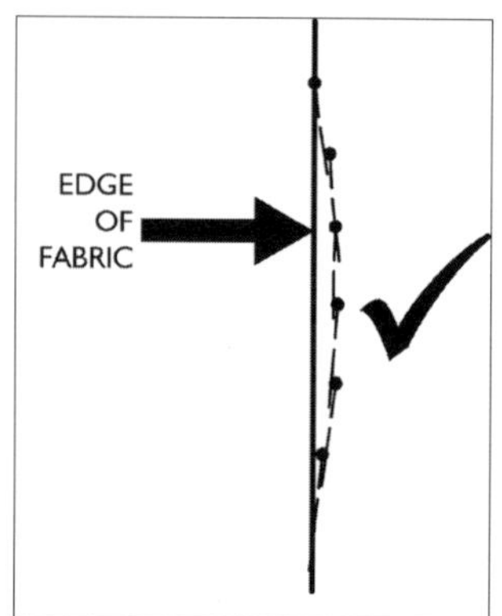

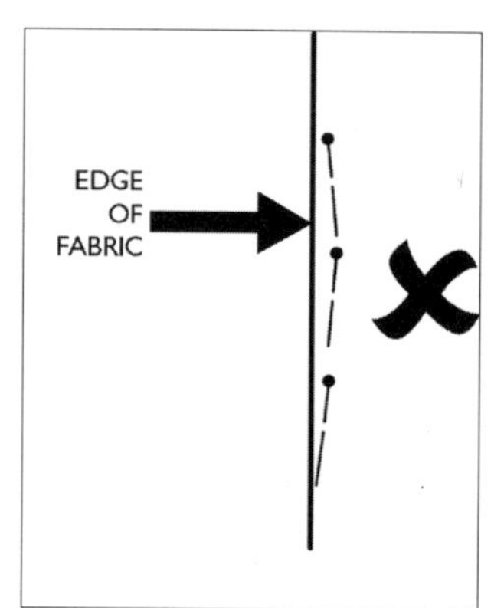

You can put darts in the front and/or back of the garment.

Step 1 - Begin pinning at the front of the dress about 1" or 2.5 cm below the nipple.

Step 2 - Place the first pin on the edge of the fabric with the pin facing down.

Step 3 - Place the second pin so that the top of the pin is below the first pin, but the bottom of the second pin is moving in towards the person's body more.

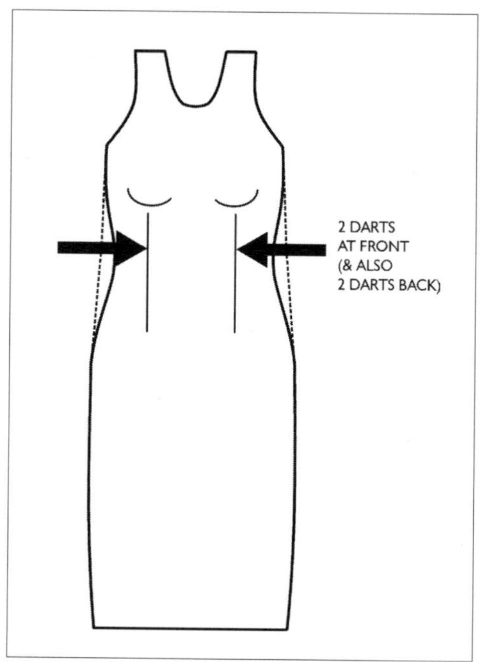

Step 4 - As you pin come in towards the body, you will notice that the garment gets tighter. Use the pins as if they are a seam. In the illustration the pins come out to a wide point, then they gradually move back in until there is no fabric in the pin.

Step 5 - The centre of a dart should be ½" or 1 cm.

Step 6 - Once you reach the waist, begin to move back out so that the garment has shape.

Step - Pin both sides trying to keep the darts even.

Step 8 - Create back darts by following the same procedure as per front darts. Use Taking in Technique.

Option 6 - Shortening straps

Straps come in different sizes and can be very wide straps to very narrow like the shoe string straps (also called spaghetti straps). Some straps have dimonties attached.

No matter what type of straps they should be pinned in a similar fashion.

Step 1 - As a rule, you should shorten straps from the back.

Step 2 - Ask the person to try the dress on. Pin the straps first if the hem is being taken up because shortening straps will affect the hem.

Step 3 - I prefer to have the person stand in front of a long length mirror. Stand behind the person.

Step 4 - Take a hold of one strap and bring the excess strap down and over the garment at the back.

Step 5 - Place a pin through the strap making sure to keep the sharp edge of the pin away from the person's body. I prefer to use two pins in a cross. If one pin is over the other, then the pins are not likely to fall out.

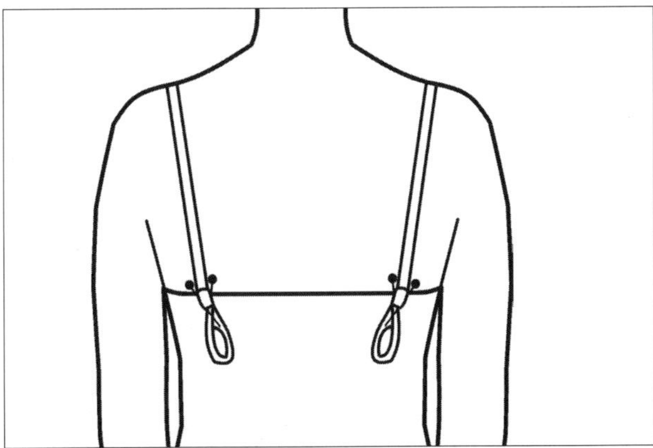

Step 6 - Measure the amount that you have pinned and follow the same procedure on the opposite side.

Step 7 - Write the amount down on a piece of paper. Some peoples shoulders are different, and it may be that you need to pin the straps different amounts.

Step 8 - Write this on the piece of paper i.e.

Right strap =

Left strap =

When you write down the measurement keep in mind that the strap has been doubled over.

Write down the total amount.

Example

1" fold = 2" total
or
1 cm fold = 2 cm total

Step 9 - Place a dot on the inside of the strap at the amount it is being taken up. For example if you had the strap folded over and it measured 1" folded, then it is two inches total. Put a dot at 2" from the position that it is sewn into the garment.

Step 10 - Straps can be sewn into a garment in a number of ways. The simple way is for the straps to be stitched to the fabric at the back and hanging loose.

Step 11 - The most common way straps are constructed in a garment is to have the straps attached between the outer fabric and the facing or lining.

Step 12 - Always unpick the under stitching at least 1" either side of the strap.

Step 13 - Turn the garment inside out so you can get at the seam between the fabric and the lining or facing. Unpick the few stitches that support the strap.

Step 14 - Pull the strap through until the dot appears.

Step 15 - Pin the strap into place and stitch it back on sewing through the original seam. Stitch a second time a little higher to strengthen the stitching.

Step 16 - Re sew the under stitching.

Option 7 -Raise shoulders - Sleeveless

There are a number of reasons why the shoulders should be raised on a sleeveless dress.

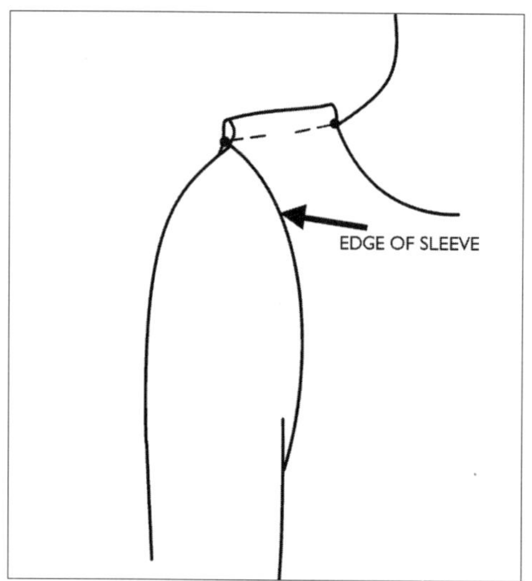

1. The dress has long straps, which causes the dress to hang too low at the bust.

2. The dress is tight at the hips, and raising it at the shoulder solves this problem. (see Option 9)

Because garments are constructed differently, there are two main styles of shoulders.

A. Front and back sections are similar
B. Back section is higher than the front

We will begin with Option (A)

A. Front and back sections are similar

Step 1 - Stand in front of the person and take hold of the excess fabric on BOTH shoulders.

Step 2 - Place the centre seam at the middle fold.

Step 3 - Place a pin on the outside of the shoulder with the pin facing in to the centre.

Step 4 - Place a second pin on the inside of the shoulder with the pin facing towards the centre.

Step 5 - If the width of the shoulder is more than

the width of the two pins, then place a third pin in the centre between the two pins.

Step 6 - Pin the opposite shoulder, following the same procedure as Step 5.

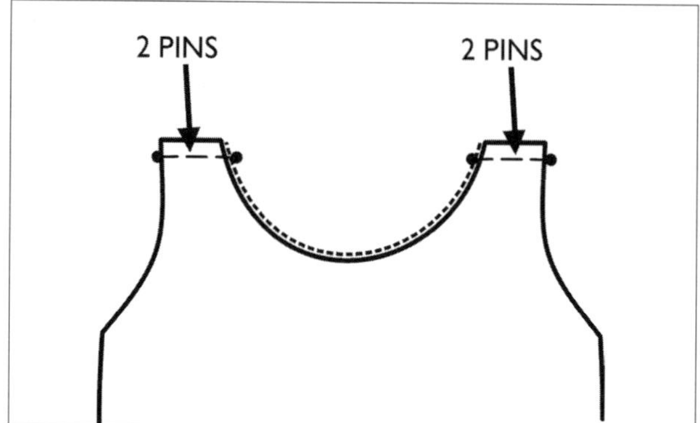

I will sometimes use the tape measure to make sure I am pinning the same amount on both shoulders. However, please note that we have all been to school and carried very heavy bags. Many people have one shoulder lower than the other does. This means you may find that one shoulder will need to be taken up more than the other is.

Step 7 - If one shoulder is lower, point this out to the person because you will have to take one side up differently from the other.

B.   Back section is higher than the front

Step 1 - Most garments are easy to alter because the front and back panels are the same, however if the back seam is wider than the front, then the back seam will have to be reshaped to the same width as the front.

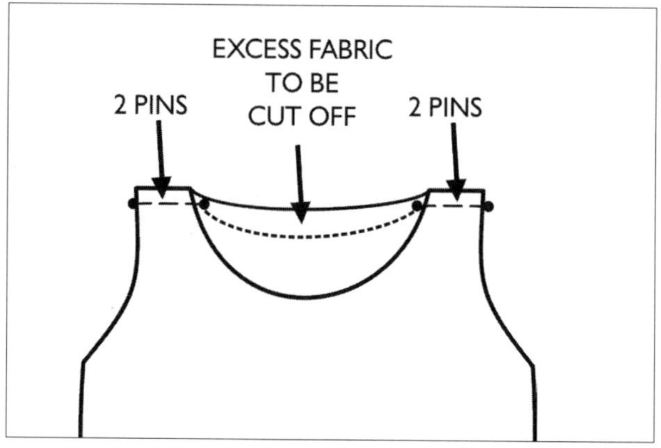

Step 2 - In a few cases, you may find that the whole back of the dress will have to be altered.

Step 3 - Write down the amount that you have pinned on the outside, centre and inside section.

Step 4 - If the garment is lined, begin by unpicking the under stitching at least 2" more on either side than the amount being taken up.

Step 5 - Turn the garment inside out and pop the shoulder through so you have access to the seams. The back section is usually bigger than the front, so I pop the shoulder through from the back section.

Important - Do not unpick the shoulder seam. Always remember that you sew your new seam first.

Step 6 - Unpick the shoulder seams where it is attached to the inside neck seam and the outside arm seam.

Step 7 - You want to unpick this section just enough to take it up the amount that you had pinned.

Step 8 - Pin the front and back panel of the outer fabric. Always have the armhole seam fitting correctly. If there is any reshaping needed, it will be the neck section.

Step 9 - Repeat this process for the lining.

Step 10 - Sew the outer and the lining, and cut excess away. Fold the seams flat.

Step 11 - Sew the side seams in the original position if possible. Reshape the neck section if necessary.

Step 12 - Iron shoulders on the right side when finished.

Step 13 - If the shoulders have bias binding on them, unpick the bias making sure you unpick under stitching or top stitching before you alter.

Step 14 - I also find that the bias should not be taken in quite as much as the shoulder.

Option 8 - Raise shoulders - With sleeves

Some dresses fit perfectly except that the neckline is too big. It may be that the dress hangs off the shoulder, or that the neckline is too low.

You can take up shoulders without taking out sleeves so long as it is not a large amount being taken out.

Step 1 - You can take up the shoulders of a dress with sleeves (without taking the sleeves out) if the amount of fabric between the neck and the sleeve is approximately 4" or 10 cm.

Step 2 - Take hold of the excess fabric in both hands and see if this raises the neckline enough.

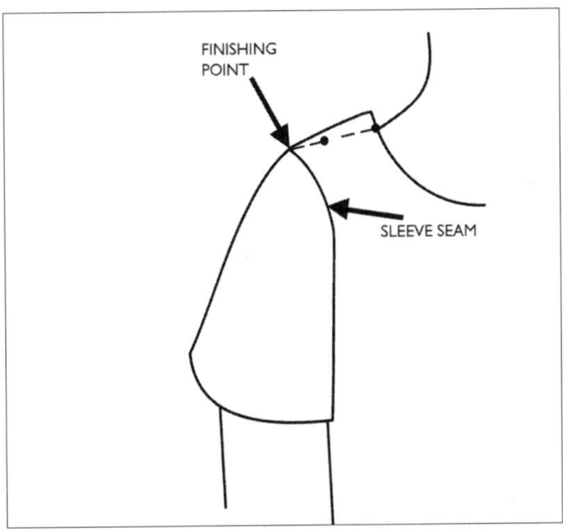

Step 3 - Place a pin on the neck edge with the pin facing towards the sleeve.

Step 4 - Place another pin about 1 ½" or 4 cm from the sleeve at the very edge of the seam fold where the shoulder joins the sleeve.

Step 5 - Fill in the gap with pins tapering from the neckline to the sleeve.

Step 6 - You can not take a lot of fabric from the neck edge (no more than 1") as the taper will be too drastic and cause the shoulder to pucker.

Step 7 - You might like to consider placing a bra strap holder on the top center seam.

You can make one out of tape with one press-stud on the garment and the other half of the press-stud on the tape.

Hook the bra strap through and secure by closing press-stud.

Step 8 - Draw a picture of the shoulder, and write down the measurement at the neck area.

Step 9 - Unpick any under stitching on the facing or lining.

Step 10 - Always undo the seam that attached the facing or lining to the body of the garment. If you try to cut corners and do not undo this seam, then you will find that you can not re-shape properly.

Step 11 - Turn the garment inside out and place a dot at the neck section the amount that you had the garment pinned.

Step 12 - Sew from the neck to the shoulder, making sure it is a straight line.

Step 13 - Sew the facing or lining the same amount as you sew the outer.

Step 14 - Over lock away the excess and sew the facing or lining back to the outer fabric.

Option 9 - Excess fabric around waist & chest area

If a person tries on a garment and the fabric is bunching up at the shoulders, you need to first determine that the garment is not too tight over the hips.

If the garment is too tight over the hips, it will push the fabric up towards the shoulders, causing it to bunch. The garment will also twist at the hip area.

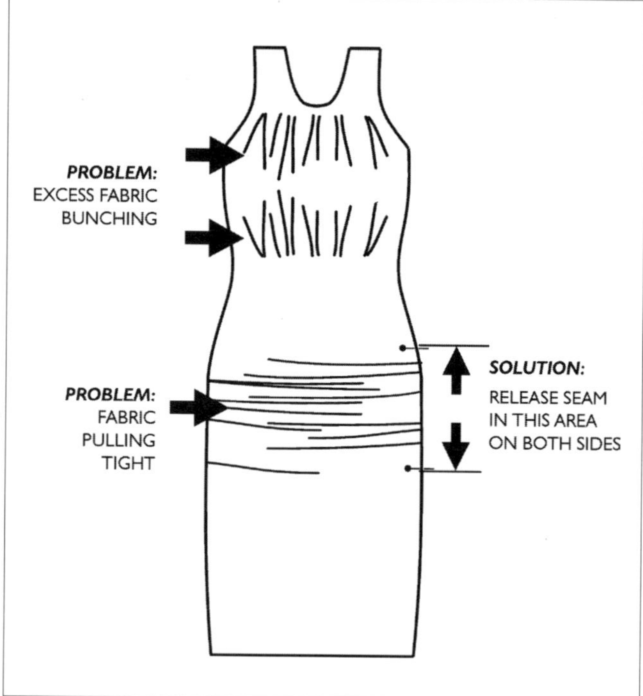

By this, I mean you will notice that the centre back seam or zip (if there is one) will be twisted.

Most women do not consider the garment is too tight at the hips when it is bunching at the shoulders.

Usually they will come in and say that the dress needs taking up at the shoulders.

I always get them to try the garment on so I can check that it is not too tight on the hips.

If the dress is tight over the hips, I will show the person what I mean by grabbing hold of the fabric around the tight area, and try to pull it down a little over the hips. I only do this if I do not think it will damage the seams.

Another method is to undo the zip (particularly over the hip area) and see if the dress falls into place.

The person will see that it stops bunching at the shoulders because the fabric DROPS over the hip.

If you are going to release the hip area proceed as follows -

Step 1 - Place a pin at the beginning of the tightness.

Step 2 - Place a second pin at the end of the tightness.

Step 3 - When you are preparing the garment, measure from under the arm, to the first pin, and put this measurement down on a piece of paper. Take the pin out.

Step 4 - Measure from the underarm to the second pin, and put this measurement down on a piece of paper. Take pin out.

Step 5 - Turn the garment inside out and place a line with a tailors pencil at the first pin measurement. The reason I use a line instead of a dot, is that dots are for taking in, and lines are for releasing seams.

Step 6 - Place a second line at the second measurement. Repeat on the opposite side.

Step 7 - Begin sewing at least 2" above where the first line is, so that by the time you get to the line, you are at the edge of the over locking.

Step 8 - Sew down the side of the garment at the edge of the over locking until you come to the second line. At this point, begin to sew back in to the seam. Taper gently so the seam does not stick out.

Option 10 - Breast enlargement cups

There are so many brilliant products to buy.

If you buy yourself a low cut dress or gown, and you need to enlarge your breast a little.

I would recommend the new oil based breast enlargement cups.

They are very natural looking, and can be sewn into the dress easily by hand.

They sell for around A$35.00 and are well worth it.

Put the dress on, and insert the cups under the breast.

Pin on the very edge of the cup at the top.

You will need to adjust the cup to your comfort.

Hand stitch bra in to garment.

Without cups

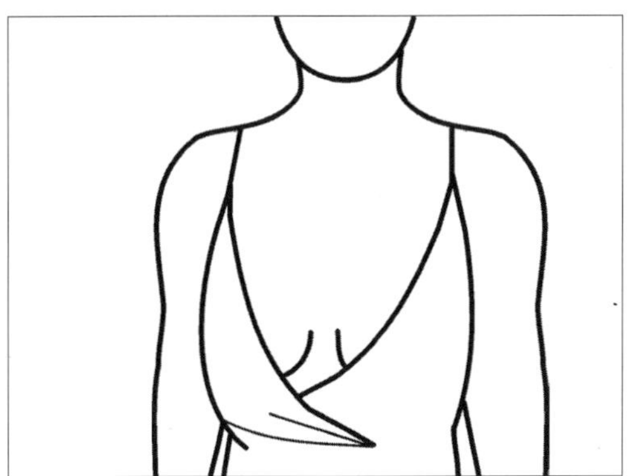

With cups

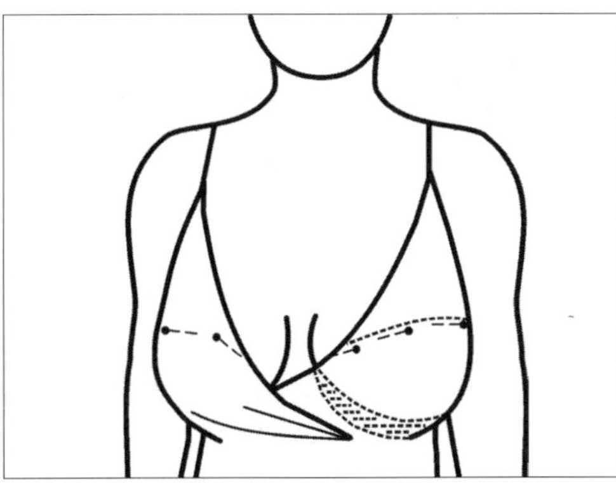

Skirts

Introduction

When you are taking up the hem on a skirt, measure from the top of the band to the new Finished Length. (F.L.)

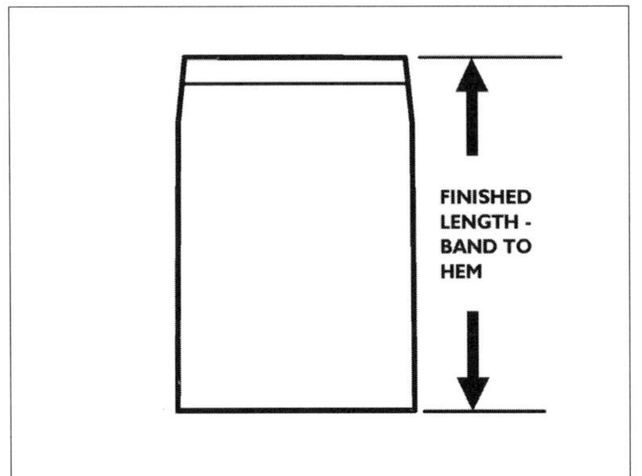

Taking up the hem on a skirt has been covered in Dresses and Gowns.

I am going to cover taking up from waist, taking in sides, taking in sides with a zip, and how to make a skirt bigger at the waist.

Take up from waist

Some skirts should be shortened from the waist. Here are a number of reasons why -

1. There is a border around the bottom of the skirt.

2. The skirt has a rolled hem and you don't have an over locker to put a new rolled hem.

3. The skirt is knitted and the knit finishes at the bottom of the skirt. If this type of skirt is shortened from the bottom the hem will not look like it is now.

Keep in mind that I am talking about a real knitted skirt and not stretch fabric. This type of skirt has been knitted on a knitting machine.

4. The person has put on weight and wants to lift the skirt at the waist. The hip area is usually wider than the waist, by raising the skirt at the waist you will have a more comfortable skirt at the waist.

Step 1 - Have the person stand in front of a full length mirror.

Step 2 - Roll the band over once, also rolling the sides and back the same amount.

Step 3 - Try to have it firm rather than loose when you are rolling so you are rolling the elastic width each time.

Step 4 - Continue to roll the band until the person is happy with the length.

Step 5 - Place two pins in a cross at the front over the folded waist.

Step 6 - Ask the person to be very careful getting out of the skirt.

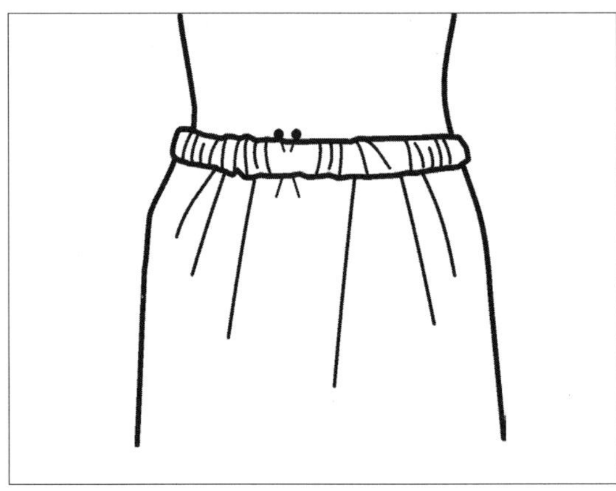

Step 7 - Measure the amount from the top of the waistband to the pin, and write this measurement down on a piece of paper.

Step 8 - Place a pin on the fold at the top and take the crossed pins out.

Step 9 - If the skirt is lined, I always mark down from the top the amount that the skirt is being taken up, then go back up for the hem allowance. You are working in reverse to a normal hem.

Step 10 - After you have marked the hem, sew a row of stitching around the waist on the inside edge of the top chalk mark. The top chalk mark is your cut line, so you want to make sure that the lining and the outer fabric stay in the same position, so you want to sew them together to hold them in place.

Step 11 - Over lock the edge of the new cut line.

Step 12 - If you are going to use the existing elastic, then you need to unpick the elastic.

If you are going to use new elastic, then you need to put the elastic around the persons waist to get the correct length.

Step 13 - Elastic always stretches by up to 2" depending on the type of elastic.

Always allow 1" minimum of stretch.

Before you cut the elastic, check it against the skirt.

I find that many people want their elastic too loose, and some times you will find that the amount they say is a lot more than the elastic in the skirt.

Step 14 - Pin the elastic at the four points, front, back and the two sides.

Step 15 - Sew the elastic on to the over locking, sewing through the centre of the over locking.

Step 16 - I then have two options for finishing:-

a. Fold the band over and stitch all the way around through the lining and the outer.

b. Fold the band down and sew on to the lining only.

Take in sides

If a skirt is too big, the obvious place to take it in is at the sides.

Step 1 - Have the person stand in front of a full length mirror.

Step 2 - Stand behind the person.

Step 3 - Take a section of fabric between your fingers on either side of the skirt.

Step 4 - This could be the band or if it has no band it will be the top of the skirt on either side.

Step 5 - If it is 1" or 2.5 cm make sure you have the same amount on the opposite side. If you take more from one side than the other, the skirt will not be correct.

Step 6 - Place a pin into the top of the skirt on each side with the pin facing down.

Step 7 - Ask the person if this feels secure.

Step 8 - Place a second pin beneath the first on either side.

Step 9 - Once you have the amount at the band correct, I usually kneel in front of the person and pin down one side with a few pins, then I ask the person to turn and face the opposite direction, so I can pin the opposite side.

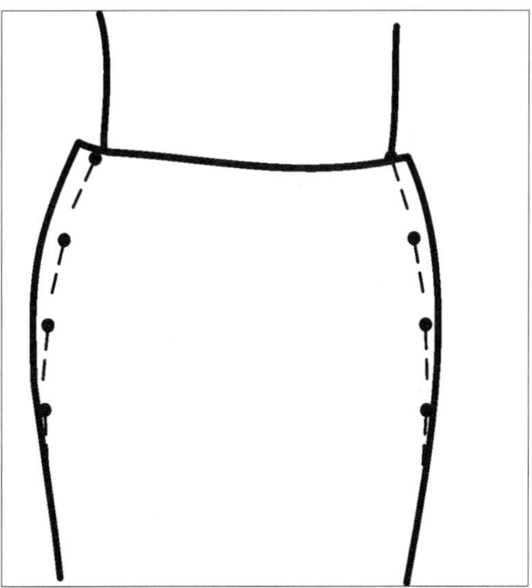

Step 10 - Continue pinning down the side over the hips with the pins following one after the other, pinning first one side then the other.

Step 11 - I have the person moving back and forward, so that I can stay on my knees in front of her.

Step 12 - If you are only pinning at the waist, and down say 5" or 13 cm. Make sure you taper off properly. Pin as if you are sewing the side seam.

Step 13 - If you are pinning through to the hem I would suggest you pin both sides the same all the way to the hem.

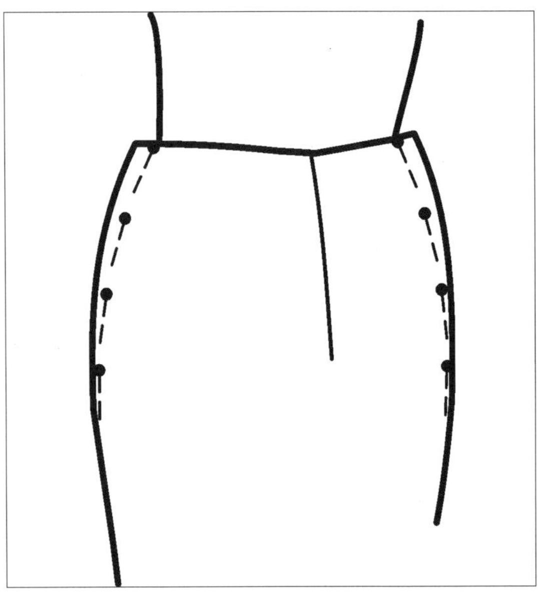

Turn the person back and forth, so you pin both sides the same.

Step 14 - Ask the person to try sitting in a chair.

Step 15 - Make sure that it is not too tight over the hip area.

Step 16 - Once you are past the thighs, you can space the pins further apart.

Step 17 - Use the "Technique for Taking In".

The sides of a skirt are the same as the sides of a pair of pants. Some skirts have bands and some have facings, and others are lined. Always keep in mind that when you are preparing something for sewing, you are working backwards from the last seam that was sewn.

Step 18 - If you are sewing through to the hem, always undo the hem enough so that you can sew through the hem. If the skirt is tapering in then you must make sure that the hem will taper out so that the hem will fit up and into the skirt.

Step 19 - After you have sewn the new seam, and over locked the excess off, iron the seam flat. I always have the seam facing towards the back.

Take in sides – with zip one side

If you have a zip on one side, pin as per the above for Take in sides however instead of having the seam in the centre you will have the zip in the centre.

Once the person is happy with the amount taken in the sides, you need to allow her to get out of the skirt by undoing the zipped side.

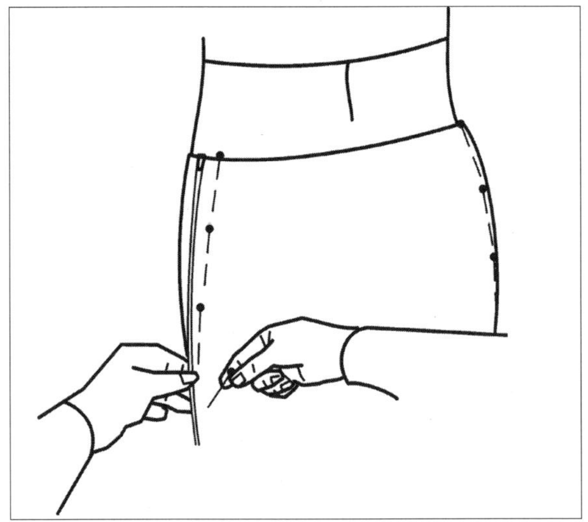

You do not want to loose the pin measurements, so you are going to release the person from the zipped garment by placing pins over the top of the existing pins.

Step 1 - Place a pin over the top of the original pin on the right hand side. Place this new pin so that it only pins one side of the skirt.

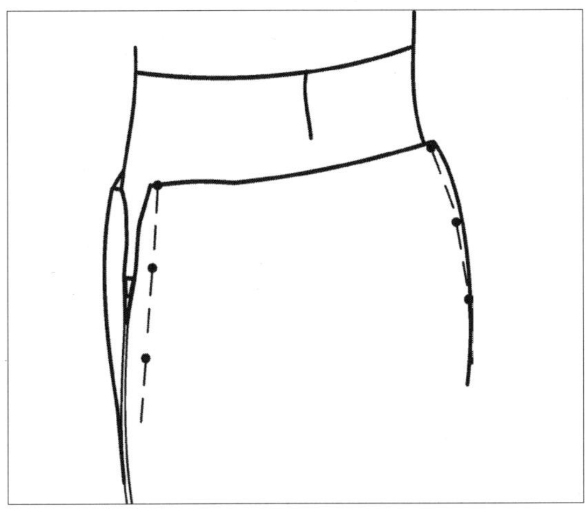

Step 2 - Continue doing this all the way down to the bottom of the zip.

Step 3 - You should be able to slide the pins out that you put in originally, thereby freeing the person to undo the zip.

Step 4 - The pins should be down one side of the zip area only.

Step 5 - All pins below the zip area should be left where they are.

Prepare the skirt with a zip in side as per "Technique for Taking In".

The only difference from the above Taking in sides of skirts is that you have the zip.

The zip must be unpicked and re inserted to the new measurement. I prefer to put an invisible zip back in but this would be your preference.

Step 1 - For the zip side place your dots on the right side of the fabric at the top of the zip, marking in on both sides of the opening. For example if you were taking in the top at 1", then place a dot at the position 1" to right on the right hand side and 1" to the left on the left hand side.

Step 2 - Place your dots all the way down on the outside of the skirt until you get to the end of the zip section.

Step 3 - Turn the garment inside out and place a dot on the wrong side of the garment next to the end of the zip.

Step 4 - When you have finished placing your dots, begin to sew, starting from the bottom of the zip following your dots to the finish.

Step 5 - Now unpick the original seam next to the new seam you have just sewn.

Step 6 - Place the garment over your ironing board (inside out), and iron the new zip section back at your dots.

Step 7 - Cut or over lock the excess fabric off, I leave about 5/8" for my seam allowance.

Step 8 - Insert your invisible zip. I use my ordinary zipper foot, with the needle moved across into a position next to the zip itself. I use my fingernails to pull the zip back so that I can sew next to the zipper. You must not sew ON THE ZIP. If you do then the zip will not work. If you do find that you catch the zip itself, then unpick and redo. Practice makes perfect.

Step 9 - Whether there is lining or facing, you should attach these to the side of the zipper using your sewing machine. Some people hand stitch the facing or lining. Get used to using your sewing machine because this is the professional way of completing alterations.

Step 10 - If you sew the lining or facing on to the edge of the zipper (right sides together) you will notice that, the lining or facing is smaller than the outer. This is correct, because when you fold the two back, you will notice that they sit flat. Then you can sew across the top where the original seam was.

Step 11 - The side without the zip, should be prepared from the inside. Unpick the top section, making sure to unpick any under stitching or top stitching before the seam that joins the outer fabric to the band or facing or lining.

Step 12 - Place your dots and sew as per "Technique for Taking in" pages 47 - 62.

Skirt too tight - Release pleats or darts at waist

Do you have a skirt in your wardrobe that has shrunk around the waist?

Well, maybe it's not the skirt that has shrunk, but the thing is that the skirt may belong to a suit. The jacket fits you great, but the skirt is just a little too tight.

There may be a way to extend the band and the area just below the band.

This will work if you only need the waist extended. It may not work if you need more at the hip or thigh area.

Step 1 - Measure the person's waist. Write this measurement down on a piece of paper. (Make sure they are not holding their breath)

Step 2 - Measure the skirt around the waistband. Make sure you close the zip first.

Step 3 - Place the beginning of your tape measure on the edge of the band.

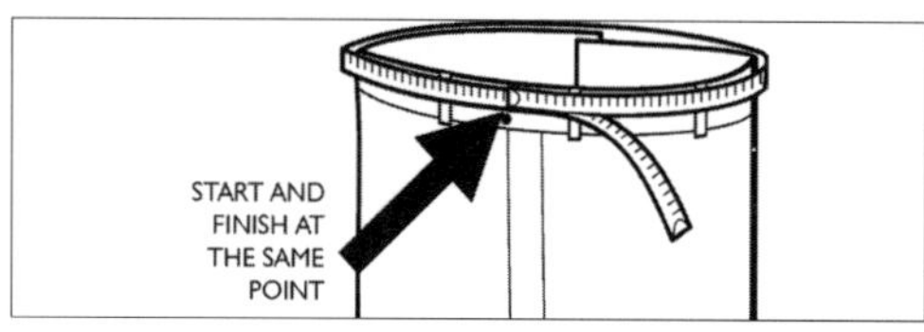

Step 4 - Carefully measure around the band until you come back to where you started.

Step 5 - Work out the difference between the person's waist measurement and the measurement around the skirts.

Step 6 - This will allow you to determine how much is needed to be let out at the pleats.

Step 7 - You now need to work out if there is enough fabric in the darts or pleats to extend the waist for the person.

Step 8 - Poke the tape measure into a pleat and measure the amount of the pleat.

You must make sure you push the tape measure up hard against the inside seam.

Let us say that the measurement is ½" or 1 cm. You now know you have 1" or 2 cm in total, because the fabric is doubled.

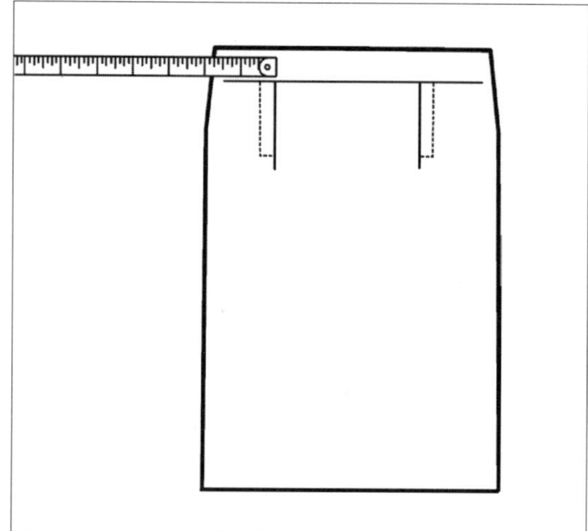

Step 9 - If you have two pleats, then you know that you have 2" or 4 cm excess fabric in the band because you have two pleats (one on each side), if you have four pleats then you can work out how much is there and use the amount you need.

Step 10 - If the skirt has darts, then measure the amount of the dart at the top next to the band. Again, because the fabric is doubled over, you will double the amount. Most skirts have four darts in the garment.

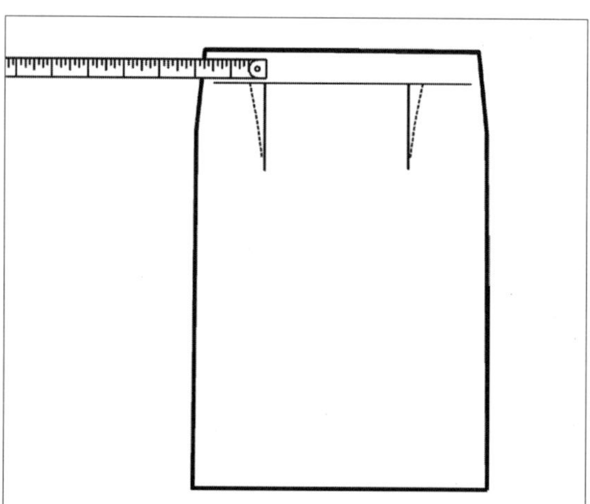

Step 11 - Work out how much you need to release at the band.

Step 12 - Take the band off beginning at the
button (not the buttonhole end) and unpick up to
the pleat next to the buttonhole.

Do not take the band off completely.

Step 13 - Release the pleats the amount needed,
and put the band back on.

Note:- pin the band back on beginning from the
button hole end which will mean you sew into
the original fold in the band starting from the
button end.

By sewing into the fold of the band, you are
guaranteeing that the band will look exactly the
way it was before you unpicked it.

Step 14 - Sew an extension onto the end of the
band and complete.

I usually look for fabric that is close to the
colour, rather than looking for the same type of
fabric.

For example I might find a linen fabric that is
the same fabric match, yet the fabric of the skirt
is cotton.

Step 15 - You can also find fabric within the
garment. For example if the skirt has a big hem,
you could cut the hem off and put a false hem
on, and use that fabric.

Step 16 - If the garment has pockets, you could
take out one pocket and use that.

Make sure you cut the fabric out the same as the
original. Some bands are cut on the bias and
some are on the straight of the grain.

Conclusion

I have tried to cover all areas of Dresses, Gowns and Skirts, however there are so many different garment styles, that I cannot provide you with it all.

The areas I have provided you with cover about 90% of the clothing alteration work I did in my shop.

If you come across a difficult alteration, I would suggest you remember what I said about working backwards.

If you are learning something for the first time, unpick one side whilst using the opposite side as a guide. Once you have one side done, unpick the second side and follow the procedure for the first.

Jackets

Taking Up

"Did you know there is a perfect jacket length for your body?"

Introduction

Jackets can be expensive garments to buy, so when they are altered, you want to know that you are getting the alteration length accurate.

If the sleeve is being shortened, take the measurement from the underarm seam to the new finished length at the end of the sleeve.

This is called the Inside Arm (I.A.)

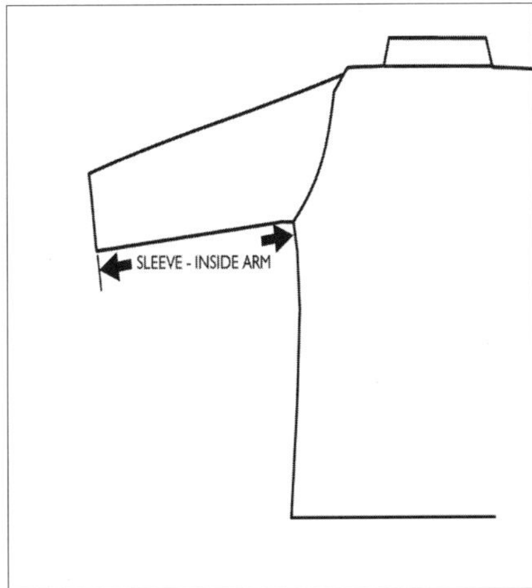

If the length of the jacket is being shortened, then you need to measure from the underarm seam to the new finished length of the hem.

This is also called the Inside Arm (I.A.)

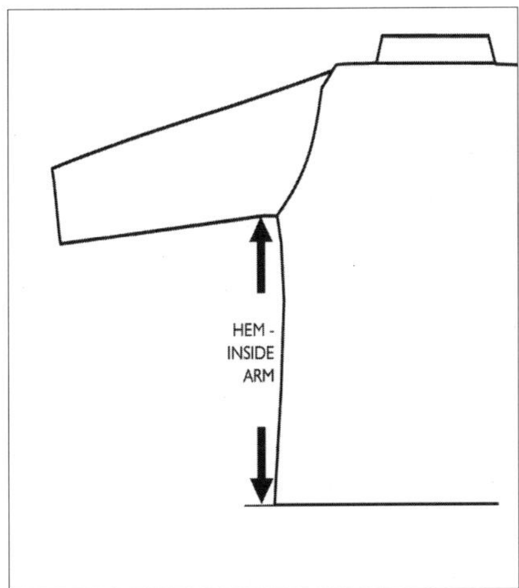

Whilst these are both called the Inside Arm (I.A.) they are both different reference points.

This is why it is important to draw an outline of what it is you are altering.

Differences between ladies and men's jackets

If you are going to do the alteration to the jacket yourself, you need to know that the construction on the shoulders of a ladies jacket is different to the construction on the shoulders of a man's jacket.

Ladies jackets

Ladies jackets have an opening in the lining in one of the sleeves. Usually it is the left sleeve, however occasionally it will be the right. By unpicking the closed seam you have instant access to the inside of the sleeve and the shoulder.

If I am working on the back or shoulders, I will unpick the seam in the inside lining, and I will pop the jacket completely through this opening.

Men's jackets - tailor made

If the men's jacket is tailor made then you will find that the lining is hand stitched around the shoulder which means no access to the shoulder without unpicking the hand stitching.

If you do unpick the shoulder then you do have the option of machine stitching the shoulder closed. It just depends on whether you or whoever you are altering the jacket for really want the original hand stitching.

I have come across men's jackets that have a label inside that says "Hand stitched" and the only hand stitching is the lining at the shoulder.

These jackets tend to have horse hair or webbing to create a structured shoulder.

Men's jackets – not tailor made.

These jackets are not hand stitched at the shoulder. You can check by just taking hold of the fabric at the shoulder and seeing if you can separate the lining from the outer fabric.

These jackets should be treated the same as the ladies jackets for alteration, although they may have more padding or wadding in the shoulder than a ladies jacket.

Hem Length

The length that a person wears a jacket is dependent on their height and shape. Whether you are a short height, average height or tall, the length that you should wear your jacket will be in proportion to your height.

Have you ever purchased a jacket only to find that you seem to be swimming in it?

Everyone has a perfect length that is proportional to his or her body type.

Fashions can change this theory, because some jackets are designed long, and are therefore intended to be worn long.

There are also some jackets that are designed with a short length, and they are intended by the designer to be worn short.

What we are looking at here is the normal styled jacket such as a suit jacket.

To work out what a persons perfect length is you need to -

Step 1 - Have the person stand facing a full-length mirror.

Step 2 - Ask them to drop their right arm down against their side.

Step 3 - Ask the person to raise their thumb so it is parallel with their wrist.

Step 4 - This is the recommended length of a jacket for your body.

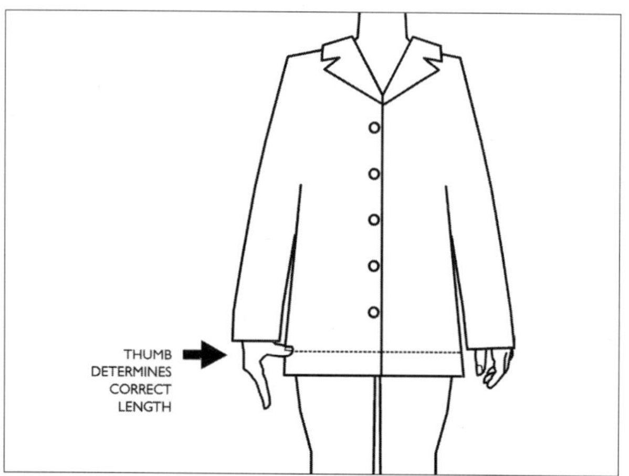

Step 5 - Fold the jacket up to this length and place a double pin in at this point.

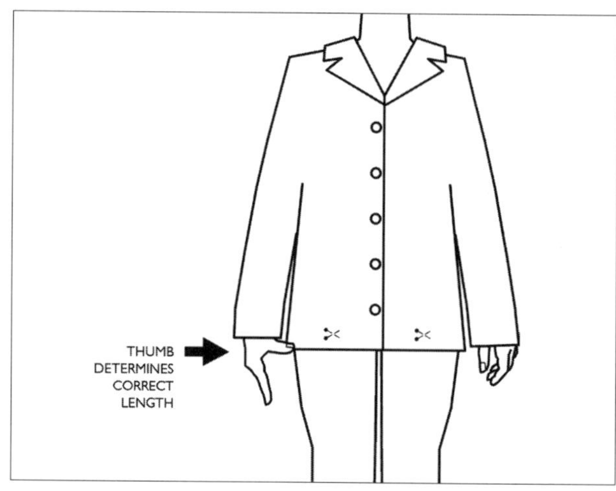

Step 6 - Check to see that the jacket is straight on the person. Because some women have big busts, it may be that the front of the jacket will sit higher than the back.

Step 7 - If you want to straighten the jacket hem, ask the person to stand with their spine straight.

You will need to find out what the reference point is from the floor. Place your tape measure on the floor, and measure up to the new hem fold under the crossed pins.

Step 8 - Move around to the back and measure from the floor up the same amount as the front.

Place a pin at the measurement, and then fold this amount up.

Step 9 - Do the same at the two side seams. Place double cross pins at these points.

Step 10 - Ask the person to stand side on to the mirror to see that it is straight all the way around.

Step 11 - Prepare the jacket as per Taking Up Technique pages 32- 36. I will explain how to prepare and sew for an unlined jacket and then a lined jacket.

Hem - Unlined Jacket

The hem on an unlined jacket is similar to the hem on a pair of pants.

Usually the hem has been over locked, then machine stitched or it has a blind hem.

The only difference is that you have a front section that is separate and sometimes you may have splits in the back or sides.

The facing, which is the fabric underneath the outer fabric down the front of the jacket, will have been under stitched.

Step 1 - Unpick the under stitching to at least 4" higher than the amount you are taking up.

If there is a buttonhole then you can only go as high as the buttonhole.

Step 2 - Mark the new hem length on the right side of the fabric and come down the amount of hem allowance you wish to have, and place another chalk mark beside the measurement of the hem allowance.

Refer to Technique for Taking up to see how to mark for a hem.

Step 3 - Usually I copy what is on the garment; however, some manufacturers put a tiny hem allowance, which I do not agree with.

Special note: Some manufacturers will have the hem faced. This is a separate piece of fabric that is sewn on to the bottom of the jacket, and it is then turned back for a hem.

If this is the case, you can unpick this facing and re attach it or take it off all together. I would personally re attach the facing, because it can make the hem sit correctly.

Step 4 - Cut on the cut line, which is the bottom of the hem allowance.

Step 5 - Over lock the edge of the hem, or sew ribbon on to the edge as per Dress pant hems.

Step 6 - Turn the jacket inside out, and lay over the ironing board. Iron up the hem and pin into place.

Step 7 - If the hem does not fit properly, then take the side seams in or out depending on what is required.   Refer to pants hems for instructions on how to do this.

Step 8 - Make sure that the fronts line up properly. Do the buttons up to make sure that they match at the bottom.

Step 9 - Bag the corners. Bagging the corners means that you turn the section back on to itself. Right sides together, and iron marks together.

Step 10 - Use tweezers or a point turner to create a sharp point.

Step 11 - Iron the corners, and place a pin through the facing and the hem.

Step 12 - Sew this section together with the machine.

You must hold the outer fabric away so that you do not catch it as you sew. This will support the hem and ensure it never falls down. If you are unsure, look at the original way it was sewn.

Step 13 - Hand stitch the hem or machine stitch depending on your needs.

Hem - Lined Jacket

To get into women's lined jackets, you will find a seam that has been closed inside one of the sleeves in the lining.

For men's jackets, you will have to make an opening in the lining in the body of the garment, because the sleeves will be closed at the top of the sleeve.

Occasionally, you will come across a jacket for men that is made in the same way a woman's jacket is.

Step 1 - Unpick the inside arm seam of the lining.

Step 2 - Pop the whole jacket out through the opening. When you first do this, you may feel a little strange, but get into the habit of altering from the inside. It is quicker and easier.

Step 3 - Most jackets are straight across. If not then refer to the next section on Lined Jackets - Curved for making templates of the curve.

Step 4 - The hem will be attached to each seam. Unpick the hem from the attached seam.

Step 5 - The front will be attached to the seam at the end of the facing. If the lining looks like it doesn't fit properly, then the alteration will be a little more complicated. I will deal with a jacket that when you have unpicked the hem from the seam, the whole section drops down. If this is the case, it is a simple process to take up the hem.

Step 6 - Mark the amount that you are going up on the fabric (not lining) side at each seam. The amount you are coming down is the exact same hem allowance that is on the jacket now. That is the amount from the fold of the hem to the edge of the fabric.

Step 7 - You will be measuring from the fold line (original hem) up to the new hem length. Mark all the way around the jacket, marking at seams and in between.

Step 8 - Lay the jacket on the ironing board, and iron the jacket flat.

Step 9 - Iron interfacing on to the hem allowance placing the interfacing in between each seam. The interfacing should be between the cut line and the new fold line. Not above the fold line.

Step 10 - Bag the two front sections together. When you ironed up the hem allowance, you will have made sure the two fronts are even.

Bag the right side front, then the left side front, and check to see they are even.

Step 11 - Pin the side facing to the outer fabric on the hem on each front section.

Step 12 - Pin the lining to the outer fabric. I do a 1/2" hem allowance.

Step 13 - For the rest of the jacket, sew just above the bottom chalk mark. This means you sew from the edge of the facing to the opposite facing.

Step 14 - Cut off the excess fabric on the cut line.

Step 15 - Iron the hem up by having the garment with the inside facing you, and iron up the hem allowance. I use the end of the ironing board.

Step 16 - Fold the hem allowance over to the lining and iron into place.

Step 17 - Do this all the way around the jacket hem.

Step 18 - Attach the hem to the seams at each section.

Step 19 - Pop the jacket out through the opening in the sleeve.

Step 20 - Re-iron the hem and if you marked correctly, the hem should be straight.

Step 21 - Close the opening in the sleeve.

Hem - Lined Jacket - Curved

With a curved hem, you need to make a template. Lay a piece of light cardboard under one side of the jacket under the curve. Trace with a pencil or pen around the curve and down along the hem line until the end of the facing. Cut out your template along the pencil or pen line.

Preparing the Jacket

Step 1 - Mark up the amount folded under and down the hem allowance on the right side of the garment BEFORE you pop it through the sleeve.

Step 2 - Mark the lining at the same time. The lining will be up the amount that you wish to shorten the jacket, but come down only 5/8".

Step 3 - Place the template of the curve over the inside of the garment and mark out the new curve. Then mark down 1/2" around the bottom of this curve.

Step 4 - Cut the hem on the bottom cut line, and cut the lining on the bottom cut line. The curve will be cut on the bottom line. At the end of the facing you will have to drop down to the hem line. This will be a vertical line down to the hem line.

Step 5 - You should still open the seam in the sleeve, because this is how you will get the jacket in the right way when you have finished the hem.

Step 6 - Have the garment inside out so you can lay the garment over the ironing board and iron up the hem allowance. For lighter fabrics and wool, cut some interfacing (1/2" more than the hem allowance) and iron on the bottom of the jacket on the inside. DO NOT IRON OVER SEAMS. Cut the facing so it fits under each seam section. Make sure the two fronts are the same length. (Do up a button to check it is straight)

Step 7 - Make sure that the under stitching is un-

picked enough that you can begin sewing from the first seam that joins the facing to the outer curved section.

Step 8 - Sew the curve on each side, but stop at the stitch line just before the lining. Cut away the excess fabric.

Step 9 - Clip the seam so that the fabric will open as it curves. Note - When ever a seam is curved, you should cut excess seam allowance so that it is about 1/8" or 1/4" only, and clip from the edge to the stitching - stopping just before the stitching. Do this every 1" or so around sharp curves. Your garment will sit flat.

Step 10 - Re sew the under stitching when you have the curve the same on both sides.

Step 11 - Pin the lining to the outer making sure to line up the seams.

Step 12 - Sew the lining to the body, but leave the last 5" either side of the facing open.

Step 13 - I usually re-iron the curve and the hem to make sure it is sitting flat.

Step 14 - Attach the edge of the facing to the hem.

Step 15 - Sew the rest of the lining to the hem of the outer.

Step 16 - At the edge, fold the lining over and sew to the facing seam.

Step 17 - Attach the hem to the back side seams and centre back seam if there is one.

Step 18 - Pop the jacket back through the opening in the sleeve.

Step 19 - Close the opening in the seam by stitching it together.

Sleeves – Without Cuffs

When the sleeves are too long on a jacket, it can make the whole jacket look too big on you.

Often I have people come in and say the jacket is too big, but after I pin up the sleeves, they are happy with the jacket.

I have two lengths that I pin my customer's jacket sleeves.

The first length is for people who work in their jackets.

The second is for people who wear their jackets out on social occasions.

Jacket sleeves for working in

Step 1 - Ask person to stand facing the mirror.

Step 2 - Stand just behind the person but on their right hand side.

Step 3 - Fold the fabric up and into the sleeve of the jacket.

Step 4 - Place the new fold so that it is approximately in the middle between the top of the thumb and the wrist.

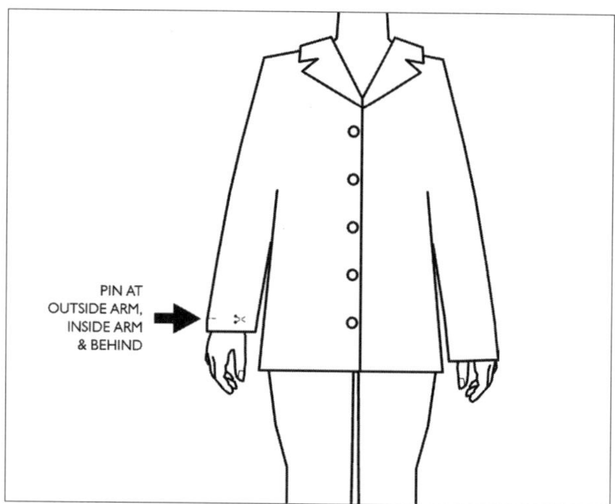

Step 5 - Move your fingers in side the sleeve and feel the amount you have folded up.

Step 6 - Place a pin on the opposite side; this will hold the fabric up.

Step 7 - Move across to the outside of the hand and fold this same amount up.

NOTE: Men's jackets slope to the outside of the hand and will continue to do this after they are altered.

Step 8 - Explain to the person that you are going to get them to raise their arm to see if it is the correct length Show the person what you mean.

Step 9 - As you raise your arm, say that you want them to raise their arm, with the elbow locked in.

Step 10 - Explain that you want them to raise it so that it is not quite level with their shoulder. Help them to do this.

Step 11 - Explain this is where the sleeve should sit from a TAILORING point of view.

Step 12 - The jacket sleeve should sit just behind the knuckle.

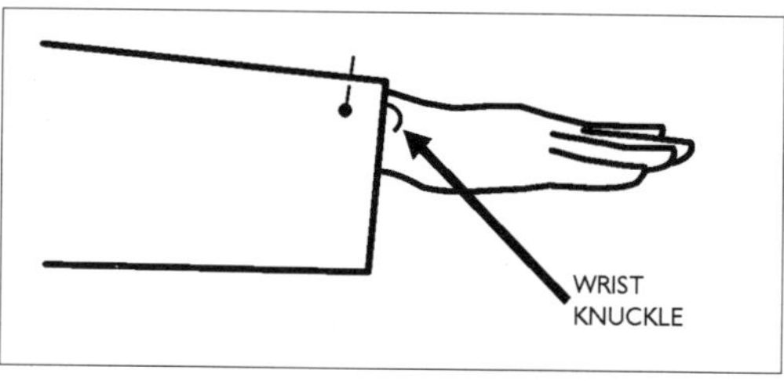

Step 13 - The only reason it will not do this is if the jacket pulls at the underarm.

Step 14 - The second way of checking is to place your left hand on the inside of their elbow, and your right hand under the small of the arm.

Step 15 - Bend the elbow so that it is laying next to their waist.

Step 16 - The jacket sleeve should sit across the wrist.

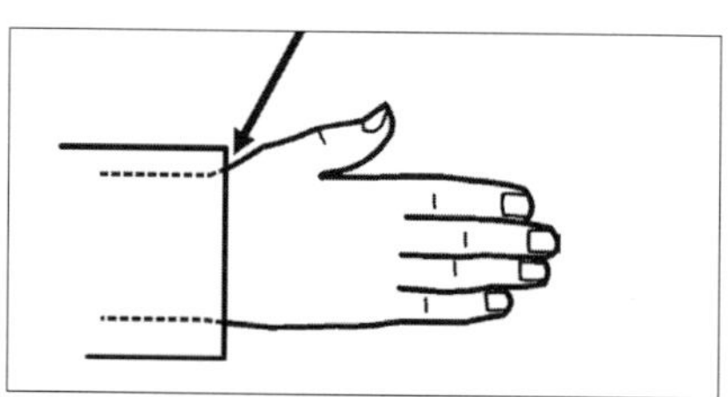

Ask the person if they are happy with length.

Jacket sleeves a little longer - social

The second length is for a person who will be wearing the jacket at social occasions rather than at work. Make the sleeves a little bit longer.

Fold the excess under and have the fold just on the first knuckle of the thumb.

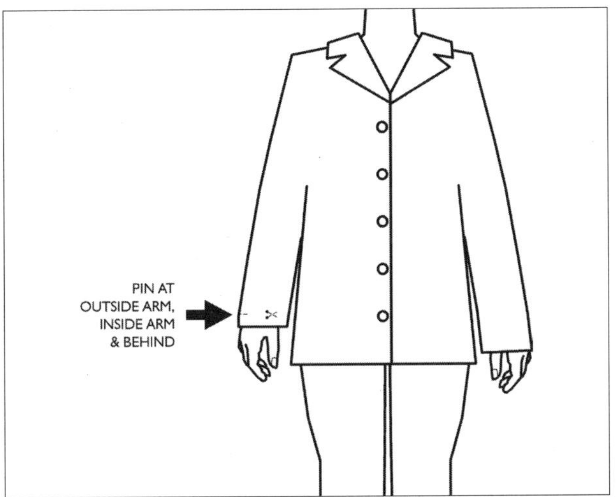

When you ask the person to raise their arm with their elbow locked, the sleeve should just cover the wrist knuckle bone.

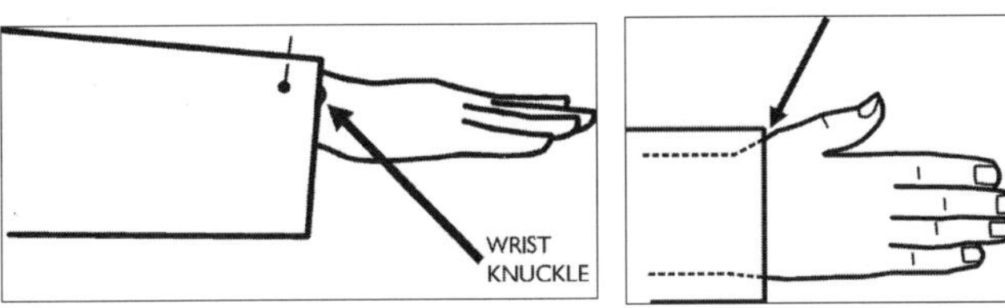

If the person bends their elbow and places their arm against their waist then the sleeve should be just on the knuckle of the thumb.

This illustration shows how to correct sleeves if persons arms are different lengths. Measure from the thumb to the new length on boths arms.

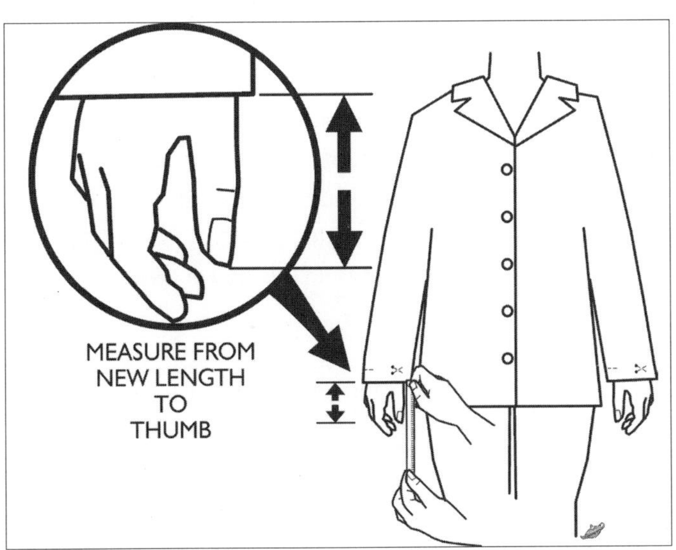

Preparing - Lined Jacket Sleeves

Step 1 - Write down the amount that you have folded under at the crossed pin. Measure the inside arm (I.A.) from the underarm to the new fold line. Make sure you are measuring the inside arm and not the outside arm. Write this measurement down.

Step 2 - Take out the pins.

Step 3 - Check both arms are the same length.

Step 4 - Check that the lining is the correct length.

Step 5 - Some linings can be too long, and an adjustment may need to be made.

Step 6 - Take any buttons off the sleeve.

Step 7 - Buttons must be unpicked from the back of the garment.

Step 8 - The reason for this is so that no one accidentally cuts the fabric on the outside.

Step 9 - Put the buttons into a little plastic bag for safe keeping.

For ladies – unpick seam on the lining on the inside arm .

Pull bottom section of sleeve through the opening.

Put your arm in to the inside of the jacket and pull the opposite sleeve through the opening.

For men's – unpick the inside arm of the lining on both sleeves and pull the bottom section of the sleeve through each opening.

Step 10 - The hem allowance will be attached to the side seams. Unpick the hem from these seams.

Step 11 - Unpick the lining from the outer fabric.

The fold line is the original hem line.

Step 12 - Place the tape measure with the amount going up at the fold line. For example, let us say the amount going up is 1". Then you place the tape section of 1" on the fold line.

Step 13 - Place a chalk mark at the top of the tape measure. Refer to Technique for Taking Up to see technique.

Step 14 - You now need to measure the hem allowance.

Whatever the hem allowance is, this is the amount you must move down the tape and mark

For example if the hem allowance is 1 ½" then come down 1 ½"" and place another chalk mark. This is your cut line.

Step 15 - Measure the lining up the same. Place the tape measure on the original seam. You should have the 1" on the original seam.

Step 16 - Place a chalk mark on the side of the end of the tape.

Step 17 - Place another chalk mark down the hem allowance.

Most linings only have a ½" hem allowance.

Even if it does not have a ½" hem allowance, make it so.

Step 18 - Cut the sleeve the same way you would cut any hem.

Step 19 - Place a nick in the side on the cut line and cut all the way around.

Step 20 - Cut the lining the same.

Once you are confident in cutting jacket sleeves, the lining can be cut quicker by just marking up 1" from the EDGE of the lining not from the seam line, or whatever the amount is that the jacket is going up.

Sewing – Lined Jacket Sleeves

Some sleeves have a split, but when the jacket is shortened, the split will not be able to be put back on. The reason for this is that the fabric used to make the split is only at the split section.

There is no fabric further up the sleeve to redo the split, so what many people do is close the split and put any buttons that are on the jacket back on.

If you have to close the split please make sure that you sew down the fold line on the sleeve.

Measure to see that the width of the sleeves is the same. By this I mean that when you close the split, you need to make sure that you have the same width on each sleeve at the bottom.

Also, check to see if you need to open side seams. See how in Pant Hems.

Step 1 - Close splits if there are splits.

I use a tailors arm to do all my jacket sleeves. You can try to work without one, but you will find it very difficult.

Step 2 - Cut interfacing that is as wide as the hem allowance.

Step 3 - Place the tailors arm on the ironing board.

Step 4 - Insert one sleeve onto the tailors arm – inside out.

Step 5 - Iron the interfacing onto the sleeve with the edge of the interfacing on the edge of the sleeve. The interfacing should be ironed on between seams, so that later you can get at the seam. Do not iron the interfacing on over the seam.

Step 6 - Fold the hem allowance up on the tailors arm – measuring the amount you are ironing up as you go.

Step 7 - If the hem allowance is 2" then you must iron up 2" all the way around.

Be careful to have only one fold mark. Try to iron up the correct amount the first time. Some fabric creases very easily.

You will have the two sleeves pulled through the one opening in the sleeve for a ladies jacket and through each sleeve for men's.

Ladies jacket – Always do the sleeve from the opposite side first.

This will be the sleeve that DOES NOT have the opening in it.

Usually it is attached at the armhole.

If it isn't you need to make sure that you have the two armhole seams joined together Pin them to make sure.

Step 8 - Begin to sew these two together with the right sides on the inside.

Have the lining on the top so it does not pucker

Step 9 - Place a tuck in the lining if the lining is too big.

Step 10 - To lock the hem up you need to attach the seams to each other. You only need to attach one side of a seam.

Place your fingers into the hem and take hold of the seam where it is folded at the new hem length. Hold them together and sew them together. Usually I sew about 1" only.

Step 11 - If you are putting buttons back on you only need to attach the inside arm seams together, because the buttons will hold the outer seam up.

If you are not putting buttons back on then you need to do the same with the outer arm seam.

Step 12 - Push this sleeve back into the jacket so it is out of the way.

Step 13 - The last sleeve is the one with the opening in it.

Step 14 - Because the lining has been pulled through the opening there is a trick to finding the right arm hole seams.

Find the seam of the outer layer that is the same seam as the lining that has the opening in it.

Now take hold of the seam of the lining that is the seam with the opening in it.

It should be underneath the opening because it is pulled through to the other side.

Step 15 - Sew these two together as per the other sleeve.

Step 16 - Sew the seams together as per the other sleeve.

Step 17 - Pop the sleeve through.

Step 18 - Turn the sleeves inside out and iron the lining flat.

Step 19 - Close the opening.

For men's jackets proceed as per the second sleeve which is pulled through the opening.

Sleeves – With Cuffs - Not Lined

The same rules apply for the length of a jacket sleeve whether you have cuffs on the sleeve or not. However, how you pin the sleeve on a jacket with cuffs is different from pinning a jacket without cuffs.

When I pin up a normal sleeve, you will have noticed that I fold the excess fabric under, so that the person can see exactly what the length will look like when the sleeve is altered.

With a jacket with cuffs on, I like to follow the same principle. That is I like to see what the cuff will look like when the sleeve is shortened. Therefore I found a way to pin the excess fabric up without folding the cuff under.

There are two scenarios with cuffs on jacket sleeves.

Option 1. There is an opening and the cuff has a button and buttonhole or similar on the cuff. This is sewn on similar to a cuff on a shirt. It is top stitched onto the sleeve.

Option 2. There is no opening. The cuff is sewn onto the sleeve of the jacket, and the seam is visible on the inside of the jacket. Usually the seam is over locked, and sometimes the edge of the sleeve is top stitched.

Whether your jacket is Option 1 or 2, the way that the jacket sleeve is pinned is the same.

So I will begin with the pinning of the jacket, and move on to the preparing and sewing of each option.

Step 1 - Have the person facing the mirror.

Step 2 - Stand just behind the person but on their right hand side.

Step 3 - Fold fabric about 10"/25 cm above the cuff.

Step 4 - Fold up sufficient that the cuff is resting on the first knuckle of the thumb.

Step 5 - Always ensure there is a little "flounce" in the arm. This means when the person raises their arm the sleeve does not move too high up the arm.

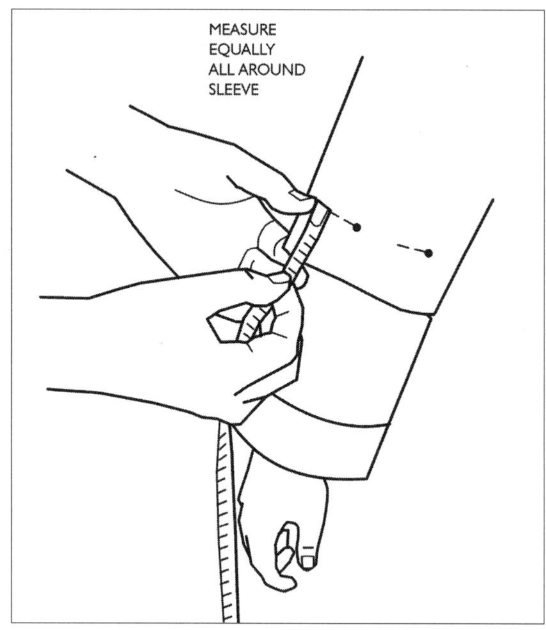

Step 6 - Place your finger nail up against the inside fabric and with your tape measure, measure the amount that you have folded as per 1st illustration.

Step 7 - Place a pin at this exact measurement. For illustration, let us say it is 1 ¼" or 3 cm.

Step 8 - Move 2" or 5cm around and follow the same procedure – fold up the same amount 1 ¼" or 3 cm.

Step 9 - Follow this procedure all the way around the arm, so that the sleeve is pinned in three places.

NOTE: Men's jackets slope to the outside of the hand and will continue to do this after they are altered.

Explain to the person that you are going to get the person to raise their arm straight out in front to see if it is the correct length (see page 174).

Step 10 - Have elbow locked.

Step 11 - Explain that the end of the sleeve should sit just behind the knuckle. Some people

like it a little longer, so for them have it resting on the knuckle.

Step 12 - Explain that this is where the sleeve should sit from a TAILORING point of view.

The only reason it will not do this is if the jacket pulls at the underarm.

Step 13 - The second way of checking is to place your left hand on the inside of their elbow, and your right hand under the small of the arm. (see Jacket - Take up sleeves)

Step 14 - Bend the elbow.

Step 15 - The jacket sleeve should sit across the wrist.

Step 16 - Ask the person if they are happy with the length.

This illustration shows the sleeves pinned a little longer. The cuff is resting on the knuckle above the thumb.

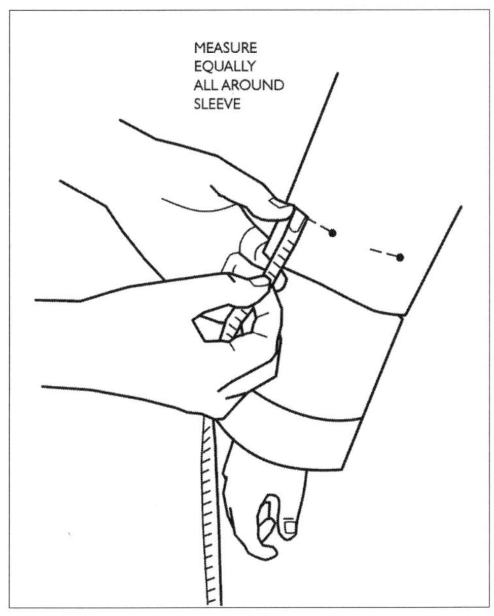

When the arm is raised, the knuckle on the wrist will be covered.

Preparing

Step 1 - Measure the amount you have folded and pinned. Double this amount, because it is folded, and write this amount down on your piece of paper.

Step 2 - Unpick the cuff from the sleeve of the jacket. If the cuff is top stitched on, unpick the top stitching first.

Step 3 - Pin the right cuff to the right sleeve, up the top near the shoulder.

Step 4 - Pin the left cuff to the left sleeve, up the top near the shoulder.

Step 5 - Mark up the amount that the sleeve is going up by.

Step 6 - Mark down 1/2" or 1 cm for the hem allowance.

Special note - The amount you are going up by is the position you will place the tape measure on the original stitching that attached the cuff to the sleeve.

The same principle was applied when shortening pants. You had the amount you were taking up the pants resting on the original length, so that the top of the tape measure was laying over the garment, and you placed a chalk mark at the top of the tape measure.

You should have the amount that the sleeve is going up by and another mark below that which represents the amount of seam allowance that is on the jacket.

Step 7 - Mark around the sleeve every 2 - 3 ".

Step 8 - Cut on the bottom chalk mark which is your cut line.

Sewing

No opening

Step 1 - Pin the cuff back on to the sleeve.

If the the sleeve was inserted inside the cuff, then push the sleeve seam allowance INSIDE the cuff.

Your pins should be positioned so that as you sew on the sewing machine you will pull the pin out towards you. That means the pin head should be facing towards you.

Step 2 - Place the tucks or pleats next to each other. I usually have no more than 1" total in a pleat or tuck. That means 1/2" folded.

Step 3 - Sew the cuff on.

If the sleeve was not inserted inside the cuff, then attach the cuff to the sleeve.

The width of the sleeve will be wider now, so you have the option of taking in the inside arm, beginning at the underarm and tapering down, or you can put tucks in the sleeve. The tucks should go on the panel on the outside arm. Personally I would taper the sleeve in.

Step 4 - Over lock two sections together.

Step 5 - Top stitch the sleeve.

With opening

Step 1 - Pin one side of the cuff to the sleeve.

Step 2 - Move around to the other side and pin the other end of the cuff to the opposite end of the sleeve.

This means you will have the opened section pinned on both sides of the cuff.

You are doing this because you want to work back towards the opposite end and place the tucks or pleats.

The panel with the tucks or pleats is the panel that runs down the outside arm.

Step 3 - Sew the cuff to the sleeve.

Note:- If the jacket is lined, have the sleeve turned inside out and pin the cuff to the lining and the sleeve, and sew all three together.

If you are not sure on this, sew the cuff to the sleeve first, then sew the lining to the cuff and sleeve second. Under stitch the lining after the cuff is sewn on.

Take Up Sleeves - With Ribbing

Step 1 - Ask the person to stand facing the mirror.

Step 2 - Stand to the right of the person.

Step 3 - Fold fabric about 10"/25 cm above the ribbing.

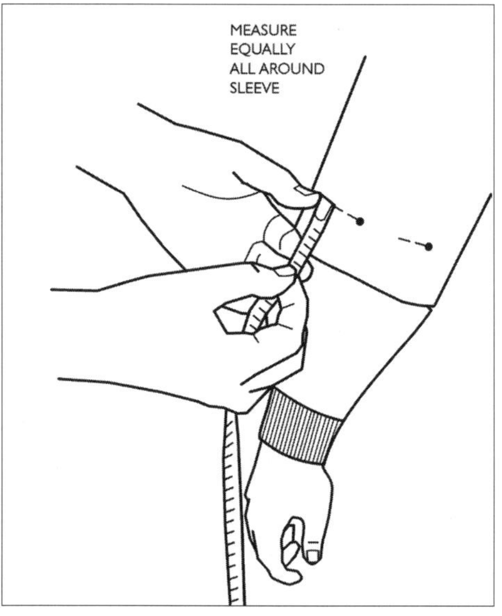

Step 4 - Take up the excess fabric in the arm so that there is just a small amount of flounce above the ribbing.

Step 5 - Place your finger nail up against the inside fabric and with your tape measure the amount that you have folded.

Step 6 - Place a pin at this exact measurement.

Step 7 - Move around the sleeve and follow the same procedure by folding the same amount and placing a pin at this amount.

Step 8 - Pin around the sleeve at least three times – front, side and back seam.

Explain to the person that you are going to get them to raise their arm to see if it is the correct length.

Step 9 - Show the person what you mean. As you raise your arm, say to the person that you

want them to raise their arm, with the elbow locked in. Explain that you want them to raise it so that it is not quite level with their shoulder. Help them to do this.

Explain that the end of the sleeve should sit just behind the knuckle. Some people like it a little longer, so for them have it resting on the knuckle.

Explain that this is where the sleeve should sit from a TAILORING point of view.

The only reason it will not do this is if the jacket pulls at the underarm.

The second way of checking is to place your left hand on the inside of their elbow, and your right hand under the small of the arm. Bend the elbow.

The jacket sleeve should sit across the wrist.

Preparing

Step 1 - Measure the amount that is folded on the sleeve. Place the tape measure on the fold and measure to the pin. Write this amount down on a piece of paper, and then double it. I usually write something like 1" = 2".

Step 2 - Take out pins.

Step 3 - Check to see that the sleeves are the same length.

Step 4 - Before unpicking the ribbing from the sleeve check to see if the garment is lined.

Step 5 - Unpick right sleeve and pin ribbing to right sleeve.

Step 6 - Unpick left sleeve and pin ribbing to left sleeve.

Step 7 - Mark up from the original stitch line that attached the cuff to the sleeve. The amount up is the amount you folded, and then mark down for the 1/2" seam allowance.

Step 8 - Use the same technique for Taking Up

as per Taking up pants.

Step 9 - Cut around the bottom chalk line.

Step 10 - Pin the ribbing back on to the sleeve. Fold the ribbing into quarters and the bottom of the sleeve into quarters.

Step 11 - Pin each quarter together.

Step 12 - Make sure the pin heads are away from the seam so that the person sewing can sew over the top of the pins.

Step 13 - Follow the same procedure for the second sleeve.

Sewing

Step 1 - Sew the ribbing on to the outer.

If the garment is not lined, you can top stitch, or just leave as is.

If the garment is lined, attach the ribbing in between the outer and the lining and sew together.

Step 2 - Over lock edge of sleeve and ribbing together.

Raise Shoulder At Top Of Sleeve

There are two ways of pinning the sleeves up onto the shoulders of a jacket.

Option 1 - Pins highlight where to raise sleeve. Use this option when shoulder pads are bulky.

Option 2 - Folding the sleeve up and onto shoulder – Use this option if the shoulder pads were not so bulky, and the sleeve can be raised up to the shoulder.

Option 1 - Pins highlight where to raise sleeve

Step 1 - Ask the person to put the jacket on and stand in front of the mirror. I prefer a full length mirror.

Step 2 - It is preferable to have the jacket buttoned up.

Step 3 - Stand to the right of the person.

I usually pin the right shoulder. The reason I only pin the right shoulder is that I prefer to have a fitting before I complete the whole garment. I take the right shoulder up (not the lining), and I do not cut the fabric away.

This way they can see the difference between the right shoulder and the left shoulder. It gives them a reference point.

This is a big alteration, so it is better to check they are happy with the amount taken up before you cut and or alter the other side and the lining.

Step 4 - When a jacket shoulder is too wide, you need to work out where the shoulder should finish for the person.

As a rule, the sleeve should join the shoulder in line with the outside arm.

Step 5 - Look at the person in the mirror, and follow an imaginary line from the outside arm to the top of the sleeve. This is where the sleeve should join the shoulder.

Step 6 - Place the first pin at this imaginary line on the centre shoulder seam. Place the pin at the top of the shoulder with the knob of the pin at the front and the sharp end of the pin pointing towards the back.

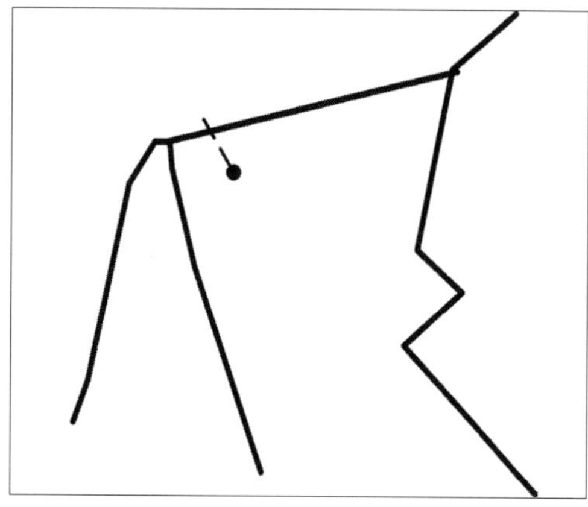

Step 7 - This pin should be in line with the outside of the arm.

Sometimes you will have a person whose arm is very rounded and this theory does not apply. If this is the case you need to imagine where the sleeve should join the shoulder.

Step 8 - When you are happy with your first pin, you need to fill in from the first pin at the top shoulder seam around to the front of the armhole.

Step 9 - The pins should follow one another around to the front.

You will see that the shoulder will jut out more at the top. Taper the pin in to the front finishing about 8" to 10" or 20 cm to 25 cm from the top shoulder seam.

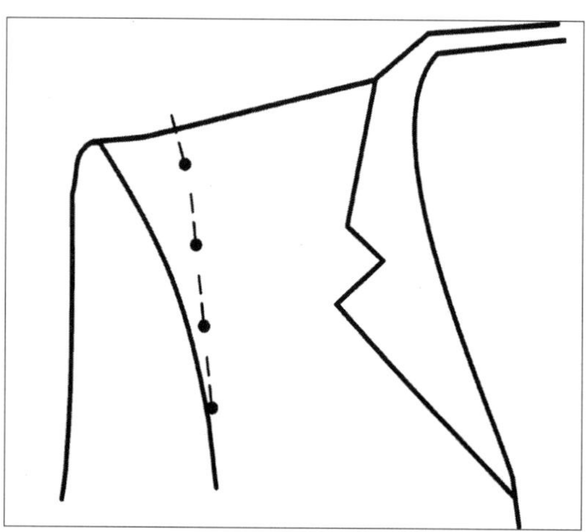

Step 10 - Move around to the back of the jacket and follow the same procedure as the front.

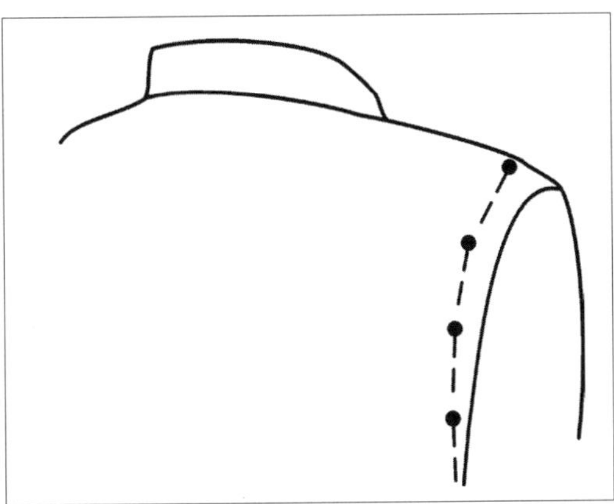

Option 2 - Folding the sleeve up and onto shoulder

Stand to the right of the person. Pin the right shoulder as per "Pins highlight where to raise sleeve".

Step 1 - Look at the person in the mirror, and follow an imaginary line from the outside arm to the top of the sleeve. This is where the sleeve should join the shoulder.

Step 2 - Starting at the top, fold the sleeve up to where the sleeve should be on the shoulder.

Step 3 - Pin the sleeve into place with the pin tip facing away from the person. When you pin you must be careful not to pin the person.

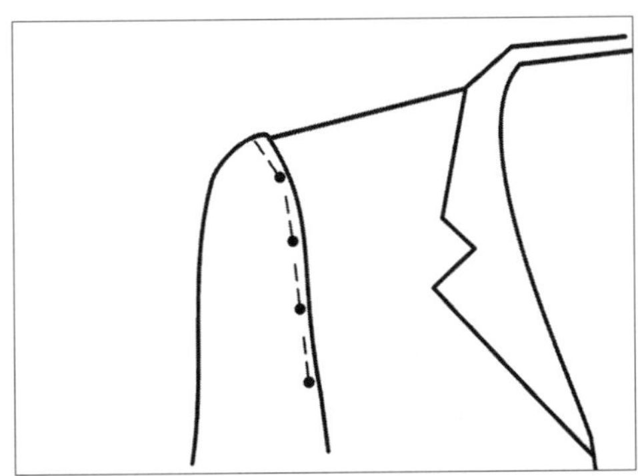

As you put the pin into the fabric, look to see where it comes out and only catch enough of the shoulder fabric to hold the sleeve in place.

Step 4 - Fold the sleeve up to the shoulder at the front moving down towards the armhole.

Step 5 - As you get closer to the armhole, take less from the sleeve, as if you are tapering off to nothing. Look at where you feel it should stop and place a pin on the edge only. It will probably be about 8" to 10" or 20 cm to 25 cm from the centre seam at the top of the shoulder.

Step 6 - Repeat the same process for the back.

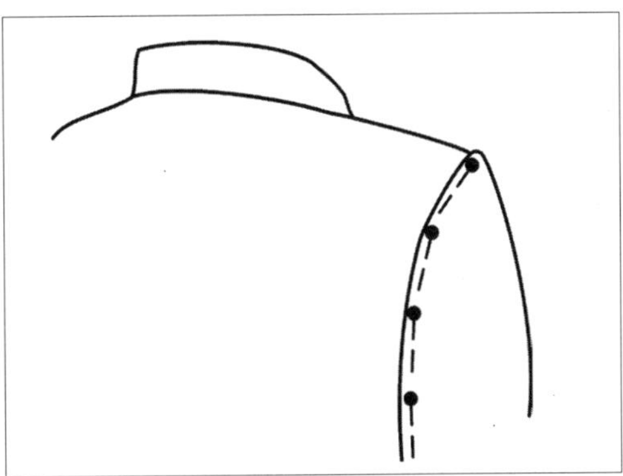

Preparing

I will begin with Option 2, which will lead into Option 1.

Jacket has been pinned by folding the sleeve up and onto the shoulder.

Step 1 - Leave the pins in the sleeve, until after you have placed pins on the shoulder section.

Step 2 - Place a pin on the shoulder section against the folded sleeve, but not in the sleeve. I usually begin at the top and work around the front. Then when I have finished the front, I work from the top and around the back.

Step 3 - When you have pins around the shoulder next to the folded sleeve, take the pins out that are supporting the sleeve. The pin will now outline where you had folded the sleeve onto the shoulder, and will look the same as Option 1.

Step 4 - Start taking your measurements from the centre shoulder seam. If the jacket does not have a centre shoulder seam, then use the front or back seam as your start point.

Step 5 - Draw an outline of a shoulder, and draw in the seam running across the shoulder to the collar.

Step 6 - Write down the word Front – in front of the shoulder seam, and the word Back at the back of the shoulder seam.

Step 7 - Measure the amount from the existing sleeve seam to the pin at the centre shoulder seam. Write this measurement down at the same position on your drawing.

Step 8 - Measure 2" from the shoulder seam going towards the front.

Step 9 - Write down the amount from the sleeve to the pin at 2".   I write down 2" = (the amount from the sleeve to the pin).

Step 10 - Now measure down 4" and write down 4" = (the amount from the sleeve to the pin).

Step 11 - Proceed every 2" and write these measurements down.

Step 12 - Follow the same procedure for the back section.

Step 13 - Turn the Jacket inside out and unpick the seam on the lining on the inner arm seam.

Step 14 - You now have the measurement of the pins on the shoulder.

Step 15 - Take out the pins.

Step 16 - Open the seam in the inside arm lining.

Step 17 - Pop the jacket through the lining so that it is inside out.

Step 18 - For men unpick the shoulder seam (this will be a hand stitched seam) The shoulder lining will drop away.

Step 19 - Remove any shoulder pads and wadding.

Step 20 - Unpick the sleeve from the shoulder BUT ONLY unpicking to the section where the measurements stop i.e. down 8" on the front and down 9" on the back.

Step 21 - Usually the under arm section will remain attached.

TIP - If you are going to take in all the way around the sleeve, save yourself some time, by leaving a small section under the arm attached, and sew the rest, then come back to the under-arm and take in.

I have seen people take the whole sleeve out, and then become totally baffled on which way to re attach.

If you always leave the sleeve attached at the underarm you will never insert the sleeve incorrectly.

Step 22 - Using a tailors pencil place a dot on the shoulder at the centre shoulder seam the same measurement you have on your piece of paper.

Step 23 - Measure down 2" and place a dot for the measurement at this point.

Step 24 - Follow this procedure at the front down to where the measurements stop.

Step 25 - Follow this procedure at the back to where the measurements stop.

Step 26 - Take the centre of the sleeve and pin it at the centre shoulder seam.

Step 27 - Proceed to pin the sleeve into the shoulder working around the front to the end.

Step 28 - Apply the same principle to the back section.

Step 29 - If you find there is more fabric on one side than the other, move the centre around slightly.

Step 30 - Do not have any gathering at the top of the shoulder.

Step 31 - Any gathering should be on either side on the bias section.

Step 32 - The person sewing can EASE the ex-

cess fabric in at the bias section thereby reducing any puckering.

Step 33 - If you find that by following the dots at certain sections the sleeve will not sit correctly, make the adjustment.

Step 34 - Pinning a shoulder is difficult, and it may have been slightly off.

Step 35 - If the customer is not having a fitting, then proceed to do the same on the opposite shoulder and unpick the lining and apply the same procedure.

Step 36 - It is extremely important that the seam FLOWS rather than stick in or out in the wrong places.

Step 37 - When you put the shoulder pads back in you may find that, you may have to cut the shoulder pad down in size. Alternatively, you may find that the pads are too big and bulky, in which case, change the pads to a smaller type.

Step 38 - Hand stitch the shoulder pads onto the shoulder seam. You can sew it on with the machine, however I find hand stitching gives a nicer finish.

Step 39 - Attach the top section of the shoulder pad to the centre shoulder seam.

Step 40 - I usually attach the lining to the underarm seam of the outer fabric. Cut a piece of fabric about 2" long and ½" side. Attach to the inside arm seam under the arm and the same to the lining.

Step 41 - Pop the jacket back through and iron the shoulder. If you are happy with the new shape, close the inside arm seam.

Conclusion

Taking the mystery out of what length you should have your jacket sleeves is great.

I have people come in to see me, worried about what length they should have the sleeves on their jackets, and when I explain the procedure they breath a sign of relief, and go away feeling relaxed.

Buying a jacket is a big expense usually, so its good to know that you are not going to make a mistake with your expensive garment.

Jackets

Taking In

"Jackets can be challenging to take in, but you can achieve a good result if it's only coming down a size or two."

Back - Take In

When someone looses weight, the first priority is to find clothes that fit.

It can be a lot of fun shopping for a new wardrobe. However, that doesn't mean that you can go into your wardrobe and throw everything out because it is too big.

There will always be garments that are old favourites. And these old favourites can be resurrected.

One of the most common alterations I do for people who have lost weight is take in suit jackets that are too big.

It may seem like an ominous job, but if you try taking the jacket in through the centre back seam first, you may find that it is all that is required to make the jacket fit the body again.

If the jacket does not have a centre back seam, you can create one. Pin down the centre back in the same way as if there is a centre back seam.

When you begin sewing at the very top at the back of the neck, begin to sew as close as possible to the collar. When the collar is folded back, it will more than likely cover the start point.

The jacket will look like it always had a centre back seam.

Therefore, to begin, you need the person to stand in front of a long length mirror, and you need to be standing behind the person.

Ask them to do the buttons up on the jacket. This is important, because if the buttons are not done up, then you could take the jacket in too much.

It is extremely important to begin the pinning at the very top of the centre back seam, as close to the collar as possible.

Sewing hint – When you begin to sew the centre back seam, you will not be unpicking the collar from the back panel.

I clip either side of the seam at the very top of the centre back seam, which lays the seam flat and allows me to begin sewing at the very top of the back seams.

Step 1 - Begin with the pin right on the edge of the seam with the pins facing down. The knob will be at the top.

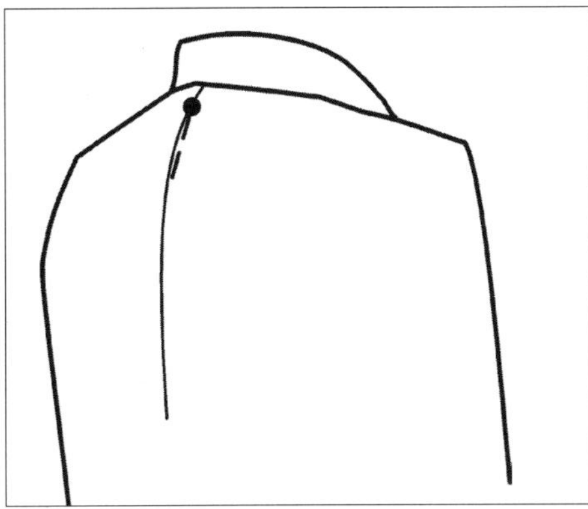

Step 2 - Place the second pin about 2" or 5 cm lower and about ¼" or ½ cm in from the seam.

Step 3 - The third pin can be about 1 ½" or 3.5 cm down and about ½" or 1 cm in.

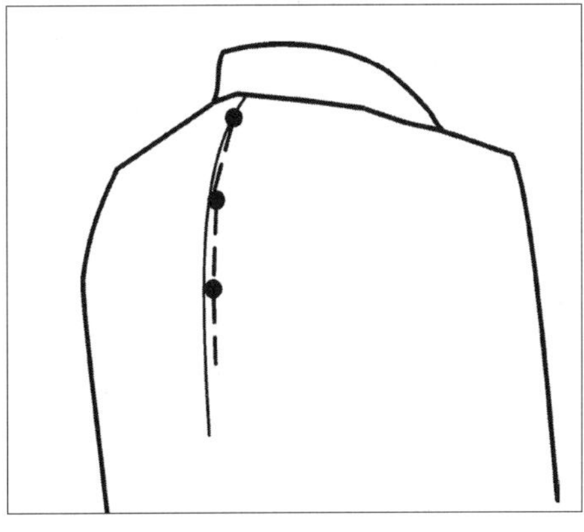

Step 4 - Pin in towards the body. Continue pinning all the way through to the hem if that is what is required.

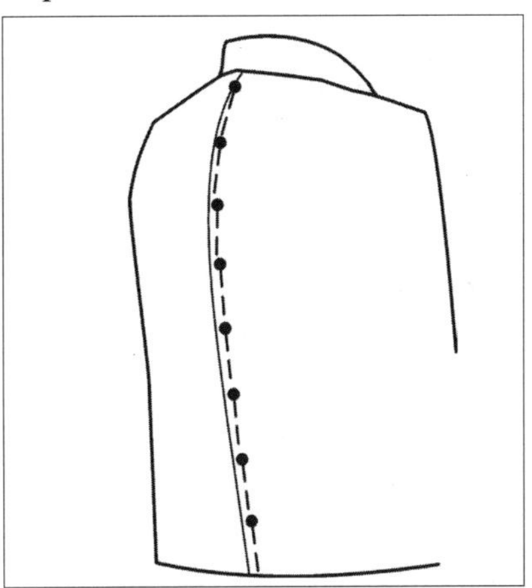

Step 5 - If you find that the jacket is really big, and you don't want to take in the centre back seam any more, consider taking in the side seams.

Step 6 - If you take the back seam in too much it will not sit properly.

Step 7 - Always pin as if you are sewing it.

Step 8 - Make sure you leave sufficient fabric over the hip area.

Step 9 - When you have finished pinning, turn the person side on to the mirror so they can see how the jacket will fit them.

Step 10 - Write down measurements as per Taking In Technique.

The opening on woman's jackets is in the lining of the sleeve on the inside arm seam.

For men's jackets, I would suggest the side seam of the lining be opened when doing the centre back seam. This way you can sew the lining of the centre back seam without worrying about closing the seam later.

When you have finished, you should open the bottom of the breast pocket of the lining. Pull the side seam through, and sew from the inside. Then close the lining pocket by sewing across from the outside. No one will know where you opened the jacket.

Step 11 - Pop the jacket inside out to do this alteration.

Step 12 - Unpick the hem from the lining. It should have some stitches holding the hem up. Unpick this, but re attach after you take in.

Step 13 - Mark your dots, and sew down the dots. Line up the hem fold at the bottom.

Step 14 - Cut away excess fabric. Iron seams open.

Step 15 - Sew lining to the outer fabric and re-stitch hem up. Pop the jacket through and close.

Sides - Take In

Jackets are constructed in different ways, so some sides of jackets will be easier to take in than others. There are two styles used when making a jacket or coat.

Option 1 - Side seams under the arm

It is much easier to alter a jacket with the side seams coming from under the arm, than it is for option 2.

Option 2 - Side seams at back and on back of arm

This option can be a difficult one. There will be some jackets that you may not be able to do like this.

Option 1 - Side seams under the arm

Step 1 - The person should do the buttons up on the jacket and face a full-length mirror.

Step 2 - Stand in front of the person.

Step 3 - Ask the person to raise their arms slightly.

Step 4 - Using your thumb and index finger, take hold of the excess fabric under the arm. Begin pinning from the join in the underarm moving down the body of the jacket.

Step 5 - A jacket is not worn tight fitting. When you take the excess fabric, you need to allow for room for the person to wear other clothes under the jacket or coat.

Step 6 - The pin should be facing down with the knob on top.

Step 7 - Pin the opposite underarm with the same amount you have pinned on the first underarm.

Step 8 - The reason you should pin the opposite side, is to determine that the pinning is not too tight.

Step 9 - Place second pin beneath the first.

Step 10 - Move back to the right side and place the second pin.

Step 11 - Move back to the left side and place two more pins working down the jacket.

Step 12 - Move back to the right side and do the same.

Step 13 - Keep moving back and forward so that the pins will be the same width down the seam.

Step 14 - Pin both sides through to the hem. Check to see it is not tight on the hip area.

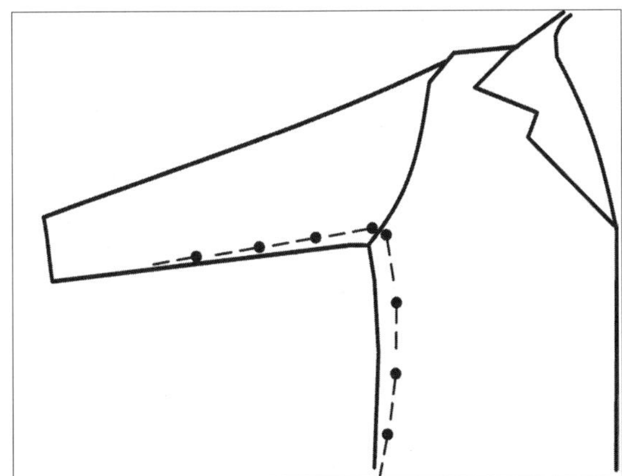

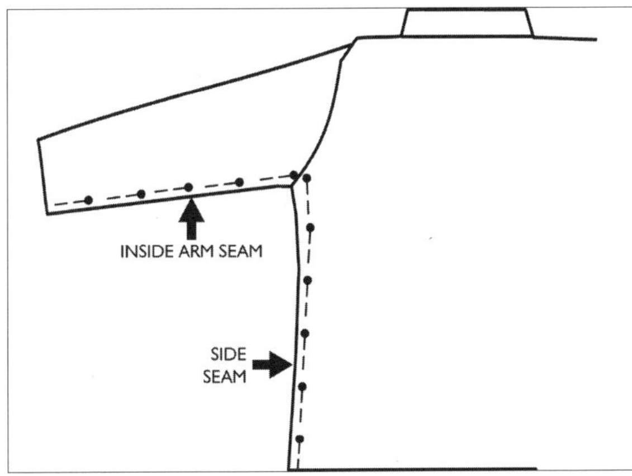

Step 15 - Ask the person to raise their arm and begin pinning along the sleeve.

Step 16 - The pins should be facing away from the person. Generally you should stop about 8" from the end, but if the jacket is too wide in the sleeve you may have to pin through to the sleeve hem.

Step 17 - Prepare and sew the jacket as per Taking In Technique pages 47 - 62.

Option 2 - Side seam at back and on back of arm

Step 1 - Look at the jacket on the person and determine if the sleeves are too large as well. It is important that the sleeves are not tight on the person. If they are then you cannot take the jacket in at the side seams.

Step 2 - Pinning this type of jacket can be difficult and in some cases, I would recommend not doing it at all.

Step 3 - You cannot take in a lot around the armhole area.

The sleeve would not sit correctly when reset.

The only way to know is to pin first and see how much is needed to be taken in.

I would consider creating a false back seam, or taking in the back seam BEFORE doing this type of alteration.

Step 4 - Begin by pinning the side seam next to the sleeve on both sides and move down the seam to the hem. Ensure that the seams are pinned the same on both sides.

Step 5 - Move back up to the sleeve and pin the fabric moving across to the sleeve side seam.

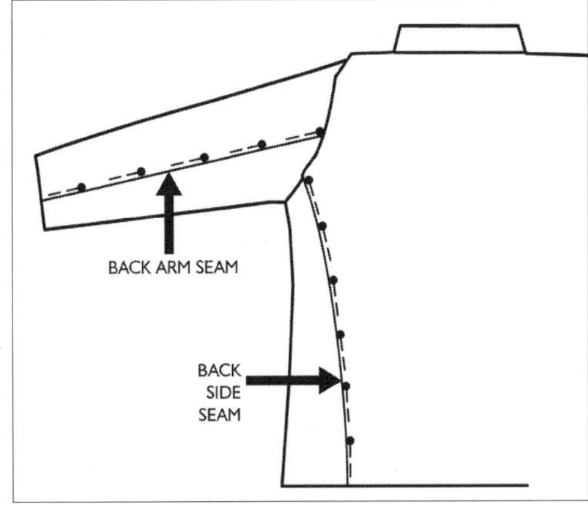

Step 6 - Pin as far as is appropriate on the sleeve.

Step 7 - When pinning the back seam, you will have to be careful you do not take the seam in too much.

Step 8 - The two panels are cut differently, and one panel will not sit properly into the other panel if you take in too much. A small amount on each side only if this is the case.

Step 9 - Explain that if you do this alteration you have to reset the sleeve at the back of the jacket, and it will change the width of the sleeve at the top.

Step 10 - Prepare and sew the jacket as per Taking In Technique.

With this alteration, you will have to reset the back section of the sleeve.

If you have never done this before, I would suggest you practice on an old jacket of your own first.

If you do not have one, consider buying one from a second hand store for a few dollars and try the alteration out before you do this on an expensive jacket.

When preparing the jacket, write down the measurement every 2".

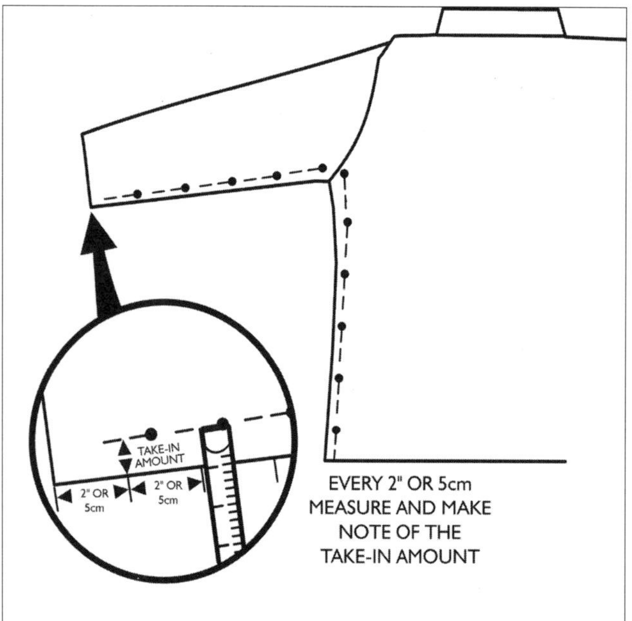

If you have never taken in a jacket before, you may like to practice on a second hand jacket that you can buy cheap from an Opportunity Shop.

If this is a ladies jacket, then unpick the inside arm seam in the lining, and POP the jacket inside out.

This is the only way to alter a jacket when you are taking in the sides.

To try it any other way would be disastrous.

The inside arm seam at the bottom of the sleeve will be attached to the lining, so you will have to unpick these two and separate them so that you can sew them individually.

You must also unpick the underarm seams so that this is taken in properly.

And last you need to unpick the hem and detach the lining from the outer.

After you have taken the jacket in, re attach the lining to the body of the jacket at the sleeve and the hem, and tack the folded body of the garment so that the hem does not drop down when you are wearing it.

Pop the jacket back the right way and stitch the lining seam together.

Shirts & Tops

Taking Up

*"Turn a long sleeve shirt or top
into
a short sleeve shirt or top."*

Introduction

I have put shirts and tops together, because there are a number of similarities to them.

Taking up the sleeves on a shirt, is the same as taking up a sleeve on a jacket with cuffs, however, I have included it in this section again, because you may want to just refer to the shirts and tops section, rather than flipping through the book.

One of the biggest problems for woman with big busts is the fact that their shirts and tops will be higher in the front than the back.

If you would like the hem to be even, I have explained my technique for achieving this.

Another alteration I had a lot of was shortening a long sleeve shirt to short sleeves. There is a quick and easy way to work out what the length should be without trying on the shirt.

I hope that you find this section helpful with your alterations.

Front higher than back

For women who have large busts, a shirt or blouse will have the hem higher at the front than the back, because the bust will cause the garment to fill out at the front, which will pull the front higher.

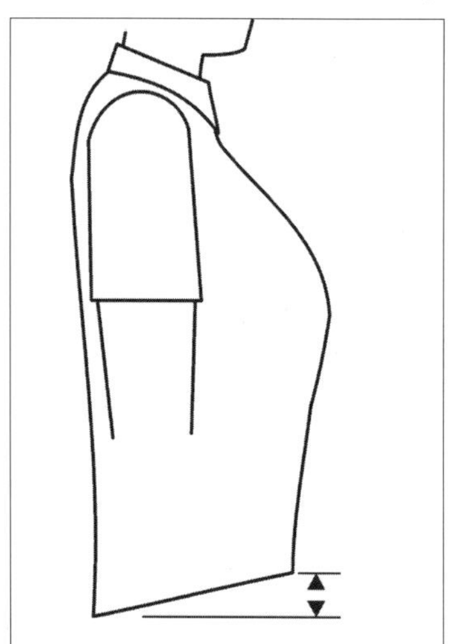

The only way to guarantee a straight hem is to measure from the floor up to the new fin-

ished length. This needs to be done all the way around the garment, or at least to the sides seams, front and back.

Step 1 - I always find it best to have the person stand in front of a full length mirror.

Step 2 - Ask the person to stand with their spine straight, and ask them to look directly into the mirror, looking into their own eyes. This ensures they keep their spine straight.

Step 3 - If you are straightening the garment, then you need to work from shortest point which is usually the front of the shirt or blouse. Measure from the floor, to this shortest point at the front.

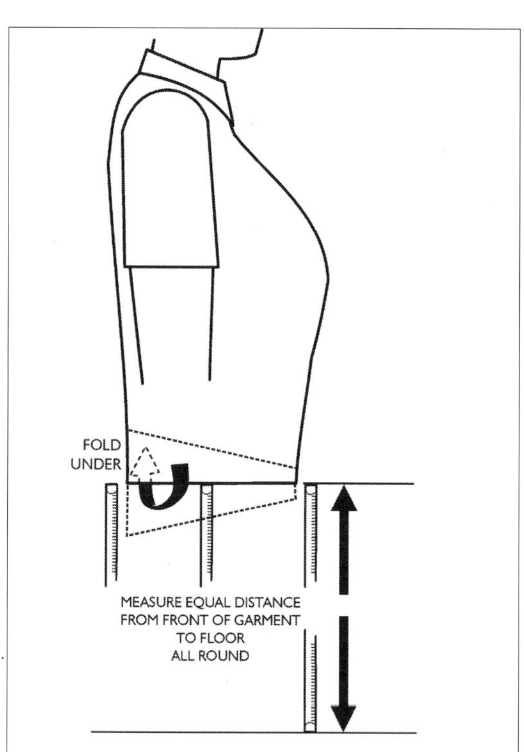

If you are finding a new length for the person, then fold the front excess fabric under, and pin to the new length. Measure from the floor to this new length.

Step 4 - Move around to the back of the person and using the same measurement as the front shortest length, measure from the floor to the centre back and place a pin.

Step 5 - Move around to the sides and do the same thing, so that you have the same length all the way around the garment.

Step 6 - You may need to pin up sections in between so that the person can see what the finished length will look like all the way around the garment.

Step 7 - At each point that you measure from the floor to the new length, place two crossed pins.

Step 8 - To prepare the garment for sewing, place a pin on each fold below each set of crossed pins. Take the crossed pins out, and lay the garment on your prepare table.

Step 9 - Using your chalk, rub the chalk across the section of the pin where the fabric is. Continue doing this all the way around the hem line. Take the pins out.

Step 10 - The hem allowance should be small for this type of alteration. I would only put a ½" hem, because sections of the fabric are on the bias, and that means the fabric could twist when sewn. Place another chalk mark ½" below the first chalk mark. This is your cut line. Cut all the way around, making sure to line up the two fronts.

Step 11 - Fold the hem up to see if it will fit (see Technique for Taking up on pants). If the hem does not fit, you may need to open the seams out.

Step 12 - Over lock the edge. Use your buttonhole foot. Sew topside.

This means the right side of the garment is on the top and the hem allowance is underneath.

I find that sewing topside on bias cut fabric means it will not twist as much.

Shirt To Be Tucked In

The length that a person wears a shirt will vary from person to person.

Men wear shirts tucked in, and some shirts are just way too long for tucking in.

If you need to shorten some shirt hems, here's a quick technique.

Step 1 - Have the person stand in front of a long length mirror.

Step 2 - Stand in front of the person and measure approximately 6" or 15 cm down from the waist.

Step 3 - Place a pin on one of the front panels at this point and then fold the fabric under beginning at the front panel.

Step 4 - Place double pins at the front section where you measured the amount up.

Step 5 - Pin the side. I usually ask the person to stand side on to the mirror and ask if they are happy with the length. Then get them to turn side on with the long length facing the mirror.

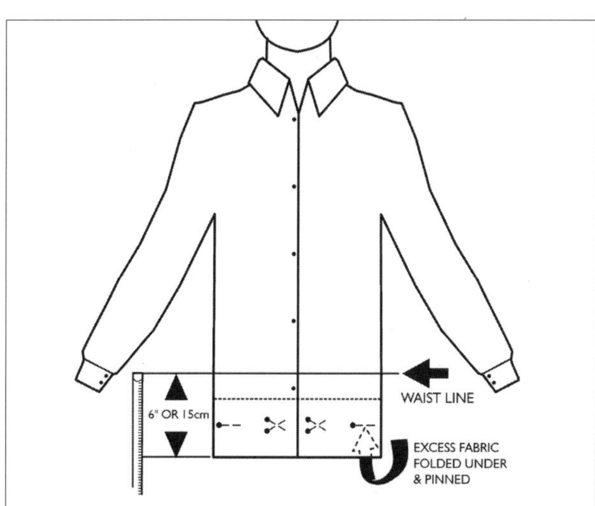

Step 6 - Prepare the garment as per Taking Up Technique pages 32 - 39 allowing for shirt not pants.

Step 7 - Sew the garment topside as per previous section on Front higher than back.

Long Shirt Length

Everyone has a perfect length that a shirt should be, in proportion to his or her body.

This is the same rule that applies for jackets, but I will repeat here for those who have skipped jackets and come straight to shirts. To work out what a persons perfect length is you need to -

Step 1 - Have the person stand facing a full-length mirror.

Step 2 - Ask the person to drop their right arm down against their side.

Step 3 - Ask the person to raise their thumb so it is parallel with their wrist.

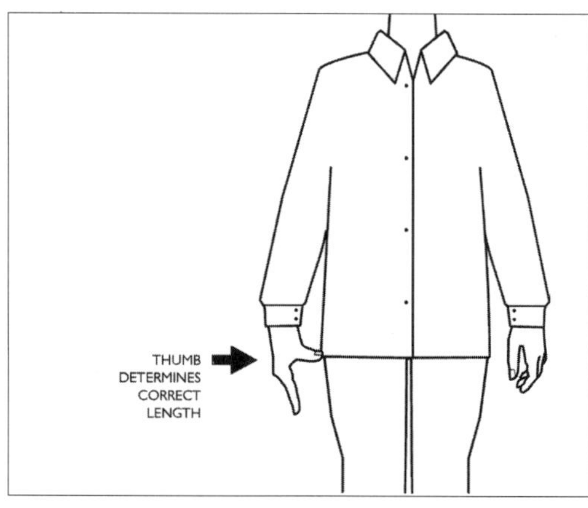

Step 4 - This is the recommended length of a long shirt for most people's bodies.

Step 5 - Fold the excess fabric up to this length and place a double pin in at this point.

Step 6 - Check to see that the shirt is straight on the person.

Step 7 - Because some women have big busts, it may be that the front of the shirt will sit higher than the back. See section on Front higher than back for details on how to straighten.

Step 8 - Prepare and sew as per Taking Up Technique.

Step 9 - Always bag the corners at the front so that the garment sits well.

Perfect Length For Top

Follow the same procedure as long shirt length when trying to work out the correct length for a top.

I do find it helpful to stand the person in front of a full length mirror.

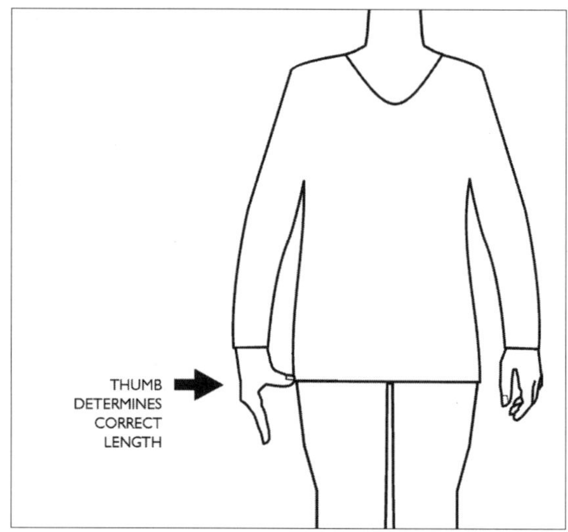

Splits at sides

After you have worked out the new hem length, have a look to see whether the splits are still there, or whether the split has been folded under.

Most splits are 2" or 5 cm long. If the split is folded under, then you could open out the side seam and put new splits in.

Prepare the garment as per Taking Up Technique pages 32 - 39 allowing for shirt not pants.

When preparing the sides for the splits, it is important to open the seam at least 6" higher than the end of the split. You can have less, but I find that if you want the split to sit properly without puckering, you are better to have the seams open at least 3 – 4" above the split. When you re over lock the sides you will over lock the sides separately. You will over lock the sides together closer to the armhole. You loose about 2" doing this.

Always consider bagging the corners of the splits, or at least sew the hem topside from edge to edge, then sew the splits last. The finish is neater and more professional this way.

Curved Length

Taking up the hem on a shirt that is curved only requires a little extra time, because you have to take into account the height that the curve will go to at the side.

Step 1 - Have the person stand facing a full-length mirror.

Step 2 - Have the person raise the shirt hem to the height they would like to see the finished length.

Step 3 - Now stand in front of the person, fold the excess fabric up to this length, and place a double pin in at this point.

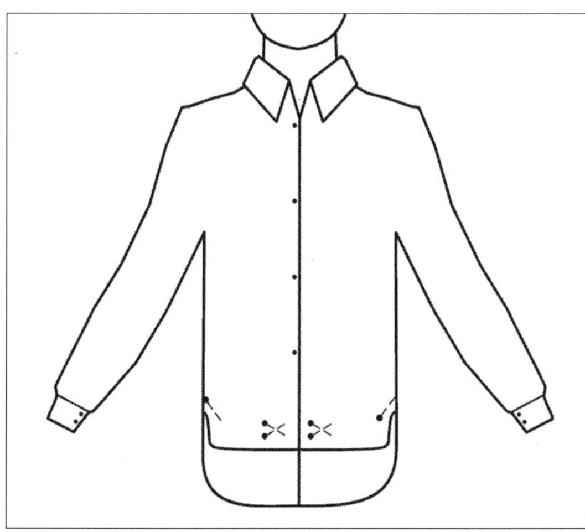

Step 4 - Move around to the side. Most curves are 2" – 3" or 5 cm – 7 ½ cm higher than the front. Fold the side up this amount.

Step 5 - Ask the person to stand side on to the mirror to see if they are happy with how high the curve is.

Step 6 - If the curve is too high, come down a little, but the person may want to consider lowering the hem height as well, otherwise they will not have much of a curve in the shirt.

Step 7 - Check to see that the shirt is straight on the person. Because some women have big busts, it may be that the front of the shirt will sit higher than the back.

Step 8 - To straighten the shirt, measure from the floor to the new hem fold.

Step 9 - Move around to the back and measure from the floor up the same amount as the front. Place a pin at the measurement, and then fold this amount up.

Step 10 - Prepare the garment as per Taking Up Technique pages 32 - 39 allowing for shirt not pants.

Step 11 - Put a small hem on for curved hems. Always sew topside, and use your buttonhole foot because it will hold the fabric down as you sew. I find the normal sewing machine foot slips on some fabrics.

Conclusion

Tops can be worn at any length. Depending on your body type and the design of the top, you might like to wear the top short around the waist area.

Some shirts are better to be worn very long.

Put the top or shirt on and experiment using your pins to fold the fabric under and have a look in a full length mirror to see the effect.

Hem With Ribbing

Ask the person to put the ribbing on the position of their body that they want it to be.

Step 1 - Take the excess fabric in your fingers about 4" or 11 cm from the band.

Step 2 - Fold the excess fabric over and place a pin to hold the fold together.

Step 3 - Measure the amount from the fold to the pin.

Step 4 - Go all around the garment at this point taking in the same amount as you pinned in the first place.

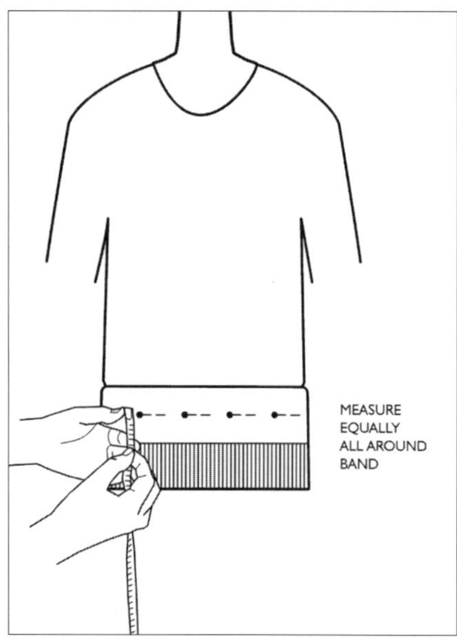

Step 5 - Always allow for flounce.

Step 6 - Have the person raise their arms to see that the ribbing doesn't rise too high for them.

Step 7 - When preparing, measure the amount pinned and double the amount because it is folded over.

Step 8 - Unpick ribbing off body of garment.

Step 9 - Cut amount from body, but leave hem allowance - usually 1/2".

Step 10 - Re attach ribbing to body and over lock.

Sleeves - Long Length

The finished length of a sleeve will be dependent on the person's personal preference.

If I was going to work in a top I would have the finished length at the end of the wrist, but if I was only going to wear the top out to a restaurant or the movies, I would probably have the length a little longer.

The reason for this is the fact that when you are working, you don't want the sleeves to get in the way.

When you are wearing the top for a social event, it is fashionable to have it longer.

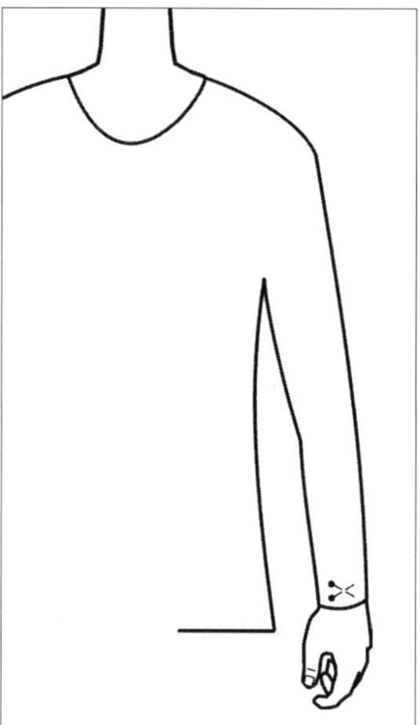

Prepare and sew the sleeves using the Taking Up Technique pages 32-39.

Sleeves - ¾ Length

Summer comes around and you have many long sleeves tops that you aren't wearing.

Why not consider shortening them to the ¾" sleeve length.

I bought a top once that I thought would look OK on me. It was a paisley fabric, and it was long sleeved.

I found that there was just too much paisley colour for me, so I converted the long sleeve to ¾ and I wear it all the time now.

Just by taking some of the fabric away, you can change the whole appearance of the top.

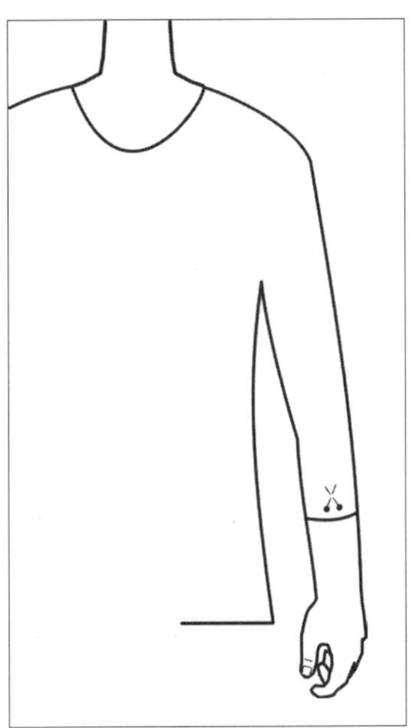

Prepare and sew as per Taking Up Technique pages 32 - 39.

Sleeves - Short Length

Convert a long sleeve into short sleeve.

Option 1

I find it easier to use a top that is the correct sleeve length.

Step 1 - Lay the short sleeve top out on a table with the back facing you. Place the beginning of the tape measure at the centre back and measure to the end of the short sleeve.

Step 2 - Now lay the long sleeve top out on the table and measure from the centre back to the finished length of the short sleeve top.

Step 3 - Place a pin at this point.

Option 2

If you can't fold the sleeve up because its too tight, use the following technique.

Step 1 - Put the top on and place a pin into the fabric at the elbow.

Step 2 - Cut the sleeve at the elbow making sure to measure up from the bottom all the way around so you get it straight.

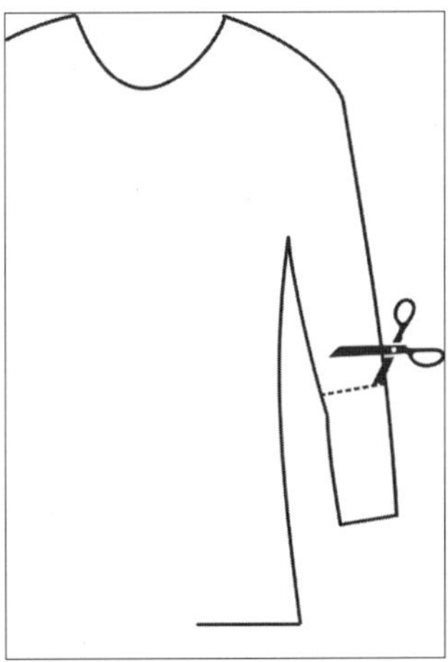

Step 3 - Try on, and fold fabric up to get the correct length.

Prepare and sew as per Taking Up Technique pages 32-39.

Sleeves - With Ribbing

Step 1 - Ask the person to stand facing the mirror.

Step 2 - Stand to the right of the person.

Step 3 - Fold fabric about 10"/25 cm above the ribbing.

Step 4 - Take up the excess fabric in the arm so that there is just a small amount of flounce above the ribbing.

Step 5 - Place your finger nail up against the inside fabric and with your tape measure the amount that you have folded.

Step 6 - Place a pin at this exact measurement.

Step 7 - Move around the sleeve and follow the same procedure by folding the same amount and placing a pin at this amount.

Step 8 - Pin around the sleeve at least three times – front, side and back seam.

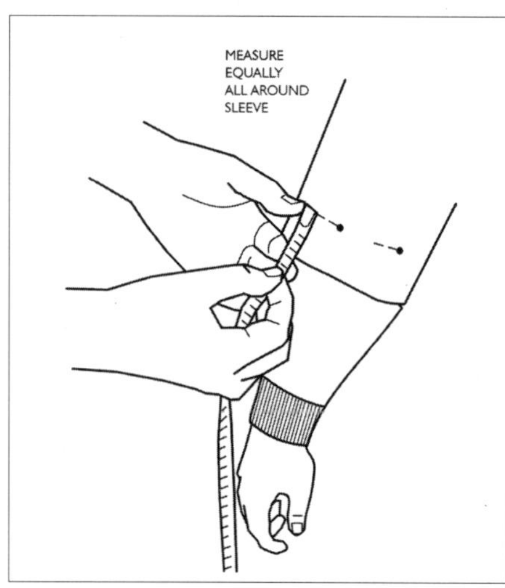

Step 9 - When preparing, measure the amount pinned and double the amount because it is folded over.

Step 10 - Unpick ribbing off body of garment.

Step 11 - Cut amount from body, but leave hem allowance - usually 1/2".

Step 12 - Re attach ribbing to body and over lock.

Sleeves – With Cuffs

When you are shortening sleeves on a shirt, the first thing to do is to have the person button up the cuff, so that it is sitting on the wrist.

Step 1 - Check the width of the cuff on the wrist.

Step 2 - Ask the person to button cuffs.

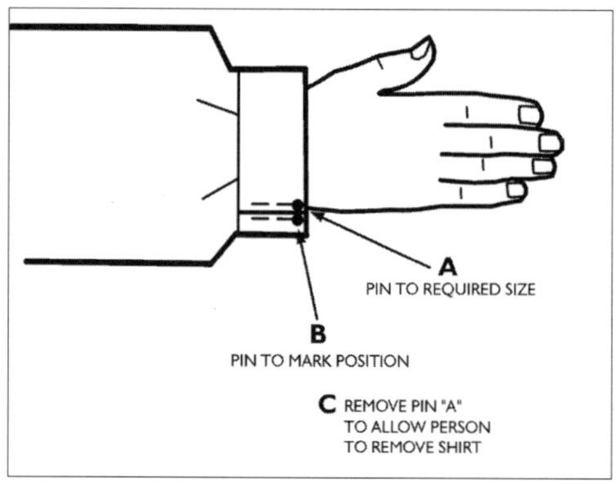

Step 3 - If the cuff width is too wide, you need to pin the cuff in so it is fitting loosely on the wrist. This means undoing the buttons and pinning to the new position.

Step 4 - Do not pin the cuff so it is too tight. The person needs to be able to raise their arm and have the cuff move around slightly. If you pin it too tight, the person will feel restricted in their movement.

Step 5 - Pin the cuffs together so that you pin through the top and bottom section of the cuff. So that you will know where to move the buttons too when the garment is being altered, you should place a pin beside the edge of the cuff as per the illustration. This shows where to place the finished width of the cuff so you can move the buttons over.

Step 6 - As you begin to pin the excess fabric, be aware that you need to allow for flounce. When the customer raises his/her arm, the sleeve will not ride up the arm.

Step 7 - Grab hold of excess fabric approximately 4" above the cuff.

Step 8 - Measure the amount you have between your fingers.   Place a pin side ways, holding

the amount taken up. For example you have folded 2".

Step 9 - The pin is 2" from the fold.

Step 10 - This means you are taking up the sleeves a total of 4" because the fabric is folded.

Step 11 - Move around the sleeve, placing a pin at 2" at each section.

Step 12 - You should have about 4 pins placed around the sleeve.

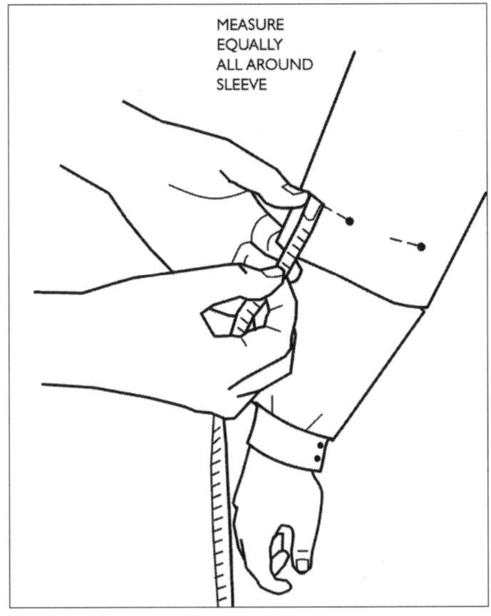

Step 13 - Check to see that the inside pin does not raise the sleeve too high.

Step 14 - If it is too high, lower the other pins. Try 1½" and see if there is enough flounce.

Step 15 - When the customer raises his/her arm, the cuff should sit just behind the knuckle.

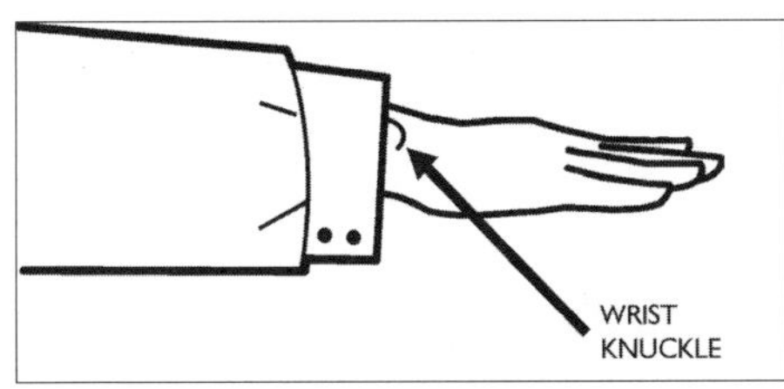

Step 16 - When the arm is down the cuff should sit on the end of the wrist, covering the knuckle.

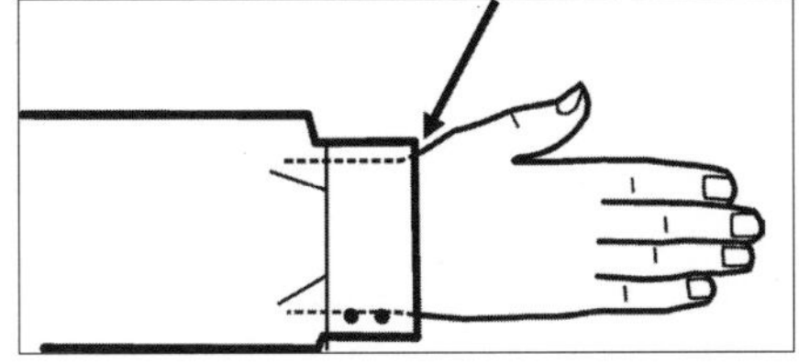

Step 17 - I have clients who work in their shirts, so they prefer their sleeves to be a little higher than a person who does not work in their shirt.

Step 18 - The first illustrations is of a shirt that is a little higher, which means that when the person raises their arm the edge of the cuff will sit just behind the knuckle.

Step 19 - The second set of illustrations is of a shirt sleeve pinned a little longer. This would be for someone who is wearing the shirt more for social occasions than at work.

Step 20 - Notice that when the arm is down the cuff hangs lower over the wrist.

Step 21 - When the arm is raised the knuckle is covered.

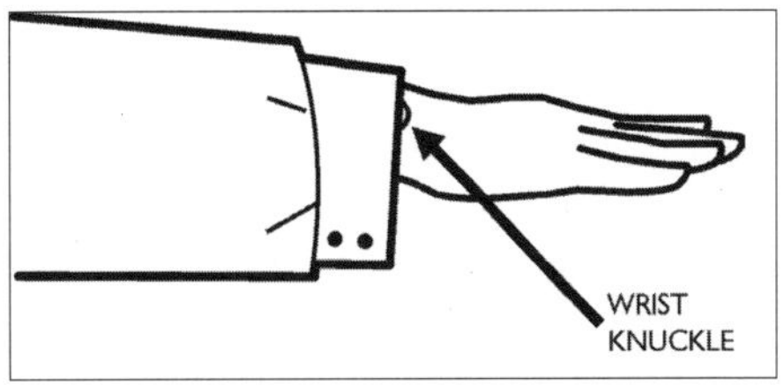

Step 22 - When the arm is at a right angle in front of the body the cuff is sitting on the wrist.

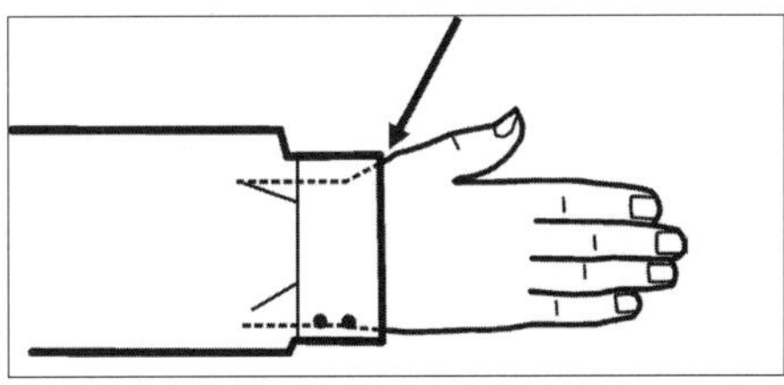

Step 23 - Write down the amount that you have folded at the sleeve. If you are measuring from the edge to the pin, then you need to double this amount because the fabric is folded.

Step 24 - Unpick the cuff, but unpick from the wrong side.

Just in case you slip and nick the cuff, at least it would not be on the right side.

Pin the cuff to the sleeve up the top. For example, right cuff pinned to right sleeve at the top, and left cuff pinned to the left sleeve at the top.

I say at the top only to get the cuff out of your

way for the time being. Just pin it to the fabric for safekeeping.

Step 25 - Measure up from the stitch line the amount you are taking up. Place your chalk mark and come down the hem allowance, which is usually 3/8" on cuffs.

Step 26 - Cut on the bottom line.

Step 27 - Pin the cuff back onto the sleeve beginning at the end with the buttons on the cuff.

Step 28 - Move around to the opposite end with the buttonholes on the cuff, and pin the cuff on to the sleeve.

Step 29 - You will notice on all sleeves, that there are pleats on one end only. You must now re pleat the sleeve. To make it easier, I use pins and have two or three pleats which are usually about 1/2" wide.

Step 30 - Move back to the opposite end from the pleats and pin the cuff back on.

Note. Have the pins pinned in such a way that when you sew on the machine, you can pull the pins out towards you.

Long Sleeves To Short Sleeves

When someone wants a long sleeve shirt turned into a short sleeve shirt, you are better off to shorten in two stages.

The first stage is to cut below the elbow. Then you can fold the fabric up from there to get the correct short sleeve length.

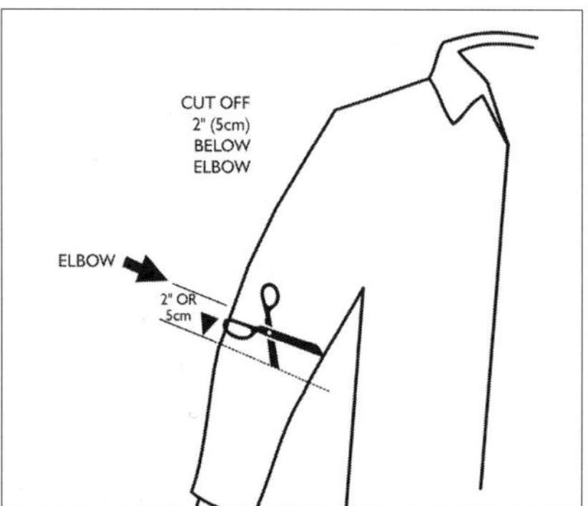

The reason you cut at the elbow first, is because the sleeve is very long, and not very wide, which means it may not fit over the arm.

DO NOT CUT WHILE ON THE PERSON.

Pin the length and cut when off the body.

The second way to get the short sleeve measurement for a shirt is to use another shirt that is already short sleeved.

Step 1 - Lay a shirt out on a table with the back facing you and the sleeves laid out flat.

Step 2 - Find the centre point on the back of the collar.

Step 3 - To do this measure the collar from edge to edge and divide the amount by 2.

Step 4 - Now measure this amount to the centre of the collar at the back and place a pin at this point.

Step 5 - Measure from this pin to the finished length of the existing short sleeve shirt.

Step 6 - Place a pin on the inside arm seam of the sleeve.

Step 7 - Write this measurement down on a piece of paper.

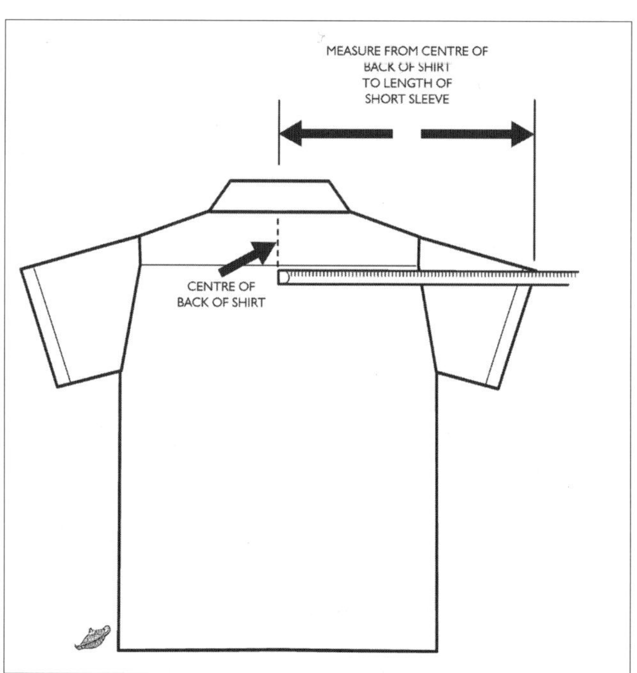

Raise Sleeve Onto Shoulder

If the shoulders are too wide on a shirt, then you can pin the sleeve up onto the shoulder. The pinning is the same as for a jacket.

Step 1 - Stand to the right of the person.

Step 2 - Make sure the buttons are done up on the shirt.

Step 3 - Pin the right shoulder. This way they can see the difference between the right shoulder and the left shoulder.

Step 4 - Imagine where the sleeve should be on the shoulder. Fold the sleeve up onto the top of the shoulder. Start pinning the sleeve up beginning from the top and working around to the front.

Step 5 - Continue folding the sleeve up and pinning into place around the front.

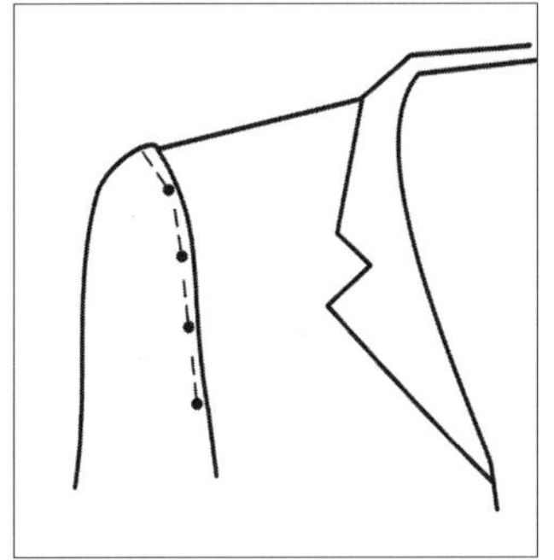 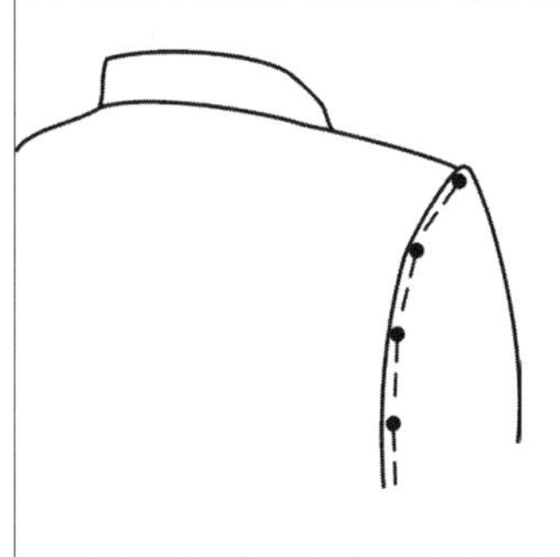

Step 6 - Pin the sleeve into place with the pin tip facing away from the person.

Step 7 - As you get closer to the armhole, take less from the sleeve, as if you are tapering off to nothing.

Step 8 - Look at where you feel it should stop and place a pin on the edge only.

Step 9 - It will probably be about 8" to 10" or 20 cm to 25 cm from the centre seam at the top of the shoulder.

Step 10 - Repeat the same process for the back.

Prepare in the same way as for raising jacket sleeves.

Halter neck - Take Up

Most halter neck tops have a join in the centre of the halter at the back of the neck. This is where it should be altered and where it should be pinned.

Step 1 - Take up the excess fabric at the back of the neck.

Step 2 - You can either use pins or a safety pin depending on the thickness of the band.

Step 3 - If the band is wide, place one pin at the top of the band pointing down towards the floor.

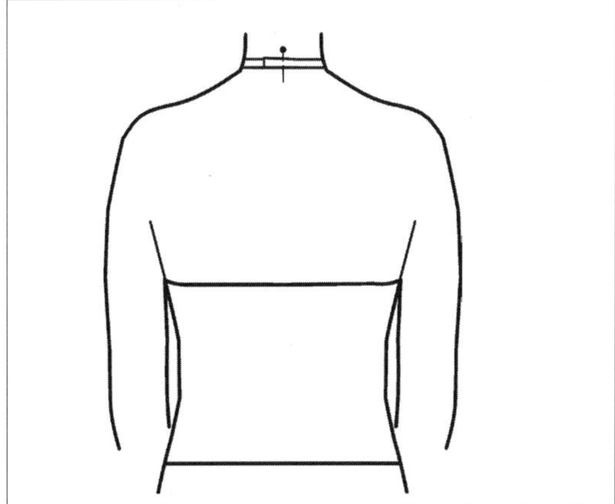

Step 4 - If there is any likelihood of pinning the person, use a safety pin.

Step 5 - Ask the person how comfortable the top feels.

Step 6 - If the halter neck is too tight, the person will be uncomfortable when wearing it, and if it is too loose, they will definitely feel insecure wearing the garment.

Straps - Take Up

Straps should be altered from the back.

Step 1 - Stand behind the person.

Step 2 - Take a hold of one strap and pull it down towards the floor.

Step 3 - When it feels comfortable on the person, place a pin through the strap and the back of the garment joining the two together.

Step 4 - Place a second pin over the first to secure the strap.

Step 5 - Pin the opposite shoulder.

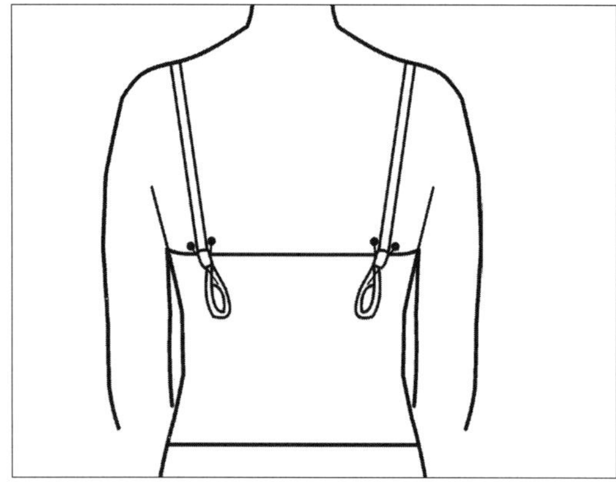

Step 6 - One thing I have found over the years is that most people have shoulders that are different.

Step 7 - The reason for different shoulders is often from carrying school bags full of books. So usually you will find that the right shoulder is lower than the left for right handed people, and it will be the left shoulder for left handed people.

Step 8 - Have the person facing the full length mirror and look at their shoulders in the mirror.

Step 9 - You should be able to tell if one is higher than the other.

Step 10 - Pin the opposite shoulder by taking the excess strap and pulling down towards the floor.

Step 11 - Place a pin in this strap, then a second pin to cross the first to secure the strap.

Step 12 - Because the pins could fall out, if it important to write down the measurements.

RS (right shoulder) = X
LS (left shoulder) = X

Step 13 - The amount is from the top of the back section to the fold on the strap.

Because the strap folds back up again, you need to double the amount.

Step 14 - If it is folded say 1' or 2.5 cm then the total measurement will be 2" or 5 cm.

Reshape Neckline - Using Pins As Guide

I think it is best to have the person face a full-length mirror.

Once the person has explained to you the shape they want, use pins to create the new neck line shape.

This allows the person to see if they are happy with the finished shape.

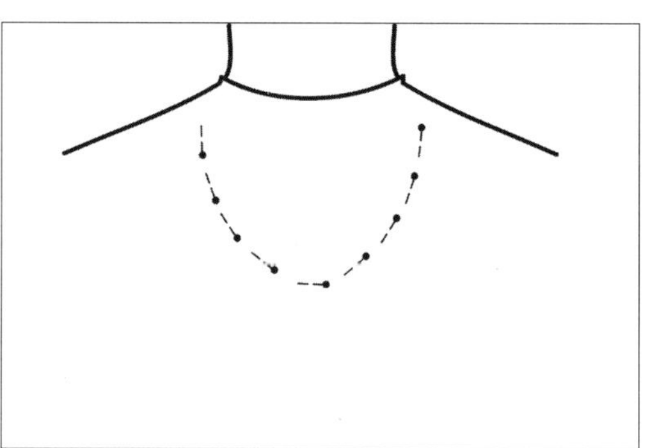

Shirts & Tops

Taking In

"Tailor your shirts and tops
to your body shape,
by taking in the sides,
or putting darts
in the front and back."

Introduction

Pinning the sides of a shirt is similar to pinning the sides of a light weight jacket, and the same principles apply to how the garment is prepared and sewn.

Taking in the sides of a sleeveless top is similar to taking in the sides of a sleeveless dress. Again the principles are the same for preparing and sewing.

Sides - Taking In

Step 1 - Ask the person to do the buttons up.

Step 2 - When you are pinning the sides of any garment, including a shirt, always check to make sure you are not causing the buttonholes to gape open or that it pulls across the bust/chest.

Step 3 - Check to see if the shirt has a French seam. See page 211 for explanation.

Step 4 - If it does have a French seam, you should advise the person, and explain that the seam needs to be opened from cuff to hem and redone with over lock instead of French seam.

Step 5 - Begin pinning from the armhole working down towards the hem.

This pin should be facing down towards the floor. The knob on the pin should be at the join in the underarm seam.

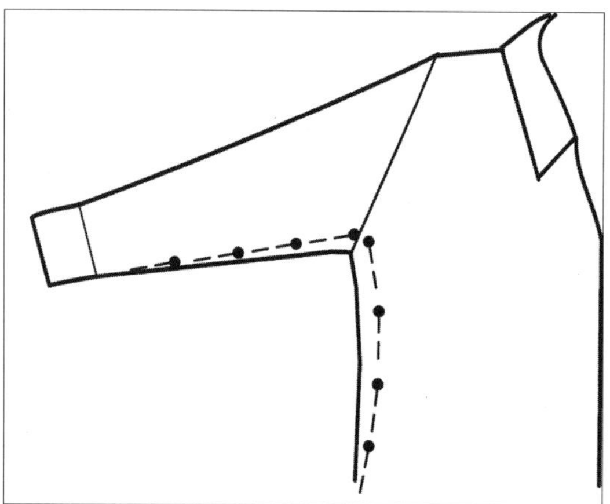

Step 6 - Place the second pin after the first with the sharp point facing the floor.

Step 7 - Move around to the other side and place a pin at the armhole section in the same way you did the first.

Step 8 - Place a second pin under the first. Place another two pins on this side.

Step 9 - Move around to the first side and place another two pins. Continue moving back and forth pinning until you come to the hem.

Step 10 - If the garment is still too loose, go back and move the pins in towards the body more.

Step 11 - Now you need to pin down the arm. These pins should be facing towards the hand, with the sharp point facing the hand.

Step 12 - Pin down the sleeve slowly tapering off to nothing near the cuff. Pin the other sleeve the same.

Step 13 - Prepare using the Taking In Technique.

Step 14 - Some shirts will be sewn through the armhole and others will require you to unpick the armhole and sew the sleeve and the body of the shirt separately.

Step 15 - For shirts with French seams, you will have to unpick the French seam and convert to normal seam and over lock.

Step 16 - Always unpick the hem and sew through the hem, then redo the hem after you have over locked off the excess.

Step 17 - If you are taking all the way to the cuff, then unpick the cuff section at the inside arm and sew right to the edge of the seam where it joins on to the cuff. Make sure not to take any in at or past where the cuff joins to the sleeve. If you do then your cuff will not fit back on.

Sides – Top Sleeveless - Take In

Taking in a top can be simple, however this would only be true if the front and back panels were the same.

If the back panel is different from the front then you need to look at another option.

Let's say that the front and back panel are the same.

Step 1 - I would stand behind the person and take the excess fabric in the fingers under both armholes.

I would look to see how much I have in both fingers.

Step 2 - Place a pin at the top of the armhole with the pin facing down towards the floor.

Step 3 - Place a pin in the opposite armhole the same amount as the first armhole.

Step 4 - Place a second and third pin under the first on the first armhole.

Ask the person to turn and face in the opposite direction and place two pins under the first on the opposite armhole.

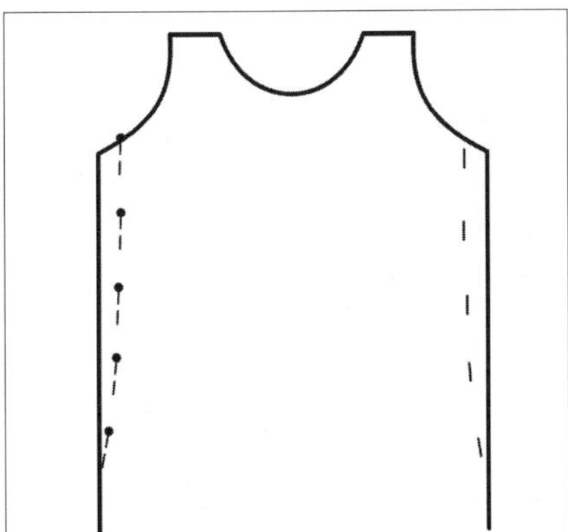

Step 5 - Continue turning the person back and forward placing two or three pins at a time until you come to the hem.

Step 6 - Stand behind the person and pull the fabric back so they can see what it will look like

with the excess fabric taken away.

Step 7 - Make sure it is not tight across the bust. If it is then adjust the pins accordingly.

Prepare and sew top the same as Taking In Sides in a sleeveless dress pages 149 - 151.

Creating darts

If you don't want to take in the sides, pin some darts at the front or the back, which will also reshape the garment.

See Dresses, Gowns and Skirts where we covered creating darts page 156.

Types
of
Seams

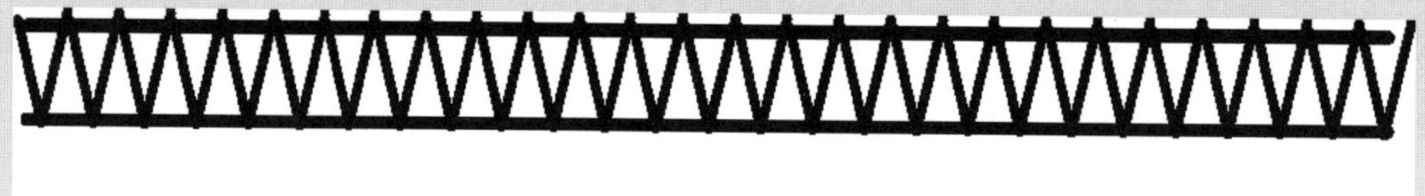

*"In every alteration
you will have to unpick seams."*

*"Learn how to unpick seams
easily and quickly."*

Introduction

When you are altering a garment, you will come across a few different seam types.

You may have to unpick one of these types of seams to shorten a hem, so I have set out below some of the seams you may need to work with and how to unpick them quickly.

Single seam with over locking

This type of seam is the most common.

The garment panels are sewn together using a straight stitch seam, then the two seams that have been sewn together are over locked together.

In some cases the seams will be over locked separately, and in this instance it will not be as difficult to alter, because you will only be unpicking the straight stitched seam, not the over locking.

The usual scenario is that the seams are over locked together.

If you have to unpick the straight seam and the over locking, there are a number of ways this can be done.

Let's deal with the straight seam first.

Straight seam

For soft fabrics like chiffons cut the thread every 6" or so, and pull the thread through. It should come out easily.

Make sure that you don't damage the fabric when you do this.

If the fabric does look like it is going to be damaged, then pull out each stitch with a quick unpick.

For fabrics like linen and satin I use a quick unpick and pull out the stitches one at a time until the thread is long enough for me to get hold of. I then pull on the thread (sort of like a jerking motion) and I break the thread as I pull. Turn the fabric over, and take a hold of the thread at the back and pull, and jerk the thread so you break it again. Then move back to the front and go back and forth snapping the thread.

Cotton fabrics are a lot stronger. I use a quick unpick and I slide the quick unpick along the seam in between the two layers. I usually have the garment out in front of me, so that I can slice in one go.

For heavy fabrics like denim I use a razor blade or stanley knife.

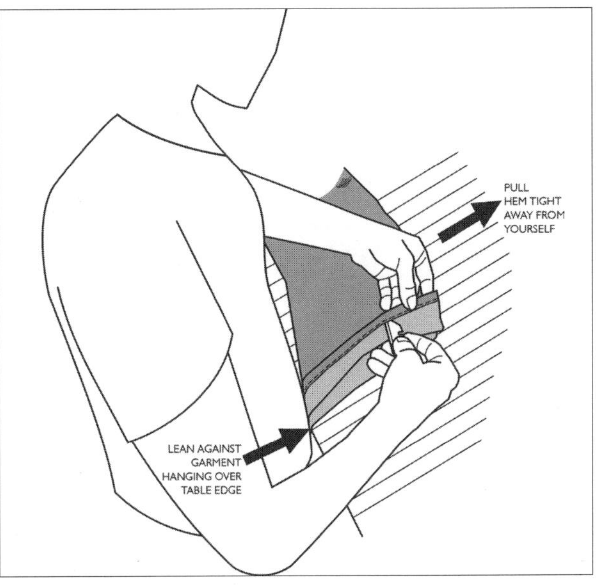

I have a prepare table that I stand at. It is quite high, so I lean against the table with a section of the garment between me and the table. The rest of the garment is in front of me.

I put the razor blade into the seam and I slice towards my body with the blade in an upwards position so it is against the hem and not the body of the garment.

The best type of razor blade to use is the blade used in the Stanley knife. I just buy a packet of those and they work fantastic. - Be careful though.

Over locking

Unpicking over locking can be easy if you pull on the right threads.

There is one particular thread that if you pull it through, then all of the over locking will fall off.

I had some illustrations made so I hope they help you.

There are a number of threads used in over locking.

Some manufacturers use a four thread machine and some use a three thread machine.

These illustrations are for a three thread machine. There is a stitch on the inside of the over locking which runs through each loop.

Step 1 - Break the thread about 3" along. Make sure you break all the threads.

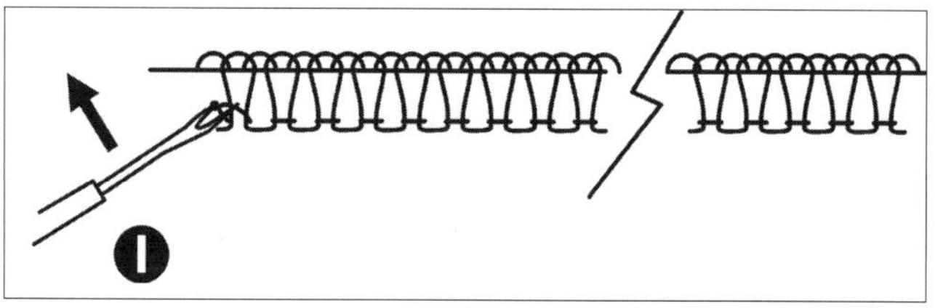

Step 2 - Using your quick unpick, flip the loop out of the bottom of the over locking as per the illustration.

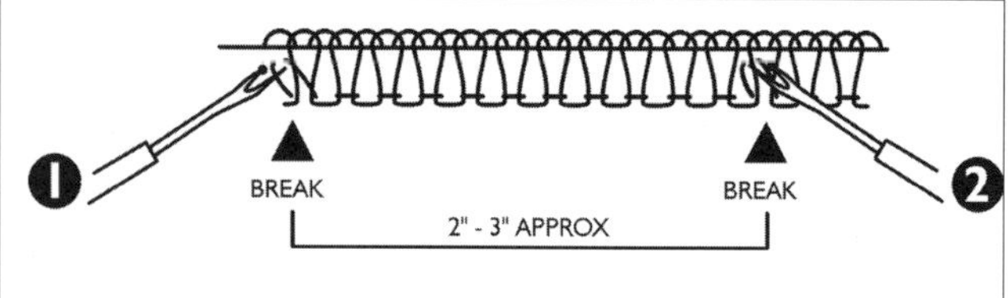

Step 3 - Pull on this thread and pull it towards you.

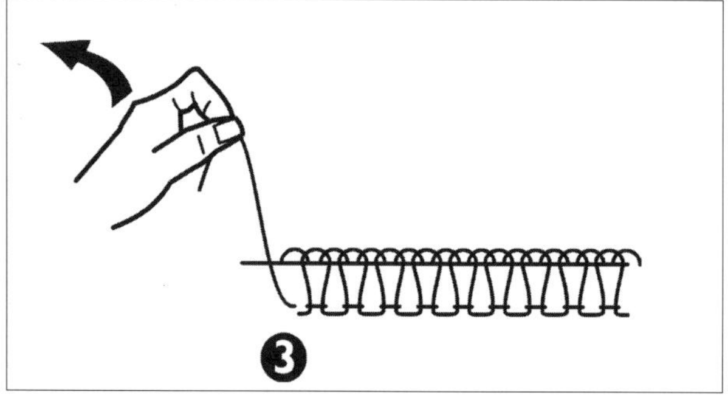

Step 4 - All the over locking should fall away or can be pulled away if you pulled the correct thread.

Step 5 - Repeat this process until all the over locking is off the garment.

The weight and type of fabric will determine how easy it is to unpick over locking.

I have unpicked over locking quickly with light fabric, and taken a long time with some heavy fabrics.

Some manufacturers will use a four thread over locker, which means that you will also have to unpick the second seam.

Unraveller and overlocking

When you look at the seam on one side it will look like a normal seam, but on the other side it will seem like a very thick seam.

This type of thick seam I call an Unraveller, because it will unravel if you do it correctly.

You can save yourself a lot of time by knowing how to unpick the unraveller.

The edge of the seam is usually overlocked. To unpick the over locking refer to the previous section.

To unpick the unraveller proceed as follows -

Step 1 - You need to work from left to right with this kind of seam.

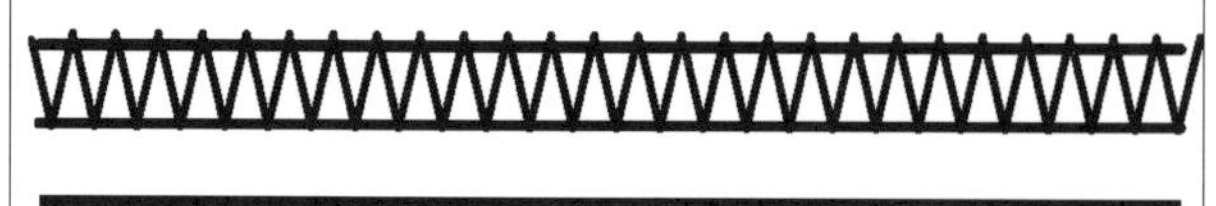

If you try to work from right to left it will NOT unravel.

Step 2 - Have the thick seam facing you.

Step 3 - Flick the quick unpick under the first stitch and cut the stitch.

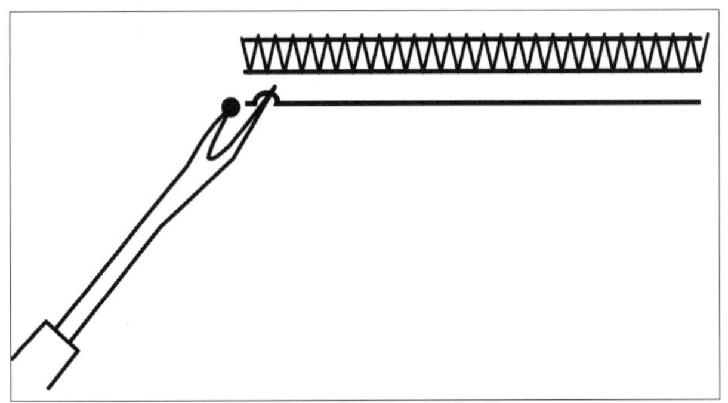

Step 4 - A small piece of the seam should come up. Using your fingers try to grab hold of the little bit of seam that has come up.

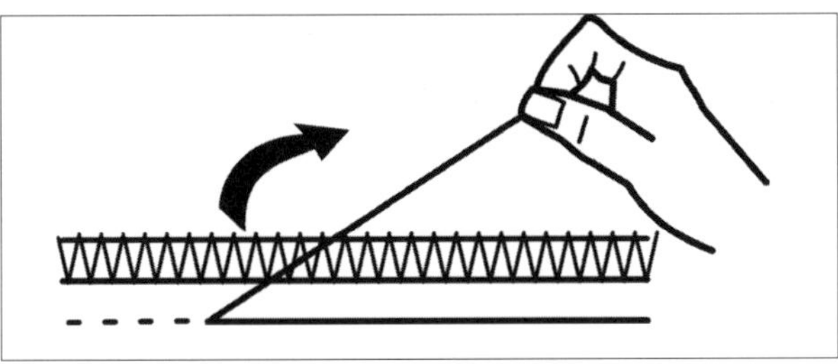

Step 5 - Pull this towards you. It should unravel.

Step 6 - If it doesn't unravel the first time, follow the first procedure until it does unravel.

Step 7 - Some stretch fabrics are harder to unravel because the stitching gets caught on the stretch fabric.

Another reason you may have difficulty is if the pants have been worn and washed a lot. The stitches may have matted together.

Cover stitch

This method of sewing is used for hemming stretch fabrics like hems on track suits etc.

Two rows of stitching show on the outside of the garment and over locking appears on the inside.

You can buy twin needles anywhere and run two threads through your domestic sewing machine to achieve the same stitch, however when you

do it on a domestic sewing machine it will not unpick as easily as an industrial cover stitch machine will.

If you need to unpick this type of seam, here is a quick easy way to unpick a cover stitch.

Step 1 - Place fold of seam on your left hand with the fold in the crease of your hand.

Step 2 - Locate the beginning of the stitching and unpick just past this working towards your body.

Step 3 - Unpick 3 or 4 stitches on each row.

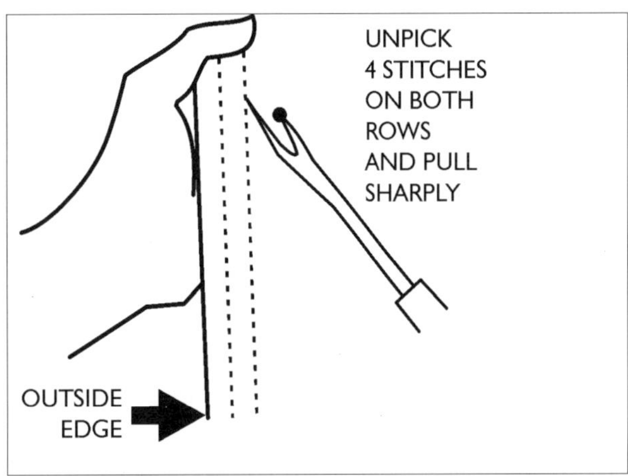

Step 4 - Pull sharply towards your body.

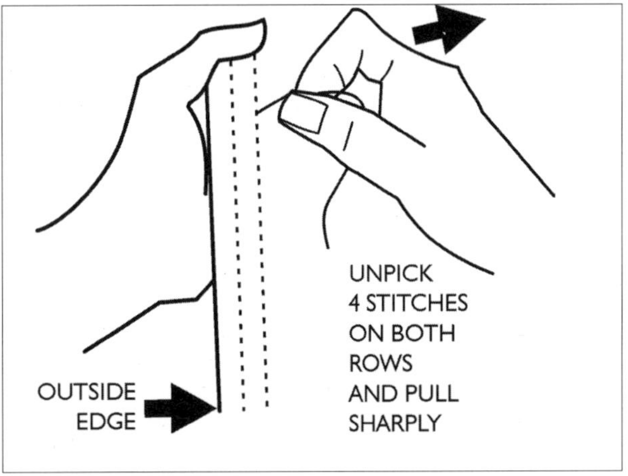

Step 5 - Flip over and stretch fabric in the direction of the stitching. You are actually stretching the stitching as much as possible.

Step 6 - Grab hold of the loose thread and pull.

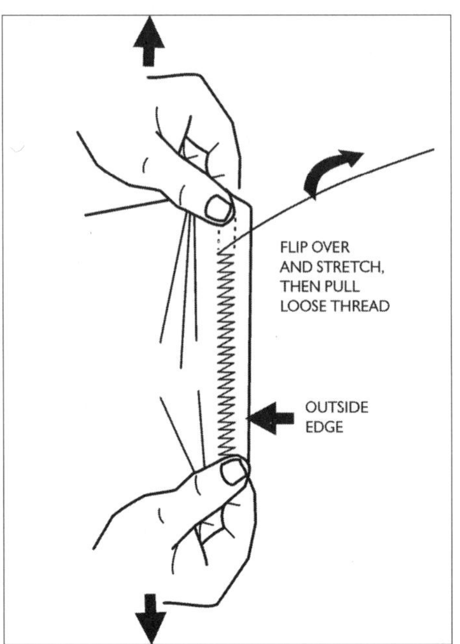

Step 7 - It should unravel. If it doesn't first time, persevere, it does work.

Please note:

There are a few stretch fabrics that will ladder if you stretch them. Try a small section first to make sure it doesn't ladder like a stocking.

If the pants have been worn long, the stitching may have matted together at the back of the leg. This may make it difficult to unravel.

Persist with the unpicking and you will get there. If it's really matted, slice the under side with the quick unpick.

Cover stitch - triple seam

Three rows of stitching appear on the outside of the garment with threads connecting the three rows. Over locking appears on the inside.

Unpicking a three thread seam is similar to the cover stitch – double seam.

Single top stitched seams

Some garments are top stitched using a single row of stitching. Jeans can have a single row of stitching down the first 8" or 20 cm from the band and towards the thigh. This ensures the seam sits flat.

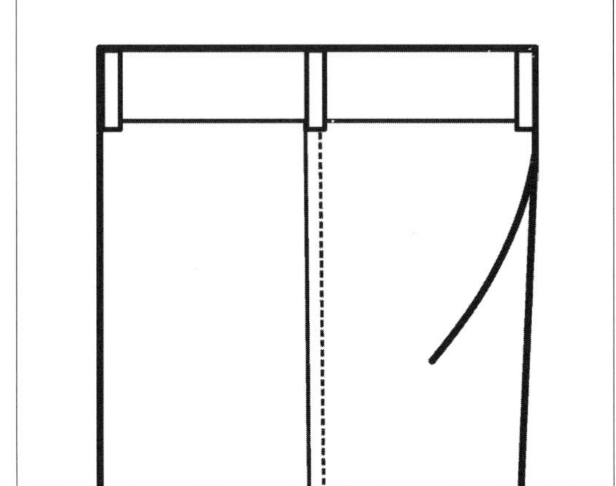

Double top stitched seams

Many garments can have a normal over locked seam on the inside, but can be double stitched on the outside.

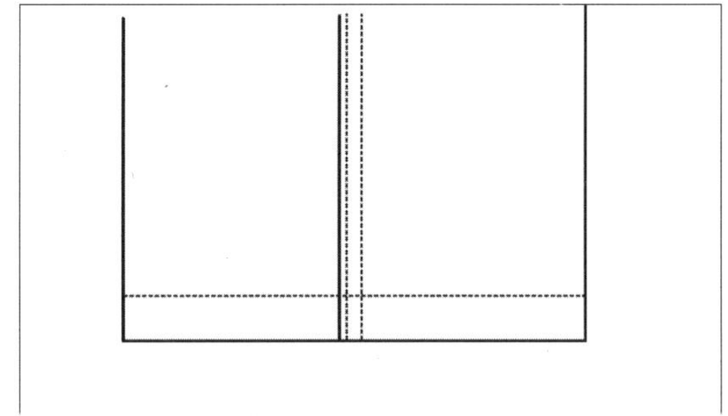

Jeans usually have double top stitching down the inside leg and the back seam. The double stitching can be by a normal industrial sewing machine, but it could also be by an unraveller.

Unpick the normal seam using a quick unpick and slicing. If you feel concerned about nicking the fabric then work slowly. If it is an unraveller, then use the technique for unpicking an unraveller.

To unpick these I turn the garment inside out because I find it gives me greater access to the seam.

Blind hem

Most manufacturers have a blind hemming machine.

I am sure you have had one of these hems fall down on you. If the right stitch is released, then the whole stitching will unravel. Not great when you have a pair of pants that you want the hem to stay up on, but great when you are unpicking a hem, and are in a hurry.

Grab hold of the right thread and its unpicked in seconds.

This stitch has to be pulled out of the loop for you to release the rest of the stitch. I hope the illustration helps you in practicing how to unravel a blind hem.

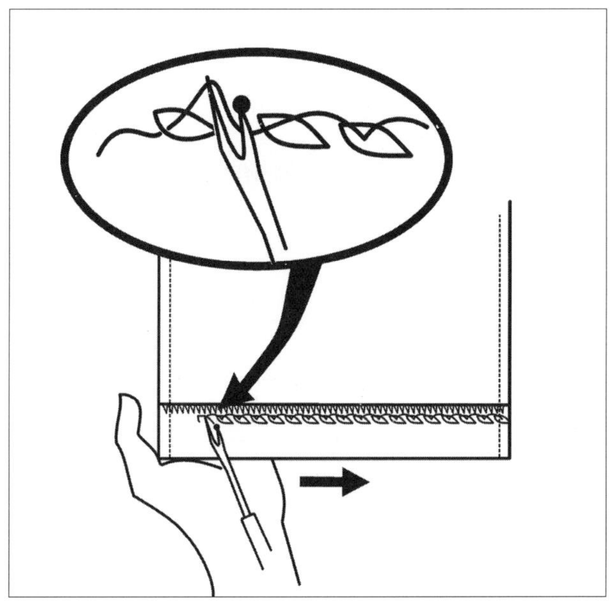

French Seam

French seams were used back in the Victorian era before over lockers were invented.

Altering a garment with a french seam can be difficult because it is hard to get the seam back together, particularly on thick denim.

I usually change the seam from french seam to over locked seam on denim.

If I was sewing a shear fabric, I would stitch with the french seam. That means I would unpick it, take the garment in, and re french seam the garment.

Here is how a french seam is constructed.

Step 1 - Place the wrong sides of the panels together and sew the seam joining the pieces together.

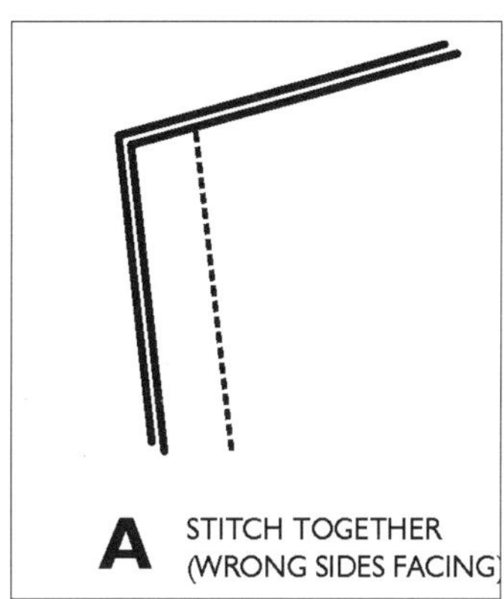

Step 2 - Turn the pieces in the opposite direction with the right sides facing and re sew the seam making sure that the frayed or cut section is encases in the last seam.

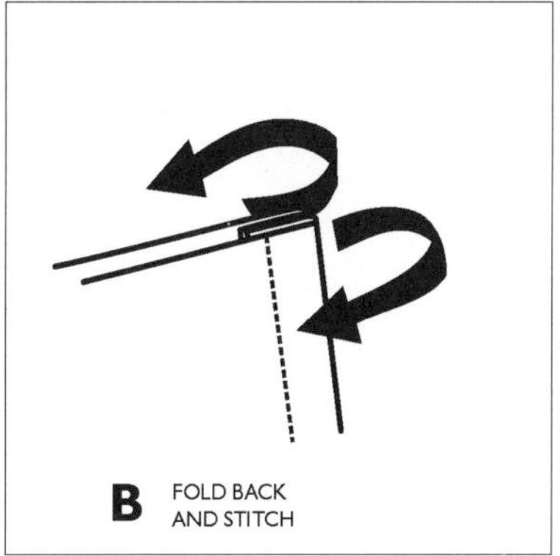

In these modern times, we join the sections together, sew the seam and over lock the edge.

As previously stated, if you come across a pair of jeans that has a french seam at the back, and you need to take the back in, then unpick the french seam, re pin the back, take in the back by a normal stitch, then over lock off the excess. Cut the excess off first before you over lock, or seam ribbon or bias onto the edge.

Garments that come from countries like India and Indonesia usually have french seams, because they don't have over lockers yet.

Imperial & Metric Explained

"Whether you are Taking Up or Taking In, the measurement must be accurate."

Measurements

When you are altering a garment, it is all about measurements.

You need to get the pinning correct, but you also need to transfer those measurements down onto a piece of paper.

I grew up with imperial measure, so when I write the measurements down I use the imperial measure.

The United States still uses imperial measure, but England and other countries use metric. I found it more accurate to use imperial.

I often got asked by customers why I used imperial measures and why I don't convert to metric. It's really quite simple. When you are altering a garment, for example taking in the sides of a skirt, you will be pinning the sides. Let's say that you pin the sides in ¼". This would be a total of ½" in total on the right side and ½" on the left side.

Let's take the same garment and pin it in 7 mm. This is a total of 14 mm on one side and 14 mm on the other side.

I mark my garments when I am taking them in with a tailor's pencil. I place a dot at the ½" position, and so on down the garment. Have you ever tried to put a dot against a millimeter mark? It is almost impossible to be accurate.

The tip of the tailors' pencil is bigger than 1 millimeter!!

To those of you who don't understand imperial, I have provided some illustrations and explanations.

Imperial measurements explained

The imperial measure has sections in 1/8" (said as one eighth of an inch).

If a garment is being taken in, and the amount is 1/8" then the tailors' pencil can be dotted right on the 1/8" of an inch, which is really ¼" total

because it is the side of a garment which is front and back.

This first illustration is of a tape measure in imperial measure. I always buy the imperial tapes, which have 1/8" sections. You can get tape measures that are 1/16" but I find they have the same problem as metric tape measures.

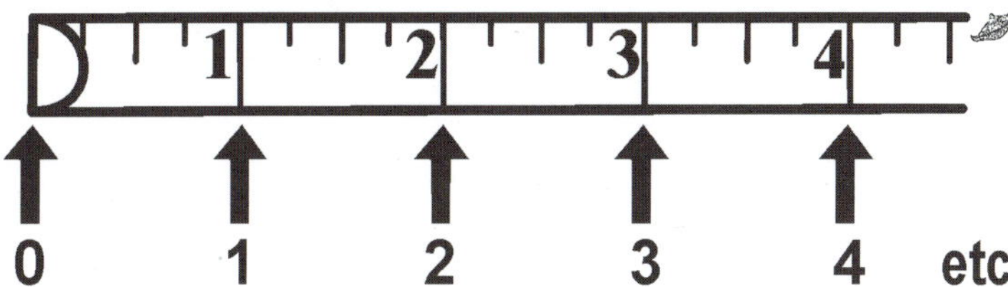

The following illustrations are a guide to understanding imperial measure.

If you have never used a tape measure before, then you need to begin at the beginning. The end of the tape has a metal section. This does make it hard to see the first few segments, however this is where you begin to measure from.

When I say place a mark beside the top of the tape measure, I mean at the top next to the end of the metal section.

If you have never worked in imperial before, then basically you will notice that an inch is broken down into 8 parts.

If you are taking a garment up and it reads half way between the 1 and the 2, then it would be 1 ½". (one and a half inch)

If the amount is going up 1" plus five bars past the 1 it would be 1 5/8". (One and five eighth of an inch)

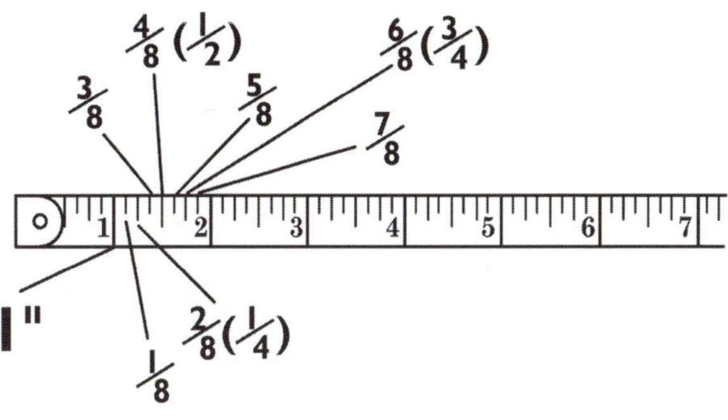

This apple will also illustrate how one inch is broken down into 8 segments.

By cutting the apple in half on one side you now have a half an apple. this is the same with an inch. Half of an inch is called "half an inch' or 1/2".

On the opposite side at the bottom right, the apple has been cut into a ¼ . An inch is the same, because in the middle of the beginning of one inch and 1/2" is a 1/4".

And finally, if you split the 1/4 into half you get 1/8th.

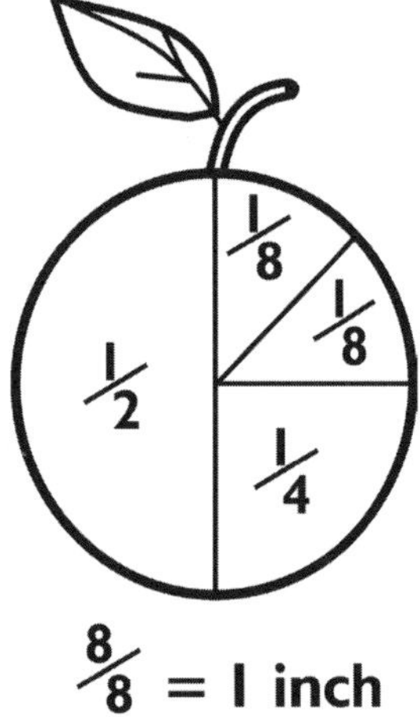

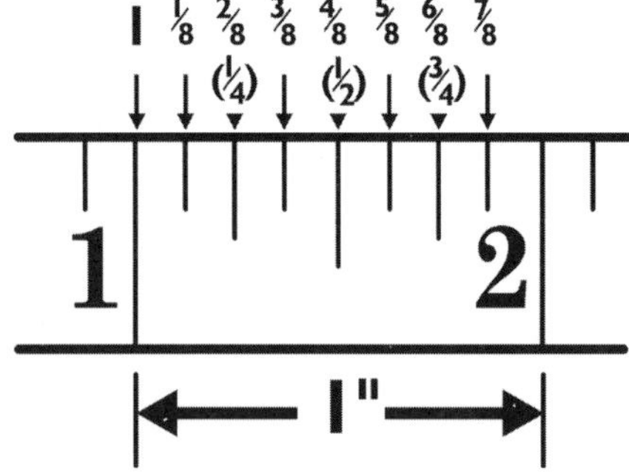

So one inch has 8 segments to it.

For the above illustration, I have begun at the end of 1". I did this because of the metal section at the beginning of the tape.

I hope this helps you to understand Imperial measure if you have not worked with it before.

Metric Explained

In one of my shops, I had a drycleaning agency. The Drycleaning people worked in metric, so I began using metric so that we were all on the same page.

I assumed that they knew how to read a tape measure.

Never assume anything.

They were not measuring from the end of the tape.

They were counting the beginning of the tape as 1 centimetre. So we were always out by 1 cm.

It took a while of explaining, but we got there.

So for all those people out there who don't know about metric here we go.

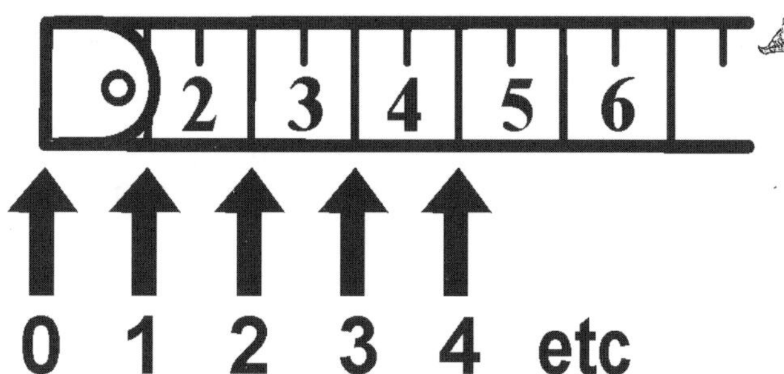

The end of the tape is "0", and the first full line you come to is 1 centimetre. The second full line is 2 and so on.

The sections in between are 1/2 centimetre or .5.

Hope that helps you with metric.

Helpful Hints & Tips

"These Hints and Tips may help you save time and money on your clothing alterations."

Introduction

Over the years I have come across, and developed some ideas and concepts to help with clothing alterations.

I thought I would put together some helpful hints and tips to help you.

I decided it was better to put it into alphabetical order. If you need a quick reference, go to the Table of Contents at the back of the book and you will be able to find what you are looking for easily.

B

Belt loops

When you take in the back of a garment, you sometimes need to sew the belt loops back on.

Rather than inserting into the band, you can sew on in such a way that the belt loops look like they are inserted into the band.

Step 1 - Lay the belt look over the band with the right side facing up, and stitch across the bottom about 1/8" from the bottom.

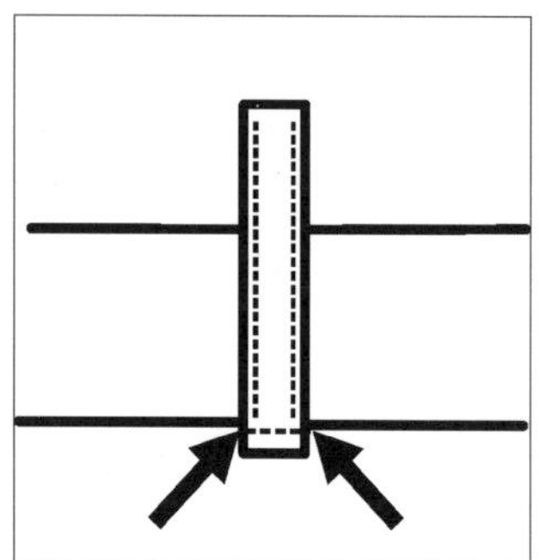

Step 2 – Fold the belt loop down and stitch across the bottom, making sure your stitches are encasing the raw edge of the material underneath.

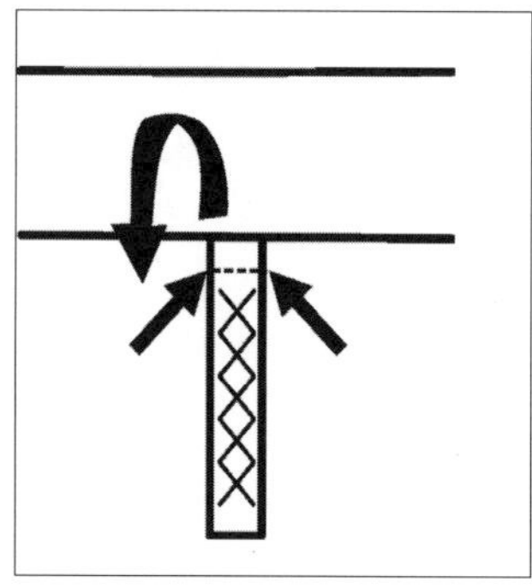

Step 3 – Fold the belt loop back up and stitch across the top.

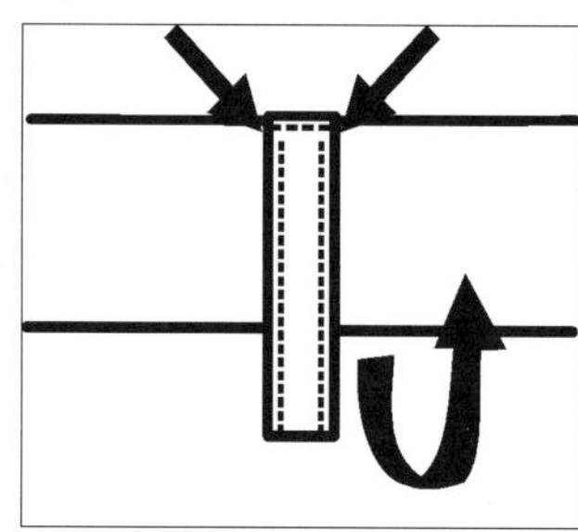

Step 4 – (Optional) Stitch across the bottom of the belt loop.

Blade - slicing jeans or thick hems

The jury is out on this one. Some people find this technique quick and easy, and others are not so sure.

I use this technique because I find it saves me an incredible amount of time if I have to unpick a jeans hem.

If you are not sure, go to the Opportunity Shop and buy an old pair of jeans to practice on.

Step 1 - Turn the jeans inside out.

Step 2 - Lean into the table and hold some of the hem against the table with your tummy.

Step 3 - Place the edge of the blade into the stitch and cut one or two stitches.

Step 4 - Turn the blade on an angle towards your face and slice along the hem.

Step 5 - The blade should not be touching the outside fabric of the hem.

Step 6 - Slice up to the thick seam and slowly work across.

Step 7 - Continue to slice until you come to the second thick seam, and repeat Step 6.

Step 8 - Unpick all the fluffy bits of cotton.

The straight stitching on one side should pull away cleanly.

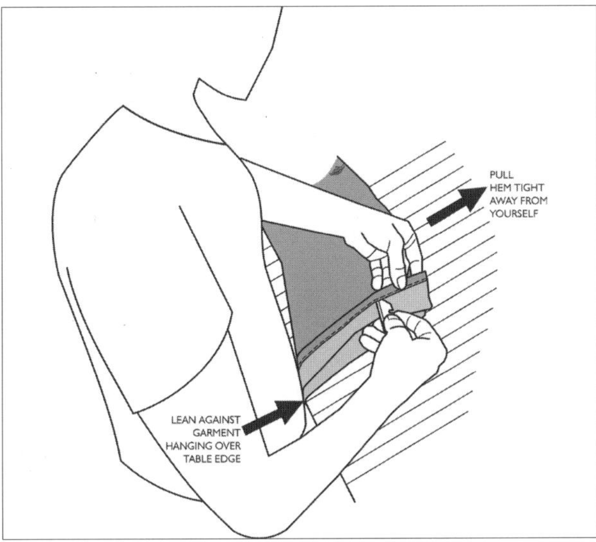

Blood on your clothes

Have you ever been working on a garment, and you accidentally get blood on the garment because you have pricked your finger on a pin or a needle? Try this little exercise. It must be done immediately you get blood on fabric.

Wet your finger with your own saliva and dab it onto the blood.

The saliva must be from the person whose blood is on the garment.

Normally the blood will disappear.

It's like magic.

If someone else tries to use their saliva it will not work.

Buttons - Sewing on with machine

You can sew buttons on to any garment with your sewing machine. It is quick and easy once you know how.

I find that if I use the button hole foot (single one) that it holds the button in place. If I use the standard foot, the button seems to slip.

Mark out where you want your buttons.

Pull the thread so you begin to sew with a long piece of thread.

Place your straight stitch to zero (0).

Place your zig zag at around 3. You will find out exactly where to have the zig zag when you begin to sew on the button.

Line the garment up on the machine, with the dot or mark where the button is to go under the zipper foot.

Buttons – Sewing by hand - Easy technique

I have so many people come into my shop saying something like – I can't even sew on a button. How sad it is that a whole generation has lost out on learning how to do just the basic skills of sewing.

Sewing buttons on to clothes doesn't have to be difficult. In fact I take just a few minutes to sew them on.

Follow these steps and you will have your buttons on in no time at all.

1. Pull the thread from the reel and pull out to arms length.
2. Now take your arm back in and pull the thread. out a second time, so that you have a very long piece of cotton.
3. Fold the cotton into two making sure the ends are even.
4. You now have a fold one end and two joins the

other end.

5. Thread the two joins into the eye of the needle. (Lick the ends if necessary to moisten)
6. You will now have four threads in the needle.
7. Knot the end of the four threads.
8. Sew the knot onto the fabric where you are going to sew the button going from the right side through to the wrong side.
9. This means that the knot is where the button will go.
10. Bring the needle back through the fabric to where the knot is.
11. Put the button on to the needle and push the button down on to the fabric, covering the knot.
12. Now put the needle through the opposite hole on the button and back through to the opposite side of the fabric.
13. If you want to come back through one more time you can or you can knot off by putting the thread through itself and pulling the thread. Do this twice and cut the thread.

Buttonholes

When a customer comes in wanting buttonholes, I generally pin the garment with them at the counter.

Notice that the pins are placed so that the centre pin can be pulled out as you sew.

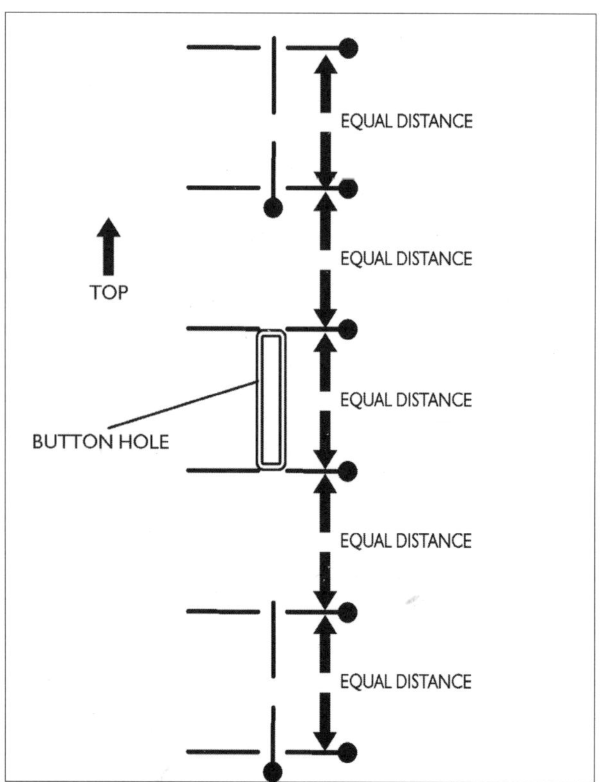

C

Clothes - Protecting clothes against moth and silverfish

I don't particularly like the smell of camphor in my wardrobe. I find that it goes through the clothes. There are a number of different products for hanging in your wardrobe to ward off silver fish and moths.

My favourite is cedar balls. You can buy them in most department stores, and they smell nice. There's nothing like the smell of timber, and the silver fish and moths hate it. So – no more holes in your woollen jumpers and suits.

D

Denim – Sewing denim

Thread two cottons side by side on the top of the machine, and normal single cotton in the bobbin. Invest in a packet of Jeans needles. I prefer size 90/12.

Sew what I call top side. This means that you fold the hem under but the right side of the fabric is facing you. Use the foot impression as your guide for sewing the hem.

Hem Allowances

The following hem allowances are a guide only. This is the amount that you will come down AFTER you have marked up the amount that was folded UNDER and pinned into place.

Types of hems	Imperial
Men's Suit/Dress Pants	2"
Men's pants with cuff	1 1/2" + 1 1/2" + 1"
Ladies Dress Pants-Box style	1 1/2"
Ladies Dress Pants-flared	1" - 1 1/4"
Ladies Dress Pants-With split	2"
Casual/Track Pants	1" - 1 1/2"
Jeans - Designer	3/8" + 3/8"
Jeans - Normal	5/8" + /8"
Cargo/Casual Pants	1" + 1/2"
Cargo/Casual Pants	1 1/4" + 2"
Cargo/Casual Pants	1 1/2" + 1/2"
Cargo/Casual Pants	2" + 1/2"
Flared Pants	1" - 1 1/4"
Skirts - Outside fabric	1 1/4" - 1 1/2"
Skirts - Lining	1"
Skirts - Lining	1/2" + 1/2"
Rolled hem	1/4"
Girls School Uniform	3"
Boys School Uniform	3"
Gown - Over locked	3/8"
Gown - Turn twice	1/4" + 1/4"
Jacket Lined - Outer fabric	1 1/2" - 1 3/4"
Jacked lined - lining	1/2"

Hem Allowances

Metric hem measurements are rounded off to the nearest 5 mm or 1/2 cm. I do not bother trying to get within a millimeter of a measurement.

Types of hems	Metric
Men's Suit/Dress Pants	5 cm
Men's pants with cuff	3.5 + 3.5 + 2 cm
Ladies Dress Pants-Box style	4
Ladies Dress Pants-flared	2.5 - 3
Ladies Dress Pants-with split	5
Casual/Track Pants	2.5 - 4
Jeans - Designer	1 + 1
Jeans - Normal	1.5 + 1.5
Cargo/Casual Pants	2.5 + 1
Cargo/Casual Pants	3 + 1
Cargo/Casual Pants	4 + 1
Cargo/Casual Pants	5 + 1
Flared Pants	2.5 - 3
Skirts - Outside fabric	3 - 4
Skirts - Lining	2.5
Skirts - Lining	1 + 1
Rolled hem	.5
Girls School Uniform	7.5
Boys School Uniform	7.5
Gown - Over locked	1
Gown - Turn twice	.5 + .5
Jacket Lined - Outer fabric	4 - 4.5
Jacked lined - lining	.5

Explanation

Where there is a + it means that the fabric is turned twice. This means no over locking. The hem allowance is folded once, then folded a second time, to create a turned twice effect.

Where there is no + it means that I am assuming you are going to use an over locker, or sew ribbon on to the cut edge, and hand stitch or machine stitch, depending on your preference.

Hem - false

When pants need to be let down because they are too short, I would recommend you sew a fabric false hem on rather than using bias binding.

The reason I use fabric (and fabric a similar weight and colour to the pants) is because it allows the hem to stay up, whereas bias binding is soft and tends to droop.

For ladies pants I cut a piece of fabric 2" wide and a little bit longer in circumference than the pants. That would mean I end up with a 1 ½" hem allowance and a ½" seam allowance.

For men's pants I cut a piece of fabric 2 ½" side and a little bit longer in circumference than the pants. That would mean I end up with a 2" hem allowance and a ½" seam allowance.

Unpick any over locking.

Close any seams that have been opened. If the pants are tapered the seams would have been opened so the pants would lie flat when folded up. If you don't close the seams again, you will have a seam that sticks out.

Begin sewing at the inside-leg. Start to sew ½" from the end of the fabric. When you come around to the beginning again, fold that ½" over. That means you will lay the extra fabric over the top of the ½" folded over. Lock off.

Now under stitch the seam allowance to the new false hem. You will notice that at the join of the fabric it will be open. This will give you flexibility when you turn the false hem up into the pants.

Hem Off Cuts

If you have purchased my book you will notice that when I cut the excess hem from the pants, I cut in a circle, rather than cutting up from the bottom and around. This way if a mistake is made the circle can be sewn back onto the pants, becoming a false hem.

In the shops I save my off cuts for six weeks. I figure this is enough time for people to come in and ask for them if they want them for something.

I used to return off cuts to customers, but the bulk of them didn't want them, so I began saving them. I put them into a plastic bag every week with the date on the outside of the bag. That way I can look for the off cut in the bag that is the date the person had the alteration completed.

If you are going to begin doing your own clothing alterations at home, I would suggest you begin saving your off cuts. There are three reasons why I keep them.

1.   If you make a mistake and don't realize it straight away, you can use the off cut as a new false hem.

2.   You can use old off cuts in similar colours for false hems on pants that are too short. Like I said before, using bias binding as a false hem is ok, but it doesn't provide the same drop in the fabric as a piece of cotton or linen fabric will.

3.   If you need to repair a garment, you will still have the original fabric, which means a better repair job, than using fabric that is not the right colour.

Hems – Small hem on evening gowns

I don't know about you but those rolled hem feet on the domestic sewing machine can be very hard to work out.

Here are two techniques you can try.

1. Sew a seam around the edge of the hem first; making sure the seam is about ¼" from the edge of the fabric. Now sew around the hem using the stitch line as your fold. Also use your finger

nail to push the fabric in. You should have a much easier turn twice small hem.

2. Convert your over locker to three threads, and have one needle in the right hand side of the over locker. Make sure the stitch width is wide not close together. Over lock around the edge of the fabric, then turn the fabric twice.

Some times I come across an evening gown which has the small turn twice hem, but the fabric is quite thick or heavy. If I am shortening the hem, I change it to an over locked hem and just turn the over locking over and sew topside. This means I sew from the top through the middle of the over locking. It means the fabric is not so rigid and has a softer fall to it.

J

Ironing – Why you should iron seams flat on garments

Have you ever worn a garment where the seams look like they are bulking out? This can happen around a hem area such as the bottom of a dress, skirt, pants or around the sleeves or even around a neckline.

Whenever I am taking in the sides of a garment, I make sure that the seams are going in the same direction. Let's say I am taking in a dress from the underarm to the hem. When I re attach the facing or lining to the outer fabric under the arm, I have the seam lying in the direction of the back of the person. I follow this practice down at the hem area as well. To make sure that you do this, turn the garment inside out and iron the seam flat with it lying in the direction of the back of the garment. Iron it flat all the way to the hem. Repeat this process on both sides.

When the garment is tried on, the seams will be sitting flat against the person's body, rather than pocking out.

Iron - Using your iron

Using your iron will almost guarantee that your workmanship will be correct. I remember when I first started doing clothing alterations for my friend Carol's business, she said to me – IRON EVERYTHING. Every time you have a seam to sew onto another seam, iron the seams together. If you just follow this one tip, you will truly become a professional seamstress.

When you are extremely busy as we were in our shops, there were times you thought to yourself – I'll just iron it later. I can almost guarantee that if you do that, the garment will not sit correctly.

Taking in the back of pants is a good example of using the iron. When you are re attaching the waist band, it is important to open the seams out on the band and iron them before re attaching. This is very important if your band is in two sections. Cut the excess fabric off (leave about 5/8" either side) and splay the seams flat. Iron them flat, then fold the seams together and iron. This makes your sewing so much easier.

I would also turn the garment inside out and iron the centre back seam flat (in the correct direction so check the crotch area to see which way the seam is lying) and iron the back over the back seam as if it is sewn back on. If your band is too big or too small, you will notice this in this ironing stage, and can make an adjustment then.

Jacket sleeves- sewing interfacing before ironing on

Shortening jacket sleeves can be complicated if you don't know how. But for those of you who are experienced and would like another little tip on how to ensure the sleeve does not DROP, read on.

Measure the amount of hem allowance on the sleeve. It is always important to repeat the same amount of hem allowance that was there before. (The same obviously applies to the lining, though I usually allow ½" or 1 cm) Cut your interfacing so it is ½" or 1 cm more than the hem allowance.

Before you iron on your interfacing, fold the interfacing at the hem allowance – glue side out – and sew a row of stitching along the fold edge about ¼"" or ½ cm in from the fold.

Using a tailors arm - have the sleeve turned inside out and iron the interfacing on to the sleeve, but only iron up to the folded section. Do not iron this part, or it will stick to your iron.

Now fold the hem allowance back at the new fold line. Because you had folded the interfacing with the sticky side out, it will adhere (stick) to the two sides of the new hem and secure it in place.

If you try to open the fold you will see stitching. This stitching will hold the sleeve up.

If you have trouble finding a tailors arm, send me an email and I will see if I can get one for you judith@geniecentre.com

Jeans - Marking

I have provided you with the jean genie for marking, preparing and sewing your jeans, however, just in case you misplace the jean genie, I will include how to mark up a pair of jeans using your normal tape measure.

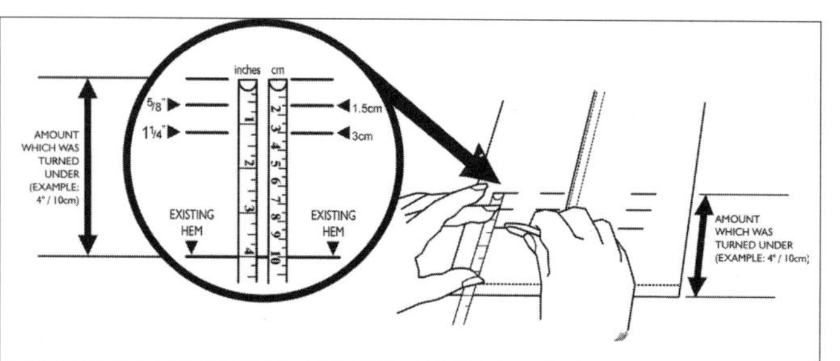

Mark up the amount you are taking the jeans up and mark down the hem allowance = 5/8" + 5/8" or 1.5 + 1.5 cm.

Jeans – Replacing jean buttons

You can replace the jean button in two ways. But before I mention those two ways you may have to repair the hole.

Cut a piece of fabric about 1" square and push it in the hole. Lay flat in between the band. I use tweezers to push it in. Thread your sewing machine with a cotton colour similar to the denim.

Put your stitch length to very small. Look at the denim and you will see the way the grain goes on the fabric. Stitch in this same direction going back and forward, but moving across as you sew. I always sew from left to right. This will darn the hole.

1. Go to your local fabric/haberdashery store and buy a packet of jean buttons. They usually come in a packet of 5 or 6. The instructions are on the back. You need a hammer and a piece of wood to rest the back of the button on. Don't lay the button on concrete or a tile.

2. Sew an ordinary button on in its place.

Jeans - Making jeans smaller

Taking jeans in can be difficult. Usually I will take jeans in through the back seam, however from time to time you will come across jeans with a French seam as the centre back seam. I would not recommend taking in and trying to re sew as a French seam.

Undo the whole seam from the top of the band to the crotch.

Unpick the seam and re pin the seam back to the original position it was in as a French seam with the fabric now loose at the side.

Take in the amount you need to and over lock the excess fabric off before re stitching with a double seam. I find it easier to cut off the excess fabric BEFORE over locking. (If your blade is a little blunt it will not cut through the thickness.) Over lock carefully over the thick fabric.

L

Labels - Unpicking labels

If you are like me, there are some labels that stick into the back of your neck, and there is no way you are going to leave the label there. To any clothing manufacturer reading this, can you take note, and have nice soft labels for people like me that had the prickly labels.

If you want to take the label off, you must be very careful not to rip or tear the fabric or knit.

One of the biggest mistakes people make is trying to take a label off a knit and making a hole.

Knits ladder just like stockings, so you have to be very careful. This is where the quick unpick comes in handy.

It has a very pointed end on it which you can slip into the stitch, and then it is also very sharp at the end of the point.

Don't try and take a label off in a hurry. Take your time, and you won't ruin the garment.

Labels - Sewing on

I used to have people bring in bag loads of clothes that needed name labels put on.

Just a tip. Most labels are white. Put white cotton on the top of your sewing machine, and use the colour of the garment on the bobbin.

For example if you are sewing on a label on a navy jumper.

Have the white on the top, navy on the bobbin, and sew the label in a position that will be seen, but not itchy for the person wearing it.

Machine plate – Fabric catches on plate.

It happens to all of us. You are sewing away, and somehow you manage to smash the needle into the sewing machine plate under the garment.

If you have a look at your plate, you will probably notice that it has a few dents on it. If it doesn't, then I take my hat off to you. Mine gets a little mangled sometimes.

Now I know that we all should get our sewing machines serviced regularly, but I find that in some cases I can fix problems that come up. One of my problems is the plate gets a little damaged, and it can grab hold of certain fabrics, particularly chiffons or knit fabrics.

Get yourself some very light weight sand paper, or use a nail file, and file the plate where it is mangled. Finish the sanding with the finest paper you have. If that doesn't solve the problem, you may have to buy a new plate.

"My Notes - blank for you to use

N

Needles – How to sharpen

Your hand sewing needles can become blunt. By this I mean that when you push the needle through fabric, it is hard to push through.

I think that this happens because when they are pushed through fabric, they can pick up residue onto the tip of the needle. I find that if you run the needle through your hair a few times it will put oil on the needle, which allows it to run through the fabric easily.

You need to have longer length hair for this to work, because you are running the needle through your hair say from the side to the end of the hair. Don't poke yourself in the head. Be careful when you do this.

This wouldn't work on needles that have been dropped or have lost part of their tip.

Needles - Self Threading needle

Many people are not aware that they can buy self threading needles. The top of the needle is open, so that all you have to do is push the thread down and onto the needle.

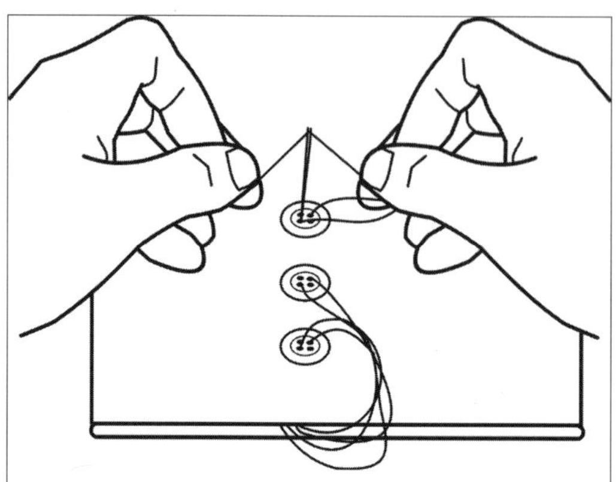

Try doubling the thread through the needle so you have four threads on the needle. Now you only need to sew into the buttonholes twice and lock off. If you want the button to look neat, have the knot of the thread underneath the button. Do this in the beginning, and when knotting off lock under the button.

O

Oil on clothes

If you get oil on your clothes, sprinkle with talcum powder as quickly as possible. It has still worked for me if I sprinkle with Talcum Powder a few hours after I get oil on my clothes.

The most common problem for this is for a seamstress who is making a garment, and the machine spots machine oil onto the garment. In this case you can sprinkle the talc immediately.

If you get cooking oil or food oil on your clothes whilst you are cooking or eating your food, then you will need to wait until you can change your clothes.

Over locking

When I opened my first clothing alteration shop I began with a small domestic over locker that I borrowed from my sister in law. It was old, but it worked well.

It was set up as a four thread, but I didn't want to use it that way.   Most manufacturers use a wide over locking stitch. You can achieve this professional look on your domestic over locker by doing the following -

1.   Take the threads off on the left hand side spool. You need to leave the looper (far right) and the thread next to the looper on.

2.   Take the right hand needle out Make sure you tighten the screw up securely so it doesn't get lost, because if you are sewing Lycra or stretch, you may like to go back to four threads.
Now when you use your over locker, you will have a nice wide over lock stitch, just like manufactures use.

If you want to ever sew Lycra or stretch, just go back to four threads. The fourth thread is only for such occasions because it gives you the seam on the left hand side of the over locking.

If you want to understand which stitch is which, put three different colours on the over locker and sew onto white fabric. Now you will see which stitch is which.

I found that when I was doing my clothing alterations in the shop, my domestic machines did just as well as any industrial. If you are going to do clothing alterations, I would recommend getting two over lockers. Have one set up all the time in black, and use the second for changing colours.

I do switch to an industrial for all my black work. But then I am doing hundreds of alterations a week.

Pants - Take in the back

If you have lost weight or purchased a pair of pants that are too big for you, try pinning the back first. If the centre back does not turn into a "V", then you can take in the back, but if it does turn into a "V", try pinning the sides.

If the sides have pockets, then try pinning the back section between the side seam and the back seam.

If this works, I would take the band off at the back, put darts at the side back section and take the centre back of the band in only at the one position at the back.

The back should not "V" doing this.

Rajah Cloth

This cloth is specially impregnated with a chemical to assist in the ironing of your clothes.

With a rajah cloth you could re-pleat a skirt, or just to use over the top of your hems after you have done an alteration. When you put the cloth over a hem and use your iron on steam, the hem will become very sharp and the fabric looks great.

The cloth is very big, so I cut it in two. I sew a piece of tape onto one end so I can hang it with my other items I use near the iron.

Have you ever ironed a garment and left an iron mark on the garment? Well with the Rajah cloth you will eliminate this ever happening again. You should be able to buy one from your local haberdashery shop.

Rolled hem – Sewing rolled hem twice

For those of you who do rolled hems on your over locker, I thought you might like this tip. For very soft chiffon fabric or similar, I find that if I do a second rolled hem OVER the top of the first rolled hem, it gives an excellent finish.

If you want the type of hem that is ruffled then I do only sew once, and I give the fabric a pull as I sew. Always practice on a scrap piece of fabric to get the settings right.

S

Satin garments

If your satin garment needs to be ironed, try this technique. Hang the garment in the bathroom while you have a shower or bath.

The steam will cause the creases to drop, and you won't have to bother with the iron.

Seams – Laying seams in correct direction

If you are shortening a pair of pants or taking in the waist, always ensure that the seams are laying flat in the same direction from the top of the garment to the bottom of the garment. If you twist the seam, then it will not sit flat against the body of the person.

I usually have the seam facing backwards towards the back of the person, rather than having it laying towards the front of the body.

Sequins – Sewing over sequins

How often have you brought a garment or fabric to make a garment, and the fabric has sequins on it. You will find it almost impossible to sew a straight line trying to sew over the sequins. Some people actually go to the trouble of undoing the threads holding the sequins and re sew them back on later. That is a very long and tiresome way of sewing sequin fabric.

Go to the hardware store (or look in your husbands tool box) and get yourself a small hammer. This particular hammer has a very small head, about the size of a sewing machine foot.

The fabric should be turned inside out. Mark out where you are going to sew. Place the fabric on the machine as if you are ready to sew, but just before you sew into the sequins, hit that section with the hammer, breaking the sequins. Now sew over the section. Smash the next section in front of you with the hammer, and then sew that section. It is slow going, but it is faster than unpicking them all.

It is a little messy, but what you are doing is breaking the sequins rather than cutting the threads and having to re sew.

None of the threads should break, and you are only hammering the section that the sewing machine foot needs to sew through.

Sewing - If you are having trouble sewing a straight line

I just had a lady send me an email saying that she had a sewing machine, but didn't know how to use it. I have met a lot of people over the years that have sewing machines, but can't sew a straight line.

I have also trained a lot of ladies in my time, and one of the things I found would help them sew a straight line was to get them to NOT look at the needle or the seam that they were sewing.

I hardly ever look at the needle or the seam. I look at where the sewing machine foot is in relation to the side of the fabric or the distance from the side of the fabric. If I keep the sewing machine foot at the same distance, then I am guaranteed a straight line.

Sewing - Two rows of stitching

When you are doing what I call double machine stitch, after you have sewn your first row, line the sewing machine foot up against the first row and sew the second row concentrating on the foot being next to the first row.

Do not look at the seam, because you will more than likely sew a wonky line.

Some sewing machines have a measurement guide on the right hand side of the needle which will allow you to get the same distance apart all the way around.

Sewing – Stitch width

I was asked a question recently about what I thought stitches per inch or 2.5 cm should be. The answer to that question is that it depends on the fabric. Try out this exercise
Get three types of fabric.

1.   A heavy denim or cotton
2.   A polyester
3.   A knit or stretch fabric

Set the machine stitch so that it is about 1/8th of an inch long or 3 mm. Sew a row of stitches with the heavy denim or cotton, then a row on the polyester and finally a row on the knit or stretch fabric.

Put a pin at the end of 1" or 2.5 cm of stitching on each row. Now count the stitches on each piece of fabric. I found that on the denim or cotton I had 9 stitches, on the polyester I had 10 and on the knit I had 11.

So what this is saying is that you should be adjusting your stitch width depending on the fabric you are sewing.

Sewing – Stitch width – tiny stitching

When you do as many clothing alterations as I have, the stitch width becomes a major issue.

Have you ever tried to unpick a seam that someone has done using the smallest stitch width possible? It is extremely difficult, and besides which it can be lethal because you have to try and unpick the seam without making a hole in the fabric.

Never ever sew a garment in a small stitch. Always have your machine set at around 3 or at the middle range width.

Do a little demonstration for yourself. Use two pieces of fabric. Set the stitch width at a low number and sew a row of stitching joining the pieces together. The first thing you will notice is that it will probably grab the fabric as you sew. The fabric will probably pucker or be pulled closer together. If you try to iron this seam, it will look like it has been gathered together.

Now try to unpick this small seam.   Good luck!!!!!!! Now set the stitch width at the middle range or around 3 and sew the fabric together. Iron the seam and I am sure you will see that the seam will be sitting flat.

Try to unpick the seam. It should be quite simple to do. Having a normal stitch width will save you a lot of time when altering clothes.

The other reason is that your seams will sit flat if you use the normal range stitch width.

Sewing topside on stretch fabrics

Pin the hem up with the pin head on the right hand side. This way you can remove the pins as you sew.

I always use the button hole foot when sewing stretch fabric, as I find that it seems to hold on to the fabric better than the standard sewing machine foot.

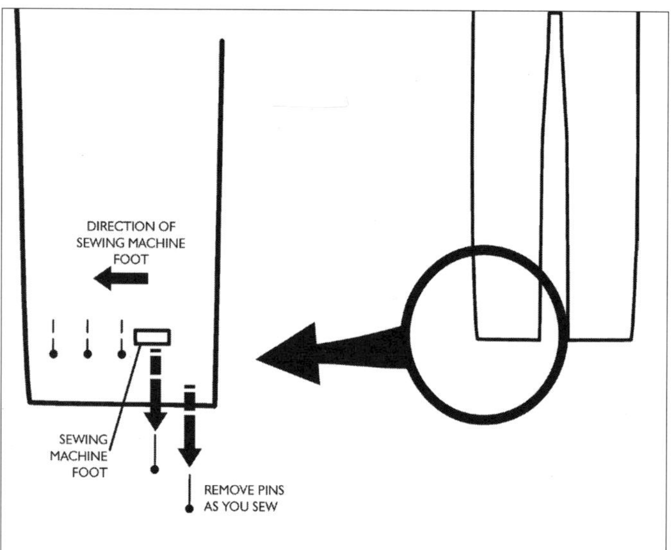

Stretch fabric – Sewing stretch fabric on your domestic sewing machine

Sewing stretch fabric does not need to be a nightmare. There are just a few things you need to do before you jump on the machine and sew. First of all you need to buy a packet of Stretch needles. They are called 75/12 and I find them the best for sewing stretch. 75/11

The second thing you need to do is use your buttonhole foot if it is plastic. I find that the bottom of the zipper foot grabs a hold of the fabric so that means that it doesn't slip on the fabric like a normal foot does. I have sewn thousand s of stretch fabric garments with my buttonhole foot. In fact it is actually broken now on one side and it still works a treat.

The third thing you need to know is to have your stitch length towards the longer length rather than the small stitch. On my machine it is around No. 3.

The fourth thing I do is sew what I call topside.

This means that I have the hem underneath and I sew on the right side of the fabric. I can see the ridge of over locking underneath, and I sew through the over locking.

T

Tailors arm

This is the greatest invention since sliced bread for seamstresses and tailors.

When you are shortening the sleeves on a jacket, you really must have a tailors arm. You place the sleeve over the arm, and it allows you to iron on interfacing and/or iron up seams etc.

It also comes in handy when ironing shirts. See Jacket sleeves page 221-222.

Tummy bloating

Women's bodies change every month. If you are going to pin a wedding gown or evening gown, I would suggest that the gown be pinned at the same time of the month that the person is going to wear it.

For example if the wedding is on a date where she is in the middle of her cycle, I would suggest that if it needs altering, have the pinning at the same time of month.

I have had women have a pair of pants taken in when they have their period, and find that a week later their tummy is not so bloated and the garment is loose.

Tummy bloating can cause the hem on a pair of pants to rise, because the pants get tighter. This tightness will cause the hem to rise higher than it would normally.

Unpicking

I use a quick unpick for unpicking seams. Unpicks can become blunt, and I would suggest that when this happens, buy a new one. Trying to unpick with a blunt quick unpick will only take you a lot longer, and you may find you could make a regrettable mistake by pushing too hard, and damaging the fabric.

Velvet

As a general rule, you should never iron velvet. My mum suggests you hang the velvet dress in the bathroom (the same as satin) and have a shower or bath, letting the steam do the work for you. Apparently it gives the velvet a great shine.

Zips - Shortening a long zip

Sometimes you will find a zip that is the right colour for your garment, but it is too long.

Because I come across of a lot of broken zips, I have over the years noticed that one of the main culprits is when a manufacturer used a long zip, but the seamstress making the garment only tacks across the bottom and cuts the zip down to the length they want.

If any pressure is put on the zip at the bottom it will just break.

So when I shorten a zip I use a piece of fabric. It could be any type of fabric.

Bias binding is good. I sew it on once, then cut the zip and wrap the bias around to the back of the zip and sew it again.

My zips never break at the bottom.

Zips – How to save them from breaking

I have never broken a zip!!!!!!!!! It's true. But there is only one reason why this is true.

I always close the zip and do the button up before putting into the washing machine.

Just imagine what happens to a zip that is left open in the washing machine.

The pants could get caught with something else, and the agitation of the machine could see the zip get broken because it gets caught with something else.

The second reason a zip will break for men or women is when they wear their pants too tight. You will see where the zip is straining about 1" from the top of the pants. If its pants that can be released at the back I would recommend getting the pants let out so that the pressure is off the zip.

Zips – Metal versus nylon

I have a lot of people wants metal zippers put into pants that are a light fabric. They think that the metal zip will last longer. I do not hold to this theory.

A dress zip will last just as long, in fact longer in some cases, because it does not become dry and hard to open over the years. A nylon dress zip can last you the life of the garment if you look after it.

A metal zip can also last a long time if they are looked after as well, but I don't believe they would last as long as a nylon dress zip. Keep metal zips away from harsh water or salt water, as this would begin the corrosion process.

I have had people bring in a zip that has been sitting around for years, and it is corroded and mouldy. Finally, remember before washing - close zip and do button up.

Zips – Nylon versus Invisible

Personally I find sewing invisible zips easier than sewing dress zips. I often have people say that they prefer a dress zip to an invisible zip.

A dress zip is not stronger than an invisible zip. To prove this take a look at the back of a dress zip.

Does it look familiar? It should because it's the same as the back of a dress zip with some minor alterations to it.

The only reason a invisible zip will break is if too much pressure is put onto it, or threads get caught in it.

Zips – Repairing jacket zip sliders

Zippers can break in a number of ways.

•	The teeth can break, which means that you would have to replace the whole zip.

•	The bottom section of a jacket zip where you slide the zip on can break off, and in this instance you will probably have to replace the zip. You could try crimping a piece of soft tin onto that section, and if you are lucky it will stay there, which means your zip is fixed.

•	But the most common problem for jacket zips is the jacket slider coming off.

This can really only be done for metal jacket zippers. I have not tried with plastic, but if you are game to try it, it may work.

The first thing you need to know is that the slider is placed onto the zip from the TOP. So if you have lost your slider, you need to go out and buy yourself a new slider.

It is cheaper to buy a new zip the same size and use the slider than take it to a clothing alteration shop and pay to have it replaced, or spend hours taking an old zip out and replacing it.

Step 1 - Unpick the top section holding the zip in place on the zip slider side only.

Step 2 - Carefully take the top metal piece off the new zip. It is situated on the same side as the slider at the top.

I find a knife is best, because you can slide the knife in under the metal and twist the knife so the metal opens and it comes off.

Step 3 - Put it aside in a safe place.

Step 4 - Slide the zip slider off the zip.

Step 5 - Follow the same procedure as you did for the new zip and take the metal piece off at the top of the old zip on the side the slider should be on.

Step 6 - Slide the new zip slider on and push it down to the bottom of the zip.

Step 7 - Zip the jacket up. It should zip up if the slider is the same size as the one you originally had.

Step 8 - Put the metal piece back on at the top of the zip

Step 9 - Put the top section of the zip back into the garment and sew back up.

Fabrics

Everything you do in clothing alterations is with fabric. There are a lot of different fabric combinations, but I thought I would provide you with some of my tips on the most common fabrics I come across in clothing alterations.

Stretch fabrics

The fabric could be a standard stretch or a two way stretch, which means that the fabric will go back into shape after bending. When pinning garments with a stretch fabric combination, you will be able to pin closer to the body knowing that the fabric has the stretch to move with the body.

Cotton fleece fabrics are used for track suits. One of the most common alterations is the length of track suit pants. Be very careful in the quality of fabric that you purchase here. A good quality cotton fleece should have a mix of polyester in it to prevent shrinkage.

A poor quality cotton fleece could see your garment shrink by 2" or 5 cm and sometimes a lot more upon washing. I bought a pair of cheap fleece pants once, and I took the hem up before I washed them. Those pants shrunk 5"!!!!!!! Honestly they were nearly at my knees after I washed them. So be cautious, and if in doubt, pre wash.

Wool – Natural fibre

I love working with wool, because it has such a good feel to the fabric. Unless the wool has been blended with a stretch fibre, I would suggest you pin carefully, making sure to allow for movement.

Wool may wrinkle, but usually the wrinkles will fall out.

Silver fish and moths love wool. My preferred protection for woollen garments is cedar balls; however there are many products on the market which will assist in the protection against these nasty creatures. They love wool, and if you don't protect woollen garments against silver fish you may find that one day you will go to put on that expensive wool suit only to find it covered in tiny little holes.

Linen – Natural fibre

Linen is a vegetable fibre that comes from flax. It is nearly 3 times stronger than cotton. Whilst linen looks great on, after a few hours of wearing, the fibre will become wrinkled.

You will need to take care when pinning a garment made of linen. The fabric is very unforgiving. This means always allow for movement. This fabric should never been pinned too tightly. If it is taken in too much, the seams are likely to burst.

Linen will normally wrinkle, however some manufacturers may treat the linen to cause less wrinkling. I would recommend hand washing and hanging to dry, however this fabric has a tendency to shrink and stretch out of shape. Linen needs ironing to look great. I would recommend dry cleaning linen so that it maintains that crisp finish.

Polyester – man made fibre

Polyester comes in many types, the most common is Microfibre. This fabric feels great on the skin, and almost feels like you don't have clothes on. Manufacturers can blend with stretch fabrics; however the most common one you will come across is Microfibre pants.

Micro fibre is an extremely unforgiving fabric when it comes to sewing. The weave is very tight, which means it is difficult to put a hem up without noticing the thread mark. If you have a blind hemming machine, you may be able to adjust to a depth in the stitch that will allow the hem to be relatively unnoticeable.

Microfibre has a very smooth feel to it, and to maintain its shape, I would recommend machine wash and hanging to dry. This fabric dries very quickly.

Generally there is no shrinkage with any type of man made fibres including Microfibre.

Silk

Silk is a strong wrinkle resistant fabric. Silk has no stretch at all, so when you pin this type of garment be sure not to take it in too much. Always allow a little room to move.

Silk can be washed by hand in mild soapy water, but dry cleaning is always recommended.

Knit

There are three different types of knit fabrics that you may deal with. The first type is commonly used for track suits. The knit pile is very close together and can be sewn on a domestic sewing machine easily. I would recommend pre washing the garment before altering.

The second type of knit comes from an industrial knitting machine. Like a hand knitted jumper, this type can ladder very easily. Care must be taken when altering this type of garment. Try not to pull this garment after cutting. Usually I sew a seam above the cut line, just in case it decides to ladder on me, then hopefully it will stop at the seam.

The third type is a hand knitted garment. I personally stay away from altering with a domestic sewing machine. Alter by hand.

Technical Abbreviations

The following technical details can be used for people who will be doing a lot of clothing alterations and would like to start to abbreviate.

BH	Blind Hem - No stitching can be seen on outside of fabric
CW	Customers waist - This is the customers waist measurement
DMS	Double Machine Stitch - Two rows of stitching can be seen on outside of fabric
FL	Finished length - Measurement from top of band to new hem length on skirt or fabric
FS	French Seam - Fabric is turned in on itself and stitched single or double
IA	Inside arm - Measurement from inside arm to new hem length
IL	Inside leg - Measurement from the crotch to the new hem length
O/L	Over lock - Fabric is over locked before sewing
OL	Outside leg - Measurement from the top of the band to the new hem length
MS	Machine Stitch - One row of stitching can be seen on outside of fabric
RBP	Release between pins – same
STP	Straighten to pin
TIAP	Take in as pinned - Seams are being taken in - Follow measurements exactly
TT	Turn twice - Fabric is turned twice and stitched. Can see stitching. e.g. Jean Hem
TTC	Thru to crotch
TTH	Thru to hem
TUAP	Take up as pinned - Hem is being taken up - Follow measurements exactly

Table of Contents

Pants

Taking Up Technique

Taking In Technique

Table of Contents